Religious Intolerance in America

EDITED BY JOHN CORRIGAN AND LYNN S. NEAL

A DOCUMENTARY HISTORY

Religious Intolerance in America

The University of North Carolina Press   Chapel Hill

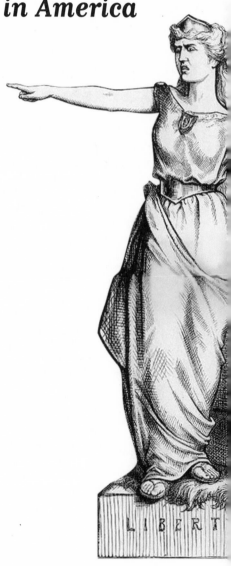

© 2010 The University of North Carolina Press
All rights reserved
Manufactured in the United States of America

Designed by Courtney Leigh Baker and set in Matrix Script and Arno Pro
by Rebecca Evans. The paper in this book meets the guidelines for perma-
nence and durability of the Committee on Production Guidelines for Book
Longevity of the Council on Library Resources. The University of North
Carolina Press has been a member of the Green Press Initiative since 2003.

Library of Congress Cataloging-in-Publication Data
Religious intolerance in America : a documentary history / edited by John
Corrigan and Lynn S. Neal.
p. cm.   Includes bibliographical references and index.
ISBN 978-0-8078-3389-6 (cloth : alk. paper) — ISBN 978-0-8078-7118-8
(pbk : alk. paper)
1. United States — Religion. 2. Discrimination — United States.
3. Religious tolerance — United States. I. Corrigan, John, 1952–
II. Neal, Lynn S.
BR517.R45 2010
200.973 — dc22   2009044820

cloth   14 13 12 11 10   5 4 3 2 1
paper   14 13 12 11 10   5 4 3 2 1

For Patrick Palermo and our students

I believe in an America that is officially neither Catholic, Protestant, nor Jewish—where no public official either requests or accepts instructions on public policy from the Pope, the National Council of Churches or any other ecclesiastical source—where no religious body seeks to impose its will directly or indirectly upon the general populace or the public acts of its officials—and where religious liberty is so indivisible that an act against one church is treated as an act against all.

For, while this year it may be a Catholic against whom the finger of suspicion is pointed, in other years it has been, and may someday be again, a Jew—or a Quaker—or a Unitarian—or a Baptist. It was Virginia's harassment of Baptist preachers, for example, that helped lead to Jefferson's statute of religious freedom. Today I may be the victim—but tomorrow it may be you—until the whole fabric of our harmonious society is ripped at a time of great national peril.

Finally, I believe in an America where religious intolerance will someday end—where all men and all churches are treated as equal—where every man has the same right to attend or not attend the church of his choice—where there is no Catholic vote, no anti-Catholic vote, no bloc voting of any kind—and where Catholics, Protestants and Jews, at both the lay and pastoral level, will refrain from those attitudes of disdain and division which have so often marred their works in the past, and promote instead the American ideal of brotherhood.

"Text of Senator John F. Kennedy's Speech to the Greater Houston Ministerial Association, September 12, 1960," in Patricia Barrett, *Religious Liberty and the American Presidency* (1963)

CONTENTS

Acknowledgments xi   *Introduction* 1

ONE   Religious Intolerance in Colonial America 17

TWO   Anti-Catholicism 49

THREE   Anti-Mormonism 73

FOUR   Intolerance toward Nineteenth-Century

              Religious Groups 99

FIVE   Intolerance toward Native American Religions 125

SIX   Anti-Semitism 147

SEVEN   Intolerance toward "New" Religions in the

              Twentieth Century 181

EIGHT   The Branch Davidians and Waco 215

              The Culmination of Religious Intolerance

Conclusion 247

Appendix: Web Resources for Combating Religious

              Intolerance 267

Notes 269   *Index* 277

ACKNOWLEDGMENTS

For a close critical reading of the manuscript and for many good suggestions I am grateful to my seminar students Cara Burnidge, Shawntel Ensminger, Daniel Dillard, Joshua Fleer, Jonathan Olson, Tammy Heiss, Adam Ware (who also logged images), Steve Adams, Barton Price, and Molly Reed (who also located an obscure illustration). Jason Leto was a great help tracking down a document. Lauren Davis did her usual great job making the manuscript look good. Barton Price prepared a superb index. Lynn Neal, collaborator extraordinaire, kept the project on track through my numerous episodes of distractedness, challenged and prodded me, and actually seemed to understand what I was saying at times. Thanks for being a mind reader and a model of coauthorial energy and good humor. It has above all been a pleasure to work with Elaine Maisner at the University of North Carolina Press. Professor Patrick Palermo opened my eyes to the power of historical narrative and taught me as an undergraduate how to look behind the story for other stories. His enthusiasm for historical study was contagious, and his insistence that historians take the "margins" seriously was a gift that has profoundly shaped my own interests as a scholar. This is a long overdue and heartfelt thank-you to him.

JC

My commitment to this project emerged from and was sustained by my students. When addressing religious intolerance in class, they fearlessly asked questions and sincerely struggled with the issues. They continually showed me the necessity of studying this topic and emphasized its salience in their lives. From the beginning, then, this book has been for them. Thus, I must thank my numerous sections of Religion 101 and recognize the students in Religion 390/690/ESE 306, who enhanced my thinking about religious intolerance in numerous ways. Individual students also served as either research assistants or conversation partners. Thank you to Allyson Doughty Blalock, Cassie Cox Evans, Maegan Neal, Jessica Devaney, Matthew Imboden,

M. Gregory Dragas, Christine Foust, and Matthew Triplett. In addition, my thanks to Elaine Maisner at the University of North Carolina Press for her consistent and unwavering support of this project from its inception. Lastly, I would like to express my appreciation to John Corrigan. We embarked on this collaboration after a brief discussion at AAR in 2003 and have met to discuss our progress at AAR in all the years since. During this time, I have been so grateful that he took a chance on a newly minted Ph.D. and this project. He has my most sincere gratitude for being both my coeditor and a gracious mentor.

LSN

Religious Intolerance in America

Narratives about Religious Freedom and Religious Intolerance

In March of 1942, the Jehovah's Witnesses learned a difficult lesson in American history. Even though they were citizens with ties to Christianity, they were not welcome in the American religious landscape. In the midst of World War II, the Witnesses encountered hostility and suspicion, intolerance and violence, for their religiously based refusal to support the war and salute the flag. This perceived disloyalty to the United States combined with their very visible evangelistic techniques sparked intolerance in numerous towns and cities across the country, including Little Rock, Arkansas, Klamath Falls, Oregon, and West Jefferson, Ohio. Despite having won a recent Supreme Court case, *Cantwell v. Connecticut* (1940), that protected their evangelistic endeavors, they were detained by police in West Jefferson, Ohio, for distributing literature and for preaching their gospel on street corners. According to the affidavit of Jehovah's Witness J. E. Lowe, "When reminded that the Supreme Court had ruled in our favor, [Officer] Wolfe replied 'We don't care for the Supreme Court and the Constitution don't apply here.'" Lowe's affidavit describes the ensuing events and the accuracy of Wolfe's statement rings eerily true.

On March 21 three car-loads of Witnesses returned to West Jefferson. Officer Wolfe was seen going in and out of different places where men generally hang out in small towns. Then the town siren blew. A crowd of men gathered in front of the barber shop immediately began pushing the Witnesses and striking them. The five male members tried vainly to protect themselves and their wives and children, but were so greatly outnumbered that it was impossible. In their viciousness they hit women members and knocked them down, one of them unconscious, and blacked their eyes. They were reminded that they were fighting against Christians and taking the law into their own hands.

They replied "That's exactly what we're doing—taking the law into our hands."

They started on us again. The Witnesses' faces were already bloody. Someone hit me with a blunt instrument. Everything went black. While in this condition, they continued to strike my head and face cutting another gash in the top of my head. At the same time they had dragged three of the Witnesses out on the highway and were pounding, beating and kicking them. Such shouts as "Kill them," "Tar and feather them," "Make them salute the flag," came from all directions. And, all this time, Officer Wolfe sat in the barber shop and watched.

Finally this gory indescribably vicious assault ceased. The Witnesses locked arms and started to walk toward their car at the far end of town. One tall young, blond fellow procured a huge American flag, held it high over our heads and marched with us. The same noble flag-bearer had only a few minutes ago twisted the arms of a young girl Witness behind her back until she thought they would break. The mobsters were at our heels singing "My country tis of thee sweet land of liberty," and shouting, "make them salute the flag."[1]

This account juxtaposes the American flag and the lyrics of "America" with the bloodied bodies of Jehovah's Witnesses. And in the 1940s, this religious group was not the only victim of supposed promoters of American liberty.

Between 1942 and 1945, more than 100,000 Japanese Americans were incarcerated in the wake of Pearl Harbor and President Roosevelt's Executive Order 9066.[2] In this order, the president granted the secretary of war the power to create internment camps or "military areas" and detain those deemed to be a threat to "the successful prosecution of the war."[3] Like the Jehovah's Witnesses, Japanese Americans were seen as un-American and unpatriotic, a danger to the war effort. However, the political actions taken against Japanese Americans also reflected religious intolerance toward both Buddhism and Shinto. In fact, scholars Thomas A. Tweed and Stephen Prothero note that "one of the first groups to be rounded up were Buddhist priests of Japanese descent." Seen as community leaders and carriers of "foreign" religious and political traditions, many priests were imprisoned in the camps, along with thousands of others who were considered to be a "threat." In response to these actions, "many Buddhists stopped practicing their faith for fear of being labeled anti-American."[4] And the Buddhist Mission of North America changed its name to the Buddhist Churches of America to appear more in-line with dominant American religio-political values. In addition, the practice of Shinto, the indigenous religion of Japan that had become increasingly politicized in the decades prior to World War II, faced censure and suspicion from various levels of the U.S. government. Then attorney general of California Earl Warren (later chief justice of the Supreme Court) testified before Congress:

> Most of the Japanese who were born in Japan are over 55 years of age. There has been practically no migration to this country since 1924. But in some instances the children of those people have been sent to Japan for their education, either in whole or in part, and while they are over there they are indoctrinated with the idea of Japanese imperialism. They receive their religious instruction [Shinto] which ties up their religion with their Emperor, and they come back here imbued with the ideas and the policies of Imperial Japan.[5]

Individuals, mobs, and governmental agencies enacted intolerance toward Japanese Americans, and Jehovah's Witnesses, for the ways their religious beliefs were believed to conflict with American values. It is difficult to fathom that these events, shocking in their violence and upsetting in their injustice, occurred in the United States little more than fifty years ago. Indeed, it challenges much of what we typically learn or hear about American religious history.

When we think of the "founding myth" of the United States, visions of pious Pilgrims fleeing religious persecution often come to mind. In the foreground of this imagined picture the "new" world of America represents liberty, as the tyranny symbolized by Europe fades into the background. In the midst of this scene stands the brave and beleaguered Pilgrim, the iconic symbol of religious freedom attained. As the story continues, the defenders of the American Republic—Washington, Jefferson, and Madison—inherited this Pilgrim legacy. They carried the banner of religious freedom to the battlefield and then to the documents framing our government, the Declaration of Independence and the Constitution. The First Amendment's protection of religious freedom, "Congress shall make no law respecting an establishment of religion or prohibiting the free exercise thereof," was the light on the hill that made the United States unique and an example to the world. Ultimately, the story culminates in the twenty-first century with a United States that prides itself on being the most religiously diverse nation in the world.

This narrative captures many of the salient features that characterize American religious history. Indeed, the story of religion in the United States is one of unparalleled diversity and the protection of religious rights. In this country, the religious landscape boasts synagogues and mosques, Zen Centers and crystal cathedrals, sweat lodges and Christian Science reading rooms. Religious variety has been a constituent feature of American history from the nation's founding. Native Americans practiced diverse religious traditions, while the Christians that quickly populated the colonial landscape, including Catholics, Pilgrims, Quakers, Anglicans, and Baptists, interpreted their faith in vastly different ways. Early on the colonies also became home to Jews in search of religious freedom, as well as enslaved Africans, some of whom brought with them indigenous African religions, while others adhered to Islam. In many ways, the United States' religious diversity and its ideal of religious freedom make its history unique and its example laudable.

Textbooks of American religious history have told this story to many generations of Americans. We should appreciate why this has been the case, beyond the obvious reason that it is a commendable story of the potential for democracy to protect the citizenry. We should remember that the history of Europe—carried in collective and individual memory to the New World—was marked by centuries of devastating religious violence. Even after the American Revolution and the sorting of governmental priorities in the early Republic, Americans remained well aware of the monumental suffering caused by wars of religion. For those whose memory needed jogging there were accounts such as Friedrich von Schiller's history of the Thirty Years' War (1618–1648), which was reprinted in translation a number of times in the nineteenth century for American readerships. It narrated a horror in which large percentages of the populations of European countries were killed (including as much as half the male population of the German states), thousands of villages and towns destroyed, nations bankrupted, and profound ecological damage spread across the natural landscape. Americans remembered Europe. Moreover Americans, after the successful rebellion against England, retained in addition to their awareness of the European past some sense of religious intolerance that had occurred in the colonies: Protestants at war with Catholics in colonial Maryland, Congregationalists torturing and executing Quakers in Massachusetts, Native Americans persecuted and massacred for being "uncivilized heathens" (or, in other words, resisting Christianity), and other bloody confrontations. The grand experiment of American democracy, in which rights and liberties were spelled out in the first ten amendments to the Constitution, gave hope that such violence was forever in the past. Americans not only created laws to avoid religious intolerance, they threw themselves into the intellectual embrace of it as a cardinal principle of nationhood. For many, the wars of religion were a thing of the past, made obsolete by a new national order in which diversity was an accepted fact of religious life. It is hard to overestimate Americans' emotional embrace of the First Amendment as the perceived solution to the problem of religious intolerance. For Americans, freedom of religion meant that from the late eighteenth century onward things would be different. Americans believed they had made a new world, and they experienced their world through that belief.

Americans continued to recall how there had been intolerance in the colonial period, but they had a harder time seeing it in the nineteenth and twentieth centuries. Americans' trust that a common morality bound the nation together, and their deep investment in the capability of law to transform life, shaped their thinking about the meanings of religious differences. When events conflicted with the belief that America had been made anew, Americans were often unable to see that minority groups suffered at the hands of majority traditions. Religious intolerance continued to afflict relations between groups, and, in fact, it worsened during the nineteenth century. Moreover, most Americans did not recognize religious intolerance for what it was. A Protestant majority was secure in its belief that extension of its morality and beliefs to the nation as a whole was its God-given destiny, and it was confident that freedom of religion in America was a fact that Protestant ambitions could in no way undermine. Protestant commentators for the most part brushed aside countervailing evidence, and Protestant historians continued to frame a narrative of American religious history that presented freedom of religion as an accomplished goal. There was no place for intolerance in such a narrative. In the same way that those who wrote about human freedom and rights in the American republic could overlook the troubling fact that African slaves were not free and had no rights, narrators of religious history overlooked the fact of religious intolerance, even when they were looking right at it.

These tales of religious freedom in America tout the fact that it had emerged earlier and advanced more rapidly in British North America than anywhere else. Daniel Dorchester's *Christianity in the United States* (1888) observed that "among the American colonies, even in those rude times, examples of religious oppression were far less numerous and severe than in countries from which they [colonists] emigrated. In respect of toleration, they were far in advance of the rest of the world."[6] Colonists might differ with regard to doctrine, pointed out *The American Nation: A History* (1907), but in terms of lived religion, America was an exception: "The ideals of theology were narrow but those of conduct were high, and no part of the world enjoyed such religious toleration."[7] Edward Eggleston agreed, declaring in *The Household History of the United States and Its People for Young Americans* (1890) that a mentality comfortable with religious diversity in fact came to maturity in the decades before the Revolution. He cited Catholic Maryland, Roger Williams's Rhode Island, and Quaker Pennsylvania as groundbreaking examples that other colonies followed, with the result that "persecution ceased in all the colonies before the revolution." The Constitution formalized that perspective, so that "all are free to worship in their own way."[8] Sometimes textbooks, and especially those around the period from 1890 to 1930, stressed a kind of "guiding mentality" in the work of the founders: "The spirit that guided the work of the founders of our government was not one that was crushed and screwed into sectarian molds by the decrees of intolerant councils. . . . This is the lesson of the development of civil as well as religious liberty in the United States."[9] That mentality transferred quickly to the American public, so that, as Albert Bushnell Hart wrote in his *American Ideals Historically Traced, 1607–1907*, "Americans are in the habit of thinking that the church has no place in political life," and "the country has completely accepted a second noble ideal, that of religious toleration."[10] The Revolution itself, which served as a major mooring for American thinking about national identity, was, for historian Edward Channing, prominent in the creation of toleration, because it helped "to weaken the old bigotry and narrowmindedness of the people."[11] In short, some historians took the Revolution as the culmination of a heroic process of gradually ending intolerance, while others emphasized the Revolution itself as the crucial event in ending intolerance, a watershed moment in religious freedom. Either way, by the end of the nineteenth century historians for the most part presented the post-Revolution constitutional provisions for religious freedom as more than the legal formalization of an ideal. They made religious freedom a realized goal, and a remarkable one at that. As Joseph Henry Crocker put it, "our fathers established, not simply universal toleration, but perfect religious equality."[12] Other writers built upon this historiographical theme to point out that wherever one looked, a "spirit of toleration" characterized the religious life of the nation. For some historians, the assimilation of different religious faiths into a harmonious American religious landscape was most striking. Ernest Hamlin Abbott, the son of renowned Protestant minister Lyman Abbott, reporting in *Religion in America* (1902) on his observation of immigrants during a national tour, declared that "to the American spirit of religious toleration I attribute the fact that nowhere in the course of my trip did I meet with evidence that the newly arrived Europeans had found occasion after their arrival for any violent readjustment of their religious life."[13] Other textbook writers celebrated the immigrant's delivery from religious persecution abroad, blending the theme of a religiously intolerant Europe with the promise of religious freedom in America. In such fashion Leo Huberman, in *We, the People* (1932), addressed the reasons for immigration: "One was religious persecution.... You might have difficulty in getting a job, or you might be jeered at, or have stones thrown at you, or you might even be murdered—just for having the wrong (that is, different) religion. You learned about America where you could be what you pleased, where there was room for Catholic, Protestant, Jew. To America, then!"[14] Such an understanding of the religious past moreover was informed by a trust that religion in America was more reasonable than in other places. The emergent mythos of American religiosity was that Americans were not a people who were superstitious, fanatical, or stupid. Americans were, rather, a thoughtful and prudent sort, able to discuss in informed ways their religious differences. As some writers explained, this was a *fruit* of religious freedom, and one that further strengthened and proved American commitment to the *principle* of religious freedom. Persons of different faiths could live in harmony because religious freedom enabled them to learn from each other in open debate. This estimation of the consequences of religious freedom emerged in the early nineteenth century and remained a central part of American self-understanding through the twentieth century. Salma Hale expressed it early on in 1840: "The consequences resulting from the enjoyment of religious liberty have been highly favorable. Free discussion has enlightened the ignorant, disarmed superstition of its dreadful powers, and consigned to oblivion many erroneous and fantastic creeds. Religious oppression, and the vindictive feelings it arouses are hardly known."[15]

Finally, in considering the ways in which narratives of the religious history of America have shaped our thinking about tolerance and intolerance, we should bear in mind the gradual disappearance of religious intolerance from textbooks. Colonial-era textbooks featured religion above all else, and although religion was treated as one of many cultural elements in nineteenth-century textbooks, it remained centrally important to historical narratives. In the late nineteenth and early twentieth centuries, the textbook narrative stressed toleration and harmony as a longstanding historical fact and juxtaposed it with early colonial instances of intolerance in order to drive home the point of the wholesale realization of the idea of freedom written into the Constitution. Such writing took for granted as well that Americans were a "chosen people" who had seized their destiny through implementation of the founders' vision. Such narratives fashioned Americans' thinking about their history, and above all about the absence of religious intolerance since the founding of the United States. Religious intolerance has been all but written out of the story for a century or more.[16] American religious history instead often reads something like a Garrison Keillor story where the religion is nice, its practitioners are upstanding, and the nation is above average.

The dominance and celebratory nature of this narrative obscures important elements in the history of the United States. It prevents us from seeing the reality and persistence of religious intolerance in the nation's past and present. Even as religious diversity has been a consistent feature of American religious life, so too has religious intolerance. Long before mobs assaulted Jehovah's Witnesses or the federal government imprisoned Japanese Americans, Pilgrims hanged Quakers, Protestants attacked Catholics, states declared war on Mormons, and the federal government attempted to eradicate Native American religious practices. Lest one be tempted to relegate religious intolerance to the distant past, current data should quickly dispel that impulse. Since the mid-1990s, hate crime statistics reveal that those acts motivated by religion ranked second only to those committed because of race.[17] Jews continue to face intransigent stereotypes (as well as vandalism and physical violence); Mormons still face suspicion and hostility (examine Mitt Romney's presidential campaign); and religion is often a primary motivation in attacks on those endorsing homosexuality, feminism, and abortion.

Failure to see and thus grapple with the persistent reality of religious intolerance in the United States is dangerous. "A story," writes J. Hillis Miller, "is a way of doing things with words. It makes something happen in the real world."[18] In this case, it creates an inability to recognize how religious intolerance is disseminated and replicated. As a result, nothing is done to prevent its proliferation. It then becomes easy to write off intolerant acts or events as aberrant and random, rather than as constituent parts of a larger historical trajectory. Equally troubling, it fuels apathy about the protection of religious rights.[19] In addition, an inability to recognize religious intolerance in our own past makes it difficult to grapple with the terrorist attacks of September 11th and the reality of global religious violence. For many, this task has been almost insurmountable as this type of religious devotion—being willing to kill and be killed—appears unfathomable and foreign. Stories of religion in America have taught us to see religious intolerance and violence as something inflicted upon the United States or something that occurs in less-civilized and -sophisticated nations than our own.

We can see this dynamic when looking at the treatment of Islam and Asian religions in the United States. During World War II, thousands of Japanese Americans fell under suspicion and were imprisoned simply because of their religio-ethnic background. Similarly, the immediate aftermath of 9/11 saw attacks on individuals assumed to be Muslim and the vandalization of mosques and Arab-owned businesses.[20] In both instances, the interpretation of these groups and their religious traditions as "foreign" justified action against them, all in the name of upholding American values and protecting American liberty. Historically, however, instances of violence toward Islam and Asian religions in the United States have been less frequent than other types of religious intolerance due to their relatively small numbers, lack of political power, and public invisibility (until current events frame them as enemies— an important pattern to look for in this volume).

That is not to say that intolerance toward Islam or Asian religions was absent prior to 9/11 or World War II. For example, in 1868 Reverend A. W. Loomis wrote an article for *Overland Monthly* entitled "Our Heathen Temples," which provided an in-depth description of the interior of a Chinese Buddhist temple—as one may suspect from the title, his analysis is less than favorable. As he concluded the piece, Loomis praised the philosophy, politeness, and shrewdness of the Chinese but lamented their idolatrous religion, labeling it "foolish in the extreme." He continued: "Sixty thousand people on this coast, who trust the keeping of their souls to such things as are here described! We read of 'the darkest places of the earth'; but here are spots which are dark enough under the droppings of our sanctuaries. But it cannot always remain so. There is light in America. Idolatry may be imported to these shores—but it cannot live for many years."[21] For Loomis, idolatry, by which he means Buddhism, is fundamentally opposed to the "light" of the Christian United States. Others also viewed those of Asian descent as forever foreign—"unassimilable"—and groups such as the Asiatic Exclusion League sought to prevent Asian immigration, a goal achieved in 1924 when Congress passed the Asian Exclusion Act, which "effectively cut off immigration from Asia."[22] Given this history of suspicion, mistrust, and intolerance—the repeated labeling of Asians as foreign and un-American—Japanese internment begins to make more sense.

Historically, Islam has been labeled in similar ways, as both foreign and violent. A letter to the editor by an "Anti-Mohammedan" in an 1845 edition of the *Cleveland Herald* highlighted these features. The letter contrasts the peaceful character of Christianity (and hence America) with the violence of Islam (and thus foreign nations) using prooftexts from sources including the New Testament and what he claims is the Koran. The letter reads:

The spirit of Mohammedanism says, "War, then, is enjoined against you, the infidels. Kill the idolators, wherever you shall find them—lay wait for them in every convenient place—strike off their heads. Verily God hath purchased of the true believers their souls and their substance, promising them the enjoyments of Paradise on condition that they fight for the cause of God." *Koran*

The spirit of Christianity says, "Love your enemies; do good to them that hate you; and pray for them that persecute and calumniate you." *Matthew*

The spirit of Mohammedanism says, "The sword is the KEY of Heaven and Hell: a drop of blood shed in the cause of God, a night spent in arms, is of more avail than two months of fasting and prayer: whoever falls in battle, his sins are forgiven—and the loss of his limbs shall be supplied with the wings of Angels." *The Koran, passion; and Gaizot's Gibbon's Rome*

The spirit of Christianity says, "Put up again thy sword into its place. For all that take the sword shall perish by the sword." *Matthew*

The spirit of Mohammedanism says, "Oh, Prophet, I am the man; whosoever rises against thee, I will dash out his teeth, tear out his eyes, break his legs, rip up his belly." *Gaizot's Gibbon's Rome*

The spirit of Christianity says, "He rebuked them saying: You know not of what spirit you are. The Son of Man came not to destroy souls, but to save them." *Luke*

The spirit of Mohammedanism says, "Ye Christian dogs, you know your option: the Koran, the tribute, or the sword. We are a people whose delight is in war." *Gaizot's Gibbon's Rome*

The spirit of Christianity says, "Blessed are the peacemakers, for they shall be called the children of God." *Matthew*

The spirit of Mohammedanism says, "Be sure you cleave their sculls, and give them no quarter." *Gaizot's Gibbon's Rome*

And the spirit of Christianity says, "Forgive us our debts as we forgive our debtors." *Matthew*

Can men, owing to their weakness, utter more atrocious and blood-thirsty language than that of the Koran? How peaceful is the word of Truth! May the spirit of Christianity teach us to shun the blood of Mohammedanism, is the prayer of him who is ever yours, AN ANTI-MOHAMMEDAN[23]

The author's hermeneutic is clear—Christianity is a religion of peace and the faith of America, while Islam is one of war and has no place in the nation. The litany sounds all too familiar in our present context. In our post-9/11 landscape, the images of Islam that permeate our modern media focus on the foreign and political threat it poses. Similar to the ways that Japanese Americans and their religious practices were deemed foreign and un-American—a move that justified intolerant action against them in the name of protecting American liberty—the contemporary media, from CNN sound bites to television's 24, depict Islam as a religion infused with violence and antithetical to the American way of life. Films such as *Not Without My Daughter* and *Patriot Games* have shaped and reinforced this interpretation. In turn, these media associations continue to define religion, intolerance, and violence as a problem of *other* nations, while the United States remains a bastion of religious tolerance and liberty.

While the desire may be to write off these instances of religious intolerance as the product of war, we must recognize that long before September 11th, indeed long before World War II, religious intolerance and violence constituted part of the American religious landscape. In part, we cannot fathom these more recent events, because we have defined mainstream American religion as necessarily "nice" and thereby failed to grapple with our own history of religious intolerance and violence. How might examining this unknown history help dispel misperceptions and shed light on present religious conflicts? We must reexamine our knowledge and assumptions about American religious history. How we chronicle history matters, and the documents in this volume seek to address this neglected dimension of American religious history.

Religious Intolerance and Religious Violence

Through a variety of primary sources, this volume interrogates the concept of religious intolerance. Seemingly more generic than the term religious violence yet more specific than either bigotry or prejudice, "religious intolerance" does not lend itself easily to definition. As a consequence, scholars often sidestep the problem of definition. For example, Martha Nussbaum's short essay entitled "Religious Intolerance" speaks to its prevalence but fails to flesh out the term, while Susan Thistlethwaite's article, "Settled Issues and Neglected Questions," hypothesizes about the causes of religious intolerance but likewise neglects to define it.[24] Relying on Supreme Court Justice Potter Stewart's "I know it when I see it" approach certainly has its merits. It recognizes the elusive and difficult character of definition, even as it allows for a wide range of possibilities. Such an approach acknowledges our common sense and implies a common morality, a shared recognition of right and wrong, just and unjust. However, in the context of American religious history, it is these very issues—seeing religious intolerance and the assumption of a common morality—that make definitional imprecision problematic. Folklorist Barre Toelken writes that "different groups of people not only think in different ways, but they often 'see' things in different ways." He explains how our culture trains us to "see things in 'programmed ways,'" or as one of his students put it, "If I hadn't believed it I never would have seen it."[25] In the United States, too many have not been "programmed" to believe or see the religious intolerance that characterizes the nation's history. The pledge of allegiance praises America's unity, and popular song lyrics describe the country as a "sweet land of liberty." In a variety of ways, the rhetoric of religious freedom permeates our culture. As a result, the "I know it when I see it approach" fails to work. Many American citizens have not been equipped with the historical knowledge and educational background to see, recognize, and acknowledge the persistence of religious intolerance in the United States (past and present). In addition, religious intolerance often occurs precisely because a religious group challenges or seeks to defend an assumed cultural morality. The second order of the Ku Klux Klan defined itself as the defenders of Christian America and its morals, and thereby justified attacks on Catholics and Jews as well as African Americans; others have labeled practices, such as polygamy and the use of peyote, as immoral and illegal acts rather than as constituent parts of religious traditions. Thus, a definition that takes its cues from understandings of right and wrong shared by a certain group tends to privilege majority religious views, namely Protestant Christianity, and thereby fails to adequately define or recognize religious intolerance. In other words, we must be careful to approach religious intolerance in ways that avoid closing down our opportunities to see it.

In order to "see" religious intolerance and understand its machinations we should adopt a working definition that provides a place for us to stand and survey the religious landscape with as little obstruction as possible. The Ontario Consultants on Religious Tolerance define religious intolerance as "not respecting the fundamental human right of other people to hold religious beliefs that are different from your own." Another group characterizes it as "refusing to acknowledge and support the right of individuals to have their own beliefs and related legitimate practices and the unwillingness to have one's own beliefs and related practices critically evaluated."[26] And another definition reads: "Prejudice against individuals or groups based on religious convictions, affiliations or practices, which can manifest as violent action and/or intimidation, with the intent to deny the right to practice religion freely."[27] These definitions share an emphasis on attitudes—respect, acknowledgement, intent—and focus our attention on how people's religious beliefs inform and influence their actions against or interactions with those who are perceived as religiously different. Our approach in this volume, then, has been to stress how religious beliefs and attitudes shape negative interactions between persons and groups. Our working definition foregrounds the linkage between the perception of religious difference and the enactment of disrespect, intimidation, or violence toward others. Sometimes that linkage is clear, while at other times it is less distinct. Our willingness to consider context matters enormously in charting it.

The frequent blurring of attitude and action, rhetoric and reality, requires that we consider for a moment the relationship between religious intolerance and religious violence. Often scholars talk about these two concepts in dualistic terms. Religious intolerance is relegated to the realm of the imagined, the symbolic, and the rhetorical, while religious violence is actual, real, and enacted. In this binary, religious violence counts, while religiously intolerant words or ideas seem unimportant or ephemeral. For example, one scholar writes that "language and violence are not the same thing," while another states, "violent stories can, under certain circumstances, generate *real* violence."[28] These authors acknowledge the power of intolerant language and ideology, yet at the same time they seem to employ a binary that relegates words to the realm of the unreal, to something less than or qualitatively different from "actual" violence. Rather than view religious intolerance as simply rhetoric that exists in contrast to the "reality" of religious violence, this volume suggests that we take the relationship between the two seriously. As Simon Wiesenthal stated, "Genocide does not begin with ovens; it begins with words."[29] Words have power—the power to define enemies, divinize heroes, and rally troops. They shape people's perceptions of the world and justify certain actions while discouraging others.

Wiesenthal and the above considerations, then, prompt us to define intolerance as a type of violence and thus broaden our understanding of violence as a category. Rather than relying on simplistic understandings of violence "as simply social action," scholars J. Gordon Melton and David Bromley urge us to view it "as relational and processual." In their study of new religious movements, they write that "it is important to abandon formulaic conceptions of violent cults in favor of pursuing a sophisticated, multidimensional understanding of movements, control agencies, and movement-societal interactions simultaneously."[30] They challenge us to see violence as a multidimensional process. If we view it in these terms, we can reconceptualize the relationship between religious intolerance and religious violence. Instead of relying on a dualistic understanding of the two, conceiving of religious violence as a continuum or process helps us attend to the ways hateful ideas, words, and acts are related to violent practices. It illuminates the variety of ways violence is disseminated and enacted. No one would dispute that lynchings, murders, and bombings are violent acts and that in certain historical contexts they have been motivated by religion. However, this broader definition helps us see how cross burning, vandalism, hate speech, public protests, threatening notes, written treatises, and the propagation of false allegations can also be viewed as religiously violent acts. The documents in this volume highlight all of these manifestations and more. By taking this approach, we can then analyze how these different violent actions, whether ideas, words, or physical conflict, reinforce and strengthen each other. Writing a treatise against the Pope and calling him the antichrist is not the same thing as burning a convent to the ground; however, what this broader definition allows and asks us to consider is how these two types of violence work together in a symbiotic manner to create a context in which it becomes plausible (if not acceptable) for some to act in these ways against their perceived enemies.

Not only does this approach allow us to consider how different types of intolerance or violence work together, it also provides the means to examine the ways and conditions that prompt people to move back and forth (or not) along this spectrum from intolerant rhetoric to physical conflict. Why do some people write an intolerant book or preach a hate-filled sermon but take no further steps toward physical violence, while others gun people down or torch buildings? There are no singular explanations or easy answers to this question, but utilizing this processual vision of violence may help illuminate how and why people enact violence in different ways. In addition, this reconceptualization highlights the variety of ways people express and chronicle their experiences of intolerance. Facing a burning cross in one's front yard or confronting a harmful stereotype at work, then, counts. A court decision that denies the legitimacy of one's religious practice or a stereotypical portrayal of one's faith in a film may not be interpreted as mere rhetoric but instead experienced as an "attack," as violent. It is not the same as being tarred and feathered, raped, or lynched, but these acts may still intimidate and inhibit the practice of one's faith and be defined by victims as violent.

Reading This Book about Intolerance

Religious intolerance is ugly. A story about America without it is a more attractive story, one that more easily pleases and inspires us, one that seems a better fit with what we believe are our ideals, and one that makes us prouder than we might be otherwise. A national narrative without reference to religious intolerance is also a fake. It not only misrepresents the past but it misorients us to our lives today and deprives us of valuable knowledge of our national experience that we should be able to draw upon as we plan our future. In a global environment where religious frictions are constant and deadly, would we be better equipped to act wisely if we pretended that we as a nation have not had such experiences? Or would we understand better what is at stake, and how complicated religious violence is, if we were able to recall that our own past has been marred by such violence as well? Would we be a better nation if we recognized that our ideals of freedom and equality, precious as they are, are hard to live up to, and that even though we have founded our government on law that guarantees them, we sometimes fall short of realizing them in practice? We intend that this book inform debate about these issues and a host of others bearing on religion in America and American roles in a religiously diverse world.

This is a documentary history. We have organized the documents thematically, collecting some under the heading of a particular historical period, such as the colonial period or the nineteenth century, others with reference to specific religious groups, and others according to a broader religious category, such as new religious movements. We begin each chapter with introductions that survey relevant background for appreciating the import of the documents in that chapter, and we comment on each document or cluster of documents in ways that we expect will help readers interpret them. We have tried as much as possible to avoid forcing our own interpretations upon readers. Certainly our choice of documents and our introductory writing will frame religious intolerance in a certain way. But we have left leeway for readers to interrogate the documents in their own ways, to ask different kinds of questions, and to draw their own conclusions. A documentary history should leave as much as possible to the voices of the documents, for they ultimately will provoke the reader to thoughtfulness about American religious history and persuade the reader to experiment with different historical interpretations of our national effort to make religious freedom a reality. So, this volume is a starting point of inquiry, not an endpoint of interpretation.

It can be easy to dismiss the idea that there has been religious intolerance throughout American history if one has not experienced it. For a nation that frequently has touted its record of cross-denominational reform initiatives and assorted multifaith social and political ventures, religious groups remain distinct in America, separated by doctrinal boundaries, moral sensibilities, aesthetics, ethnicity, region, and other factors. It can be hard to see what others believe and experience when one lives apart from them, and especially so when one is sure that one's own position is superior. It is also the case that groups occasionally claim religious intolerance where there is none. The radical Christian Right, for example, began complaining in the late twentieth century that Christianity in America was a persecuted religion. Originating in White Supremacist circles and rippling outward from there, such a claim was based upon a tortured definition of intolerance that mistakes separation of church and state for persecution. It was also plainly ignorant, based upon a profound misunderstanding of intolerance in American religious history. This volume hopefully will inform those for whom the history of religious intolerance has been obscured by other narratives, and in so doing lead to corrective vision for persons who see no intolerance, as well as for those who are careless in their invocation of it.

CHAPTER ONE

Religious Intolerance in Colonial America

The Europeans who crossed the Atlantic and colonized the Americas, and who fashioned through their explorations and migrations an Atlantic World that interconnected Africa, the Americas, and Europe, were not tolerant. Much has been written, and much has been said in speeches and sermons, about how the earliest English settlers of North America came to the New World seeking refuge from religious intolerance in England. It is true that English Puritans had suffered misfortunes beginning with the reign of Queen Elizabeth I, and minority religious groups from the Continent—from German- and French- and Spanish-speaking lands, especially—likewise sought relief from mistreatment by dominant churches and by the state apparatus that was joined to those churches. The idea of toleration, however, as historian Perez Zagorin has observed, had not yet coalesced in the West.[1] The pioneering efforts of the Dutch humanist Erasmus (d. 1536), particularly his imaging of Jesus as a loving, generous, and appealingly simple manifestation of God, were lost in the theologically and politically driven preoccupation with heretic hunting and the persecution of religious minorities, as well as the ongoing horror of massive religious warfare. In the climate of acute religious fear and fury that shaped the times, other visions of toleration also were kept cloistered within the sterile confines of intellectual debate, far removed from implementation. The Geneva-trained humanist scholar Sebastian Castellio's *Concerning Heretics*, occasioned in 1553 by the author's revulsion at the burning of the heretic Michael Servetus earlier that year in Geneva, argued passionately against the notion of heresy and persecution and proposed that toleration was beneficial to a society. Castellio criticized the Calvinists for playing God and ignoring the conscience of individuals, and he challenged Calvin directly by maintaining that reason and religion worked together in bringing about the good society. Europe was not ready to hear him, however. Nor was Europe prepared to embrace the ideas of the Dutch writer Dirck Coornhert (d. 1590), a somewhat unorthodox Catholic who fashioned in several publications a plea for toleration in which he claimed that religious freedom, the exercise of individual conscience, and pluralism were good for the state. Hugo Grotius (d. 1645) and Jacob Arminius (d. 1609) added arguments critical of state religion and the notion of God as a tyrant, but it was not until the beginning of the Enlightenment, in the writings of John Locke and Pierre Bayle, that the idea of toleration began to acquire the momentum that would lead to its formalization as a policy advantageous to the state. In the meantime, Jews, expelled from Spain in 1492, struggled, like other persons accused of infidelity and heresy, under the brutal machinery of the Inquisition. Catholics found themselves at war with Protestants across a vast and shifting front, and Protestants attacked each other—as in the case of the Church of England's campaign against the Puritans—with cannon and sword as well as preaching and writing.

The ideas of John Milton, the Puritan advocate of toleration, were rudimentary in the seventeenth century, and in any event did not translate easily to the American environment, where Indians and Catholics vigorously competed with Puritans for space. Puritans arrived in the New World persecuted, and intolerant. Catholics, in New Spain and New France, brought their own brands of intolerance, not only of Protestants but of Indians and Jews. European Christians also brought with them to the Americas interpretations of the Bible that supported not only intolerance of non-Christian religions (and intolerance of brands of Christianity that differed from their own) but supplied guidance about how to deal with those who were different. Intolerance, after all, is not merely an abstract intellectual position. Intolerance, in reality, is practice as much as theory. It is the implementation of a theory of difference in the form of actions taken against religious opponents. Accordingly, one of its components is an argument for the vigorous and unrelenting persecution of others, and that argument typically is made in bold terms, in actions as well as words. For many of those who crossed the Atlantic to the New World, the trope or story that informed their practice of intolerance was the Old Testament account of God's dealings with the Amalekites.

The Amalekites, according to Biblical accounts, had always been the enemies of the Jews. They were especially reviled because in spite of some manner of blood relationship to the Jews, they raided the weak and slow at the rear of the column of Jews who were fleeing Egypt and attacked the Jews at other times as well. The Old Testament reports that God commanded the

Jews to annihilate the Amalekites, to utterly destroy them without mercy—their men, women, children, and animals—leaving no trace of them. The Jews were to exterminate the Amalekites, to cleanse the world of them, and of any memory of them as well. According to Biblical sources, the Jews eventually accomplished that mission.

English writers during and after the English Reformation adopted the image of cowardly, duplicitous, menacing Amalekites to illustrate for their readerships the dangers posed by Roman Catholics to Protestantism in England. Theological differences between Catholics and Protestants (and between different Protestant groups) led to a long period of terrible violence in Europe beginning in the early sixteenth century. The Reformation was as much a revolution in social and political life as it was religious innovation, and the sudden and profound changes that took place in all of those areas produced an environment that was exceedingly volatile and frequently ripe for the enactment of violence when ideological support could be mustered for that. The rhetorical justification for such violence invariably was drawn from the Bible, and in the case of the English, the Amalek story proved particularly effective as a motivating image for dealing with religious enemies. English Protestant writers cultivated an anti-Catholic perspective that blossomed, poisonously, into characterizations of Catholics as evil, plotting traitors to England and to God. They compared them to Amalekites, noting that Catholics, as at least nominal Christians, should have embraced the Protestant emphasis on the word of God in the Bible and Protestant criticism of Roman Catholic Church government, and ritual, as corrupt. Because they did not, they existed as a deadly element inside the tent of Christianity, and by means of conspiracies and deceptions were spreading their malignancy throughout the newly reformed church. They were Amalekites—seeming kin, but not truly kin—whose influence posed such a danger to the fledgling Protestant churches that extreme measures were required to ensure that through their plottings of evil they did not subvert the purified Christian church. The inflammatory rhetoric of writers such as Thomas Taylor and John Flavel informed and reinforced English Protestant thinking about intolerance of Roman influences, and it traveled to the New World with the earliest Puritan colonists. John Winthrop, best known for his speech about God's providence that he delivered while aboard the vessel bringing the first Puritans to Massachusetts Bay, invoked in that very speech the story of God's command to the Jews to annihilate the Amalekites. Once ashore, the story was adapted to the new circumstances and marshaled in campaigns against Indians, Catholics, and non-Puritans.

The religious people who crossed the Atlantic to settle in New England in the early seventeenth century inhabited an enchanted world. For them, earthquakes were not the shifting of tectonic plates, violent storms were not the accidental meeting of weather fronts, and fires that burned down houses, towns, or even cities were not random tragedies. All such events were ordained by God, who punished and rewarded as he pleased. God's ways sometimes bewildered men and women who placed their trust in Him, but faith led persons to embrace the events that shaped their days on earth as part of God's plans for their lives as individuals and for the good of the Christian church as a collective body. The religious worldview of the colonists in New England led them to picture Native Americans in various ways, but always through a lens ground by colonists' investment in the idea of a world where divine providence and demonic evil shaped events and influenced lives. Some colonists sought out missionary success among the Indians, believing that conversion of Indians was a condition in the covenant that God had made with New Englanders for their survival in the New World wilderness. Other colonists regarded Indians suspiciously, and at times that suspicion was distilled into fear and hatred of Indians as demonic, warlike, and meant by God for extermination.

Native Americans posed a particularly challenging ideological problem for colonists. Speculation about who they were and where they came from frequently made its way to the conclusion that Indians were descendants of the Jews, the surviving remnant of Lost Tribes that had been dispersed in ancient Jewish history to far-flung lands. English Christians' understanding of the historical unfolding of God's plan for the world, grounded in suggestive but often vague biblical references to peoples, places, and events, demanded of them an effort to link Native American history to Old Testament accounts of the populating of the world. The Americas, the territory that Indians inhabited, was the territory to which Indians were led by God long ago, in the aftermath of a Jewish crisis of faith and identity in the eastern Mediterranean. By such reckoning, Indians were assessed as distant religious kin of the Puritans, and in some more elaborate English imaginings of Indian history, as a people very much like the Britons who occupied England in an earlier age. The English, moreover, were not alone in reflecting on the Jewish origins of Indians. Spanish and French writers offered up similar analyses of the Indian presence and past, sometimes suggesting (like some English) that they were in fact lapsed Christians. In the writings of the renowned Dominican missionary Bartolomé de Las Casas and Spanish writers such as Garcilaso de la Vega, Pedro Cieza de León, and José de Acosta, Native Americans were linked to

Judaism and Christianity through interpretation of their mythologies, rituals, and material cultures. Indians, said some writers, had over time "forgotten" the Jewish revelation. Other writers argued that Indians had fallen away from Christianity over time, and that Amerindian religion in general was, accordingly, *praeparatio evangelica*, that is, preparation for the gospel. The Capuchin Pacifique de Provins echoed this theological rumination when he expressed the view that the role of the missionary was to recover the faith, to reawaken it, in Amerindians. In his words, the missionary labored to "bring these savage people *back* to the knowledge of the true God we adore." The abbé Bobé in 1719 likewise explained how "Israelites under the dispersion by Salmanasar passed into North America," and he linked them specifically with the Sioux. Among Puritans, the missionary John Eliot embraced the theory that Indians were descended from the Lost Tribes, and he was joined in that cause by the Jewish Rabbi Menasseh ben Israel in Amsterdam, who authored *Hope of Israel* (1650), and in Norfolk, England, by Presbyterian clergyman Thomas Thorowgood, author of *Iews in America; or Probabilities that the Americans are of that Race* (1650). Boston minister Cotton Mather, Rhode Island founder Rodger Williams, the Quaker William Penn, and the theological giant Jonathan Edwards all adopted the theory in whole or in part.[2]

The crucial element in colonial theories about the linkage of Indians to Judaism and Christianity was the colonists' sense that Indians were, in some fashion, part of a global and transhistorical family of believers in God. Indians were lapsed, perhaps, or had come to be degraded in their faith over time, but they were relatives nevertheless. They were, in short, religious kin to Christians, and when things did not go well between Indians and colonists, Indians were not just opponents but, in the Puritan world of interwoven religion and society, religious traitors. Like the Amalekites, they were deserving of the penalty of extermination that God long ago had ordained as judgment on those who, in spite of their kinship with a people favored by God, betrayed their relatives. Such reasoning, refined in English anti-Catholic religious writings and transmitted to the colonies in the seventeenth century, was applied to the interpretation of relations between Indians and New Englanders. Those applications led to rhetorical adaptations that could be exploited for generations in campaigns against Indians, Catholics, Mormons, Quakers, persons identified as witches, and others. Moreover, those patterns were reinforced in English Protestant relations with Catholics in the New World. In the seventeenth century, for example, French Catholics who settled the St. Lawrence Valley and other areas west of New England met with stiff opposition from the English. When territorial and commercial disputes, framed by already difficult relations between the English and French in Europe, gathered momentum and issued in armed conflict, religious imagery shaped the rhetoric of violent encounter. During the French and Indian War (1754–63) and at other times, New Englanders cast the French as minions in the army of the papal Antichrist, and the French retaliated with depictions of the Puritans and their descendants as people seduced from the true church by demonic influence.

English settlers in the Chesapeake found themselves, like New Englanders, periodically in conflict with Native Americans. The colonial enterprise in the Chesapeake differed from that of New England, however, in that the people who settled Jamestown, and their Virginia Company overseers in England, were not infused with zeal born of a sense of religious destiny. The prospect of commercial profit weighed more heavily than religion in their calculation of reasons to carry forward the colonial enterprise. That did not mean, however, that religion was unimportant in Virginia and the surrounding plantation territories. Keenly aware that the work of building a colony required the realization of some measure of order, discipline, and common cause among the persons involved, officials at Jamestown and elsewhere in the region enforced religious statues that served the purpose, at least in their minds, of fostering progress toward those goals. An early instance of the subsequent codes governing behavior were the statutes enforced under Governor Thomas Dale several years after the founding of the colony in 1607. Dale considered the English undertaking in Virginia to be a species of "religious warfare" that involved the enforcement of severe penalties for immoral behavior among the settlers as much as battle against the Indians. Dale's laws represented intolerance of any drift from Anglican moral standards or theological tenets. Heresy, the public pronouncement of religious ideas contrary to Anglican theology, was punishable by death. Although the standard for behavior for colonists became less rigid over time, the tone of that earliest code set the terms for Protestant thinking about Catholics who settled nearby Maryland (as well as others who came later). By the end of the seventeenth century in Maryland, with Catholics a religious minority, the Church of England officially established, and Virginia exercising de facto rule of the colony, Catholics there suffered under the enforcement of statutes that forbade them from holding office, voting, or worshipping publicly. The anti-Catholic mood was still strong in the colonies when the Georgia charter of 1732 forbade Catholics the practice of their religion.

Dissenting Protestants also suffered at the hands of the Anglican ecclesiastical establishment in the Chesapeake. Thomas Jefferson, who led the cause of religious freedom in Virginia in the 1780s, observed that the execution of Quakers—which came to a head when Puritans put to death Quaker missionaries in Massachusetts in the mid-seventeenth century—likely would have happened as well in Virginia had historical circumstances conspired more actively with hatred of Quakers there. As it happened, Quakers were fined and banished but not executed in Virginia. Religious conflict among other Protestants—involving Methodists, Baptists, Presbyterians, and Anglicans—was intense and sometimes violent in Virginia and the Carolinas.

Jews were not treated as badly in the American colonies as they were in Europe. This was due in part to their very small presence in America: they were barely visible and did not strike observers as capable of the kinds of subversive plottings of which they were constantly accused in Europe. Also, in the difficult colonial environment, cooperation among persons of different backgrounds—in the interest of advancing common commercial and social projects—was generally more important than the cultivation of animosity toward potential partners in those enterprises. In New England, Quakers suffered misfortunes, however unearned, because they violated religious laws regarding public preaching and the espousal of heretical doctrines. Jews were not evangelical. They were disinclined to convert others to their faith, and they made no effort to enforce their view of religion upon others through manipulation of law or custom. Jews, however, brought with them from Europe the baggage that for centuries had plagued them. They were conceived in much religious literature primarily as Christ killers, and in some writings as fiends who required the blood of innocents for their rituals. Moreover, the image of the Jew as a sneaky commercial fraud, as a person duplicitous in commercial transaction with others and single-minded in a determination to fleece trading partners, followed Jews wherever they were dispersed around the globe. Jews were cast as enemies of Christ and were linked with Catholics, Indians, and Muslims in blasphemy of Christian truth. With some exceptions, they were left alone during colonial times; but in later centuries, as their numbers grew larger from immigration, Jews experienced overt and violent persecution.

The vast and extraordinarily wealthy Spanish empire in the Americas was built upon the search for gold, the desire to convert Indians to Christianity, and the hope of achieving military glory. Beginning with Columbus's voyages after 1492, the Spanish treated American indigenes in ruthless fashion, killing, torturing, and enslaving them, shipping Indian gold back to Spain, and systematically constructing a brutal regime of colonial exploitation of the human and natural resources of the Americas. Conversion to Christianity was a crucial component of the Spanish plan of acculturation and integration of Indians into the economic machinery of the colonial territories. Dominicans, Jesuits, and Franciscans came to the New World in large numbers, bringing with them some measure of hopefulness for baptizing Native Americans as Roman Catholics, and bringing the everyday lives of the converts under close and constant moral supervision. The records of missionary activities in New Spain indicate that sacrifice and devotion to religious ideals were not generally lacking in the efforts of the clergy. But the religious enterprise was mingled with the economic rationale for Spanish exploration and dominion, and the resistance of Indians to the Spanish demand for submission was viewed as resistance to Christianity as much as to Spanish political will. Accordingly, the fundamental ends of Spanish exploration and colonization—conversion of Indians and the extraction of wealth through military dominance—were intertwined from the very beginning of the Spanish presence in the Americas. To resist Christianity was to resist politically, and to resist politically was to offer offense to Christianity. This understanding of the complexity of religious encounter was redolent in Spanish documents of the colonial period, and especially in landmark legal pronouncements such as the *Requerimiento* of 1510, a statement read in Spanish to Indians that demanded of them assent to Catholic doctrines and submission to the authority of the Roman Church and its representatives, the Spanish clergy and government officials.

The bloody history of Spanish repression of Indian religions and the vicious tenor of Spanish colonialism in general has been narrated by historians in books written over several centuries, beginning in fact in the sixteenth-century writings of some clergy, such as Bartolomé de Las Casas, whose published laments about the inhumanity of Spanish rule in the New World gained him a reputation as a reformist in Spain. The Spanish treatment of Protestants and Jews in the Americas was not characterized by the kind of cruelty that marked Spanish treatment of the Indians (and Protestants and Jews were rarely numbered among the inhabitants of Spain's overseas possessions). Spain officially barred Jews from immigrating to its American colonies, but Jews were present in the Caribbean in the 1490s and some even served as soldiers in Spanish expeditions in subsequent decades. The Inquisition was installed in New Spain in the early sixteenth century, and it went about its business of rooting out heretics, apostates, Jews, and Protestants with its usual grim efficiency, burning two Jews at the stake in Mexico as early as 1528.

French Catholics in North America did not deploy an Inquisition to ferret out faith traitors or heretics. The French nevertheless were no strangers to religious intolerance, their history on the European continent having been punctuated at regular intervals with violent episodes of religious warfare. The French colonial enterprise in the Americas was never as expansive or as well organized as that of Spain or England, and the integration of religion, commerce, and government, which was crucial in New Spain and in some of the British colonies, was poorly articulated in New France. Indians were seen not so much as a threat because of their non-Christian religious ways as ripe candidates for conversion. Religiously motivated violence of the sort practiced in Spanish and British colonial settings was less common in French-controlled areas of the St. Lawrence Valley, Great Lakes, and Mississippi River Valley. The French, however, did carry with them across the Atlantic a suspicion of Jews and non-Catholics. Anti-Catholic rhetoric flavored French writing during the French and Indian War, and disputes between Protestants and Catholics in the maritime provinces sometimes took on the character of Protestant-Catholic religious battles. Jews were not welcome in New France, and in fact were expressly prohibited from residing in French colonies by a series of decrees beginning in the early seventeenth century.

In this chapter, we will examine documents that illustrate some of the ways in which Europeans imagined religion to be a central part of their colonization of North America, and how they imported from Europe an assortment of prejudices which they deployed against Native Americans and against other religious opponents who likewise had migrated from Europe. The earliest ventures of Europeans in the Americas were characterized by religious intolerance. This was the case in spite of the fact that some of the groups migrating to the New World sought refuge from persecution in Europe. That search for refuge, part of the collective memory of early regional Euro-American culture, had some effect, in the eighteenth century, on American advocacy of religious liberty. But the colonial mentality, which was constructed out of greed, fear, pride, and certainty in one's superiority to the colonized people, was prone to violence in encounters with Others. The flashpoint for violence sometimes was religion. In the rapidly changing and volatile social situation of the colonial world, in a setting where rules for social engagement and economic relations periodically were rendered ambiguous by unexpected developments, enactments of frustration over failure to realize goals often took the form of religious intolerance. Religious opponents were sometimes made scapegoats for the defects in colonial life. Intolerance nevertheless was always carried forward explicitly on the platform of religious difference, and violence against religious Others was explained as precisely that: religiously motivated. This pattern of blame, intolerance, and willingness to entertain the idea of the utter annihilation of religious opponents was set deeply into American culture during the colonial period and continued to inform religious conflict in America throughout the nineteenth century and into the twentieth.

DOCUMENTS

The Amalekites in Old Testament Accounts

Biblical references to the Amalekites are found largely in the Old Testament books of 1 Samuel and 2 Samuel, Judges, and in the Pentateuch (Genesis, Exodus, Leviticus, Numbers, Deuteronomy). In the accounts given in those books, the Amalekites are pictured as a nomadic people, adversaries of, but distant relations to, the Jews. They are reviled above all for the cowardly manner in which they attacked, in the Sinai desert, those who lagged behind the main body of Jews fleeing Egypt. Their treachery is angrily condemned by God, who orders the Jews to annihilate the Amalekites and wipe their name from history. The story of the destruction of the Amalekites has not only informed Jewish reflection on Jew hating and Jewish resistance to enemies up to the present day, but the trope has become a key part of Christian-tinctured texts that call for the destruction of one's religious opponents, whoever they might be.

Then came Amalek, and fought with Israel in Rephidim. And Moses said unto Joshua, Choose us out men, and go out, fight with Amalek: tomorrow I will stand on the top of the hill with the rod of God in mine hand. So Joshua did as Moses had said to him, and fought with Amalek: and Moses, Aaron, and Hur went up to the top of the hill. And it came to pass, when Moses held up his hand, that Israel prevailed: and when he let down his hand, Amalek prevailed. But Moses' hands were heavy; and they took a stone and put it under him, and he sat thereon; and Aaron and Hur stayed up his hands, the one on the one side, and the other on the other side; his hands were steady until the going down of the sun. And Joshua discomfited Amalek and his people with the edge of the sword. And the LORD said unto Moses, Write this for a memorial in a book, and rehearse it in the ears of Joshua: for I will utterly put out the remembrance of Amalek from under heaven. And Moses built an altar, and called the name of it Jehovahnissi: For he said, Because the LORD hath sworn that the LORD will have war with Amalek from generation to generation.

Source: Exodus 17:8–16 (King James Version).

> Remember what Amalek did unto thee by the way, when ye were come forth out of Egypt; how he met thee by the way, and smote the hindmost of thee, even all that were feeble behind thee, when thou was faint and weary; and he feared not God. Therefore it shall be, when the LORD thy God hath given thee rest from all thine enemies round about, in the land which the LORD thy God giveth thee for an inheritance to possess it, that thou shalt blot out the remembrance of Amalek from under heaven; thou shalt not forget it.
>
> *Source*: Deuteronomy 25:17–19 (King James Version).

> Thus saith the LORD of hosts, I remember that which Amalek did to Israel, how he laid wait for him in the way, when he came up from Egypt. Now go and smite Amalek, and utterly destroy all that they have, and spare them not; but slay both man and woman, infant and suckling, ox and sheep, camel and ass.
>
> *Source*: 1 Samuel 15:2–3 (King James Version).

Amalek in Seventeenth-Century English Anti-Catholic Writings

The appearance of the Amalek in American colonial writings about religious opponents came about through the influence of English writers who employed the image of plotting, duplicitous, and deadly Amalekites in their characterizations of English Catholics. The trope of Amalek was focused and enriched in such writings, and the notion of Amalekites—and therefore of Catholics—as religious relatives of Anglicans who betrayed the righteous people of God was foregrounded. It was a Christian duty, argued some writers, to make war against the "Romish Amalek" until it was utterly defeated, because only then could Christians rest securely in the knowledge that remnants were not lurking in caves crafting schemes to subvert Protestant religion. Such a view of the Catholic menace played especially well in the wake of the discovery and deflection in 1605 of the Gunpowder Plot, a plan to kill King James I and the leading Protestant nobility by igniting a stockpile of gunpowder hidden beneath Parliament. Thomas Taylor's *An Everlasting Record of the Utter Ruine of Romish Amalek* (1624) and John Flavel's *Tydings from Rome or, England's Alarm* (1667) are excerpted to illustrate the rhetorical incitement of hatred of Catholicism in England.

Exodus 17:14 — *And the Lord said to Moses, Write this for a remembrance in the book, and rehearse it for Joshua, for I will utterly put out the remembrance of Amaleck from under Heaven....*

Now from this first part of the Text wee may note, ...

That in our way to heavenly Canaan, we must make account of many Amalekites as Israel cannot set forth towards Canaan but Amalek will meet them. Israel going into Egypt had no enemies, but in their way to Canaan never wanted them. A man may goe to hell merily, and never meet with Amalekites to hinder him; hee hath wind and tide with him. But let all the Israel of God resolve in their way to meet with Amalek, to fight with Amalek, to overcome Amalek, else there is no hope of ever seeing Canaan; wee must not expect rest till we be thorow the Wildernesse....

In this second part of the text are two things....

The Author of the revenge....

The severitie of this revenge, in that the Lord will utterly destroy him with a totall and finall destruction; and is not satisfied in overthrowing the kingdome and dominion only, unlesse he put out the name and memorie of them from under heaven. All which noteth a great detestation and an utter abolishing of this people.

Quest. Why? what cause was there of such severitie in this execution?

Answ. The cause was the fierce wrath of *Amalek,* against Gods people the Israelites; if *Amalek* bee fierce against the people of God, God will bee fierce against *Amalek.* Now the fierce wrath of *Amalek* appeared against Israel, because, ...

It was *unnaturall,* for *Amalek* was of the same bloud and neere kinred with Israel: *Amalek* was the sonne of *Eliphaz,* the sonne of *Esau* by *Tymnah* his Concubine; as *Esau* and *Iacob* were brethren: so as they forgetting bloud and kinred, nourish an unnaturall wrath, and raise an unnaturall war against the people of God....

It was *Crafty* and *Cowardly* done: they give Israel no warning, nor offer faire termes of war, but steale upon them, and fall upon the weakest; and when they were weake and weary, *and scattered the remnant of Israel, Deuteronomie* 25.20. Thus because they ioyne with force, fraud in spoyling Israel, the Lord taketh his peoples part, and scattereth them with a terrible revenge....

If we looke to the enemies, they are many and mighty, but *Amalekites;* we have to doe with cruell enemies, but accursed in their persons, in their enterprises, and in all the wicked meanes of accomplishing the same: and if we looke a little into the resemblance, we shall see that as Romish *Amalek* have notably expressed the like cruelty with these in our text; so shall they meet with the same certaine perdition: they being written by God to destruction as truly as the former. For, ...

Amalek signifieth a smiting people, and of all Religions, never was any so fierce or smiting as Romish *Amalek*, their cruelty transcendeth the barbarous cruelty of Turkes or Scithians; no degrees of men could avoid their strokes with both their swords: they make no difference of men, but strike at Princes and people, Kings and kingdoms, they smite the living and the dead, and make no bones to blow up three whole kingdomes at once with one terrible blow or stroke. The blowes of the old *Amalekites* were gentle and soft to the blowes of this smiting *Amalek*.

Source: Thomas Taylor, *An Everlasting Record of the Utter Ruine of Romish Amaleck* (London: J. H., 1624), 1–19.

---

1 COUNSEL. Abhor Popery, and be eminent in your zeal against it. *Rome* is that *Amalek*, with whom God will never make peace; neither should we: It was *Queen Elizabeths* Motto, *No peace with Spain* and it should be ours. No peace with *Rome*. My dear Countreymen, I beseech you, be not deceived with vain words; suffer not your selves too be circumvented by a Stratagem of the Enemy let not prejudice, and discontents which they endeavour to beget and foment in you against your real friends, cause any of you to fall in with the Design and Interest of your Enemies: it is a dangerous thing to comply with that Interest which God hath engaged himself against, and as sure as Christ sits at his Fathers right hand, shall be destroyed: and what cause you have to abhor Popery: you will see by that time I have shewed you, that it is a FALSE: BLOODY: BLASPHEMOUS: UNCOMFORTABLE: AND DAMNABLE RELIGION.

Source: John Flavel, *Tydings from Rome, or Englands Alarm* (London, 1667), 18–19.

John Winthrop's *A Modell of Christian Charity* (1630)

John Winthrop organized the migration of a group of Puritans to Massachusetts Bay in 1630 and served as the first governor of the colony. His speech delivered at sea aboard the *Arbella*—republished in history textbooks so many times as to be iconic—is frequently cited for its references to the group's trust that their colony would be like "a city on a hill," a shining example of Christian devotion made visible to the rest of the world. The Puritans who made the Atlantic crossing with him came to believe that they had entered into a covenant with God, and that God would protect and bless their enterprise in the New World as long as they were vigilant in enforcing the practice of purified Christianity (i.e., "Puritans"). What is overlooked in historical commentary on the speech, however, is evidence of Winthrop's easy familiarity with the story of Amalek. Directly preceding the statement regarding a covenant with God is Winthrop's reminder that just as God had given Saul a commission to utterly destroy the Amalekites, and punished Saul for falling short of that, God would punish the Puritans if they failed in their commission. Of the many biblical references that he might have chosen to drive home the importance of meeting the challenge of God's call to holiness in America, Winthrop chose an image that he knew his audience would readily appreciate and understand. The speech accordingly evidences the strong awareness among the earliest Puritan settlers of New England of biblical grounds for the ruthless extermination of religious opponents. It also raises the question of the extent to which Puritans, even before landing near Boston, had imagined the possibility of pursuing a deadly agenda in their relations with American indigenes.

First, in regard of the more near bond of marriage between him and us, wherein he hath taken us to be his after a most strict and peculiar manner, which will make him the more jealous of our love and obedience. So he tells the people of Israel, you only have I known of all the families of the earth, therefore will I punish you for your transgressions. Secondly, because the Lord will be sanctioned in them that come near him. We know that there were many that corrupted the service of the Lord, some setting up altars before his own, others offering both strange fire and strange sacrifices also; yet there came no fire from heaven or other sudden judgment upon them, as did upon Nadab and Abihu, who yet we may think did not sin presumptuously. Thirdly, when God gives a special commission he looks to have it strictly observed in every article. When he gave Saul a commission to destroy Amalek, he indented with him upon certain articles, and because he failed in one of the least, and that upon a fair pretense, it lost him the kingdom which should have been his reward if he had observed his commission.

Thus stands the cause between God and us. We are entered into covenant with him for this work, we have taken out a commission, the Lord hath given us leave to draw our own articles, we have professed to enterprise these actions, upon these and those ends, we have hereupon besought him of favor and blessing. Now if the Lord shall please to hear us, and bring us in peace to the place we desire, then hath he ratified this covenant and sealed our commission, [and] will expect a strict performance of the articles contained in it. But if we shall neglect the observation of these articles, which are the ends we have propounded, and, dissembling with our God, shall fall to embrace this present world and prosecute our carnal intentions, seeking great things for ourselves and our posterity, the Lord will surely break out in wrath against us, be revenged of such a perjured people and make us know the price of the breach of such a covenant. . . .

Now the only way to avoid this shipwreck, and to provide for our posterity, is to follow the counsel of Micah: to do justly, to love mercy, to walk humbly with our God. For this end, we must be knit together in this work as one man, we must entertain each other in brotherly affection, we must be willing to abridge ourselves of our superfluities, for the supply of others' necessities, we must uphold a familiar commerce together in all meekness, gentleness, patience and liberality; we must delight in each other, make others' conditions our own, rejoice together, mourn together, labor and suffer together, always having before our eyes our commission and community in the work, our community as members of the same body. So shall we keep the unity of the spirit in the bond of peace. The Lord will be our God, and delight to dwell among us as his own people, and will command a blessing upon us in all our ways, so that we shall see much more of his wisdom, power, goodness and truth, than formerly we have been acquainted with. We shall find that the God of Israel is among us, when ten of us shall be able to resist a thousand of our enemies: when he shall make us a praise and glory that men shall say of succeeding plantations: "the Lord make it like that of New England." For we must consider that we shall be as a city upon a hill: The eyes of all people are upon us, so that if we shall deal falsely with our God in this work we have undertaken, and so cause him to withdraw his present help from us, we shall be made a story and a byword through the world: we shall open the mouths of enemies to speak evil of the ways of God and all professors for God's sake. We shall shame the faces of many of God's worthy servants, and cause their prayers to be turned into curses upon us, till we be consumed out of the good land whither we are going.

Source: John Winthrop, *A Modell of Christian Charity*, in *The American Puritans*, edited by Perry Miller (New York, 1956), 82–83. Written on board the *Arbella* on the Atlantic Ocean, 1630.

Colonial Depictions of Native Americans as Amalekites

English depictions of Catholics as Amalekites provided an image of evil and a basic inventory of corrupt practices and beliefs that could be applied to other groups. In stressing Catholic deviousness, barbarity, cunning, and cowardly tactics, among other things, English writers articulated a set of attributes that could be applied to other religious opponents who might then also be judged worthy of annihilation. Seventeenth- and eighteenth-century New Englanders, long familiar, as we have seen, with the story of the Amalekites, discovered over time the relevance of the trope to their reflection on relations with the Indians. Cotton Mather, never one to miss a chance to publicly bless the New England Puritan cause or to foretell its destiny, called up Amalek to rally colonial forces to battle in King William's War against the French and Indians (*Souldiers counseled and comforted* [1689]). Because the Indians were in league with the French, and the French were Catholics, it was not a difficult intellectual maneuver to tar the Indians with the same brush that had painted the Catholics as Amalekites. Exhorting his audience to "in the name of God be daring enough to execute that vengeance on" the "Tawny Pagans," he urged the soldiers departing to battle to "turn not back till they are consumed." The intertwining of seventeenth-century Puritan rhetoric about papal plots and the call for extermination of the Indian continued to develop in New England thinking so that by the early part of the eighteenth century, the contagion was complete: fears of Catholic power could be detached from fears of Indian power, and the Amalek trope be kept intact in its application to Indian enemies. The process was advanced especially by the picturing of Indians increasingly as practitioners of witchcraft. Against such a background, Thomas Symmes could elegize soldiers killed in a lost battle with the Indians (without mentioning Catholics) by reminding his audience that the mortally wounded commanding officer had resembled Joshua, Moses' "Renowned general, in his wars with the Aborigines of Canaan," the Amalekites.

> At the first Appearance of the Tawny Pagans, then Courage brave Hearts; Fall on! Fall on Couragiously, with that Appearance in Psal. 3.6,7. *I will not be afraid of ten thousands of the people that have set themselves against me. O my God, thou hast smitten all mine Enemies.* Yea, when once you have but got the Track of those Ravenous howling Wolves, then pursue them vigorously; Turn not back until they are consumed: Wound them that they shall not be able to Arise; Tho' they Cry Let there be none to Save them; But beat them small as the Dust before the Wind, and Cast them out, as the Dirt in the Streets. Let not the Expression seem Harsh, if I say unto you, Sacrifice them to the Ghosts of the Christians whom they have Murdered. They have horribly Murdered some scores of your dear Country-men, whose Blood cries in your Ears, while you are going to Fight, Vengeance, Dear Country-men!

Vengeance upon our Murderers. Let your Courage, in the Name of God be daring enough to Execute that Vengeance on them. . . .

The Barbarians may (as 'tis by Escaped Captives reported that they have) by their Diabolical Charms, keep our Dogs from Hurting of them, but they shall not so keep our Swords from coming at them. Faith and Prayer among us, hath wonderfully made the Divels themselves to fly before it; so shall These too find unto their Cost. Tho' the Papists may likewise contribute what Help they can unto these Miscreants, and say Mass with them (as of Late) after their Little Victories, yet we need not be disanimated; but the rather from thence prognosticate their Approaching Ruine. For we too much Distrust our own Observation, if we do not now think, that the whole Papal Empire, (which was of late replanting a Tabernacle in the Glorious Holy Mountain between the Seas) is very near its End when none shall help it; and that the twelve Hundred and sixty Years, during which the people of God, were to be harassed by it, are not far from their Expiration. In a word, you may go forth with such a Triumph as that in Psal. 20.7,8: *Some Trust in Chariots, and some in Horses* (Some in Satan, and some in Antichrist) *But wee will Remember the Name of the Lord our God. They are brought down and fallen; but wee are Risen and stand Upright.*

And for a close, Let me mind you, that while you fight, Wee'l pray. Every good man will do it, in secret and in private every day; and publick supplications also will be always going for you. We will keep in the Mount with our Hands lifted up, while you are in the Field with your Lives in your Hands, against the Amalek that is now annoying this Israel in the Wilderness. It was the Watch Word which a Battel once Commenced withal Now for the Fruit of Prayer! Now for the Fruit of Prayer. To gather that Fruit will be your Errand.

Source: Cotton Mather, *Souldiers counseled and comforted. A discourse delivered unto some part of the forces engaged in the just war of New-England against the northern and eastern Indians* (Boston: Samuel Green, 1689), 28–31.

When Joshua with his chosen Soldiers had Discomfited Amalek, with the Edge of the Sword; (while Moses with the Rod of GOD in his up-lifted hands, supported by Aaron and Hur, made intercession to the GOD of Armies, on the Top of the Hill) the Lord said to Moses, *Write THIS for a Memorial in a Book, and rehearse it in the Ears of Joshua*, Exod. XVII.14. For this would be an unspeakable Encouragement to that Renowned General in his Wars with the Aboriginies of Canaan.

Source: Thomas Symmes, *Historical Memoirs of the Fight at Piggwacket* (Boston: B. Green, 1725), 1.

Witchcraft

Fear of witches was common in early modern Europe. In England alone, approximately one thousand suspected witches—persons accused of bargaining with the Devil—were hanged from the middle of the sixteenth century to the end of the seventeenth. In the English colonies, and especially in New England, where rapid growth begat social change and ruptures with the original visions of the colonies' founders, witchcraft fears were a regular part of the seventeenth-century religious worldview. Most of those accused of witchcraft were women, and they often were persons whose place in the social order was ambiguous—a widow, or a commercially successful woman, or a woman who dared to publicly air her dissenting theological positions. New England witch hunting reached its peak at Salem, Massachusetts, in 1692 with the hanging of nineteen persons accused of witchcraft. The hysteria evident at Salem represents the commitment of local leaders to enforcing strict religious standards for conduct and thinking. A measurement of religious orthodoxy, it reveals how intolerance can take the form not only of opposing other seemingly official religions (e.g., Protestants' opposition to Catholics) but can flare up as an attempt to root out seeming heterodoxy within the religious community itself. Margaret Jones, hanged for witchcraft in Charlestown, Massachusetts, in 1648, was known for her herbal remedies for illnesses. Perhaps she was too much of an adept, however, because she came under suspicion of deriving her power from a compact with the Devil and was brought to trial when a witch hunter testified that she had been in the company of a child who could vanish from sight. The account of the evidence marshaled against her, taken from John Winthrop's *Journal*, illustrates the ease with which religious fears could lead to violence, in this case her execution.

At this court one Margaret Jones of Charlestown was indicted and found guilty of witchcraft, and hanged for it. The evidence against her was 1. that she was found to have such a malignant touch, as many persons, (men, women, and children,) whom she stroked or touched with any affection or displeasure, or, etc., were taken with deafness, or vomiting, or other violent pains or sickness, 2. she practicing physic, and her medicines being such things as (by her own confession) were harmless, as aniseed, liquors, etc., yet had extraordinary violent effects, 3. she would use to tell such as would not make use of her physic, that they would never be healed, and accordingly their diseases and hurts continued, with relapse against the ordinary course, and beyond the apprehension of all physicians and surgeons, 4. some things which she foretold came to pass accordingly; other things she could tell of (as secret speeches, etc.) which she had no ordinary means to come to the knowledge of, 5. she had (upon search) an apparent teat in her secret parts as fresh as if it had been newly sucked, and after it had been scanned, upon a forced search, that was withered, and another began on the opposite side, 6. in the prison, in the clear day-light, there was seen in her arms, she sitting on the floor, and her clothes up, etc., a little child, which ran from her into another room, and the officer following it, it was vanished. The like child was seen in two other places, to which she had relation; and one maid that saw it, fell sick upon it, and was cured by the said Margaret, who used means to be employed to that end. Her behavior at her trial was very intemperate, lying notoriously, and railing upon the jury and witnesses, etc., and in the like distemper she died. The same day and hour she was executed, there was a very great tempest at Connecticut, which blew down many trees, etc.

Source: Winthrop's Journal: "History of New England" 1630–1649, vol. 2, edited by James Kendall Hosmer (New York: Charles Scribner's Sons, 1908), 344–45.

Enforcement of Orthodoxy in Colonial Virginia

The enforcement of orthodoxy by extreme means is as much an indication of religious intolerance as campaigns against religious opponents outside one's own community. The establishing of draconian measures to force conformity to standards of religious behavior discloses a keen sense of boundary separating religious insiders from all others. It is a signal of acute intolerance of any competing worldview. Governor Thomas Dale, in a 1611 letter to a minister in London in which he discusses relations with the Indians, refers to the colonial undertaking in Jamestown, Virginia (founded in 1607), as "religious warfare." The religious code of conduct that the governor enforced—known as "Dale's laws"—with its lengthy listing of offenses punishable by death, underscored the fortress mentality of the colony's overseers. "Hereticks" and "Idolaters" in this case were considered much like witches.

Right Reverend Sir:

By Sir Thomas Gates, I wrote unto you, of such occasions as then presented themselves; and now again by this worthy gentlemen, Captain Argall, I salute you; for such is the reverend regard I have of you, as I cannot omit any occasion to express the sincere affection I bare you. You have ever given me encouragements to persevere in this religious warfare, until your last letters; not for that you are now less well affected thereunto; but because you see the action to be in danger, by many of their non-performances, who undertook the business. I have undertaken, and have as faithfully, and with all my might, endeavored the prosecution with all alacrity; as God that knoweth the heart can bear me record. What recompense, or what rewards, by whom, or when, I know not where to expect, but from Him in whose vineyard I labor, whose church with greedy appetite I desire to erect.

Source: "Thomas Dale," in Edward Giddings, *American Christian Rulers or Religion and Men of Government* (New York: Bromfield & Company, 1890), 154.

And first, of such as deserve capitall punishment, or cutting off from a mans people, whether by death or banishment.

1. First, Blasphemy which is a cursing of God by Atheisme or the like, to be punished with death.

2. Idolatry to be punished with death.

3. Witchcraft which is fellowship by covenant with a familiar Spirit to be punished with death.

4. Consulters with Witches not to be tollerated, but either to be cut off by death, or by banishment.

5. Heresie which is the maintenance of some wicked errors, overthrowing the foundation of Christian Religion, which obstinacy if it be joined with endeavour, to seduce others thereunto to be punished with death: because such an Hereticke no less than an Idolater seeketh to thrust the soules of men from the Lord their God.

6. To worship God in a molten or graven Image, to be punished with death.

7. Such members of the Church, as doe willfully reject to walke after due admonition, and conviction, the Churches establishment, and their Christian admonition and censures, shall be cut off by banishment.

8. Whosoever shall revile the Religion and Worship of God, and the Government the Church as it is now established, to be cut off by banishment.

Source: "Of Crimes," in *Tracts and other papers relating principally to the origin, settlement, and progress of the colonies in North America from the discovery of the country to the year 1776,* 4 vols. (Washington, D.C.: Peter Force, 1836–46), 3:12–13.

Official Intolerance

The colonial charter of Georgia (1732) officially withheld religious freedom from Catholics. The state constitution of New York (1770) prohibited clergy from holding civil or military office. The latter case evidences the ways in which religious intolerance could be carried forward seemingly in the cause of religious freedom, the framers arguing that priests and ministers historically had been the leaders in fomenting intolerance and so were to be denied positions of power from which they could continue to prosecute that agenda.

And our will and pleasure is, that all and every person and persons, who shall from time to time be chosen or appointed treasurer or treasurers, secretary or secretaries of the said corporation, in manner herein after directed, shall during such times as they shall serve in the said offices respectively, be incapable of being a member of the said corporation. And we do further of our special grace, certain knowledge and mere motion, for us, our heirs and successors, grant, by these presents, to the said corporation and their successors, that it shall be lawful for them and their officers or agents, at all times hereafter, to transport and convey out of our realm of Great-Britain, or any other of our dominions, into the said province of Georgia, to be there settled all such so many of our loving subjects, or any foreigners that are willing to become our subjects, and live under our allegiance, in the said colony, as shall be willing to go to, inhabit, or reside there, with sufficient shipping, armour, weapons, powder, shot, ordnance, munition, victuals, merchandise and wares, as are esteemed by the wild people; clothing, implements, furniture, cattle, horses, mares, and all other-things necessary for the said colony, and for the use and defence and trade with the people there, and in passing and returning to and from the same. Also we do, for ourselves and successors, declare, by these presents, that all and every the persons which shall happen to be born within the said province, and every of their children and posterity, shall have and enjoy all liberties, franchises and immunities of free denizens and natural born subjects, within any of our dominions, to all intents and purposes, as if abiding and born within this our kingdom of Great-Britain, or any other of our dominions. And for the greater ease and encouragement of our loving subjects and such others as shall come to inhabit in our said colony, we do by these presents, for us, our heirs and successors, grant, establish and ordain, that forever hereafter, there shall be a liberty of conscience allowed in the worship of God, to all persons inhabiting, or which shall inhabit or be resident within our said provinces and that all such persons, except papists, shall have a free exercise of their religion, so they be contented with the quiet and peaceable enjoyment of the same, not giving offence or scandal to the government.

Source: "The Georgia Charter of 1732," in Francis Newton Thorpe, *The Federal and State Constitutions Colonial Charters, and Other Organic Laws of the States, Territories, and Colonies Now or Heretofore Forming the United States of America* (Washington, D.C.: Government Printing Office, 1909).

XXXVIII. And whereas we are required, by the benevolent principles of rational liberty, not only to expel civil tyranny, but also to guard against that spiritual oppression and intolerance wherewith the bigotry and ambition of weak and wicked priests and princes have scourged mankind, this convention doth further, in the name and by the authority of the good people of this State, ordain, determine, and declare, that the free exercise and enjoyment of religious profession and worship, without discrimination or preference, shall forever hereafter be allowed, within this State, to all mankind: Provided, That the liberty of conscience, hereby granted, shall not be so construed as to excuse acts of licentiousness, or justify practices inconsistent with the peace or safety of this State.

XXXIX. And whereas the ministers of the gospel are, by their profession, dedicated to the service of God and the care of souls, and ought not to be diverted from the great duties of their function; therefore, no minister of the gospel, or priest of any denomination whatsoever, shall, at any time hereafter, under any presence or description whatever, be eligible to, or capable of holding, any civil or military office or place within this State.

Source: "The Constitution of New York: April 20, 1777," in Francis Newton Thorpe, *The Federal and State Constitutions, Colonial Charters, and Other Organic Laws of the States, Territories, and Colonies Now or Heretofore Forming the United States of America* (Washington, D.C.: Government Printing Office, 1909).

Colonial Anti-Quakerism

Members of the Society of Friends, nicknamed Quakers because of the physical manifestations of prayer that some Friends displayed, were persecuted in England and in America. They eventually found a safe haven in Pennsylvania, which was founded by the Quaker William Penn in 1681. They were reviled in New England, especially, in the first part of the seventeenth century. Quaker missionaries to Massachusetts were treated harshly, whipped, imprisoned, hanged, or deported. Mary Dyer was a supporter of Ann Hutchinson, who had been convicted as a heretic for her moderately unorthodox theological opinions and had fled Massachusetts in 1638. She joined a community founded by Roger Williams in 1633 that was more tolerant of religious difference than other New England communities, and she was joined there eventually by Mary Dyer, who had been chased from Massachusetts for preaching Quakerism. Dyer returned to Massachusetts several times to preach and finally was convicted and executed. The excerpt from an account by Samuel Morton, which begins with a report of her stillborn fetus, which was exhumed in 1638 just after her first banishment from Massachusetts, not only demonstrates the nature of intolerance toward Quakers because of their beliefs, it suggests how heretics, devils, witches, and Quakers (and, if we look to other documents, Indians as well) were joined together as related evils in the colonial imagination. Below, Thomas Jefferson's observation that Quakers escaped execution in Virginia merely by chance follows the Morton document calling for the suppression of Quakers in New England.

This Year there was a hideous Monster born at Boston in New-England, of one Mrs. Mary Dyer, a Co-partner with the said Mrs. Hutchinson in the aforesaid Heresies; the said Monster (as it was related to me) *It was without Head, but Horns like a Beast, Scales or a rough Skin like the Fish called the Thorn-beck, it had Leggs and Claws like a Fowl, and in other respects as a Woman Child*: the Lord declaring this detestation of their monstrous errors (as was then thought by some) by this prodigious birth. . . .

Having noted before, That in the Year 1657, there arrived in the Colony of New Plimouth many of that pernicious Sect called Quakers, the Reader may take notice, That by this time, for some years after, New-England (in divers parts of it) abounded with them, and they sowed their corrupt and damnable Doctrines, both by word and writings, almost in every Town of each Jurisdiction; some whereof were, *That all men ought to attend the Light within them to be the Rule of their Lives and Actions*; and, *That the holy Scriptures were not for the enlightening of man, nor a settled and permanent Rule of life.* They denied the Manhood of the Lord Jesus Christ, and affirmed, *That as Man he is not in Heaven.* They denied the Resurrection from the dead. They affirmed, *That an absolute Perfection in Holiness of Grace is attainable in this life.* They placed their Justification upon their Patience and Suffering for their Opinions, and on their righteous life, and retired demurity, and affected singularity in both word and gesture.

As to Civil account, they allowed not nor practiced any civil respect to man, though superiours, either in Magistratical consideration, or as Masters or Parents, or the Ancient, neither by word nor gesture. They deny also the use of Oathes for the deciding of Civil Controversies, with other abominable Opinions, Dreams, and Conceits, which some of them have expressed, tending to gross Blasphemy and Atheism.

This efficacy of Delusion became very prevalent with many, to as the number of them increased, to the great endangering of the subversion of the whole, both of Church and Common-wealth, notwithstanding the endeavours of those in Authority to suppress the same, had not the Lord declared against them, by blasting their Enterprizes and Contrivements, so as they have withered away in a great measure; sundry of their Teachers and Leaders which have caused them to err, are departed the Country, and we trust the Lord will make the folly of the remainder manifest to all men more and more. Errour is not long-lived; the day will declare it. Let our deliverance from so eminent a danger, be received amongst the principal of the Lords gracious Providences, and merciful loving kindnesses towards New-England; for the which let present and future generations celebrate his Praises.

Source: Nathaniel Morton, *New England's Memorial* (Boston: John Allen, 1721), 142, 197–98.

The first settlers in this country were emigrants from England, of the English church, just at a point of time when it was flushed with complete victory over the religious of all other persuasions. Possessed, as they became, of the power of making, administering, and executing the laws, they shewed equal intolerance in this country with their Presbyterian brethren, who had emigrated to the northern government. The poor Quakers were flying from persecution in England. They cast their eyes on these new countries as asylums of civil and religious freedom; but they found them free only for the reigning sect. / Several acts of the Virginia assembly of 1659, 1662, and 1693, had made it penal in parents to refuse to have their children baptized; had prohibited the unlawful assembling of Quakers; had made it penal for any master of a vessel to bring a Quaker into the state; had ordered those already here, and such as should come thereafter, to be imprisoned till they should abjure the country; provided a milder punishment for their first and second return, but death for their third; had inhibited all persons from suffering their meetings in or near their houses, entertaining them individually, or disposing of books which supported their tenets. If no execution took place here, as did in New England, it was not owing to the moderation of the church, or spirit of the legislature, as may be inferred from the law itself; but to historical circumstances which have not been handed down to us. / The Anglicans retained full possession of the country about a century. Other opinions began then to creep in, and the great care of the government to support their own church, having begotten an equal degree of indolence in its clergy, two-thirds of the people had become dissenters at the commencement of the present revolution. The laws indeed were still oppressive on them, but the spirit of the one party had subsided into moderation, and of the other had risen to a degree of determination which commanded respect.

Source: Thomas Jefferson, *Writings* (New York: Viking Press, 1984), 283.

Jews in North America

Twenty-three Jews arrived in New Netherlands (known today as New York City) in 1654. They were not welcomed by the governor of the Dutch colony there, Peter Stuyvesant. He wrote instead to Dutch West India Company officials who oversaw the business of the colony and urged them to approve his proposal to expel the Jews. He offered standard arguments that their religion was "abominable," that they cheated in commerce, and that if they were admitted it would set a precedent that might lead to the immigration of Roman Catholics to the colony. After taking stock of the substantial stake of Jewish investors in the company, the overseers refused Stuyvesant's request. Jews remained under suspicion in the colonies, however. New England minister Cotton Mather's reminder to his readers in 1669 that the Jews murdered Jesus Christ and his emphasis on Jews as blasphemers of the name of Jesus represented the general mood of Christians toward Jews in the colonies, even though such suspicion of Jews rarely led to overt acts of intolerance.

The Jews who have arrived would nearly all like to remain here, but learning that they (with their customary usury and deceitful trading with the Christians) were very repugnant to the inferior magistrates, as also to the people having the most affection for you; the Deaconry also fearing that owing to their present indigence they might become a charge in the coming winter, we have, for the benefit of this weak and newly developing place and the land in general, deemed it useful to require them in a friendly way to depart; praying also most seriously in this connect, for ourselves as also for the general community of your worships, that the deceitful race—such hateful enemies and blasphemers of the name of Christ—be not allowed to further infect and trouble this new colony to the detraction of your worships and the dissatisfaction of your worships' most affectionate subjects.

Source: "Peter Stuyvesant to the Amsterdam Chamber of the Dutch West India Company," in Samuel Oppenheim, "The Early History of the Jews in New York, 1654–1664," *Publications of the American Jewish Historical Society* 18 (1909): 45.

3. *Blasphemy is a most fearful sin.* It is a crime to be punished by the Judge. Now the Fears lie under the guilt of blasphemy, as it is said concerning the Papists, Rev. 13.6. *That they blaspheme the tabernacle of God*, i.e. the humane nature of Christ in respect of their Idolatrous Mass, Transubstantiation, etc. So it is true concerning the Jews, that they blaspheme the tabernacle of God. In another sence, they speak evil of the man Christ Jesus. Yea they are (some of them at least) guilty of the most hideous and horrid blasphemy against the Son of God, the only God-man Jesus Christ, that ever was heard of. For they are wont to curse that blessed name in their Synagogues. In their Lyturgies they pray, that the name of Jesus of Nazareth may be rooted out of the Earth. O fearful blasphemy; whose heart trembleth not at the hearing of it? In this respect some of the Jewish Lyturgies are worse than the Turkish Alcoran; For that speaketh honourably of Christ: Likewise they are wont to call the blessed Gospel a Volume of lies, or falsehood. One would think it impossible that such sinners should ever be saved.

. . . 4. *Murther is a most horrid sin.* The cry of blood is heard from Earth to Heaven. Now, the Jews lie under the guilt of Bloud and Murther. Some have laid a most hydeous fact to the charge of the Jews, so that they have been wont once a year to steal Christian children, and to put them to death by crucifying out of scorn and hatred against Christians. But inasmuch as those in dark and Popish times, it may be questioned whether truth be in them or no. So it hath been laid to them they poisoned the waters of some Countreys that they might be the death of those that lived therein. However, it is certain that the most prodigious Murther that ever the Sun beheld (yea such Murther as the Sun durst not behold) hath been committed by the Jews, and that the guilt thereof lyeth upon the Jewish Nation to this day, even the guilt of the bloud of the Saviour of the world, of him that is the Prince of life, and Lord of glory. See Acts 2.23 & 7.52. Oh! To be guilty of bloud, though it were but the bloud of the meanest person in the world, is a sad thing; but to be guilty of him that is God as well as man, how doleful is that?

Source: Increase Mather, *The Mystery of Israel's Salvation* (London: John Allen, 1669), 174–76.

Intolerance in New Spain

The Spanish colonial regime in the Americas was built upon the extraction of wealth from the land and the people and the conveyance of that wealth back to Europe in many forms, from gold bricks to violins crafted by indigenes. In the northernmost settlements of New Spain—an area that included what today are California, Arizona, New Mexico, Texas, and eastward along the Gulf to Florida—Indians were treated harshly, although the worst atrocities occurred further south. Spanish domination of Native Americans was a complex and sometimes contradictory historical process: notable acts of sacrifice on the part of Spanish missionaries alternated with the clergy's complicity in vicious acts of cruelty carried out by the military. The *Requerimiento* of 1510, read to Indians in a language they did not understand, was little more than a legalistic charade that set Indians up for the forceful imposition of Spanish rule on them. It demanded their conversion to Christianity and acceptance of the authority of the Pope and Spanish rulers, and it stated the terrible consequences (which generally followed) if Indians did not submit to Christianity and the Crown. Bartolomé de Las Casas's complaint, *Short Account of the Destruction of the Indies*, published in 1542, catalogued (though sometimes in embellished accounts) Spanish atrocities toward Indians in the New World and led to reforms, some of which were limited and temporary. The long-term influences of the Spanish policy of forced conversion continued to influence the American treatment of Native Americans after the founding of the United States, and its residue remains present, alongside of other colonial residues, in American thinking about religious difference.

On the part of the King, Don Fernando, and of Doña Juana, his daughter, Queen of Castille and León, subduers of the barbarous nations, we their servants notify and make known to you, as best we can, that the Lord our God, Living and Eternal, created the Heaven and the Earth, and one man and one woman, of whom you and we, all the men of the world, were and are descendants, and all those who came after us. But, on account of the multitude which has sprung from this man and woman in the five thousand years since the world was created, it was necessary that some men should go one way and some another, and that they should be divided into many kingdoms and provinces, for in one alone they could not be sustained.

Of all these nations God our Lord gave charge to one man, called St. Peter, that he should be Lord and Superior of all the men in the world, that all should obey him, and that he should be the head of the whole human race, wherever men should live, and under whatever law, sect, or belief they should be; and he gave him the world for his kingdom and jurisdiction.

And he commanded him to place his seat in Rome, as the spot most fitting to rule the world from; but also he permitted him to have his seat in any other part of the world, and to judge and govern all Christians, Moors, Jews, Gentiles, and all other sects. This man was called Pope, as if to say, Admirable Great Father and Governor of men. The men who lived in that time obeyed that St. Peter, and took him for Lord, King, and Superior of the universe; so also they have regarded the others who after him have been elected to the pontificate, and so has it been continued even till now, and will continue till the end of the world.

One of these Pontiffs, who succeeded that St. Peter as Lord of the world, in the dignity and seat which I have before mentioned, made donation of these isles and Tierra-firme to the aforesaid King and Queen and to their successors, our lords, with all that there are in these territories, as is contained in certain writings which passed upon the subject as aforesaid, which you can see if you wish.

So their Highnesses are kings and lords of these islands and land of Tierra-firme by virtue of this donation: and some islands, and indeed almost all those to whom this has been notified, have received and served their Highnesses, as lords and kings, in the way that subjects ought to do, with good will, without any resistance, immediately, without delay, when they were informed of the aforesaid facts. And also they received and obeyed the priests whom their Highnesses sent to preach to them and to teach them our Holy Faith; and all these, of their own free will, without any reward or condition, have become Christians, and are so, and their Highnesses have joyfully and benignantly received them, and also have commanded them to be treated as their subjects and vassals; and you too are held and obliged to do the same. Wherefore, as best we can, we ask and require you that you consider what we have said to you, and that you take the time that shall be necessary to understand and deliberate upon it, and that you acknowledge the Church as the Ruler and Superior of the whole world, and the high priest called Pope, and in his name the King and Queen Doña Juana our lords, in his place, as superiors and lords and kings of these islands and this Tierra-firme by virtue of the said donation, and that you consent and give place that these religious fathers should declare and preach to you the aforesaid.

If you do so, you will do well, and that which you are obliged to do to their Highnesses, and we in their name shall receive you in all love and charity, and shall leave you, your wives, and your children, and your lands, free without servitude, that you may do with them and with yourselves freely that which you like and think best, and they shall not compel you to turn Christians, unless you yourselves, when informed of the truth, should wish to be converted to our Holy Catholic Faith, as almost all the inhabitants of the rest of the islands have done. And, besides this, their Highnesses award you many privileges and exemptions and will grant you many benefits.

But, if you do not do this, and maliciously make delay in it, I certify to you that, with the help of God, we shall powerfully enter into your country, and shall make war against you in all ways and manners that we can, and shall subject you to the yoke and obedience of the Church and of their Highnesses; we shall take you and your wives and your children, and shall make slaves of them, and as such shall sell and dispose of them as their Highnesses may command; and we shall take away your goods, and shall do you all the mischief and damage that we can, as to vassals who do not obey, and refuse to receive their lord, and resist and contradict him; and we protest that the deaths and losses which shall accrue from this are your fault, and not that of their Highnesses, or ours, nor of these cavaliers who come with us. And that we have said this to you and made this Requisition, we request the notary here present to give us his testimony in writing, and we ask the rest who are present that they should be witnesses of this Requisition.

Source: Arthur Helps, *The Spanish Conquest in America and Its Relation to the History of Slavery and to the Government of Colonies*, 4 vols., edited by M. Oppenheim (London: John Lane, 1900), 1:264–67.

This governor and his men dreamed up new ways of tormenting the native population and whole new techniques for torturing them in order to force them to reveal the whereabouts of their gold and to hand it over. A Franciscan friar, Francisco de San Roman, witnessed at first hand an expedition, mounted by the governor and led by one of his right-hand men to wipe out the natives and rob them of everything they possessed. His report suggests that this expedition alone resulted in the deaths of over forty thousand natives, who were variously put to the sword, burned alive, thrown to wild dogs, or subjected to torture of one form or another.

From the very beginning, Spanish policy towards the New World has been characterized by blindness of the most pernicious kind: even while the various ordinances and decrees governing the treatment of the native peoples have continued to maintain that conversion and the saving of souls has first priority, this is belied by what has actually been happening on the ground. The gulf that yawns between theory and practice has meant that, in fact, the local people have been presented with an ultimatum: either they adopt the Christian religion and swear allegiance to the Crown of Castile, or they will find themselves faced with military action in which no quarter will be given and they will be cut down or taken prisoner. It is as though the Son of God, who gave His life for every living soul, when He instructed His followers with the words: "Go ye therefore and teach all nations," intended heathens, living in peace and tranquility in their own lands, to be confronted with a demand that they convert on the spot, without their ever hearing the Word or having Christian doctrine explained to them; and that, should they show any reluctance to do so and to swear allegiance to a king they have never heard of nor clapped eyes on, and whose subjects and ambassadors prove to be cruel, pitiless and blood-thirsty tyrants, they should immediately surrender all their worldly good and lose all rights to their land, their freedom, their womenfolk, their children and their lives.

Source: Bartolome de Las Casas, *Short Account of the Destruction of the Indies*, translated by Nigel Griffin (New York: Penguin Classics, 1999), 32–33. Reprinted with the permission of Penguin Books, Ltd.

New France

French authorities created the Code Noir (Black Code) in 1685 as a step toward systematizing policy regarding slave owning and slave trading. It decreed the expulsion of Jews from French colonial territories, outlawed the public practice of any religion other than Catholicism, and limited ownership of slaves to Catholics. Originally applied to French colonies in the Caribbean, it was adopted in Louisiana in the early part of the seventeenth century and remained in force there until 1803. The Code Noir consisted of a total of fifty-four articles. Like Spanish colonial views of the superiority of Catholicism, the French view, and French repression of other religions, survives in traces within American thinking about religion, and especially religion and race.

Edict of the King:
On the subject of the Policy regarding the Islands of French America
March 1685
Recorded at the sovereign Council of Saint Domingue, 6 May 1687.

Louis, by the grace of God, King of France and Navarre: to all those here present and to those to come, GREETINGS. In that we must also care for all people that Divine Providence has put under our tutelage, we have agreed to have the reports of the officers we have sent to our American islands studied in our presence. These reports inform us of their need for our authority and our justice in order to maintain the discipline of the Roman, Catholic, and Apostolic Faith in the islands. Our authority is also required to settle issues dealing with the condition and quality of the slaves in said islands. We desire to settle these issues and inform them that, even though they reside infinitely far from our normal abode, we are always present for them, not only through the reach of our power but also by the promptness of our help toward their needs. For these reasons, and on the advice of our council and of our certain knowledge, absolute power and royal authority, we have declared, ruled, and ordered, and declare, rule, and order, that the following pleases us:

Article I. We desire and we expect that the Edict of 23 April 1615 of the late King, our most honored lord and father who remains glorious in our memory, be executed in our islands. This accomplished, we enjoin all of our officers to chase from our islands all the Jews who have established residence there. As with all declared enemies of Christianity, we command them to be gone within three months of the day of issuance of the present [order], at the risk of confiscation of their persons and their goods.

Article II. All slaves that shall be in our islands shall be baptized and instructed in the Roman, Catholic, and Apostolic Faith. We enjoin the inhabitants who shall purchase newly-arrived Negroes to inform the Governor and Intendant of said islands of this fact within no more that eight days, or risk being fined an arbitrary amount. They shall give the necessary orders to have them instructed and baptized within a suitable amount of time.

Article III. We forbid any religion other than the Roman, Catholic, and Apostolic Faith from being practiced in public. We desire that offenders be punished as rebels disobedient of our orders. We forbid any gathering to that end, which we declare to be conventicle, illegal, and seditious, and subject to the same punishment as would be applicable to the masters who permit it or accept it from their slaves.

Article IV. No persons assigned to positions of authority over Negroes shall be other than a member of the Roman, Catholic, and Apostolic Faith, and the master who assigned these persons shall risk having said Negroes confiscated, and arbitrary punishment levied against the persons who accepted said position of authority.

Article V. We forbid our subjects who belong to the so-called "reformed" religion from causing any trouble or unforeseen difficulties for our other subjects or even for their own slaves in the free exercise of the Roman, Catholic, and Apostolic Faith, at the risk of exemplary punishment.

Article VI. We enjoin all our subjects, of whatever religion and social status they may be, to observe Sundays and the holidays that are observed by our subjects of the Roman, Catholic, and Apostolic Faith. We forbid them to work, nor make their slaves work, on said days, from midnight until the following midnight. They shall neither cultivate the earth, manufacture sugar, nor perform any other work, at the risk of a fine and an arbitrary punishment against the masters, and of confiscation by our officers of as much sugar worked by said slaves before being caught.

Source: *Édit du Roi, Touchant la Police des Isles de l'Amérique Française* (Paris, 1687), 28–58.

CHAPTER TWO

Anti-Catholicism

The roots of anti-Catholicism in America stretch back to late antique Europe. Religious movements born in Europe and the Mediterranean that challenged the authority of the Roman Catholic Church or its teachings were common in the first few centuries after the Emperor Constantine (d. 337). Gathering momentum in terms both of their numbers and their ability to attract followers, such movements increasingly emerged as permutations of Roman Catholicism, and especially as representations of altered Catholic doctrine. Because of that, they were considered heretical. Heretics and their followers, as apostates or traitors to the faith, posed a particular danger to Roman leadership as "wolves in sheep's clothing," or a kind of malignancy thought to be growing in the body of the true church. Rome was ever watchful against heresy, rooting it out wherever it could be found, brutally punishing or exterminating heretical communities. Believing that secret organizations of apostates, under the controlling influence of Satan, existed undercover within Christendom, biding their time and gaining strength with the aim of ultimately overthrowing the Catholic Church, Roman officials invented various kinds of machinery to destroy such cancers. The most notorious initiative in that regard was the Inquisition, devised to root out persons who claimed to be Christians but who secretly practiced another religion, whether it be a form of Judaism or Islam or—and this was especially important to Inquisitors—a corrupted Christianity. When the Protestant Reformation began in the early sixteenth century, the Catholic Church fought it tooth and nail but could not contain it. Near-genocidal wars of religion followed in which both Catholics and Protestants proved their capability to act out sadistic, unbridled dramas of human butchery, out of fear as well as arrogance. Protestants and Catholics were engaged in such wars even as Europeans were settling North America. The bloody Thirty Years' War, for example, raged in Europe from 1618 to 1648, and the Puritan Revolution in England took place in the 1640s. In North America, Protestants and Catholics were wary of each other. The St. Lawrence River Valley and some adjacent territories were a flashpoint for violence between the French, who were Catholic, and the largely Protestant settlers of British colonies. Among Protestants, the image of Catholics as power-hungry, morally depraved despots prevailed, and it was that image of the Catholic that permeated English anti-Catholicism. Protestants cast Catholics, and especially the Roman leadership, as enemies in terms strikingly similar to the ways that Catholics had pictured Protestants in Europe: as secretive, conspiratorial, deadly, morally unregenerate, bent on political domination, cruel, duplicitous, and seductive.

Many European religious groups immigrated to British North America seeking to escape religious persecution. Some brought with them fairly well-developed ideas about religious toleration. Others embraced a rhetoric of religious freedom but responded violently to groups of persons who adhered to even slightly different religious views. Some were especially keen on limiting the rights of Catholics. After the Glorious Revolution in England (1688) replaced a Catholic ruler with a Protestant, the legal status of Catholics in the English colonies changed significantly. In the late seventeenth and early eighteenth centuries most of the colonies passed laws against Catholics, forbidding either the practice of Catholicism, or being a member of the Catholic clergy, or other kinds of offenses derived from Protestant anxieties about religious difference. In some colonies, Catholics were disenfranchised, in others, actively hunted and prosecuted. Some were sentenced to whippings and banishment, others to removal to England to be more ambitiously prosecuted there; and in a few cases Catholics were sentenced to death and executed. French Catholicism in North America was crucial background to the French and Indian War (1754–63), fought on the British side largely by New Englanders exercising vigilance in their efforts to ensure that Catholics not be given a foothold in the region. In the South, early eighteenth-century English military campaigns against Franciscan missions had largely erased the string of over fifty mission towns and settlements across the Florida Panhandle. That prepared the region for English control when the Treaty of Paris (1793), which marked the end of the French and Indian War, committed the French to surrendering Canada to the English, and the Spanish to ceding Florida.

Intolerance of Catholics during the nineteenth century took a variety of forms, some physically violent, some not. As the Catholic population of the United States increased, intolerance grew more fevered in its pitch; and as

Catholics became more visible demographic blocs—as Catholic neighborhoods coalesced in cities, for example—violent encounters between Protestants and Catholics reached a peak. In the several decades before the Civil War, anti-Catholic violence broke out regularly in cities where immigration had increased the Catholic population. In Boston during the 1830s, a series of rhetorical and physical confrontations between Catholics and the Protestant majority culminated in the burning of the Charlestown convent by a Protestant mob in 1834. In Philadelphia the spring and summer of 1844 were marked by escalating conflict that was fueled by Protestant nativist rumors that Catholics had laid plans for taking the Bible out of public school classrooms. In early May, a mob set fire to and destroyed St. Michael's and St. Augustine's Churches, numerous residences, and the local fire station in the Irish Catholic Kensington neighborhood on the edge of the city, with loss of life and dozens of injured. Several months later, in July, the Native American Party planned an Independence Day parade, and, suspecting that it might end in further violence, Catholics persuaded the sheriff and governor to station police and militia to protect the church of St. Philip Neri. Over the next several days, a mob of thousands attacked the church, which was defended by several cannons supplied by the militia. The rioters brought their own cannons, which they had removed from the wharf, and a subsequent pitched battle between Protestants and Irish Catholics killed as many as twenty persons and injured dozens. The deployment of thousands of militia ended the weeklong violence. Official reports about the battles in May and July were mixed in their assessment of what had happened, some concluding that Catholics had incited the violence, others pointing to the incompetence of the civil authority in keeping the peace, and a few holding the Protestant mob culpable. The episode, like much religious violence in America, and especially in the nineteenth century, was complex in its causes and in the shifting dynamics of its enactment. Each side suspected the other of secrecy, subversion, and corruption of both religion and government. Each had a hand in inciting the violence. Each, in fact, was a mirror to the other. Violent confrontation between Irish Catholics and Irish Protestants likewise made the summer of 1870 a dangerous time to be a New Yorker. Dozens of Catholics died there in the so-called Orange Day riot. Again, the encounter was not a matter of sniping and scattered instances of violence, but of massed force in battle.

On the national front, anti-Catholicism coalesced in the form of nativist political parties and movements such as the American Republican Party in the 1840s and the secretive Know-Nothing movement (whose members supposedly responded "I know nothing" when asked about their political activities), which won victories in the 1855 elections. Anti-Catholic nativist organizations increased in number as waves of immigration greatly enlarged the Catholic population in the last decades of the nineteenth century. The American Protective Association (APA), founded in Clinton, Iowa, in 1887, built directly upon the ideological base that had been established by the Know Nothing movement. The APA called for the end of immigration and advocated the removal of Catholics from public office and from teaching positions in public schools. While its claim of a membership of 2.5 million surely was inflated, the movement was strong and, in spite of its secretive style, highly visible in both urban and rural settings until the end of the century. The largest and most organized anti-Catholic group, the Ku Klux Klan, was relaunched in the early twentieth century in Georgia (an earlier post–Civil War incarnation had floundered). The Klan, like earlier groups, conceptualized its mission as the defense of white Protestant traditions against challenges posed by Catholics, Jews, African Americans, and some others. Believing that modernity had brought a crisis of faith and a dangerous drifting of America from its Protestant foundations, the Klan numbered several million members nationwide. It carried on a war of words in print against its enemies and staged the notorious nighttime gatherings of hooded members to intimidate, assault, and sometimes murder those whom it considered threats to its vision for America. That vision, like the ones of the Know Nothings and APA, included a nation where the Catholic population was not allowed to grow and where Catholics were relegated to second-class citizenship, quarantined in social spaces from which they could not influence the nation as a whole. Klan rhetoric and protest resulting in the lynching of Leo Frank, a Jewish man in Atlanta, served notice in 1915 that Klan nativism was intensely appealing to white Protestants and that the Klan could recruit and organize an active membership based on that appeal. The Klan sent a particular message to Catholics in 1924, when thousands of Klansmen gathered outside New York City to burn in effigy New York governor Al Smith, a Catholic, and to celebrate the power of the Klan in defeating Smith's bid for Democratic candidate for president.

The lively tenor of Klan opposition to Catholicism had much to do with the emergence in the 1920s of a robust print culture (and later a radio campaign) that built communities of anti-Catholics through a vigorous elaboration of the evils of Catholicism and the beauties and truths of American Protestantism. By 1914 as many as sixty national anti-Catholic weeklies were being published. Regional and local magazines throughout the South and Midwest built large subscription bases preaching the dangers posed by Catholicism. The *Liberator,* based in the town of Magnolia, Arkansas, circulated 15,000 copies in 1915. In 1913, *Watson's Magazine,* in Thompson, Georgia, printed 80,000 copies of each issue, and its sister magazine there (from the same publisher), the *Jeffersonian,* circulated 45,000 copies. In 1915 the *Menace,* in the Ozark town of Aurora, Missouri, claimed a circulation of 1,469,400. (In comparison, the tabloid *National Enquirer* had a circulation of less than 1,000,000 in 2006.) The *Menace* had one mission: to attack the Catholic Church and to strip it of any power it had in America. It had "Absolute Proof That Romanism Desired the Death of Abraham Lincoln," that Catholics had tried to poison President Warren G. Harding, that the church had started World War I, that women were enslaved and abused in convents (a claim that led to bills being introduced in some state legislatures allowing for un-announced "convent inspections"), and that "nobody ever got a dollar out of these tax-gatherers from the Pope's garden and nobody ever will except assassins they hire to get presidents out of the way." Although persons in the United States and Canada (where the magazine was banned from the mail in 1920) pursued libel cases against the *Menace,* it continued to publish well into the 1930s. All of these magazines reinforced and detailed the perspective of widely circulated Klan publications such as the *Imperial Night-hawk* (Atlanta) and the *Dawn* (Chicago).[1]

The subsequent presidential campaign of Al Smith in 1928, in which he succeeded in winning the Democratic nomination, was a flashpoint for anti-Catholicism of all sorts, whether organized through groups such as the Klan or in terms of a more diffuse, ground-level antipathy to Catholics. Newspaper and magazine articles cast Smith as a puppet of the Pope, as "Rome's Tattooed Man" who would use his power as president to make America a Catholic nation where Protestant traditions would be downplayed and progressively removed from the public square. Smith's loss to Herbert Hoover was also related to his opposition to prohibition ("Alcohol Smith") and regional factors, but the opposition to him was unrelentingly religious in tone. By the same token, John F. Kennedy, who successfully ran for president in 1960, was accused by anti-Catholic opponents of looking to Rome for his leads in governing the nation. Evangelical Protestant leaders actively organized against him, repeating, but in subtler language, accusations that had been leveled against Catholics for two centuries.

Although the anti-Catholicism represented by the Klan or the campaign against Al Smith is an important kind of religious intolerance—organized, ambitious, violent—the everyday experience of Catholics was arguably even more significant a marker of intolerance because it could include performances of intolerance that were habitual and unrelenting. Immigrants of all sorts typically are cast as outsiders, and as such face serious obstacles in their attempts to make a living, educate their children, find a comfortable place in the social order, and participate fully in political life. Religious difference complicates what already is a difficult life for immigrants and often retards progress that immigrants might otherwise make—that is, if their religion was that of the dominant social group. In other words, being Catholic and immigrant (or, as we shall see, Jewish and immigrant) brought with it a set of challenges that Protestant immigrants, and especially English-speaking Protestant immigrants, did not have to confront. Oral histories of Catholic immigrants overflow with stories of being chased from stores, government buildings, and other public sites and of enduring firings from jobs, vandalism to their homes and businesses, songs that mocked their religion, and other offenses, large and small, that made up a day in the life of a victim of intolerance. Those enactments of intolerance were fostered in part by an anti-Catholic print culture and the campaigning undertaken by anti-Catholic groups. It is, nevertheless, a view of the everyday reality of living in a place where religious difference led to concrete disadvantage that is key to understanding the depth and breadth of anti-Catholicism.

Campaigns against Catholics were grounded in deep-seated fears that had coalesced in medieval and Reformation Europe, were driven by slanderous rhetoric, and were embodied in mob violence. It is important to keep in mind, however, that Rome did American Catholics few favors during the worst of the conflicts with Protestants in the nineteenth and twentieth centuries. The leadership of the church in Rome had great difficulty coming to terms with the demise in its status as modern nations took shape, religious authority was superseded by civil authority, and the wealth of the church progressively diminished. One response to those events was for the church to protest ever more emphatically the mistake of "modernism" in official publications, such as encyclicals and other formal announcements. Among those announcements, several were particularly threatening to American Protestants. The *Syllabus of Errors*, issued by Pope Pius IX in 1864, included language condemning free speech, separation of church and state, free public schools, Bible societies, and Protestantism itself. Subsequent pronouncements from Rome, made over a period of fifty years, reinforced certain aspects of the Syllabus, or added new emphases. *Immortale Dei* (the Christian Constitution of States) in 1885 explicitly affirmed the right of the papacy to judge when the civil order must yield to the superior authority of the Roman Church. Inspired by such writings, Catholics in America sometimes followed with their own applications of Catholic doctrine. The *American Catholic Quarterly Review* in 1877 caricatured the Declaration of Independence as a mess of ambiguity and cliché, and in 1882 a letter from the bishops of Cincinnati to the churches in their region questioned the prudence of a political system in which people ruled themselves.

In the late twentieth century, some observers of the American religious scene argued that anti-Catholicism was alive and well and that it was flourishing in popular culture and popular media. The ambitious efforts of the twentieth-century popes Paul VI and John Paul II to reinforce Catholic tradition in America did not include denouncements of democracy, however, or an insistence on a favored place for Catholic education in America. Their agendas did not inspire mob violence. Nevertheless, Catholics found themselves in an uneasy situation, in a predicament that hearkened back to nineteenth-century troubles prompted by reports of the sexual abuse of women in convents. That predicament, caused by disclosures of widespread abuse of children by Catholic priests, recalled and reanimated for Catholics and non-Catholic alike a historical matrix of issues that informed previous episodes of American anti-Catholicism.

DOCUMENTS

Anti-Catholic Rhetoric in Eighteenth-Century Boston

When Judge Paul Dudley of the Massachusetts Supreme Court died in 1750, he left his alma mater, Harvard College, a fund that, according to his will, was to support among other things an annual lecture "exposing the idolatry of the Romish Church, their tyranny, usurpations and other crying wickedness." The lecture would continue the theme that he had addressed in 1731 when he took the Roman Catholic veneration of relics as a point of departure for a sweeping anti-Catholic polemic. His accusatory rhetoric was similar to that of other anti-Catholic outbursts on both sides of the Atlantic, but not yet as inflamed as that of one of the best-known Dudleian lecturers, the Reverend Jonathan Mayhew of Boston's West Church, whose vitriolic *Popish Idolatry*, delivered in 1765, was particularly pointed.

> He must be a Stranger to the British History that does not know how fre-
> quently our Holy Religion, together with the Civil Liberties of the Nation,
> has been in the utmost danger from the Days of Queen Elizabeth; some-
> times by secret Attempts, at other times by open Violence, thro' the Influ-
> ence of the Jesuits, with their Associates, and other Emissarys of the Church
> of Rome. . . . Let it suffice here only to take notice of the *Fraud* and *Injustice*
> that runs tho' the whole. . . . The many and various ways the *Romish* Church
> has of defrauding and cheating the Nations. . . . Not only the open Violence
> & Robbery of the Bishops and Popes of *Rome*, in the Plunders and Depreda-
> tions they have made on their Neighbours, both Princes and People, of their
> *Civil* Rights and Properties; but likewise their *Spiritual and Religious* Thefts,
> if I may so call 'em. . . . The *Romish* Church, with the Pope at the Head of
> it, is *That Man of Sin, that wicked one, that was to be revealed,* of whom the
> Apostle in his Prophecy, of the great Apostacy of the Christian Church gives
> so large and particular an Account in his 2nd *Epist[le]* to the *Thes[salonians]*
> 2nd *Chapter*—Our Protestant Divines are generally agreed, that by the *Man
> of Sin* here spoken of, we are not to understand, as the Papists would have us
> believe, a *single Person,* but a *Compages of many,* or a System of Men either
> Existing together, or Succeeding one another. Now among other Signs or
> *Indicia* of this Man of Sin or Antichrist, here set down by the *Apostle,* we are
> told, That *his coming should be with all Deceivableness of Unrighteousness.*
>
> Source: Paul Dudley, *An Essay on the merchandize of slaves & souls of men*
> (Boston: B. Green, 1731), ii, 34–36.

Violence in the Colony of Maryland

Further south, Puritans and Catholics likewise found themselves engaged in
wars of words, and wars of blood as well. In an episode fueled by the clash
between Puritans and royalists in England in the 1640s, Richard Ingle, captain of the ship *Reformation,* attacked Catholics in Maryland—which had
been founded as a Catholic colony—in a campaign that came to be known
as "the Plundering Time" of 1644–46. Joining religious and political causes
(as was the case in England), Ingle and his band of militants chased most of
the Catholic inhabitants out of Maryland, and that included the Catholic
governor, Leonard Calvert. The Protestants destroyed property, kidnapped
clergy and returned them to England for trial, and fomented violence. That
violence continued well after Ingle was captured and executed by a returning
Calvert. The annual letter from the English Province of the Society of Jesus
in 1655/56 recounts continued problems stemming from differences between

Protestants in Virginia and Catholics in Maryland. While indicating ongoing violence, the letter also illustrates the way in which persecuted clergy took the opportunity to imagine themselves engaged in a larger, timeless drama against untruth.

In Maryland, during this year and the next preceding, Ours have escaped grievous dangers, but have had to contend with great difficulties and straits, and have suffered many unpleasant things as well from enemies as from our own people. The English who inhabit Virginia made an attack on the colonists, themselves Englishmen too; and safety being guaranteed on certain conditions, received indeed the Governor of Maryland, with many others, in surrender. But in treacherous violation of the conditions, four of the captives, and three of them Catholics, out of extreme hatred of our religion were pierced with leaden balls. Rushing into our houses, they demanded for death the impostors, as they called them, intending inevitable slaughter to those who should be caught. But the Fathers, by the protection of God, unknown to them, were carried from before their faces in a little boat; their books, furniture, and whatever was in the house, fell a prey to the robbers. With almost the entire loss of their property, private and domestic, together with great peril of life, they were secretly carried into Virginia and in the greatest want of necessaries, scarcely and with difficulty do they sustain life. They live in a mean hut, low and depressed, not much unlike a cistern, or even a tomb, in which that great defender of the faith, St. Athanasius, lay concealed for many years.

Source: From the Annual Letter of the Jesuits of 1655 and 1656, in Clayton Colman Hall, *Narratives of Early Maryland, 1633–1684* (New York: Scribner's Sons, 1925), 141–42.

New York Act against Jesuits and Popish Priests

Protestant anxieties about Catholics in the colonial Northeast often were interwoven with the suspicion that Jesuits in the British colonies were in league with Catholic New France just to the north to incite Indian rebellions against British rule. Protestants also were concerned that Catholics might foment other kinds of unrest among slaves or other subalterns. There also were deep-seated specifically religious reasons for Protestant unease, including differences in doctrines, conceptions of religious authority, and, in the opinion of Protestants, ideas about the role of individual conscience. After the Glorious Revolution (1688) in England, which resulted in the deposition of the Catholic ruler, King James II, English investors and royal overseers urged colonial governors to reduce the influence of Catholics in the colonies through various legislative acts. Colonial governing bodies subsequently enacted laws excluding Catholics from toleration, prohibiting them from holding office and preaching Catholic doctrines, and other such measures. The laws against Jesuits in New York, passed in 1700, were tested almost immediately, in 1701, when Father John Ury was arrested for being a Catholic priest, practicing Catholicism, and sedition, the last charge in connection with the complaint that he had told African American slaves that God was able to forgive them all their sins, including rebellion. He was sentenced to death and executed by hanging. There were very few Catholics in New York at the time, but even through two subsequent centuries of large-scale Catholic immigration to New York, anti-Catholic violence periodically punctuated the relations between Protestants and Catholics.

Whereas divers Jesuits, priests and popish missionaries have of late come and for some time have had their residence in the remote parts of this Province and other his majesty's adjacent colonies, who by their wicked and subtle insinuations industriously labour to debauch, seduce and withdraw the Indians from their due obedience unto his most Sacred majesty, and to excite and stir them up to sedition, rebellion and open hostility against his majesty's Government, for prevention whereof be it enacted ...

That all and every Jesuit and seminary priest, missionary or other spiritual or ecclesiastical person made or ordained by any authority, power or jurisdiction derived, challenged or pretended from the Pope or See of Rome, now residing within this province or any part thereof, shall depart from and out of the same at or before the first day of November next in this present year seventeen hundred.

And be it further enacted by the authority aforesaid, That all and every Jesuit, seminary priest, missionary or other spiritual or ecclesiastical person made or ordained by any authority, power or jurisdiction derived, challenged or pretended from the pope or See of Rome, or that shall profess himself or otherwise appear to be such by preaching and teaching of others to say any popish prayers, by celebrating masses, granting of absolutions, or using any other of the Romish ceremonies and rites of worship by what name, title or degree soever, such a person shall be called or known, who shall continue, abide, remain, or come into this province or any part thereof after the first day of November aforesaid shall be deemed and accounted an incendiary and disturber of the public peace and safety and an enemy of the true Christian religion, and shall be adjudged to suffer perpetual imprisonment, and if any person being so sentenced and actually imprisoned shall break prison and make his escape and be afterwards retaken, he shall suffer such pains of death penalties and forfeitures as in cases of felony.

Source: New York Act against Jesuits and Popish Priests (1700), in Francis X. Curran, *Catholics in Colonial Law* (Chicago: Loyola University Press, 1963), 76–77.

A Letter from the Devil

The American Protestant was the organ of the American Protestant Association, formed in 1842 for the purpose of curtailing the growth of Catholicism in the United States. The APA, following the lead of anticlericalists a half-century earlier (such as Tom Paine, who otherwise is known to Americans as author of the incendiary revolutionary tract *Common Sense*), sought to discredit the Catholic Church by raising suspicions about the motives of its ecclesiastical leadership and especially by offering evidence that church leaders sought to frighten people into obedience to them. The magazine published a commentary on a letter that seemed to illustrate the seriousness of the Catholic program of deception: "The first thought of the reader as he glances at this letter, may be that it is published merely as a burlesque on the Roman Catholic Church. This is not the object. It is an authentic document. It illustrates the 'pious frauds' of the Priests, by which they inspire their people with terror, not in the dark ages, but in the nineteenth century. Yes! At the present day. . . . "

Source: "Letter from the Devil to the Venerable Sister Maria Crocefissa, from a manuscript account of her life, exhibited by the Priests and Canons of the Cathedral of Girghenti," *American Protestant* 1 (October 1845): 154.

The Burning of the Charlestown Convent

In the middle decades of the nineteenth century the Catholic population grew rapidly as a result of the immigration of several million Catholics, mostly from Germany and Ireland. As Catholics became more visible, the violence against them escalated. *Awful Disclosures of Maria Monk, or, The Hidden Secrets of a Nun's Life in a Convent Exposed*, a book purporting to reveal the sexual enslavement of nuns to priests in a convent in Montreal, became a bestseller when it was published in New York in 1836. In Boston, Rebecca Reed, a young Protestant woman, had published her own tell-all volume the previous year, in which she complained that at the Ursuline convent in Charlestown, Massachusetts, girls such as her (most of the girls in the convent school were Protestant) lived as prisoners, abused by the nuns and desperate to escape. The story of her *Six Months in a Convent* likely was discussed and circulated well prior to publication, and by many accounts set the stage for the burning of the convent by a mob in the late summer of 1834. After demanding unsuccessfully that the "imprisoned" woman be handed over to them, the mob destroyed the convent and grounds, but that did not deter the local Protestant press from expanding their publication of anti-Catholic propaganda. The *Boston Evening Transcript* account of the fire, however, attempted more-even coverage of the event and prefaced its report with the observation of "a respectable and well-known citizen of Charlestown—not a Catholic," who testified that his own investigation into the rumors of the imprisonment of girls in the convent led him to disbelieve them.

The attention of our citizens was first called to the proceedings at Mount Benedict, by an alarm fire given from the vicinity of the Convent a little after eleven o'clock, and caused by tar-barrels and other combustible materials having been set on fire, as is supposed, to draw together those who had undertaken to aid in the work of destruction, or whose aid was expected to be obtained by the display of this signal. We have been informed that some time previous to this a small party, of the same description with those who subsequently constituted the mass of the assailants, had ascended the hill, reconnoitered the premises pretty carefully, and apparently satisfied themselves that no suspicion was entertained, or, at all events, no deference prepared within the walls, from which serious difficulty or delay might be apprehended in the prosecution of the plan. This was no doubt suggested by the circumstance of certain, or rather uncertain, designs against the Convent having been for some days the subject of general report. Immediate action or attempts, however, on the part of the disaffected, were not anticipated either by the municipal authorities, or the citizens generally; and this impression of at least present security had been artfully confirmed by a hand-bill yesterday posted up and extensively circulated in Charlestown, which intimated, substantially, that what was proposed to be done would be done on Thursday evening next.

A few moments after the signal was given, as above described, a gang of about fifty persons—as nearly as we can ascertain—but certainly at no time sixty—having gathered about the front door of the Convent, and made considerable noise by way of warning the inmates to flee, proceeded to affect a forcible entrance.

The whole party, we should observe here, were disguised. All of them, so far as we can learn, had their faces painted—some after an Indian fashion, and others in other ways; and a part of the number employed devices and disguises of various other description, adapted to conceal the individuals concerned in the outrage, from recognition, at the time of its execution, and of course from punishment hereafter.

Meanwhile, the inmates of the Convent had all, we believe, effected their escape from the house, as admonished to do by the assailants in their first demonstrations about the entrance. These were the Lady Superior, five or six Nuns, three servant maids, and fifty-five or fifty-six children, the latter being pupils under the instruction of the Nuns, and placed there by their parents and other friends—the majority of whom we understand to be Protestants—belonging in this city and other places in Massachusetts generally, but some of them resident at greater distance. All of the inmates had retired when the alarm was given, and most were probably asleep; but the Nuns exerted themselves in rousing the children as fast as possible, and were successful in getting them all out of the Convent. . . .

Of the destruction of all the buildings by fire, however, there is no doubt. The fire was set, in different parts of the Convent, probably about 12 o'clock, after considerable time had been spent in breaking up the furniture, including three pianos, an elegant costly harp, and other musical instruments. The whole establishment was in a blaze before one, and was reduced to ashes in the course of an hour or two.

Source: "Burning of the Charlestown Convent," *Boston Evening Transcript*, August 12, 1834.

A Jewish Woman Fears the Religious Riots in Philadelphia

Rebecca Gratz (1781–1869), an observant Jew and leading Philadelphia social reformer, observed the Protestant anti-Catholic riots in Philadelphia in 1844 that destroyed two churches, left at least a dozen Catholics dead, and wasted several blocks of a Catholic neighborhood. In her voice we can hear her fears about the "scene of war" that threatened not only Catholics—represented by St. John's Church, which was for a while surrounded by cannons to defend it—but Jews as well, even though Jews were not specifically targeted by the mob.

> The present outbreak is an attack on the Catholic Church, and there is so much violent animosity between that sect and the Protestants that unless the strong arm of power is raised to sustain the provisions of the Constitution of the U.S., securing to every citizen the privilege of worshiping God according to his own conscience, America will be no longer the happy asylum of the oppressed, and the secure dwelling place of religion.
>
> Intolerance has been too prevalent of late, and many of the clergy of different denominations are chargable with its growth. The whole spirit & office of religion is to make men, merciful & humble & just. If such teaching was preached by the pastors to their own congregations and the charge of others left to their own clergy, God would be better served, and human society governed more in accordance to His holy commandments. But this is not what I intended to say to you, my dear brother. I thought you would like to hear something from the scene of war, and sat down merely to tell you that we were safe. St. John's, one of the threatened [?] chapels and our very near neighbour, is still standing and we depend on the measures now taking to secure it.
>
> Source: Letter from Rebecca Gratz to Benjamin Gratz, July 11, 1844, in *The American Jewish Woman: A Documentary History*, compiled by Jacob R. Marcus (New York: Ktav Publishing House, 1981), 1047. Reprinted with the permission of the Jacob Roder Marcus Center of the American Jewish Archives, Cincinnati, Ohio.

The Orange Riots in New York City

Religious and political animosities incubated in Europe continued to mature on American soil in acts of violence between Protestants and Catholics. In New York in 1870, a parade celebrating the victory of the Irish Protestant William of Orange over the seventeenth-century Catholic King James II erupted in violence in which eight persons died. On Orange Day the following year, the Protestant-versus-Catholic violence was larger in scale, with sixty-one Catholics dying in a pitched battle with the state militia and police and hundreds wounded. Religious hatreds were linked to some degree with class and political differences in the riots, as Protestants wished to break the grip of the largely Irish-Catholic Tammany Hall on the levers of power in the city.

Source: "New York City—Scene of the Riot at Elm Park, Eighth Avenue and Nineteenth Street, between Protestant and Catholic Irish, on Tuesday, July 12, 1870," *Frank Leslie's Illustrated Newspaper*, July 12, 1870, 313.

Wide Awake Yankee Doodle

Songs such as this were part of nineteenth-century Protestant resistance to Catholicism. Although not likely to replace hymns or psalms in church services, such songs nevertheless encoded a nativist position that blended hatred of "papists," love of American "liberty," and homage to George Washington, whose saintly image loomed large in the early nineteenth-century American Protestant calculation of the meaning of America.

WIDE AWAKE
YANKEE DOODLE.

BY WM. C. MARION.

Come Uncle Sam, be " Wide Awake,"
Too long you have been sleeping,
Be on your guard, to crush the snake,
That round you has been creeping.
For it has almost charmed your eyes,
To such imprudent blindness,
That it could take you by surprise,
And crush you for your kindness.

      Yankee Doodle, Wide Awake,
      Be silent you should never,
      Until you drive the popish snake,
      From off the soil, FOREVER.

Our forefathers were " Wide Awake,"
When liberty was dawning,
They saw what foreigners would take,
And gave us timely warning.
Of foreign influence, beware;
Our Washington has told us,
And time indeed, there's none to spare,
His words they shall embold us.
      Yankee Doodle, &c.

Americans should be " Wide Awake,"
For surely you must know,
That for our country's own dear sake,
Each man his worth must show.
For we are free, and wont submit
To intolerance and aggression,
From papists, who from foreign lands
Come here to rule this nation.
      Yankee Doodle,&c.

Brave Washington bequeathed to us,
The liberty we enjoy,
Shall we not claim our rights, and thus
Prove worthy, without alloy.
For is he not the father of
The country that we love,
Shall we then stand and blush with shame,
For foreigners who disgrace the same.
      Yankee Doodle, &c.

Source: William C. Marion, "Wide Awake Yankee Doodle" [n.p., n.d.], in American Song Sheet Collection, Rare Book and Special Collections Division, Library of Congress, Washington, D.C., Digital ID: as114980.

Lyman Beecher's *Plea*

Lyman Beecher (1775–1863) was the patriarch of a distinguished New England family of intellectuals, writers, and clergy. As the pastor of a Presbyterian church in Cincinnati and the president of Lane Theological Seminary there, he was concerned that westward movement of the American population include a robust Protestantism. His opposition to Catholicism lay especially in his fear that growing Catholic power would lead to restrictions on the free practice of Protestantism. His widely circulated *Plea for the West* (1835), while modulated at points in his tone toward Catholics, polemically linked the undermining of American religious and political liberties to a mass immigration of Catholics who took their marching orders from a Roman leadership eager to extend its rule over North America.

It is to the political claims and character of the Catholic religion, and its church and state alliance with the political and ecclesiastical governments of Europe hostile to liberty, and the tendency upon our republican institutions of flooding the nation suddenly with emigrants of this description, on whom for many years European influence may be exerted with such ease, and certainty, and power, that we call the attention of the people of this nation. Did the Catholics regard themselves only as one of many denominations of Christians, entitled only to equal rights and privileges, there would be no such cause for apprehension while they peaceably sustained themselves by their own arguments and well doing. But if Catholics are taught to believe that their church is the only church of Christ, out of whose inclosure none can be saved,—that none may read the Bible but by permission of the priesthood and no one be permitted to understand it and worship God according to the dictates of his own conscience,—that heresy is a capital offence not to be tolerated, but punished by the civil power with disfranchisement, death and confiscation of goods,—that the pope and the councils of the church are infallible, and her rights of ecclesiastical jurisdiction universal and as far as possible and expedient may be of right, and ought to be as a matter of duty, enforced by the civil power,—that to the pope belongs the right of interference with the political concerns of nations, enforced by his authority over the consciences of Catholics, and his power to corroborate or cancel their oath of allegiance, and to sway them to obedience or insurrection by the power of life or death eternal: if such, I say, are the maxims *avowed by her pontiffs, sanctioned by her councils, stereotyped on her ancient records, advocated by her most approved authors, illustrated in all ages by her history, and still*

UNREPEALED and still *acted upon* in the armed prohibition of free inquiry and religious liberty, and the punishment of heresy wherever her power remains, unbroken: if these things are so, is it invidious and is it superfluous to call the attention of the nation to the bearing of such a denomination upon our civil and religious institutions and equal rights? It is the *right of* SELF-PRESERVATION, and the denial of it is TREASON or the INFATUATION OF FOLLY.

It is the duty also enforced by the unparalleled novelty and urgency of our condition, for since the irruption of the northern barbarians, the world has never witnessed such a rush of dark-minded population from one country to another, as is now leaving Europe, and dashing upon our shores. It is not the *northern* hive, but the *whole* hive which is swarming out upon our cities and unoccupied territory as the effect of overstocked population, of civil oppression, of crime and poverty, and political and ecclesiastical design. Clouds like the locusts of Egypt are rising from the hills and plains of Europe, and on the wings of every wind, are coming over to settle down upon our fair fields; while millions, moved by the noise of their rising and cheered by the news of their safe arrival and green pastures, are preparing for flight in an endless succession.

Source: Lyman Beecher, *Plea for the West* (Cincinnati: Truman and Smith, 1835).

The American Protective Association's "Secret Oath"

In the late nineteenth century, in the early years of the largest wave of Catholic immigration to America, Henry F. Bowers, a lawyer, organized his fellow Iowans into the American Protective Association (APA) in Clinton, Iowa. In costumed ceremonies and through secret oaths, the organization initiated members throughout the Midwest, New England, and California, and was a powerful force in the politics of a number of large cities. Spreading fear of Catholicism through its strident rhetoric and circulation of phony Catholic documents (including a spurious letter from the Pope calling for Americans Catholics to rise up and exterminate Protestants on the feast of St. Ignatius in 1893), the movement managed to place some of its members in Congress in spite of the condemnations of governors, political party conventions, and public figures such as Theodore Roosevelt. The oath of allegiance was published in the *New York Times* and other newspapers in December 1893.

I do most solemnly promise and swear that I will always, to the utmost of my ability, labor, plead and wage a continuous warfare against ignorance and fanaticism; that I will use my utmost power to strike the shackles and chains of blind obedience to the Roman Catholic church from the hampered and bound consciences of a priest-ridden and church-oppressed people; that I will never allow any one, a member of the Roman Catholic church, to become a member of this order, I knowing him to be such; that I will use my influence to promote the interest of all Protestants everywhere in the world that I may be; that I will not employ a Roman Catholic in any capacity if I can procure the services of a Protestant.

I furthermore promise and swear that I will not aid in building or maintaining, by my resources, any Roman Catholic church or institution of their sect or creed whatsoever, but will do all in my power to retard and break down the power of the Pope, in this country or any other; that I will not enter into any controversy with a Roman Catholic upon the subject of this order, nor will I enter into any agreement with a Roman Catholic to strike or create a disturbance whereby the Catholic employees may undermine and substitute their Protestant co-workers; that in all grievances I will seek only Protestants and counsel with them to the exclusion of all Roman Catholics, and will not make known to them anything of any nature matured at such conferences.

I furthermore promise and swear that I will not countenance the nomination, in any caucus or convention, of a Roman Catholic for any office in the gift of the American people, and that I will not vote for, or counsel others to vote for, any Roman Catholic, but will vote only for a Protestant, so far as may lie in my power. Should there be two Roman Catholics on opposite tickets, I will erase the name on the ticket I vote; that I will at all times endeavor to place the political positions of this government in the hands of Protestants, to the entire exclusion of the Roman Catholic church, of the members thereof, and the mandate of the Pope.

To all of which I do most solemnly promise and swear, so help me God. Amen.

Source: "The Secret Oath of the American Protective Association, October 31, 1893," in Michael Williams, *The Shadow of the Pope* (New York: McGraw-Hill, 1932), 103–4, reprinted in John Tracy Ellis, ed., *Documents of American Catholic History* (Milwaukee: Bruce Publishing Company, 1956), 500–501.

Thomas E. Watson on the Confessional

A larger-than-life bronze statue of Thomas E. Watson (1856–1922) stands on the lawn of the Georgia State Capitol, honoring the former United State senator from Georgia. A populist and influential writer and politico in the early twentieth century, Watson was also anti-Catholic, anti-Semitic, and racist, and played an important role in the resurrection of the Ku Klux Klan in the second and third decades of the twentieth century. Publisher of *Watson's Magazine* and the *Jeffersonian*, Watson produced anti-Catholic writings that were fearful and tormented, and imbued with a suspicion that Catholics plotted in secret against Protestantism and American liberties. Like some other writers, he fixed his gaze upon the confessional—a confidential booth where Catholics met with a priest to confess their sins—as the representative example not only of Catholic secrecy but of Catholic sexual impropriety as well.

The iniquity of Romish priests in the Confessional can scarcely be imagined. There is nothing else like it; it is a thing by itself; there is a chasm between itself and other crimes which human depravity cannot pass. Could I state them all as I have known them my readers would feel themselves almost insulted: an ocean and a sea of wonders, and waters of grief and sadness for fallen humanity would ebb and flow around them. Just fancy an innocent female on her knees before an artful unbelieving priest. But why is she there? Why does not instinct warn her off? Why does not conscious innocence tell her to fly from him? Why does not innocence—native conscious innocence—if, in reality there is such a thing, teach women to flee from those incarnate demons, Romish confessors? Why will they entrust themselves alone and unprotected by father or mother, brother or honorable lover with those scheming artful seducers? Why will mothers, married women, go to confession to these men, or why will husbands be such inconceivable dupes as to permit it? Have husbands any idea of the questions which a confessor puts to their wives? They have not even the remotest. Let me give them a few of these questions and I assure them as I have more than once done before that I state nothing but what I know of my own knowledge. The following are a few of them. 1st. Have you been guilty of adultery or fornication and how often? 2nd. Have you desired to commit either and how often? 3rd. Have you ever intended to commit fornication or adultery? 4th. Have you ever taken pleasure in thinking upon these subjects? 5th. Have you dwelt upon them for any length of time? 6th. Have you ever endeavored to excite your own passion? 7th. Have you ever taken indecent liberties with yourself or with your husband? . . .

The Roman Catholic Hierarchy! The most damnable group of interlocked secret societies that ever met in darkness, and took hellish oaths to a compact of greed, and lust, and crime, for the sordid purpose of grasping uncontrollable power, boundless wealth, and a never ceasing supply of the most enjoyable women.

Religion? These secret societies, which constitute the real machinery of the Roman Catholic Church, have the same sort of *religion* that Satan would have, were he able to leave hell, and take human shape on earth.

Source: Thomas E. Watson, *The Roman Catholic Hierarchy*, 5th ed. (Thomson, Ga.: Jeffersonian Publishing Co., 1915), 220–54.

The Ku Klux Klan

The Ku Klux Klan, founded at the end of the Civil War by Confederate veterans, was reorganized in Atlanta in the early twentieth century. In Indiana, it claimed as many as a million members, and the national membership approached 5 million. Klan campaigns against blacks, Jews, and Catholics frequently were violent, with many lynchings attributed to Klan hatred of non-white, non-Protestant groups. The Klan was particularly threatened by Catholic organizations such as the Knights of Columbus, a Catholic fraternal and charitable society founded in Connecticut in 1882. Klan leaders believed that the Knights of Columbus was the advance guard of a growing Catholic conspiracy bent on militant takeover of the United States and the extermination of Protestantism in North America, and rallied its members to anti-Catholic activities through fictional disclosures about the progress of Catholic subversiveness. *Knights of the Klan versus Knights of Columbus*, a pamphlet published in Oklahoma City in the early 1920s, purported to contain an oath taken by Knights of Columbus members. The extreme language of this fictional oath represents the state of fear out of which Klan anti-Catholic rhetoric emerged.

I will defend this doctrine [Roman Catholic positions on Jesus, the Virgin Birth, the papacy, etc.] and His Holiness's right and custom against all usurpers of the heretical or [P]rotestant authority. . . . I do further promise and declare that I have no opinion or will of my own or any mental reservation whatsoever, even as a corpse or cadaver . . . but will unhesitatingly obey each and every command that I may receive from my superiors in the militia of the Pope, and of Jesus Christ. . . . I do further promise and declare that I will when opportunity presents, make and wage relentless war, secretly and openly, against all heretics, Protestants and Masons, as I am directed to do, to extirpate them from the face of the whole earth; and that I will spare neither age, sex or condition, and that I will hang, burn, waste, boil, flay, strangle and bury alive these infamous heretics: rip up the stomachs and wombs of their women and crush their infants' heads against the walls in order to annihilate their execrable race.

Source: *Knights of the Klan versus Knights of Columbus* (Oklahoma City: Reno Publishing Company, n.d.), n.p., Special Collections, University of Georgia Libraries, Athens, Ga. Thank you to Dr. Kelly Baker for this citation.

The Kennedy Presidency

In 1960, a Catholic Senator from Massachusetts, John F. Kennedy, campaigned as the Democratic candidate for president of the United States. Norman Vincent Peale (1898–1993) was the Protestant pastor of the Marble Collegiate Church in New York City, and one of the most celebrated Protestant clergymen in the nation. In the late summer of 1960, he met with a group calling itself the National Conference of Citizens for Religious Freedom, and shortly thereafter that group—named the Peale Group by journalists—published in the *New York Times* a statement on the presidential race. That statement appealed to traditional anti-Catholic reasoning in its alarm about the likelihood of a Catholic president taking his orders from the Vatican, and observed the prospect of ruin for an American democracy that separated church and state. Condemned by religious leaders of different faiths (including Protestants) Peale's view nevertheless remained strong in public statements made by the National Association of Evangelicals, among other Protestant organizations.

The President has the responsibility in our Government for conducting foreign relations, including receiving and appointing ambassadors. It is inconceivable that a Roman Catholic President would not be under extreme pressure by the hierarchy of his church to accede to its policies with respect to foreign relations in matters, including representation to the Vatican.

The Roman Catholic Church has specifically repudiated on many occasion the principle sacred to us that every man shall be free to follow the dictates of his conscience in religious matters. Such pronouncements are, furthermore, set forth as required beliefs for every Roman Catholic, including the Democratic nominee. Binding upon him, as well as upon all members of this church, is the belief that Protestant faiths are heretical and counterfeit and that they have no theoretical right to exist.

The record of the Roman Catholic Church in many countries where it is predominant is one of denial of equal rights for all of other faiths. The constitutions of a number of countries prohibit any person except Roman Catholics from serving as president or chief of state.

The laws of most predominantly Catholic countries extend to Catholics privileges not permitted to those of other faiths.

In countries such as Spain and Colombia, Protestant ministers and religious workers have been arrested, imprisoned and otherwise persecuted because of their religion. No Protestant church or Jewish synagogue can be marked as such on its exterior. . . .

The Roman Catholic Church in the United States has repeatedly attempted to break down the wall of separation of church and state by a continuous campaign to secure public funds for the support of its schools and other institutions. In various areas where they predominate, Catholics have seized control of the public schools, staffed them with nun teachers wearing their church garb, and introduced the catechism and practices of their church. . . .

By recommendation, persuasion and veto power, the President can and must shape the course of legislation in this country. Is it reasonable to assume that a Roman Catholic President would be able to withstand altogether the determined efforts of the hierarchy of his church to gain further funds and favors for its schools and institutions, and otherwise breach the wall of separation of church and state?

Under the canon law of the Roman Catholic Church, a President of this faith would not be allowed to participate in interfaith meetings; he could not worship in a Protestant church without securing the permission of an ecclesiastic. Would not a Roman Catholic President thus be gravely handicapped in offering to the American people and to the world an example of the religious liberty our people cherish?

CHAPTER THREE

Anti-Mormonism

Members of the Church of Jesus Christ of Latter-day Saints (LDS) have been known as Mormons since shortly after the publication of the *Book of Mormon* in 1830. The term "anti-Mormon" appeared at almost the same time, a sign of the conflict between Mormons and other Americans that has marked the history of Mormonism from its beginnings. Joseph Smith (1805–1844), the founder of Mormonism, grew up in the excited religious environment of early nineteenth-century New York. In an area that was experiencing growth and rapid social change—especially after the completion of the Erie Canal in 1825—religious innovation and an inclination to form new kinds of religious communities were strongly in evidence. The flourishing Shakers, the apocalyptic Millerites, the Oneida community, early Spiritualist groups, enthusiastic revivalism, and intense interest in local Native American traditions were some of the indicators of the religious mood of what came to be called "the burned-over district." The religious enthusiasm of the region indeed might have pleasantly scorched the religious lives of some New Yorkers, but some persons took pause in the midst of all of the commotion. Joseph Smith was drawn into the excitement at the same time that he was ambivalent toward it, dissatisfied with a proliferation of religious groups and viewpoints that seemed to undercut the possibilities for unity. In 1820, he had a vision of the first two persons of the Christian Trinity, God the Father and Jesus Christ, who informed him that humanity had misunderstood previous revelations. The local community did not receive with generosity Smith's report of his vision, and so began a history of intolerance toward Mormons. Smith continued to report encounters with supernatural beings and eventually claimed to possess golden plates on which historical and religious truths were inscribed. Community opposition to his assertions of contact with the divine (and his claim of being able to use "seer stones" to locate valuables) included accusations of his being in league with the devil as well as legal charges against him for being an impostor and for vagrancy. In 1830, Smith published what he called a translation of the writing on the golden plates, titling it the *Book of Mormon*. Smith immediately sought converts and founded the Mormon movement, which eventually became the Church of Jesus Christ of Latter-day Saints. Smith ran into more legal trouble, reported additional visions, and began to look westward, where he anticipated establishing a community of the faithful, the "City of Zion." In 1831 Smith and a small group of converts fled the increasingly inhospitable atmosphere of New York and settled in Kirtland, Ohio. As Smith received more revelations and published them, and as his following grew, he came increasingly under suspicion by Ohioans who feared that he was becoming dangerously powerful. In 1832, a mob administered a severe beating to Smith and his colleague Sidney Ridgon and tarred and feathered them. Smith consequently moved to Independence, Missouri, where vigilante groups likewise tarred and feathered church officials and destroyed Mormon homes.

In the midst of this early violence against Mormons there appeared the first explicitly anti-Mormon book, *Mormonism Unvailed* (1834). Written by E. D. Howe, it presented itself as an exposé of Mormonism, a detailing of how the *Book of Mormon* was developed from an unpublished romance written by one Solomon Spalding, which Smith plagiarized as part of a far-reaching plan to deceive persons into committing their property to him and his family. Affidavits that Howe collected from persons familiar with the Smith family stressed the laziness of Joseph and his parents and siblings and their intention to create income through spurious claims of receiving revelations and organizing a following based on that deception. Numerous other anti-Mormon publications followed, such as a cluster of pamphlets in 1838 railing against the fraud that had been perpetrated upon religiously unsophisticated or uneducated persons. Such writings stressed that Mormonism was a "false religion" and that its founder was an impostor. That was the line of attack taken in *Antidote to Mormonism* by James M'Chesney and in *Mormonism Exposed*, in which author Origen Bacheler asserted, "By their deception and lies, they swindle [their followers] out of their property, disturb social order and the public peace, excite a spirit of ferocity and murder." LaRoy Sunderland also charged Smith with calculated deception, and added some analysis of the unreasonableness of Mormon ideas generally, in *Mormonism Exposed, in which is shown the monstrous imposture, the blasphemy, and the wicked tendency, of that enormous delusion, advocated by a professedly religious sect, calling themselves*

"*Latter Day Saints.*" The first sustained print attack on Mormonism published outside the United States, the Rev. Richard Livesey's *Exposure of Mormonism* (1838) detailed Smith's flawed character and charged the Smith family with being "fortune-tellers" and exploiting other occult arts in the service of treasure hunting. As J. Spencer Fluhman has pointed out, these attacks, like others on religious groups in the first part of the nineteenth century, capitalized on a widespread American belief that religion had to make sense, that it had to be "reasonable" in some ways. Mormonism was a fake because it did not make sense: its teachings were visibly phony and its founder an uneducated fanatic.[1] Other polemical works followed in the early 1840s, most embodying a perspective that is represented in the long title of a book published in New York in 1841: *The Anti-Mormon Almanac, for 1842 Containing, besides the usual astronomical calculations a variety of interesting and important facts, showing the treasonable tendency, and the wicked imposture of that great delusion, advocated by a sect, lately risen up in the United States, calling themselves Mormons, or Latter Day Saints; with quotations from their writings and from public document no. 189, published by order of Congress, February 15, 1841, showing that Mormonism authorizes the crimes of theft, robbery, high treason, and murder; together with the number of the sect, their views, character of their leaders &c., &c.*

In Ohio, and later in other states, opposition to Mormonism was enlarged beyond concerns about whether Smith actually had received revelations, whether the golden tablets existed, and how the Smith family had schemed to relieve people of their wealth. In Kirtland, Smith had a revelation to found the United Order, a religious society requiring its members to turn over their property to the church to be redistributed in a utopian spirit. The experiment, undertaken in Kirtland in 1831, failed in short order. Five years later, in 1837, Smith and other Mormon leaders organized the Kirtland Safety Society, a wildcat bank, which printed notes with Smith's signature on them. Its failure within a year intensified ill will toward Mormons in Ohio. News of the failure made its way to Missouri, where it added to the troubles Mormons were experiencing there.

In Missouri, the disputes and sometimes violent encounters that had marked the development of the LDS since its inception in New York advanced beyond informal and largely local opposition to official and statewide demand for Mormon obedience to law and conformity to custom. Non-Mormons looked at the growing Mormon population of Missouri as a concerted effort by fanatics to take over their towns, then their counties, then their state. Altercations broke out between the two groups regularly during the latter part of 1838. The state militia undertook to visit Mormon homes and

MORMONISM UNVAILED:

OR,

A FAITHFUL ACCOUNT OF THAT SINGULAR IMPOSITION AND

DELUSION,

FROM ITS RISE TO THE PRESENT TIME.

WITH SKETCHES OF THE CHARACTERS OF ITS

PROPAGATORS,

AND A FULL DETAIL OF THE MANNER IN WHICH THE FAMOUS

GOLDEN BIBLE

WAS BROUGHT BEFORE THE WORLD.

TO WHICH ARE ADDED,

INQUIRES INTO THE PROBABILITY THAT THE HISTORICAL PART

OF THE SAID BIBLE WAS WRITTEN BY ONE

SOLOMON SPALDING,

MORE THAN TWENTY YEARS AGO, AND BY HIM INTENDED TO HAVE

BEEN PUBLISHED AS A ROMANCE.

BY E. D. HOWE.

PAINESVILLE:

PRINTED AND PUBLISHED BY THE AUTHOR,

1834

collect arms from them, and as that process developed, relations worsened. In October, Mormons responded to assaults on them by attacking a militia encampment at Crooked Ridge, losing three men and killing a militiaman. The governor of the state, Lilburn Boggs, subsequently called out a force of 2,500 to take action against Mormons. His strongly worded "order of extermination" (included in the documents below) set the tone for a campaign against Mormons that captured church leaders and confiscated or destroyed the majority of Mormon properties. After a battle at Haun's Mill in October 1838 left eighteen Mormons dead, the church looked elsewhere for a place to gather and by spring of 1839 had relocated back across the Mississippi River in Commerce, Illinois, which they renamed Nauvoo.

The Mormon community in Nauvoo grew rapidly, aided by the arrival of converts from England, and soon became the second largest city in the state. Mormons were not received well in Illinois, partly because of widely circulated stories that made them out as troublemakers. During this period of time, Joseph Smith began to practice plural marriage, and may eventually have had several dozen wives. Others followed his lead, infuriating the downstate community of non-Mormons. The issue of polygamy, as it surfaced in Nauvoo, quickly became a lightning rod for criticism of Mormons. Critics offered it as evidence for the corrupted morals of the LDS, and, noting that the practice was illegal, demanded that Mormons give it up. Nearly all complaints against Mormons from the early 1840s until the end of the nineteenth century bemoaned plural marriage as a cardinal offense against Christian virtue, civility, and women. Polygamy became the stepping-off point for most polemics against Mormonism, and served as a platform on which additional criticisms could be arranged. One of those additional criticisms, and an important one, involved Joseph Smith's notions of political governance. At Nauvoo, he articulated a form of government called theodemocracy. In short, it was not much different from theocracy, a rule by the godly, whose authority trumped that of the civil power. In Smith's vision of theodemocracy, a so-called Council of Fifty would exercise responsibility for leadership, and he established such a group in Nauvoo. In so doing, he quickly earned the suspicion of persons who believed that he had organized a secret order of government that would undermine democracy and the republican ideal of civics. When William Law left the church over the issue of polygamy and in 1844 established a newspaper, the *Nauvoo Expositor*, to disclose the inner workings of the church, Smith ordered the newspaper office, including the printing press, destroyed. Non-Mormons were outraged by that act and soon managed the arrest of Smith and his brother, Hyrum. A mob attacked the jail and killed both of them in late June of that year.

The murder of Joseph Smith marked the coalescence of several key elements of American intolerance toward Mormons. Mormons had lost their lives, and many had been injured, in previous engagements with non-Mormons in Ohio and Missouri. The manner of Smith's death—accomplished by a mob against an unarmed man—provided dramatic perspective for Mormons and non-Mormons alike about the place of Mormonism in America. For Mormons, Smith's murder had the effect of solidifying both the prophetic quality of the religion's founder and confirming the depth and volatility of resistance to Mormonism and its tendency to be expressed in extremely violent acts. For non-Mormons, the assassination of Smith was viewed as a decisive step toward bringing the LDS to heel—to force them to comply with legal and community standards of government and morality—and conclusively opened the field to subsequent official acts of violence. Not surprisingly, both Mormons and their enemies became more militant in their views of each other, and more prone to violence in their encounters.

The retreat of Mormons from Illinois to Utah took place under the leadership of Brigham Young, who succeeded Smith and oversaw the migration, which ended in the Salt Lake Valley in 1847. At such a far distance from those with whom they had done battle, and at the same time more willing to assert themselves theologically and as a society, Mormons established a way of life that directly challenged the views of their opponents back East. In 1853, Young officially declared polygamy to have been a revelation to Joseph Smith, and the church progressively and energetically embraced that revelation as it fought to construct itself as a politically and economically viable religious community in Utah. To government officials in Washington, D.C., Smith's pronouncements on polygamy and many other things were like a poke in the eye. The Protestant missionaries who sought conversion of Indians in the West likewise viewed Mormonism with alarm. Missionaries and their clerical supporters came to understand Mormonism as a corruption of Christianity and conceptualized Mormon missionary efforts—which were strenuous, and had been since the founding of the religion—as a kind of "wolf in sheep's clothing." Protestants from the major denominations, such as Baptists, Methodists, and Presbyterians, among others, feared that Mormonism, because of its acceptance of the Bible as a holy book and its theological language that borrowed substantially from Christian ideas, would be confused for "true Christianity." Under cover of "true religion," Mormon missionaries would make inroads among those needing to be saved, infecting their converts with "false religion," and at the same time degrading the moral authority of orthodox Christianity by making it appear as if it, too, supported polygamy, rejected the idea of hell, and believed in ongoing revelation that came directly from God. All such doctrines were anathema to the typical Methodist missionary, and the fact of their obvious appeal to those who were converting to Mormonism was both infuriating and frightening.

Intolerance of Mormons, in the wake of Smith's death and in the midst of Young's assertive and highly public agenda for a Mormon future, coalesced in the 1850s. It represented a distaste for specifically religious differences (and especially Mormon theological ideas) alongside the rejection of what was believed to be the unpatriotic Mormon viewpoint about the nature of government and social life. News of Mormon growth in Utah made its way to the ears of increasingly uneasy Protestants back East. Protestant fears that Mormons sought to betray the nation, to acquire power, and to subvert the Constitution, intensified. Much ink was spilled in city newspapers about the dangers to both Christianity and American government posed by the LDS. Calls for government action against Mormons increased. The polemics took on the tone of the worst rhetoric of previous clashes between non-Mormons and Mormons, and the word "extermination" appeared more frequently. The election of President James Buchanan brought with it a sense of the need for action against Mormons, and in 1857 Buchanan declared the territory of Utah to be in rebellion against the United States. He dispatched federal troops to Utah to remove Brigham Young as governor. Both sides warned of bloodshed, and blood eventually was spilled in skirmishes between Mormon raiders and the troops (and supplies) moving westward. The drama was brought to a fever pitch when Mormons massacred a wagon train of Protestants at Mountain Meadows, Utah, in the fall of 1857. The following year, federal troops supervised the removal of Young as governor, but Protestant hatred of polygamy and disagreement over various theological issues, as well as suspicion of Mormon intentions to subvert the nation's government, remained as the core of ill will toward Mormons and the reason for continuing attacks against them in print and in person. In Washington, legislators railed against the twin evils of "polygamy and slavery," the latter offense a reference to the enslavement of women as well as blacks.

In 1890, in the wake of thirty years of federal legislation and Supreme Court decisions aimed specifically at polygamy, the president of the LDS received a revelation leading the church to abandon polygamy. Opposition to Mormonism remained concerned about the church's history of polygamy and suspicious about possible ways in which the practice might be unofficially continued. Such concerns informed opposition to Mormon B. H. Roberts, a polygamist, who was refused a seat in Congress after being elected a representative in 1898. In 1902, Reed Smoot, an officer of the Mormon Church, was elected a senator from Utah and spent the next four years fighting attempts to oust him by opponents in Washington who claimed he was a polygamist. Other charges of treasonous intentions were attached to the accusation of polygamy, but Smoot eventually was seated and served until 1933.

During the time that he was building the LDS Church, Joseph Smith was troubled by what he believed was an overly sectarian religious atmosphere in America. He had seen the sectarian debates and confrontations that occurred in the burnt-over district and fashioned his own message in response to that. It is ironic that one of the criticisms leveled against the LDS throughout its development has been that it is sectarian. Opponents frequently have characterized it as un-American in its fortress mentality and seeming lockstep submission to the will of church authorities—more or less the same criticism that was made of Roman Catholics, who were characterized as looking to Rome, rather than Salt Lake City, for their marching orders. Likewise, since the late nineteenth century Jews have periodically been accused of seeking first the good of Israel rather than that of the United States. LDS sectarianism historically has been pictured as driven by an agenda of social purity and exclusivity and imbued with an unwillingness to cooperate with other religions in shaping a public sphere where multiple viewpoints are accepted. The ideology of a "shared public" is at bottom a trust in a national agreement about the importance of sects and factions of all types, whether religious, political, or social, to occupy space alongside each other in the public square. It has served as a basis for one strand of American thinking about difference since the late eighteenth century. It has never been fully realized, as the national history of slavery, ethnic discrimination, gender bias, religious intolerance, and sexual discrimination all have evidenced. In many cases chauvinism, infatuation with power, and fear have driven such failures. At other times, an appeal to the principle of peaceful coexistence in the public square itself has informed the exclusion of groups who are perceived as somehow opposed to accepting that bedrock rule of public life. In other words, the ideology of inclusion and rights periodically has been interpreted as a mandate to exclude those who do not seem to accept the principle itself. In the nineteenth century and into the twentieth, the popular anti-Mormon viewpoint was that Mormons did not respect the Constitution, care for the good of the nation, revere the family as traditionally defined, or accept religious difference, and that they were not committed to defending a public square characterized by diverse opinion and practice. In other words, they were un-American. "Sectarian" was the term that opponents used to express their belief that Mormons were un-American and to identify them as a danger to society. That danger was perceived as so serious that Mormons often were characterized as deserving of "extermination."

The presidential campaign of former governor of Massachusetts Mitt Romney brought to the surface negative opinions about Mormonism that have lingered into the twenty-first century. A Pew Forum survey in December 2007 showed that only a little more than half of those polled had a favorable view of Mormonism, and fully one-fourth indicated that they would not vote for a Mormon for president. In contrast only 7 percent said they would not vote for a Catholic, and only 6 percent would not vote for an African American for president. Among evangelical Republicans, 36 percent answered that they would not be inclined to vote for a Mormon for president. White evangelicals, and especially evangelicals who attended church weekly and those whose educational attainment did not go beyond a high school diploma, were most opposed to Mormonism. When asked to provide a one-word impression of Mormonism, more respondents said "polygamy" than anything else. The next most commonly mentioned negative word was "cult."[2] The persistence of the impression that Mormons practice polygamy and submit fully and firstly to the demands of their religious leaders has not been helped by media coverage of offshoot branches of the original LDS Church. That coverage has called attention to the unorthodox family organization within those groups and often has been accompanied by charges that adherents practiced polygamy, especially through arranged marriages of very young females. When state authorities raided the Fundamentalist Church of Jesus Christ of Latter-Day Saints compound in Eldorado, Texas, in the spring of 2008, they took 482 children into custody. Almost all were later returned to their families (however those families were organized). The incident recalled not only one of the generations-old bases for actions against Mormons, but also disclosed that religious intolerance, even in the twenty-first-century United States, engenders extreme responses to perceived differences. It also indicated that the intertwining of religious differences with other forms of divergence—about the nature of civil authority, the meaning of family, sexuality, and reproduction—continues to be central to the issue of intolerance generally.

Missouri Mormon War (1838)

Having migrated from New York to Ohio, Mormons in 1831 began to settle in Missouri. As in previous places where they had formed communities, there were frictions with non-Mormons over land ownership, clannishness, local politics, and larger issues such as slavery, all of which were dramatically compounded by specifically religious difference. When Mormon leader Joseph Smith arrived in Missouri in 1837, the community had acquired land in several counties, and other Missourians had become anxious about growing Mormon influence. On July 4, 1838, Sidney Rigdon, a Mormon leader, made a speech that warned opponents that a "war of extermination" would follow from mob violence against Mormons. The speech proved a flashpoint for the escalation of conflict into violence. In October, the Battle of Crooked Ridge, fought between Mormons and the state militia, ended with deaths and injuries on both sides. Governor Lilburn W. Boggs subsequently issued what came to be known as the "Extermination Order," which is included among the documents here, alongside a newspaper report about the order that refers to Mormons as a "deluded" people. A second encounter at Haun's Mill, in which a vigilante group killed eighteen Mormons in a surprise attack on the Mormon settlement there, was enough to send Mormons fleeing across the Mississippi River to Nauvoo, Illinois. An eyewitness account by a militiaman reports the scene there. The order was rescinded in 1976, 138 years after it had been issued.

Missouri Executive Order Number 44
Headquarters of the Militia
City of Jefferson, Oct. 27, 1838.
General John B. Clark:

Sir Since the order of this morning to you, directing you to cause four hundred mounted men to be raised within your division, I have received by Amos Reese, Esq., of Ray county, and Wiley C. Williams, Esq., one of my aids, information of the most appalling character, which entirely changes the face of things, and places the Mormons in the attitude of an open and avowed defiance of the laws, and of having made war upon the people of this state. Your orders are, therefore, to hasten your operation with all possible speed. The Mormons must be treated as enemies, and must be exterminated or driven from the state if necessary for the public peace—their outrages are beyond all description. If you can increase your force, you are authorized to do so to any extent you may consider necessary. I have just issued orders to Maj. Gen. Willock, of Marion county, to raise five hundred men, and to march them to the northern part of Daviess, and there unite with Gen. Doniphan, of Clay, who has been ordered with five hundred men to proceed to the same point for the purpose of intercepting the retreat of the Mormons to the north. They have been directed to communicate with you by express, you can also communicate with them if you find it necessary. Instead therefore of proceeding as at first directed to reinstate the citizens of Daviess in their homes, you will proceed immediately to Richmond and then operate against the Mormons. Brig. Gen. Parks of Ray, has been ordered to have four hundred of his brigade in readiness to join you at Richmond. The whole force will be placed under your command.

I am very respectfully,

your ob't serv't,. . .

L. W. Boggs,

Commander-in-Chief.

Source: Lilburn W. Boggs to John B. Clark, October 27, 1838, *Document Containing the Correspondence, Orders, &c in Relation to the Disturbances with the Mormons* (Missouri: *Boon's Lick Democrat*, 1841), 61.

The latest Missouri papers, announce the marching of Gen. Clark, with the volunteers for Richmond, which place he intends to make his head quarters.

General Donophon with a force of 500 men, will reconnoiter on the south side of the Missouri river, and another General with a like force will range on the northern border of the state, from Des Moines to the Missouri river, and thus move on and concentrate their forces in the Mormon settlements, in Caldwell county. It is stated upon good authority, that the instructions from the Governor to General Clark, are to extirpate the whole fraternity of Mormons, or drive them beyond the state; it is probable there may be some little misapprehension in this, but there is no doubt that very strong measures must, and will be adopted to put an end to the wretched state of things, growing out of the disgusting conduct of these deluded people.

Source: "The Mormon War," *Atkinson's Saturday Evening Post*, November 24, 1838, 3.

Senate Chamber Nov 28th 1838

Dear Sir: In answer to your note of this morning requesting me to give you such information as was in my knowledge relative to the battle fought on the 30th October at the Mills on Shoal Creek between the citizens and Mormons.

I will state that the company I belonged to was stationed in the rear as a reserve at a distance of about 40 yards of the line of battle. As soon as the line of battle was formed and before all the troops in the line had dismounted, the fire commenced (by the Mormons as I was told by those in front). The position I occupied prevented me from seeing the commencement. As soon as firing commenced, the company I belonged to dismounted and run in the line in front. When I got sight of the position of the Mormons, they were all in the house or under the bank of the creek and the smoke of their guns from both places appeared to me to be continual. Our men took a few fires at a crack in the house when I heard the order to charge the house which order was promptly obeyed. The men run to the house. As we approached it I saw one man have out his gun in front of me. I stepped to one side & the man in front of me squatted down and pitched under the muzzle, lay still until the gun fired. He then rose and as the Mormon drew back his gun, our man shoved his gun in the house & fired. By this time our men got posses-sion of all the port holes, cracks &c and kept up such a constant fire that the Mormons could not get their guns out to shoot. They then broke out of the house and run towards the creek, but many fell in their flight. About that time I heard the cry of Quarters among our own men. I recollect distinctly of hearing one of our own men say (they called for quarters). I then hallowed Quarters! Quarters! as loud as I could which was echoed by all around me. The firing then ceased on our parts at which time a volley came from the creek. I then thought they had heard us calling for Quarters and thought we were whipped. The firing then renewed on our part and continued as long as there was any Mormon in sight, except the wounded. After the battle was near a close, I saw some of the Mormons that had reached the top of the hill south of the creek, about 300 yards from us, stopped, turned around and shot back at us and then run on.

After the battle had subsided I saw some of our men carry our wounded man into a house and laid him on a bed. The men in counting the dead found one man in the house not hurt who had fallen down in the early part of the action and was covered with the slain. I saw him and talked with him the mo-ment he was taken prisoner. Those who counted the dead said 31 was killed of the Mormons and seven of our men was wounded. We then got a waggon and horses and such of our wounded as was unable to ride was put in the waggon and we left the place.

The above is an outline of that affair as my recollection serves me.
Yours respectfully,
Daniel Ashby
To Genl J. B. Clark

Source: Letter from Daniel Ashby to General J. B. Clark, November 28, 1838, Missouri State Archives, Jefferson City, Mo.

Illinois Mormon War (1844–1846)

Resettled in Nauvoo, Illinois, which soon numbered 12,000 Mormon inhabitants (at a time when the population of Chicago was only a few thousand more), Joseph Smith and his followers came under attack by a local newspaper, especially for their polygamy. After Mormons destroyed the newspaper offices on Smith's lead, anti-Mormon feeling intensified in Nauvoo and nearby Warsaw. Smith and his brother Hyrum were arrested and jailed. On June 27, 1844, while awaiting trial, the men were shot to death by a mob that forced its way into the jail. After the state of Illinois revoked the charter for Nauvoo, Brigham Young, who succeeded Smith as leader of the church, gathered together a majority of the Mormons there and led them out of the state. The document below, representing the volatile atmosphere just after the death of the Smith brothers, repeats the message of "extermination" that had been pronounced against the Mormons in Missouri, and that would follow them eventually to Utah.

Resolution of the Citizens of Warsaw, Illinois

Resolved, That the public threat made in the Council of the city, not only to destroy our printing press, but to take the life of its editor, is sufficient, in connexion with the recent outrage, to command the efforts and services of every good citizen, to put an immediate stop to the career of the mad prophet and his demoniac coadjutore. We must not only defend ourselves from danger, but we must resolutely carry the war into the enemy's camp. We do, therefore, declare that we will sustain our press and our editor, at all hazards. That we will take full vengeance—terrible vengeance should the lives of any of our citizens be lost in the effort. That we hold ourselves at all times in readiness to co-operate with our fellow citizens in this State, Missouri, and Iowa, to exterminate, utterly exterminate, the wicked and abominable Mormon leaders, the authors of our troubles.

Resolved, That a committee of five be appointed forthwith to notify all persona in our township, suspected of being tools of the prophet, to leave immediately on pain of instant vengeance. And we do recommend the inhabitants of the adjacent township to do the same, hereby pledging ourselves to render all assistance they may require.

Resolved, That the time, in our opinion, has arrived, when the adherents of Smith, as a body, should be driven from the surrounding settlements into Nauvoo. That the prophet and his miscreant adherents, should then be demanded at their hands, and if not surrendered, a war of extermination should then be waged, to insure the entire destruction, if necessary, of the adherents. And we do hereby recommend this resolution to the consideration of the several townships, to the mass Convention, to be held at Carthage; hereby pledging ourselves to aid, to the utmost, the complete consummation of the object in view, that we may thereby be utterly relieved of the alarm, anxiety and trouble, to which we are now subjected.

Resolved, That every citizen arm himself, to be prepared to sustain the resolution herein contained.

Source: "Miscellany," Liberator, July 5, 1844, 108.

Utah Mormon War (1857–1858)

The Utah War, which was criticized in the late 1850s as "Buchanan's Blunder" because it was launched at the behest of President James Buchanan and ended as an embarrassment for the federal government, was fueled by concerns in Washington about Mormon polygamy. Mormons in the Salt Lake Valley in the late 1840s refused to acknowledge the authority of the federal government over their marital practices, and in the summer of 1857, Buchanan declared the Utah territory to be in rebellion against the United States. Concerned over reports that federal troops had been dispatched to Utah (2,500 eventually arrived in the region) the Mormon leader Brigham Young spoke of bloodshed should the government attempt to dislodge Mormons from Utah. In September, Mormons massacred a wagon train of 120 men, women, and children in Mountain Meadows, Utah. A week later troops left Fort Leavenworth in Kansas for Utah, arriving in Salt Lake in April of 1858 after a hard winter. They replaced Brigham Young as governor. About the same time, Buchanan issued a statement about the rebellion, identifying Mormons as treasonous but offering a pardon as well. John Lee was convicted of orchestrating the Mountain Meadows massacre and executed in 1877, twenty years after it had happened.

The documents here, like those above, indicate the give-and-take of religious intolerance. This has been especially true of Mormon history in the

United States. Religious intolerance does not take place in a vacuum. In the case of Mormons in Utah, polygamy was a real offense against the sensibilities (and law) of the nation; treason was a more ambiguous but serious offense; and the massacre of defenseless non-Mormons a flashpoint for federal action against Mormons in Utah. Those who wished to confront Mormons violently, however, had for many years drawn on inflammatory and often exaggerated newspaper and magazine articles about Mormonism. They also had placed their concerns about Mormonism within a framework that offered "extermination" of religious opponents as a historically certified method of addressing religious difference. President Buchanan's 1838 proclamation repeatedly stressed that the case against Mormons was not on religious grounds. Those overweening denials, while expressing some of the truth of the situation, also disclose the complex ways in which religious intolerance has been intermingled with other kinds of complaints in relations between religious groups. The religious difference was always more pronounced in the popular press than in official government communications.

Let us take a practical case, one which is not likely to create no little trouble yet, that of the Mormons. The Mormon reason and conscience are incompatible with the maintenance of the American state. Mormonism teaches that the dominion of the world belongs to the Saints, and that the Saints are the Mormons. The Mormons acknowledge, as we were instructed by two of their twelve apostles, no legitimate authority but that instituted by Joseph Smith amongst themselves, and hold that all the property of the Gentiles is given to them for their inheritance, and that they have a divine right to take and appropriate it to their use when and where they please; and if they do not yet do it, it is because they are restrained by prudential considerations, because they are not strong enough to make it prudent for them to attempt it. They hold also that they have a perfect right to slay and exterminate, in the name of the Lord, all who refuse to join their communion and submit to their authority. "You must exterminate us," said a Mormon elder to the writer, "or we, as we become strong enough, shall exterminate you," that is, the non-Mormon portion of the American people. Moreover, they hold to polygamy, and permit each man to have an unlimited number of wives. Here is the Mormon reason and conscience. Here is what Mormons hold God says to them. What will you do with them?

Source: O. A. Brownson, "Christianity and the Church Identical," Brownson's Quarterly Review, July 1857, 344.

Camp at Mountain Meadows,
Utah Territory, May 25th, 1859 . . .

They had also all the Indians which they could collect at Cedar City, Harmony and Washington City to help them, a good many in number. This party then came down, and at first the Indians were ordered to stampede the cattle and drive them away from the train. Then they commenced firing on the emigrants; this firing was returned by the emigrants; one Indian was killed, a brother of the chief of the Santa Clara Indians, another shot through the leg, who is now a cripple at Cedar City. There were without doubt a great many more killed and wounded. It was said the Mormons were painted and disguised as Indians. The Mormons say the emigrants fought "like lions" and they saw that they could not whip them by any fair fighting.

After some days fighting the Mormons had a council among themselves to arrange a plan to destroy the emigrants. They concluded, finally, that they could send some few down and pretend to be friends and try and get the emigrants to surrender. John D. Lee and three or four others, headmen, from Washington, Cedar, and Parowan (Haight and Higby [Higbee] from Cedar), had their paint washed off and dressing in their usual clothes, took their wagons and drove down toward the emigrant's corral as they were just traveling on the road on their ordinary business. The emigrants sent out a little girl towards them. She was dressed in white and had a white handkerchief in her hand, which she waved in token of peace. The Mormons with the wagon waved one in reply, and then moved on towards the corral. The emigrants then came out, no Indians or others being in sight at this time, and talked with these leading Mormons with the three wagons.

They talked with the emigrants for an hour or an hour and a half, and told them that the Indians were hostile, and that if they gave up their arms it would show that they did not want to fight; and if they, the emigrants, would do this they would pilot them back to the settlements. The migrants had horses which had remained near their wagons; the loose stock, mostly cattle, had been driven off—not the horses. Finally the emigrants agreed to these terms and delivered up their arms to the Mormons with whom they had counseled. The women and children then started back toward Hamblin's house, the men following with a few wagons that they had hitched up. On arriving at the Scrub Oaks, etc., where the other Mormons and Indians lay concealed, Higby [Higbee], who had been one of those who had inveigled the emigrants from their defenses, himself gave the signal to fire, when a volley was poured in from each side, and the butchery commenced and was continued until it was consummated. . . .

In pursuing the bloody thread which runs throughout this picture of sad realities, the question how this crime, that for hellish atrocity has no parallel in our history, can be adequately punished often comes up and seeks in vain for an answer. Judge Cradlebaugh says that with Mormon juries the attempt to administer justice in their Territory is simply a ridiculous farce. He believes the Territory ought at once to be put under martial law. This may be the only practical way in which even a partial punishment can be meted out to these Latter-Day devils.

But how inadequate would be the punishment of a few, even by death, for this crime for which nearly the whole Mormon population, from Brigham Young down, were more or less instrumental in perpetrating.

There are other heinous crimes to be punished besides this. Martial law would at best be but a temporary expedient. Crime is found in the footsteps of the Mormons wherever they go, and so the evil must always exist as long as the Mormons themselves exist. What is their history? What their antecedents? Perhaps the future may be judged by the past.

In their infancy as a religious community, they settled in Jackson County, Mo. There, in a short time, from the crimes and depredations they committed, they became intolerable to the inhabitants, whose self preservation compelled them to ride and drive the Mormons out by force of arms. At Nauvoo, again another experiment was tried with them. The people of Illinois exercised forbearance toward them until it literally "ceased to be a virtue." They were driven thence as they had been from Missouri, but fortunately this time with the loss on their part of those two shallow imposters, but errant miscreants, the brothers Smith.

The United States took no wholesome heed of these lessons taught by Missouri and Illinois. The Mormons were permitted to settle amid the fastnesses of the Rocky Mountains, with a desert on each side, and upon the great thoroughfare between the two oceans. Over this thoroughfare our Citizens have hitherto not been able to travel without peril to their lives and property, except, forsooth, Brigham Young pleased to grant them his permission and give them his protection. "He would turn the Indians loose upon them."

The expenses of the army in Utah, past and to come (figure that), the massacre at the Mountain Meadows, the unnumbered other crimes, which have been and will yet be committed by this community, are but preliminary gusts of the whirlwind our Government has reaped and is yet to reap for the wind it had sowed in permitting the Mormons ever to gain foothold within our borders.

They are an ulcer upon the body politic. An ulcer which it needs more than cutlery to cure. It must have excision, complete and thorough extirpation, before we can ever hope for safety or tranquility. This is no rhetorical phrase made by a flourish of the pen, but is really what will prove to be an earnest and stubborn fact. This brotherhood may be contemplated from any point of view, and but one conclusion can be arrived at concerning it. The Thugs of India were an inoffensive, moral, law-abiding people in comparison.

I have made this a special report, because the information here given, however crude, I thought to be of such grave importance it ought to be put permanently on record and deserved to be kept separate and distinct from a report on the ordinary occurrences of a march. Some of the details might, perhaps, have been omitted, but there has been a great and fearful crime perpetrated, and many of the circumstances connected with it have long been kept most artfully concealed. But few direct rays even now shine in upon the subject. So that however indistinct and unimportant they may at present appear to be, even the faint side lights given by these details may yet lend assistance in exploring some obscure recess of the matter where the great truths, that should be diligently and persistently sought for, may yet happily be discovered. . . .

I have the honor to be, very respectfully, your obedient servant,

James Henry Carleton,

Brevet Major, U.S.A., Captain in the First Dragoons.

Major W. W. Mackall, Ass't. Adjutant-General, U.S.A., San Francisco, California.

H. Doc. 605

Source: *Special Report of the Mountain Meadow Massacre by J. H. Carleton, Brevet Major, United States Army, Captain, First Dragoons* (Washington, D.C.: Government Printing Office, 1902), 10–11, 16–17.

Fellow-citizens of Utah, this is rebellion against the government to which you owe allegiance. It is levying war against the United States, and involves you in the guilt of treason. Persistence in it will bring you to condign punishment, to ruin, and to shame; for it is mere madness to suppose that, with your limited resources, you can successfully resist the force of this great and powerful nation.

If you have calculated upon the forbearance of the United States—if you have permitted yourselves to suppose that this government will fail to put forth its strength and bring you to submission—you have fallen into a grave mistake. You have settled upon territory which lies geographically in the heart of the Union. The land you live upon was purchased by the United States and paid for out of their treasury: the proprietary right and title to it is in them, and not in you. Utah is bounded on every side by States and Territories whose people are true to the Union. It is absurd to believe that they will or can permit you to erect in their very midst a government of your own, not only independent of the authority which they all acknowledge, but hostile to them and their interests.

Do not deceive yourselves nor try to mislead others by propagating the idea that this is a crusade against your religion. The Constitution and laws of this country can take no notice of your creed, whether it be true or false. That is a question between your God and yourselves, in which I disclaim all right to interfere. If you obey the laws, keep the peace, and respect the just rights of others, you will be perfectly secure, and may live on in your present faith or change it for another at your pleasure. Every intelligent man among you knows very well that this government has never, directly or indirectly, sought to molest you in your worship, to control you in your ecclesiastical affairs, or even to influence you in your religious opinions. . . .

But being anxious to save the effusion of blood, and to avoid the indiscriminate punishment of a whole people for crimes which it is not probably that all are equally guilty, I offer now a free and full pardon to all who will submit themselves to the authority of the federal government. If you refuse to accept it, let the consequences fall upon your own heads. But I conjure you to pause deliberately, and reflect well, before you reject this tender of peace and good will.

Source: "Proclamation on the Rebellion in Utah," in *The Works of James Buchanan* (Philadelphia: J. B. Lippincott, 1910), 204–5.

Mormon Theocracy as Anti-Republican

Criticism of Mormons was similar to that leveled against Catholics in several regards. Both groups were suspected of desiring a nation governed by a religious authority. In the case of Catholics, that authority was thought to be the Roman leadership of the church. Misgivings about Mormons focused on a Mormon "theocracy," or rule by the "godly," or saints, many of whom had immigrated from overseas after their exposure to Mormon missionizing. Conflicts with non-Mormons, were, as *Scribner's Monthly* pointed out, no "make-believe exercises," but pitched battles in which persons lost their lives, or mob actions that destroyed property as well as injured and killed Americans on each side. *Scribner's* wondered whether conflicts with Mormons were a sign of religious intolerance but quickly rejected that possibility. Instead, said the magazine, Mormonism was profoundly anti-American. It was opposed to republican American values of democratic virtue and constitutional rule and should be broken as an institution and stripped of any civil authority it possessed.

White Americans have but one native religion, and that one is the sole apparent exception to the American rule of universal toleration. In this branch of manufacture we have reversed our policy of protection; for while foreign heresies by the score have been naturalized, the only church born in this country, with American prophets and apostles, home-made miracles and revelation in the Yankee dialect, has passed through what its own historians call "ten general persecutions." In the forty-seven years since Joseph Smith translated the "Golden Bible" into what he called English, the church he founded has been engaged in no less than three regular wars with the nation, and in minor conflicts almost innumerable, during which and the forced marches attendant on them, more than a thousand persons have lost their lives. Equally strange is the fact that this, the only native American church, has lost every trace of Americanism and become an essentially foreign theocracy—drawing its entire strength from the peasantry of the Old World. If we include neighborhood wars, local raids and extraordinary mobs, the Mormons as a body have been in open conflict with the government or people no less than thirteen times; and that these were no make-believe fights may be judged from the fact that in one massacre in Missouri eighteen Mormons were killed and as many wounded, while in another, in Utah, a hundred and thirty-one Gentiles were murdered!

Of this anomaly two explanations are offered: one that the Americans are not really a tolerant people, and that what is called toleration is only such toward our common Protestantism, or more common Christianity; the other that something peculiar to Mormonism takes it out of the sphere of religion and necessarily brings it into conflict with a republican people and their institutions. . . .

It might have been possible for a good governor to reconcile the free state men and border ruffians in the territory of Kansas, for both parties held to a belief in republican government, and had many other points in common; but it is not possible for any man to reconcile the two parties in Utah. They have no common ground whatever. Either the Mormon theory of government is true in all particulars, in this case the federal officials are usurpers and the Gentiles intruders and rebels against the "Kingdom of God;" or it is false in every particular, and must be totally subverted. It is impossible that a divinely inspired priesthood, claiming civil rule and authority in all things, and a class of citizens who maintain the paramount authority of a man-made constitution, can coalesce. If the States are right, they will eventually drive us all out of Utah, just as their great exemplars, the Israelites, did the Canaanites, and set up the "Kingdom of God" in its purity; and if we are right, we will eventually break in pieces every vestige of the temporal of the priesthood, reduce the institution from a government to a church, and establish a republic in Utah like that in Colorado.

Source: "The Mormon Theocracy," *Scribner's Monthly,* July 1877, 391.

Meeting in Cincinnati to Plan to "Blot Out" Mormonism

The notion that religious opponents should be exterminated or "blotted out" remained central to the rhetoric of intolerance through the nineteenth century. Here we have an example of how anti-Mormon movements deployed language in order to characterize Mormons in the worst possible terms. Merely suggesting that Mormonism was so dangerous as to require "blotting out" was sometimes enough to foment resistance to Mormons, even in cases where there had been no local violence or unusual conflict. Literary tropes, and coded language, carried forward the mentality of intolerance from one generation or locality to another. Religiously motivated violence rarely had its facts right. Scary rumors blended with a lively rhetoric often were enough to frighten Americans into neglecting to investigate and analyze before they acted.

Cincinnati. Jan. 21. An anti-Mormon movement is being started in this city. Thus far it has been confined to the clergy, but during the coming week it will be brought before the general public. At the meeting of the Presbyterian Ministerial Association last Monday a paper was read on the subject by the Rev. Dr. Morris, the President of Lane Theological Seminary. Dr. Morris visited Utah last Summer and gathered a great deal of information relative to Mormons and Mormonism. He doubted its despotic power should be resorted by the Government. This [*sic*] auditors were in sharp disagreement with him, and his address will be answered at the meeting day after to-morrow. At that meeting resolutions will be offered providing for the preparing of petitions asking the Congress to take immediate and energetic means to blot out Mormonism. These petitions will be circulated for signature by committees of ladies who have already been selected and who expect to make thorough work of it. The subject will also be brought before the Methodist ministers at their meeting on Monday. A committee representing this association has been at work for some time and is now ready to report. It is thought that the Methodists will follow much the same plan that the Presbyterians are proposing to adopt.

Source: "Steps to Blot Out Mormonism," *New York Times,* January 22, 1882, 7.

Polygamy and U.S. Congressman B. H. Roberts

Utah entered the Union as a state in 1896 and in 1898 elected B. H. Roberts to the United States Congress. Roberts was a Mormon and, although the LDS Church had changed course and ruled against "plural marriage" in 1890, he was a polygamist. Protestant churches and mission societies resisted his being seated in Congress, fearing that it would signal approval of both polygamy and a Mormon church that undermined "American liberty and American morality." A dissenting grandson of Brigham Young, Eugene Young, addressed the Women's Board of Home Missions of the Presbyterian Church shortly before Roberts was to be seated, linked polygamy to anti-Americanism and the aspirations of the Mormon hierarchy to rule the nation as a theocratic state. This, he said, was "the new Mormonism," a blend of political sedition, immorality, and a will to power. The Congress refused to seat Roberts. When Reed Smoot was elected senator several years later, there was similar resistance in Washington. After a trial lasting four years, and much continued complaint about the Mormon Church, Smoot was seated.

Had the reiterated warnings of the Presbyterians been heeded by Congress, the Mormon problem would not have arisen to distract the nation at a moment when the war has laid fresh burdens on the shoulders of those who are engaged in the great work of redemption. Had legislators listened to the voice of reason instead of expediency, had they delayed Statehood for Utah until its people had indeed learned the principles of American liberty, a defiant polygamist, an obedient servant of the Mormon priesthood, would not now be preparing to demand a seat in the House of Representatives. Because the Mormons were forgiven too soon, however, Congress at its next session must face a great problem of national morality and the Christian men and women of the country must unite to arouse the national conscience by a demand for a proper solution of it. . . .

There is an inclination to view the election to Congress of B. H. Roberts, a three or four ply polygamist, still living in polygamy as an unavoidable outcome of old conditions in Utah and a mere question of personal morality. "What if Roberts is a polygamist?" says one. "He is no worse than dozens of men in Congress." Let those who take such views beware of the awakening. Some day they will see, as those who know Mormon ambitions see now, that Mr. Roberts is a mere instrument the representative of mighty forces. They will learn that through his election a people, three hundred thousand strong, have turned from American liberty and American morality and have taken the initial step towards the establishment of a hierarchy, foreign to our institutions and our social laws, in the midst of our republic. . . .

If Mr. Roberts were merely a common law breaker, frowned upon by his own people, it would be wasting time to make any effort against him. But if, in dragging polygamy into the House of Representatives, he is representing the defiant sentiment of the whole Mormon people, then we must not rest until Congress has cast him out as a warning to all covenant breakers and all polygamists. It is because those who know the failings of the Mormon people believe he is an embodiment of such a defiance that they are warning the nation against the new Mormonism.

Source: "Woman's Board of Home Missions," *New York Evangelist*, December 22, 1898, 69.

Mormonism and "Sectarian Hate"

By the end of the nineteenth century, criticism of Mormonism had boiled down to a cluster of issues: polygamy, Mormon tendency to theocracy, Mormon antipathy to liberty and democracy, and Mormon refusal to recognize the authority of Washington. While some continued to view Mormons as personae non gratae, a small minority began to consider the possibility that condemnations of Mormons were themselves driven by sectarian hate. That is, some Americans wondered if in fact it was the Protestant denominations— which represented the vast majority of the nation's religious membership— that were guilty of fomenting conflict because of their own narrow view of religion and its historical place in American public life. Writers questioned whether religious persecution was a matter of a long-ago past that came to an end with the ratification of the Constitution and Bill of Rights, or whether it survived in the sectarian quarrels among religious groups in America. In 1899 a Boston magazine articulated those concerns and added, in an instance of apologetic overreaching, a defense of Mormons on the grounds that they were descended from Puritans—a badge of American patriotism.

The spirit of religious persecution does not belong to an archaic and vanished past; it still embroils neighborhoods and embitters national life, gags the press and poisons the founts of literature. In this republican land, sectarian jealousy and ecclesiastical ambition kindle their baleful fires; here a union of church and state still exists, which large bodies of Christian make use of for their own advantage under pretense of the public good. The newspapers recently reported a convention of the clergy in and about Boston, at which resolutions were passed asking for "the recognition of Jesus Christ as King and Lawgiver in the Constitution of the United States, and the acknowledgement of the Almighty God and His will as revealed in the Holy Scripture as the court of final appeal." And it is from the ranks of this class of reformers that the material has been drawn for the Anti-Polygamy League, recently formed to prevent a congressman-elect of Utah from taking his seat, and "to give Mormonism a setback," as frankly stated. Col. T. W. Higginson, in giving his reason for declining the invitation to join the league, shows plainly that he thinks its charges are not based on ascertained facts, and that the movement bears the earmarks of sectarian hate; and he asks pertinently enough, "whose turn will it be next?" But such courageous utterances in such matters are like angels visits, few, and far between. President Eliot of Harvard College, which has on its roster scions of Mormon households, after a visit to the home of the Rocky Mountain Saints, saw a resemblance between the faith and the fate of the Mormon and those of the Puritan, as others of candid intelligence had done before him, and his conduct was at once made the subject of animadversion by press and pulpit.

Cultured New Englanders, proud of their descent from Puritan stock, love to dwell on the virtues and sufferings of those refugees from old-world intolerance, and condone and minimize the bigotries and cruelties of what is called the Puritan Commonwealth; and any suggestion that the experience of that band of exiles may be paralleled in this age and in this land is treated as an unpardonable sin, compounded of heresy and treason. The newspapers teem with articles attacking Mormonism in the most hostile and prejudiced way, while it is next to impossible to get a hearing for the other side.

And if these things are true today, what must it have been in those days when the Mormons were driven from Ohio, from Missouri, and from Illinois, and finally into the uninhabited wilderness? We should know that these persecutions were inaugurated before polygamy had become a part of the Mormon faith. And through it all, from first to last, these people have been represented as ignorant, superstitious, priest-ridden, and law-defying; while the truth is, as the most reliable and statistical investigations have shown, that they are among the most industrious, moral, and law-abiding communities within the confines of the Republic. "By your fruits ye shall know them." Their doctrinal tenets even are more progressive and rationalistic than the creeds of many other Christian sects. And no church organization could possibly be more democratic, and at the same time biblical.

All the leading officials of the Mormon Church are American born, and principally New England lineage, tracing their descent from revolutionary sires, some of them from the Pilgrim Fathers.

Source: Theodore W. Curtis, "A Word for the Mormons," Arena, June 1899, 17.

Mormonism as a Twentieth-Century Cult

While a strong residue of suspicion about Mormon theocratic designs on the nation survived through the twentieth century, anti-Mormonism was expanded in another direction through the activities of evangelical Christians, some of whom were ex-Mormons. Evangelicalism's enthusiasm for the supernatural, and renewed interest in the ways in which devils and demons influenced people's lives, undergirded much of the political activism of evangelicals such as Pat Robertson and Jerry Falwell, among other Protestant religious leaders. Worry about satanic influence was transmitted directly to analysis of the LDS, where outspoken critics such as Ed Decker (founder of the anti-Mormonist Saints Alive in Jesus mission) warned, for example, that Mormon founder Joseph Smith had been deeply involved in the practice of the occult, and that "the fruit does not fall far from the tree." Intolerance of Mormonism, then, was reinforced by an evangelical Protestant perspective that had accepted much of the earlier criticism of the LDS but had enriched it by casting the threat of Mormonism as more serious and urgent, as a cult that brainwashed women and children into submission to church authority. It did so by pointing out alleged Mormon diabolicism to a well-established evangelical subculture that was likely to respond instinctively, and negatively, to such kinds of claims.

In April, 2008, rumors of sexual abuse, which in most cases historically follow upon a group being branded a cult, emerged in connection with the Fundamentalist Church of Jesus Christ of Latter Day Saints (FLDS) community in Eldorado, Texas. Just as had been the case in nearby Waco fifteen years earlier, the rumors led to an overwhelming response by the state. Texas Rangers removed 482 children from the compound. The children were returned the following month when the Texas Supreme Court overruled the initial court order authorizing state action. The highly agitated prose of reporters and commentators raised traditional concerns about Mormons in the process of describing the family and marital arrangements ("plural marriage") among members of the FLDS community in Eldorado. They frequently raised the issue—so often present in debates about religious "cults"—of whether the members of the community had been "brainwashed."

Most reports of the LDS Church's problems with satanic abuse don't mention that Mormonism was originally brewed in a seething cauldron of occultism, sorcery and blood sacrifice. Contrary to the charming, Church-approved tale of the "First Vision," in which Joseph Smith was supposedly visited by two gleaming personages, the actual beginnings of Joseph Smith's spirituality were steeped in witchcraft.

First, Joseph Smith, Sr. and his entire family were casting magic circles and practiced the "faculty of Abrac," according to Joseph Smith, Jr.'s own mother, Lucy Mack Smith! Abrac is short for Abracadabra, and is a common, old-fashioned way of saying that they practiced *folk magic*.

Joseph Smith himself practiced "glass-looking," a 19th-century term for crystal ball gazing. He was even convicted of this in a Bainbridge, New York court. In fact, Joseph's annual meetings (on a witchcraft holiday) with the angel "Moroni" on the Hill Cumorah were actually attempts to conjure up a demon spirit through magic and necromancy. There is strong evidence that in 1824 he actually had to dig up the body of his dead brother, Alvin, and bring part of that body with him to the hill to gain the gold plates!

Joseph Smith was also well known in his community for using blood sacrifices in his magic rituals to find hidden treasure. . . .

Smith's participation in this kind of occult ritual is born out by several other testimonies. Additionally, after his death, Smith was found to be carrying a magic talisman on his person sacred to Jupiter, and designed to bring him power and success in seducing women.

With unbiblical practices like that at its roots, how could the tree of Mormonism be anything else but sinful and occult? As has been frequently shown, the sacred Temple rituals of the LDS Church are grounded in practices familiar to those involved in both Masonry and Witchcraft. Even many of the icons on the outside walls of older Temples are textbook examples right from witchcraft. This demonic core of Mormonism is hardly hidden from view.

Source: Ed Decker, *My Kingdom Come: The Mormon Quest for Godhood* (Longwood, Fla.: Xulon Press, 2007), 292–93.

CHAPTER FOUR

Intolerance toward Nineteenth-Century Religious Groups

The early nineteenth century evidenced in its intellectual and religious life a broad familiarity with the Enlightenment emphasis on reason and freedom that had guided the nation's founders and that had been shaping Protestantism in new ways since 1750. Religious freethinkers, called "infidels" by the orthodox and pious, formed loosely structured associations of "Deists," publishing religious manifestoes that challenged Christian ritual, doctrine, and institutions. Deists such as George Washington, Thomas Jefferson, and Joel Barlow, representing three points on the wide spectrum of Deist belief, embraced the idea of a Supreme Being and an afterlife but cared more about religion as the practice of a moral life than as divine revelation or communion with the supernatural. Partly in reaction to what they perceived as a grave danger to the future of Christianity in America, and partly for reasons having to do with the cultural changes that came with nationhood, Protestant leaders and leaders-to-be urged whoever would listen to them to forego the rationalist path and engage anew the religion of previous generations. They counseled Americans to aim instead for a religious conversion that would remake them in grace and spiritual feeling. Some Protestant ministers preached for a "revival" of Christianity, and many Americans responded, making antebellum America a singular period for religious enthusiasm in pursuit of a born-again experience.

Exactly how conversions were to occur—how persons who were religiously unexcited were to experience a life-changing event through divine grace—was the topic of much debate in the nineteenth century. Some preachers, such as Charles Grandison Finney, promoted a method of conversion that relied upon the minister's capability to set the stage for conversion through a certain style of preaching and collective worship. Others, reflecting the national mood of hopefulness in the prospect for building a free society and confidence in human capabilities to know God intimately and to choose freely to serve Him, experimented with other ways of fostering conversion. In their participation in the many revivals, camp meetings, Sunday services, and other religious activities of the nineteenth century, Americans tried out an assortment of paths that together constituted the new evangelicalism.

Just as tradition-minded Protestants sought to recover and renew doctrine (even if it was through exploration of new techniques of prayer and devotion), more liberal Americans searched for different kinds of answers to their religious questions. The nineteenth century is characterized by a remarkable efflorescence of new religious groups, ranging from the doctrinally and socially radical to those that made less sweeping but important and distinctive changes to tradition. In the alternately exultant and worrisome atmosphere of the early Republic, Americans founded and developed, alongside the mainstream denominations, groups with new revelations that placed them far from the Protestant center. Americans also remade religion in ways that directly challenged the mainstream denominations on their own turf.

Conflict between traditional Protestant denominations and new religious groups was constant in the nineteenth century. We have seen how Mormons were targeted for "annihilation" by their most determined enemies almost from the beginning of their coalescence in the 1830s. While most of the new religious groups did not experience the kind of sustained hatred that informed the campaign against Mormons, many nevertheless had their share of troubles as alternative communities of faith. Over the course of the century, Campbellites, Millerites, Adventists, Jehovah's Witnesses, Spiritualists, Christian Scientists, and others all discovered the difficulties of dissent. Some suffered periodic local harassment that grew less intense over time. Others remained the objects of scorn and discrimination that made it difficult for them to partake of life in the broader social and political worlds. Yet others experienced physical violence that lasted into the twentieth century.

It is important to take note of the degree to which Protestants were engaged throughout the nineteenth century in debates about doctrine, ritual, Scripture, religious authority, emotion, preaching, and a host of other topics. In the years between the outbreak of religious revival at Yale College in 1802 (following a course of sermons by Yale president Rev. Timothy Dwight criticizing Enlightenment infidelism) and the emergence of Pentecostalism in 1906, Protestants spilled oceans of ink and preached countless sermons against those whom they believed had erred in their vision of Christianity. In an intellectual climate that was fast absorbing the perspectives of a lively scientific culture, and in a social environment that was rapidly changing due to demographics, the market, westward migration, war—and especially the Civil War, which forced denominations to split into Northern and Southern factions—ministers and theologians were kept constantly busy as interpreters of tradition. Crucial issues emerged about which there was much disagreement. For some, the "religious affections," or a felt connection to the divine, were thought to be essential to Christian spirituality and the living of a Christian life. Opponents claimed that emotions were useful but that they were less important than Christian education, arguing that familiarity with the Bible, church doctrine, and the teachings of one's pastor were the foundation of the religious life. Much debate took place over the Bible: about its authorship, factuality, consistency or inconsistency, and comportment with science and with the narratives about the past that were emerging from academic circles. In some denominations, heresy trials were conducted in order to purify the community of opinions that were deemed antithetical to the faith of the orthodox. Ministers were fired and their writings condemned. Some sought employment in other denominations, or in new religions. Others left the ministry.

Such frictions, however, rarely issued in the kind of intolerance that finds expression in ongoing discrimination and acts of violence. A debate between rival members of a denomination, even if it was accompanied by catcalls or other disruptions, was not the same thing as setting fire to a house of worship belonging to a religious group that one hated. It was not the same as planning and executing a vicious attack on a gathering of persons who belonged to a religion different from one's own. It was not the same as rhetorically fomenting anger and fear to the point that they were expressed in misdeeds. There is a difference between theological debate—even when it led to heresy trials—and hatred that found expression in violence against members of other religious groups. The majority of religious debates and disagreements were settled by church members voting with their feet, either staying within a community or leaving it. Religious intolerance manifested itself in more dramatic fashion as physical challenges to opponents and as elaborately contrived ideological justifications for the violence that often broke out in the context of those challenges. We should not overlook the fact, however, that although religious intolerance differs from theological debate, in many cases the kinds of anxieties that were raised by intra- or interdenominational debate could be exploited in the service of more nefarious agendas. A Protestant congregation brought to the edge of its seat with worry that traditional views of Scripture, salvation, and morality were under attack within the denomination might be more receptive to intolerant views than a congregation that rested undisturbed in its embrace of tradition. In short, there is a difference between debate and intolerance. Nevertheless, in an atmosphere highly charged with concern about how tradition should be interpreted, raised emotions and the search for threats to one's religious heritage could lubricate the slippery slope to hatred and vengeance against Others.

We have seen how intolerance of Roman Catholics and Mormons developed out of complex social and intellectual backgrounds that overlapped in some ways but also how that intolerance was driven by unique complaints about each of those two groups. In this chapter, we consider the case of groups that emerged directly from Protestantism. Protestant intolerance, we should remember, was not manifested only in conflicts with Catholics, Mormons, and Indians. Protestants in America fought among themselves as well, just as they had in Europe, with disastrous consequences, for over a century following the Reformation. The issues that incited them to violent rhetoric, discrimination, destruction of property, and physical assault were many. In this chapter, four issues are of particular importance for their tendency to divide: (1) the future of the new nation; (2) the relation between science and religion; (3) the relation of individual spiritual experience to collective ritual; and (4) race.

Protestants, as well as members of other religious groups, were heirs to a vision of America as a Promised Land. Puritans who pictured America as a "city on a hill" and a light to the rest of the world passed that self-understanding down to every generation that followed them, and it became a trope for understanding the land, the people, and American destiny. Imbued with a sense of the specialness of America, the privileged place that God afforded it among all the nations of the earth, Americans believed that their covenant with God rested on their fostering and protecting a "pure" Christianity in North America. America was an enchanted land, and the hand of God was always active in ordering events for good, whether that meant rewarding the faithful with bountiful harvests and healthy children or punishing them with earthquakes and cholera. To be a good Protestant in America was to trust in God, obey the Bible, cultivate spiritual feeling, behave morally, and work to ensure that the "city on the hill" retained its luster and its commitment to its mission to bring the rest of the world, by example, to God. In colonial America, there were those who believed that the timeframe for the conversion of the world was intimately linked to the blossoming of piety in the religious revivals of the 1740s. The revivals, called the Great Awakening, were interpreted by the influential Massachusetts pastor Jonathan Edwards as an extraordinary outpouring of divine grace, the dawning of the new age, the Christian "millennium," which would begin in America and spread around the globe. In his view, the world was entering a one-thousand-year period of peace, prosperity, and communion with God, which would fulfill the American destiny. Other writers and religious leaders pointed to other events as signs that a Christian millennium (as foretold in the Biblical book Revelation to John) was beginning. In the nineteenth and twentieth centuries such prognosticating continued, albeit among a shrinking minority.

When prophecy failed—whenever the expected millennium did not materialize—American Protestants retreated from self-congratulatory views of their piety and moral uprightness and took refuge in the everyday practice that had always supplied the rhythms and meanings to their religious lives. They tried harder to live as they believed their religion required. They also distributed blame, and in the nineteenth century, they had no trouble locating guilty parties, a sampling of which would include Enlightenment rationalism and its neglect of emotional faith, greedy materialism, godless science, sexual deviancy and the decay of the family, and, not insignificantly, religious groups that were outside the Protestant mainstream. Most importantly, Protestants grew in the conviction that the destiny of the nation would not be realized without unwavering faithfulness to the terms of the covenant that their ancestors had made with God. Nothing would come easy. Traditions were sacred. The moral life was a difficult path. A nation without religion is doomed. All must strive together, joined in orthodoxy.

Some Americans in the nineteenth century kept their eyes turned toward heaven, expecting signs that the millennium was about to begin. Occasionally they saw them, and when they did, the news was mixed. The millennium indeed was imminent, but it was not for everyone. And for those who were not invited into it, there would be weeping and gnashing of teeth on a biblical scale. Visionary men and women enunciated end-time scenarios that foregrounded a selective process of salvation. Worthy individuals who had gathered into a community—not the nation as a whole—would survive an apocalyptic judgment and live a new sanctified life (in physical or soulful form, or something in-between) in the aftermath. This understanding of sacred time, a certain kind of millennialism, rejected the notion of Jesus Christ returning in a Second Coming to reward a nation that had succeeded in leading the world to a glorious thousand-year reign of perfected Christian piety. Instead, these millennialists presumed that the mission was lost, that the world had become so corrupted that only those who had managed to keep themselves apart from the tragic decay of worldly Christianity would be saved. They were "premillennialists" because they believed that Jesus would return to render judgment upon humanity before the dawning of the thousand-year period of perfected Christian community.

Groups that coalesced under the umbrella of the premillennial vision were not well tolerated by the Protestant mainstream (that is, those denominations that together wielded dominating cultural power). In the first place, the newly formed premillennial groups appeared to orthodox Protestants to have abandoned faith in the national destiny of a Protestant America. Accordingly, they were suspect not only as deviant Christians but as unpatriotic. Second, orthodox Protestants perceived in premillennial groups a drift from the commitment to established traditions of authority, worship, education, family, and work. Third, the new millennial groups were considered "fanatical" and "sectarian," or, in other words, a serious threat to Christian unity (an ideal which the dominant Protestant coalition upheld). Fourth, because premillennial groups typically emerged from within Protestantism, traditionalists imagined them as a kind of cancer within Protestantism itself. For traditionalists, those groups, in preaching erroneous doctrine and encouraging unorthodox behavior, not only misled people. They survived by feeding slowly but progressively on Protestantism itself, destroying it from the inside. In view of the particular challenges posed by premillennial groups, other Protestants—who might at the same time be involved in vexing doctrinal debates within their own churches—were primed for intolerance toward them.

Science developed rapidly in the wake of the Enlightenment. In virtually every area of life, from communications, travel, agriculture, and medicine to mathematics, biology, and the study of antiquity, science was vastly reshaping ideas and lives. The nineteenth century began on foot and horseback and ended with the automobile and airplane. It began with Sunday services at Congregational churches in New England according to an order that was established in the 1630s and ended with a generous reception for Hindus, Buddhists, Spiritualists, and Christian Scientists at the World's Parliament of Religions in Chicago. Reports of "warfare" between science and religion sometimes miss the ways in which they collaborated, but the fact remains that religion and science often were at odds during the nineteenth century. The Enlightenment, the eighteenth-century "Age of Reason" that began in Europe and made its way to America, challenged religion on several fronts, not the least of which was the claim of Enlightenment thinkers that reason alone was sufficient to know truth and to construct a workable moral code. Critics of "infidelism" in the early nineteenth century linked it to the new philosophy and science, and a parade of opponents of Enlightenment ideas followed that lead through the nineteenth century. The debate about truth acquired through the exercise of reason versus knowledge revealed in religion lost none of its edge during the century, and occasionally issues would emerge that made the debate even more pointed. The advent of more systematic and careful approaches to studying the Bible, pioneered in Germany and brought to America before mid-century, triggered a host of often bitterly fought battles between biblical literalists and those who advocated more flexible interpretation. In the latter case, scholars invoked "scientific" principles of literary criticism. They likewise sought to take the measure of the biblical narratives against the historical record as shaped by a nascent "scientific" historiography. Likewise, the publication of Charles Darwin's *On the Origin of Species* in 1859, following upon growing circulation of his ideas about evolution, challenged biblical accounts and the broader Western religious worldview about creation that had aggregated around biblical interpretation. As science enlarged its turf and gained visibility, religious criticism of atheists and agnostics, and even those who professed a "rational religion" was sharpened. Atheism soon enough was cast as un-American, as Christians developed narratives about the role of religion and divine providence in the emergence of the American Republic. As religion progressively was linked to liberty, unbelief was more surely condemned as un-American. The intolerance of unbelievers eventually found legal expression in a number of states that passed laws prohibiting atheists from holding public office. Municipal ordinances sometimes expanded that prohibition to larger ranges of activities.

Religious power was manifest everywhere in the nineteenth century. Evangelical revivals often were remarkable displays of emotions, and equally remarkable "exercises"—jerking, rolling, weeping, laughing, jumping—to go along with them. So heated could revivals, and especially camp meetings that were held in the open in the countryside, become that unsympathetic eyewitness accounts sometimes characterized the gatherings as mobs. The "foamings, faintings, groanings, and quaking" that critics of the eighteenth-century Great Awakening complained about were even more visible in the revivalism of the nineteenth century. Shakers, with their ecstatic dancing and loud, enthusiastic praying, likewise garnered the scorn of orthodox Christians. Shaker theology differed in some important ways from that of the dominant Christian denominations, but it was the emotional pitch of their meetings, alongside their self-imposed separation from the world, that most disturbed observers. Other religious groups were similarly cast as reckless in their engagement of the holy. That is, Christians who belonged to traditionally structured denominations where ritual, authority, feeling, belief, and piety itself were strictly shaped by tradition were skeptical of the free-form piety of some revivals and new religious groups. In their eyes, the powerful encounter with the sacred was not channeled as it should be into religious practice, and especially the moral improvement of self and society. It was not imbedded in tradition. Consequently, it was dangerous. It posed a threat to the standing order of Protestantism and it held the potential to undermine the promise of America as a Christian land. In the latter half of the nineteenth century, movements such as Theosophy, Spiritualism, and the Church of Christ, Scientist, were judged by some traditionalists as so reckless in their play with holy power that they bordered on witchcraft or other demonic activity. So strong was this criticism, and so deeply imbedded in culture were fears about it, that even those associated with the new religions sometimes had suspicions about their associates practicing witchcraft. The last witchcraft trial in America (thrown out by the court) involved one Daniel Spofford, who had been closely associated with the beginnings of Christian Science. Interestingly, the case against him was argued by the founder of Christian Science, Mary Baker Eddy, who accused him of physically injuring a woman with his mind.

On the other hand, there were religions or parareligious organizations that were thought to be absent real contact with the divine, empty shells made up of mechanical ritual and formal philosophy. Unitarianism, which attracted many persons in New England before spreading to other regions in the mid-nineteenth century, inspired its opponents to portray it as spiritually morbid. It raised fears in those who saw it as a wolf in sheep's clothing, a perversion of Christianity (with its rejection of the Trinity and especially its insistence on the humanity, not divinity, of Jesus) that threatened to infect and destroy the orthodox churches. Various "New Thought" movements likewise were thought empty of spiritual feeling or contact with God. Movements that focused on diet, nature, electricity, water, bumps on the head (phrenology), or a vague "divine inflow" were deemed by traditionalists to be philosophical misadventures and a potential undermining of true religion, or, in other words, Protestant Christianity. The detailed religious practice of such movements and groups, absent an informing traditional Christian spirituality, made them appear as mockery of the dominant Protestant groups, at least in the estimation of their detractors.

Race complicated every aspect of relations between persons in the nineteenth century, and especially so in the religious sphere. Euro-Americans who owned slaves or who supported slavery—and likely many who just did not think about it too much—were challenged by the emergence of black congregations and denominations. That challenge was more complex than it might first appear. Whites who were intolerant of black congregations and were threatened by the emergent African Methodist Episcopal Church and African Methodist Episcopal Zion Church in the nineteenth century were not merely opposed to blacks forming their own organizations. Because of deeply rooted beliefs about the inferiority of blacks and their status as a biblically "cursed" people (i.e., the Curse of Ham), the development of black churches was viewed as a potential undermining of Christianity itself. When Christianity took on the form of a black Christianity, it was, for some, the pollution of a sacred trust given by God to whites. Accordingly, some white Christians looked with disdain and fear on black churches, and took steps to discourage them. Such intolerance was often performed through church burnings, but other kinds of violence and intimidation were enacted as well.

DOCUMENTS

Shakers

The Shakers emerged within English Protestantism in 1757 and under the leadership of Mother Ann Lee came to America in 1774. In the first decade of the nineteenth century a dozen Shaker villages had been established, and by 1820 there were seventeen. At the peak of their growth in the 1840s they were spread out from Florida to Maine and westward to Indiana. Shakers embraced celibacy as religious practice and strived to build utopian agrarian communities, where sexually segregated "families"—some all male, others all female—lived, worked, and worshipped in an ecstatic style that included strenuous and prolonged line and ring dancing and shouting. They believed that God was both male and female, that the Second Coming already had taken place, and that they were to maintain their purity by living apart from the world. Shakers were criticized for their theology, their refusal to link themselves with other social groups, religious or otherwise, their loud and comparatively freeform worship, and their celibacy, which posed a particular problem in the cases of married converts who were required to leave their families in order to live the new life of purity. Their opponents suspected them of secret plottings and nefarious connections to European superiors—familiar complaints in many cases of religious intolerance—and of being deluded. Shakers, said their opponents, were guided by community elders to submit so thoroughly to their passions in their devotions that they lost the capability to think freely and critically. Some, including ex-Shaker Amos Taylor, whose writing is excerpted here, said their communities might be the work of witches (women were prominent in them). Shakers were the object of vigilante campaigns and mob violence in antebellum America, including an incident in Enfield, New Hampshire, in 1818, when a mob was inspired by accusations from ex-Shaker Mary Marshall Dyer that the village was keeping her converted children from her. Other mob actions erupted on simpler provocations. One report of the violence enacted against Shakers in the village of Harvard, Massachusetts, during the summer of 1782 (excerpted below) identifies the loud prayers of the Shakers as the trigger for action by opponents.

When we consider the infant state of civil power in America, since the revolution began, every infringement on the natural rights of humanity, every effort to undermine our original constitution, either in civil or ecclesiastical order, saps the foundation of independency. To see a body of more than two thousand people, having no will of their own, but governed by a few Europeans conquering their adherents into the most unreserved subjection, argues some infatuating power; some deep, very deep, design at bottom. . . .

It has been observed that persons who newly open their minds to this society, leave immediately the company of their old neighbours and acquaintances, some of their old vicious habits, and all their old religion, and experiences, and are cemented into the union of deep delusion. . . . It will be granted, however, by what has been already written, that great appearances of more than common power may proceed from the union and fellowship of such a deluded body of people, whose affections and animal spirits are cemented into a likeness of passion and transport, being bewitched, as it were, or enchanted with the splendid show of perfection: Should this be the most favourable circumstance in regard to that people, and they be ignorant of any absolute league, but only among themselves; it is most worthy of being truly distinguished from pure and vital religion, and ought to be abhorred and utterly detested by all, even as an infringement on the common rights of humanity. For there is a perpetual scene of trembling, quivering, shaking, sighing, crying, groaning, screaming, jumping, singing, dancing and turning, which strikes the animal part, operating on the nerves of the greatest opposers, in following which the adherent finds an easy transition from favour with them to go into their several exercises, to mourn and rejoice with them, to kneel, to leap, and dance, to turn and shake, and sometimes to utter forth their unknown mutter, so gibberish that a person not deluded would imagine they were a company of madmen, by whom their passions in different colours are artfully displayed.

Source: Amos Taylor, *A Narrative of the Strange Principles, Conduct and Character of the People known by the Name of Shakers* (Worcester, Mass.: By the author, 1782).

Early on the morning of the 19th while it was yet dark, the mob began to assemble round the Square-house. Their noise alarmed the people within, some of whom supposed them to be a company of Indians. . . .

The mob no sooner discovered that the Believers were on their knees, than they rushed upon the doors, which were shut and barred, burst them open, and began to size upon the brethren and sisters, as they stood upon their knees. . . .

The Believers being all embodied and surrounded by the mob, orders were given, that all who lived in the vicinity, should return immediately home; and that the distant Believers should leave the town and never be seen there again; and one hour was allowed them to prepare & eat their breakfast, & make ready for their journey. If any of the Believers attempted to address the mob, with a view to cool their rage, they were instantly answered by a stroke over the head, with a whip or a cudgel. . . .

At the expiration of the hour, they were ordered to march. The sisters were permitted to ride; but the brethren were forbidden; though many of them had horses with them. About one half of the mob formed the advance guard; the Believers, in a body, were placed next, and the remainder of the mob brought up the rear . . . If any who were aged or infirm, did not travel so fast as their drivers thought proper, their pace was soon quickened by a severe stroke of a whip or cudgel. . . .

They drove on about three miles, till they came to a level, open plain, near Still-river, where they were ordered to halt. "Now (said the leaders of the mob) we will have a little diversion;" and orders were given for James Shepard to be soundly whipped. . . .

They accordingly formed a ring, and sent one of the mob into the bushes, to cut sticks for that purpose. He soon returned with his arms full, and distributed them among the company appointed to whip him, and each one was ordered to give him a certain number of strokes. . . .

One of the ruffians, (Isaiah Whitney,) without waiting for orders, gave him a number of severe strokes with his horse-whip. Just at this instant, Eleazer Rand and Jonathan Slosson arrived; and Eleazer, seeing these strokes, suddenly leaped on to James's back. This increased the rage of the mob to such a degree, that they beat on, with their clubs, canes and whips. . . .

From the place where the mob halted, to whip James Shepard, to Lancaster, a distance of seven miles, was one continued scene of cruelty and abuse; whipping with horse-whips, pounding, beating and bruising with clubs, collaring, pushing off from bridges, into the water and mud, scaring the sisters horses, with a view to frighten the riders, and every kind of abuse that they could invent without taking lives.

Source: *Testimonies of Mother Ann Lee* (Hancock, Mass.: J. Talcott & J. Deming, 1816).

African American Churches and Denominations

In the nineteenth century, some churchgoing African Americans left the white churches that treated them as second-class congregants and founded their own denominations. Black congregations had been in existence for a long time, some on slave plantations. Black families in Wilmington, Delaware, founded the Union Church of Africans in 1813, and three years later, Richard Allen, born a slave and later the minister of an African American congregation in Philadelphia, founded the African Methodist Episcopal Church there. In 1821, the African Methodist Episcopal Zion Church was organized in New York City. For whites who already were suspicious of black congregations meeting for prayer and Bible study—many whites objected to the education of blacks, even for religious purposes—the black denominations were especially threatening. Moreover, opponents of black denominations feared that local black Baptist and Methodist congregations would be emboldened by the example of the AME and AMEZ. White intolerance took many forms, but the most common was arson. Black churches, and especially those that had schoolhouses constructed alongside them, were frequent targets for arsonists wishing to send a message to blacks about their place in society or discourage them from educating their children—which above all consisted in teaching them to read the Bible. At the same time, opponents denigrated the authority of African Americans to wield religious authority, claiming that the natural inferiority of Negroes made them unfit for church office. Intolerance of emergent black congregations and denominations accordingly was a blend of white belief that emergent black religious communities were corruptions of a pure Christianity and fears about the potential of religion to raise the social status of blacks. Intolerance was especially acute during Reconstruction and in the 1920s and 1930s. It reemerged during the 1960s, when opposition to religiously led protest against discrimination, and the churches' role in the civil rights movement generally, made African American houses of worship symbolically rich targets for white opponents, especially in the South.

The popular name for it is a "negro riot"—the true name is negro massacre. . . .

That night the riot culminated in the burning of the colored church and school-houses in the city, and many of the houses occupied by colored families in South-Memphis, and other parts of the city. The burning was systematic and thorough. Whenever a rebel dwelling was imperiled by these fires, the fireman were on hand to ward off the flames. There was no other house burned or injured in this "negro riot" but those belonging to or used for the colored people. Mounted men, some of them belonging to the fire department, spent the night in this work of destruction and hate. Only two school-houses escaped: one because it endangered the property of a rebel; and the other, the Medical College building, because it belonged to a rebel, and he was present, and "begged the *gentlemen*" not to ruin him by destroying the last dollar he had. The gentlemanly mob were considerate of their brother rebel's feelings, and rode on to Lincoln chapel, erected by Rev. Mr. Tade, agent of the American Missionary Association. They formed in line around the building, with cocked pistols and carbides while one of their number plied the match. A negro family, living in a building attached to the chapel, were fastened in, and forbidden to come out on pain of death, while their own house and furniture were burning. Fortunately the mounted citizens were satisfied with the progress of the fire, and moved off in time to allow the family to get out of the blazing but alive.

At another burning further north, where a house caught from the school building, a sick negro girl, one of the most promising scholars in Memphis, arose from her bed, and rushed out of the flames. She was shot, and thrown back into the fire and burned to a crisp.

When Mr. Tade and his missionary wife came to their chapel at daylight, they found the ashes and smoking sticks surrounded by the school children with their parents, weeping in unaffected grief over the loss of their church and school-house. Two of the churches burned were large, substantial edifices, built by the savings of the negroes in the days of slavery, and their destruction is a severe loss. One of them cost $15,000 in gold prices.

Source: "The Horrors of Memphis," *Independent*, May 31, 1866, 18.

Texas, 1877

An incendiary has fired the African Methodist church at Huntsville, Texas. This makes 15 colored churches burned in Texas this year.

Source: "General Methodist Items," *Zion's Herald,* June 14, 1877, 189.

Dorchester County, Maryland, October 1865

On the 21st of October, Addie Howard, the black teacher, writes in great haste to inform Mr. Graham of the calamity which had befallen. "Some malicious person or persons" had set fire to the church in which the school was held, and before the flames were discovered the building was entirely destroyed. Miss Howard had been with her night-school till 10 o'clock. This was not the first church that had been burned because it was used for a school-house. These people bend with such adoration before the demon Ignorance, that they will burn the image of their God on his altar. Rather than have schools, they will have no churches. If they cannot escape from instruction in any other way, they will put an end to worship. Certainly; why not? If you would quench learning, you must burn faith. That is what they did, and perhaps they did wisely in their generation. Certainly their faith had served them a wretched turn, and they could not do better than be rid of it. Their chance of getting civilized is considerably more hopeful with neither church nor school-house than it was with no school-house and a church. But what shall be done? asks Miss Howard.

Source: "A Chapter in the History of the Colored School," *Independent,* November 2, 1865.

Millerites and Adventists

During the nineteenth century, many persons became interested in biblical writings that were thought to predict the Second Coming of Christ and/or the end of the world. There were two kinds of thinking about this, including postmillennialism, which had been much discussed during the eighteenth century and was characterized by belief that Jesus would return to rule over a world where Christianity had triumphed. Nineteenth-century premillennialists, on the other hand, believed that the world had become so corrupted that only a cosmic act of God could purge the world of evil, and that only the purest "remnant" of the Christian faithful would be spared the apocalypse. Premillennialst William Miller (1782–1849) gathered around himself a group of followers in Vermont in the 1830s and 1840s and taught them to prepare to be saved from the coming tribulations. When the world did not end in 1844, as Miller had predicted, many of his followers gave up on him; but some carried the idea forward into what became the Adventist movement. Among the various groups of Adventists, the Seventh-Day Adventists, especially through the leadership of vegetarian and visionary Ellen Gould White (1827–1915), continued to draw adherents and have survived into the twenty-first century with millions of members. Another group that coalesced in the debates about the coming of the millennium was the Jehovah's Witnesses, founded by Charles Taze Russell (1852–1916) in the 1870s. Opponents of these groups ridiculed their millennialist ideas, complained about their deleterious effect on the social order, accused their leaders of a wide range of offenses, including financial misdeeds, and periodically charged these groups with conspiring to establish a theocratic order in the United States. In the case of Seventh-Day Adventists, whose Sabbath falls on Saturday, specific complaints centered on Adventists' breaking of Sabbath laws, or, in other words, working on Sunday, which is the day of the week that most Christians recognize as the Sabbath. For Jehovah's Witnesses, the doctrines of pacifism and resistance to blood transfusions, among other things, led to many instances of intolerance, including mass arrests of members of the denomination for refusing to perform military service. Rhetorical attacks on the group began in the nineteenth century and reached their peak in the twentieth century. In the 1930s the leader of the denomination declared saluting the flag to be a form of idolatry, leading to mob violence against Jehovah's Witnesses, even after a reconsidered Supreme Court decision in 1943 (reversal of *Gobitis*) declared their right not to salute to be guaranteed by law protecting the practice of religion. In the 1940s mobs of sometimes more than one thousand attacked congregations in Klamath Falls, Oregon, and in Maine, and in many places in between, burning houses of worship and beating members of the religious group. Also included in the documents below is an example of the kind of tragic incident that intolerant groups typically connected to the religion of their opponents, citing such as characteristic of their opponents' "fanaticism" and moral depravity, which sometimes was instanced as sexual abuse and at other times as kidnapping, enslavement, physical beatings, and even child sacrifice.

The following extract is taken from a highly graphic letter published in the Boston Courier, from Lydia Maria Child. . . .

I'm very sorry that the Millerites have attracted the attention of a portion of our population, who delight to molest them, though it is more from mirth than malice. All sincere convictions should be treated respectfully. Neither ridicule nor violence can overcome delusions of this sort, or diminish their power to injure. Such crowds are continually about the doors of the Millerite meetings, that it is most dangerous to life and limb to effect an entrance. Stones and brickbats are thrown in, and crackers and torpedoes exploded under their feet. The other night, while Mrs. Higgins was exhorting and prophesying, with tempestuous zeal, some boys fired a pile of shavings outside the window near which she was standing, and at the same time kindled several Roman candles. The blue, unearthly light of these fire-works illuminated the whole interior of the building with intense brilliancy, for a moment.

The effect on the highly excited congregation was terrible. Some fainted, and some screamed. Several serious accidents happened amid the general rush; and one man, it is said, was so deranged with nervous terror, that he went home and attempted to cut his throat. The Mayor, and a strong array of constables, now attend the meetings, to prevent a repetition of these dangerous tricks.

Source: "Miscellany," *Liberator*, October 25, 1844, 172.

Fanaticism in Second Adventism never had a more awful result than in the murder of a child by its father, last week, in Pocasset, Barnstable county, Mass. Charles F. Freeman deliberately killed his little daughter Edith, only five years old, her mother approving the deed. He claims that he took the life of the child "by the order of the Lord, as Abraham was ordered to sacrifice his son Isaac." The murderer is in jail, and his wife also. The child's funeral was attended on Sunday last, though the Adventists had insisted that she would rise on Saturday. We hope that this murderer would be treated as all murderers should be, and that it will not be admitted that religious fanaticism is to justify human sacrifices. The law expressly holds that crime committed while a man is intoxicated as if the man was sober; and so Mormons, Adventists, and Spiritualists should be held responsible for offences against law, notwithstanding their pretended revelations of a higher law. There is no safety in society if any other principle prevails.

Source: "Article 2," *New York Evangelist*, May 15, 1879, 7.

On May 27 the Grand Jury of Henry County indicted five farmers living on small places near the village of Springville, Tenn. The cases were tried in Paris before a certain Judge W. H. Swiggart. The prosecution did not attempt to prove that any one was disturbed by the work of these poor farmers; indeed, the witnesses for the state each declared that he was not disturbed. One of the prisoners had been seen ploughing strawberries on Sunday, another cutting sprouts, and still another loading wood on a wagon. The accused did not employ counsel, but each made a simple statement of his case, relying upon the guarantee of the Constitution and the intelligence of the judge and jury for acquittal. The following is the statement made by Mr. M. S. Lowry, whose name came first:

"I would like to say to the jury that, as has been stated, I am a Seventh Day Adventist. I observe the seventh day of the week as the Sabbath. I read my Bible, and my convictions on the Bible are that the seventh day of the week is the Sabbath, which comes on Saturday. I observe that day the best I know how. Then I claim the God-given right to six days of labor. I have a wife and four children, and it takes my labor six days to make a living. I go about my work quietly, do not make any unnecessary noise, but do my work as quietly as possible. It has been proved by the testimony of Mr. Fitch and Mr. Cox, who live around me, that they were not disturbed. Here I am before the court to answer for this right that I claim as a Christian. I am a law-abiding citizen, believing that we should obey the laws of the state; but whenever they conflict with my religious convictions and the Bible, I stand and choose to serve the law of my God rather than the laws of the state. I do not desire to cast any reflections upon the state, not the officers and authorities executing the law. I leave the case with you."

This simple, eloquent, and noble statement of a high-minded Christian gentlemen would have made an impression on any mind not blinded by bigotry, and would have rendered just any heart not dwarfed and shriveled by religious fanaticism. But like the ill-fated Huguenots of the sixteenth century, these victims of religious prejudice lacked broad-minded, liberty-loving, and constitution-revering patriots for judge and jurors. The prosecuting attorney struck the key-note of the true animus of the prosecution when in closing his speech he made use of the following significant expression:

"I cannot conceive that a man who claims to be a peaceable, law-abiding citizen can go on disregarding the day openly in the face of the law, openly in the face of the protections that are thrown around the holy Sabbath, *as we believe it and hold it*, and protected by the laws of this state; and this is a question that I presume you gentlemen will not have any difficulty in coming to a decision upon."

The accused were promptly found guilty by the jury, and on refusing to pay the unjust fine were remanded to jail on June 3, where they remained for over forty days. . . .

After lying in jail for over forty days, three of these conscientious, upright citizens were taken out, chained to three negro criminals who had been sentenced for drunkenness, shooting in the street, and fighting the city marshal, and set to work on the public highway. What a humiliating spectacle to a justice and liberty loving American!

Source: B. O. Flower, "Religious Intolerance in the Republic: Christians Persecuting Christians in Tennessee," Arena, December 1892, 120.

From an affidavit by John Q. Adams of Beaumont, Texas, dated October 30, 1940:

"On September 1st, 1940 B. P. Jones, a resident of Beaumont, Texas was visiting friends near Jasper, Texas having brought home some of the children who had been attending his wife in her illness. While he was in Jasper he performed a baptismal service for some of the colored people, he himself being a colored man and one of Jehovah's Witnesses.

"While walking from one house to another a car drew up alongside and someone said, 'Hello preacher, what are you doing up here?' While explaining that he was here to bring home the girls who had been attending his wife, two more cars drove up; one man with a shotgun got out of one of the cars and forced him into one of the cars, whereupon they drove out the highway and turned off onto a dirt road leading to a cemetery. Upon arriving at the cemetery, one of the men said, 'We ought to go and get that white son-of-a-bitch.' (Referring to one of the men who lives in that vicinity who likewise is one of Jehovah's Witnesses). The man with the gun then said 'Well, let's go ahead with him now!' The mob then tried to force Jones to say that he knew the white 'son-of-a-bitch' that they were alluding to—he did not know the man as he was only visiting and was not acquainted with any except colored people.

"The mob then tied Jones' hands behind his back and put a rope around the neck, by which one held him while another beat him with a wet rope. Two of the others cut a pole from one of the trees nearby with which they took their turn at beating him. When they quit beating him, the man with the gun said, 'Now run!' Jones replied, 'No, if you want to shoot me you can do it while I am looking at you.' At this, one of them said, 'You got a lot of nerve, eh, nigger?' Then the mob said they would give Jones three minutes to get his stuff from the house and leave Jasper, whereupon they took him back to the house where he was visiting and waited for him to get his car. The mobsters then followed him about 8 or 9 miles out of town.

"The above incident is merely one of the numerous acts of mob violence that have occurred in the past three or four months in the vicinity of Jasper and Newton counties. In June, a mob of Legionnaires dragged some of Jehovah's Witnesses from their automobiles as they were sitting in the Court House Square at Jasper and beat them up and when some bystanders attempted to come to the rescue of these people, they likewise were beaten— two of them being a frail woman and her daughter. When the woman and her daughter appealed to the Sheriff and Deputy and Town Marshall of Jasper for protection, they merely stood by and chuckled while the mob continued their 'dirty work.' This mob has been trailing and attempting to ambush various ones associated with Jehovah's Witnesses and have forced one family to leave the county."

Source: *The Persecution of Jehovah's Witnesses* (New York: American Civil Liberties Union, 1941), 9, 10.

Mary Baker Eddy and the Church of Christ, Scientist

Mary Baker Eddy founded the First Church of Christ, Scientist, in Massachusetts in 1879. Among the many unorthodox ideas that she espoused was "animal magnetism," a power that could be drawn upon to perform "mental healing" of sick persons. Certain persons, including some of those she had trained to physically heal through the power of mind, were, she believed, capable of using "animal magnetism" in a malicious way. Thus, "malicious animal magnetism," a force undetectable by any of the senses, could cause physical harm to persons, even when directed by persons at far distances from the victim. Such thinking is similar to the way in which persons think about the power of a witch, who can cast spells from afar and cause suffering, insanity, and even death through her occult power. In 1878, a woman who had experienced relief from her illness through Mrs. Eddy's agency, Lucretia Brown, suffered a relapse. She identified Daniel Spofford, a former student of Eddy's, as the culprit, and accused him in a legal complaint of using "mesmerism," which was understood to operate in a similar way to malicious animal magnetism, to persecute her from afar. Eddy became involved in the lawsuit, which was filed in Salem, Massachusetts, where two centuries earlier the witchcraft trials had taken place. The action quickly was dismissed by the court. The fact that Christian Scientists complained that witchcraft was being practiced against them—when orthodox Christian opponents at the time cast Christian Scientists themselves as experimenters with demonic powers and witchcraft—suggests how groups could mirror each other in their fears, even as they professed themselves to be profoundly different.

Humbly complaining, the plaintiff, Lucretia L. S. Brown of Ipswich, in said County of Essex, showeth unto your Honors, that Daniel H. Spofford, of Newburyport, in said County of Essex, the defendant in the above entitled action, is a mesmerist and practises the art of mesmerism and by his said art and power of his mind influences and controls the minds and bodies of other persons and uses his said power and art for the purpose of injuring the persons and property and social relations of others and does by said means so injure them.

And the plaintiff further showeth that the said Daniel H. Spofford has, at divers times and places since the year eighteen hundred and seventy-five, wrong fully and maliciously and with intent to injure the plaintiff, caused the plaintiff by means of his said power and art great suffering of body and mind and severe spinal pains and neuralgia and a temporary suspension of mind, and still continues to cause the plaintiff the same. And the plaintiff has reason to fear and does fear that he will continue in the future to cause the same. And the plaintiff says that said injuries are great and of an irreparable nature and that she is wholly unable to escape from the control and influence he so exercises upon her and from the aforesaid effects of said control and influence.

Source: Complaint against Daniel H. Spofford filed in Supreme Judicial Court, Salem, Massachusetts, May 1878, in Willa Cather, Georgine Milmine, and David Stouch, *The Life of Mary Baker G. Eddy and the History of Christian Science* (Lincoln: University of Nebraska Press, 1993), 240–41.

In the Judicial Supreme Court in Salem, on Tuesday, a bill in equity was brought more befitting the new institution in Danvers [i.e., the nearby state hospital for the insane] than the highest tribunal of the Commonwealth. The bill was nominally brought by Lucretia L. S. Brown, of Ipswich, to restrain Daniel H. Spofford, of Newburyport, from mesmeric influence over her, causing her severe pains and neuralgia; but we suspect the real complainant is Mary B. G. Eddy, of Lynn, who has a power of attorney to appear for the plaintiff in the case. . . . The witchcraft delusion is not yet dead, even officially.

Source: *Newburyport (Mass.) Herald*, May 16, 1878.

Evangelical Enthusiasm and Anti–Camp Meeting Mobs and "Disturbances"

Americans historically have taken a conservative view of religion. That is, they have been wary of religion that seems either too "enthusiastic" or too rational. For most, there is a limited spectrum of belief and practice that is consonant with commonly held ideals of democracy, civic virtue, liberty, and other core aspects of the dominant political and social ideologies. Movements that play with expression at the ends of the spectrum are suspect and poorly tolerated. Deists were disliked for their Enlightenment views about the capability of human reason to know truth and for their reluctance to accept the authority of religious institutions. Methodists, especially in antebellum America, before the movement had become rooted in the middle class, ran into trouble because of their boisterous worship and emotionally rich piety. Like Pentecostals in the twentieth century—who also began on the margins of the middle class and suffered as well for their enthusiastic performances of prophecy, speaking in tongues, healings, and other "gifts" of the Holy Spirit—Methodists confused and challenged Americans who took a conservative view of religion.

Many a newspaper report on nineteenth-century camp meetings explicitly noted that there was "little disturbance" at them, meaning that the camp meeting was not invaded by persons who sought to chase off the participants. Such reportage reflects the fact that those attending revivals in the form of camp meetings sometimes expected such disturbances. Methodists who gathered in woods or out in the countryside for extended prayer meetings over a weekend or more—sometimes weeks at a time—were loud, enthusiastic, and inclined toward expressive ritual that could involve mass barking, laughing, rolling on the ground, jumping, or other such religious "exercises." The occasion also could lead to unexpected pregnancies on the part of both married and unmarried young women, and though that did not happen often, popular understanding of the camp meeting as exotic and erotic encouraged the foregrounding of such accidents in public discussion of the meetings. In some cases, armed and, more often, drunken men attempted to disrupt camp meetings. This happened regularly enough that statutes regarding the free exercise of religion were clarified in legal proceedings to specifically include camp meetings. There were incidents in which clubs were wielded, knives were drawn, shots were fired, and person were seriously injured or killed. Critics of Methodism claimed that the emotional intensity of the meeting could lead to the moral decay of those attending. The final document below represents the fear among some Americans that evangelicals could channel their fervor into attacks on those with whom they disagreed, "infidels," and form mobs to attack them.

Every person who shall wilfully, maliciously or contemptuously disquiet, or disturb, any camp meeting, congregation or other assembly met for religious worship, or when meeting at the place of worship, or dispersing therefrom, or any school or other meeting or assembly of people met together for any lawful purpose whatever, by making a noise, or by rude or indecent behavior, or profane discourse within the place of assembly, or so near the same as to interrupt or disturb the order or solemnity thereof, or who shall wilfully menace, threaten or assault any person there being, shall be deemed guilty of a misdemeanor."

Source: Missouri Statute against Disturbing a Camp Meeting, Mo. Rev. Stat. §1528 (1879).

This little book is written *specially* for *your* benefit. The author has no pecuniary interest in its sale, nor any *party* end to answer. . . .

He has seen with much pain and regret some signs of *enthusiasm* and *error* crept into our church, which *should* have been checked by those who were our *overseers* in the Lord. He verily believes that *they* should have *restrained*, and *not fostered* the unprofitable emotions of *screaming, hallooing* and *jumping*, and the *stepping and singing* of *senseless*, merry airs. These have often prejudiced true and vital religion. And because no man hath hitherto regarded these things, in this way, the author, however deficient in his task, is disposed to contribute his mite towards the suppression of a growing evil.

Source: Methodist Error; or Friendly, Christian Advice (Cincinnati: Phillips & Speer, 1819).

We have no hesitation in saying the public ought not to encourage [Methodists], by attendance at their meetings; and this for many good reasons.

1. The powerful temptations to the practice of gross vice, especially uncleanliness. . . . We would gravely ask parents, whether they would be willing to intrust their youthful sons and daughters, during the night, in the society of the licentious and profane, who flock thither to indulge the grosser propensities of fallen human nature? . . .

3. The excitement produced, is almost, if not altogether, the effect of an appeal to the passions and the animal sensibilities of our nature.

Source: "Methodist Camp-Meetings," Evangelical Witness, October 10, 1825, 456.

DISTURBANCE OF A CAMP MEETING.—The prevailing spirit of urgency displayed itself at a Camp Meeting held last week at Northridge, Worcester county. We learn that the meeting proceeded orderly and quietly until Thursday, on which day the congregation was supposed to amount to 5000. A large gang of miscreants, supplied with *rum* from an unlicensed tavern three-quarters of a mile distant, commenced their operations a short distance from the camp ground, by making loud noises, and insulting females, and others, as they passed to and from the ground, and finally, setting themselves up as manufacturers of public opinion, pronounced it highly improper that the meeting should be allowed to proceed. Accordingly, as darkness increased, they gathered boldness, and commenced their disturbances at and near the preaching stand; which continued to increase during the religious exercises of the evening. A gentleman writing to a friend in this city, says:—

" ... A struggle ensued between the friends of good order and the unprincipled, self-appointed judges of *expediency*, which resulted in some blows, and a few moderate wounds. One of our friends was knocked down, another was struck a heavy blow in the face, and others received blows more or less severe. Several of the rioters were wounded, and one or two, I believe pretty severely. Seven or eight were arrested, and the rest soon disappeared. Of those who were arrested, two were discharged the same evening; another named Loud was delivered to a gentlemen who promised to return him this morning, but he has not yet been returned. The other four were examined this afternoon and ordered to recognize in the sum of $300 each, to take their trial at the next term of the County Court. The names of the ringleaders, and several others concerned in the mob, are known, and will be presented to the grand jury at its next session. The disturbance was purely an anti-camp-meeting one."

Source: "News of the Day," *Christian Watchman*, September 4, 1835, 143.

Let no one accuse me of exaggeration, for the sake of dramatic effect. I am speaking now of Shelby County—the home of the Lyncher—the terrible *locale*, where, ten years later, forty persons were poisoned to death at a marriage supper!

It will be obvious that in such a community, very few would be disposed to patronize camp meetings; and accordingly a dozen different trials at various times had never collected a hundred hearers on a single occasion. But even these were not allowed to worship in peace; uniformly the first day and night a band of armed desperadoes, headed by the notorious Watt Foeman, chief judge and executioner of the Shelby Lynchers, broke into the altar and scattered the mourners, or ascended the pulpit and treated the preacher with a gratuitous robe of tar and feathers! Hence all prudent evangelists soon learned to shun the west bank of the Sabine, as if it had been infected by a cohort of demons; and two whole years elapsed without any new attempt to erect the cross in so imperious a field.

Source: Charles Summerfield, "Paul Denton, the Texas Missionary," *Christian Secretary*, June 28, 1850, 1.

It is known, that the denomination [Methodists] most accustomed to camp meetings in our country, have thought best, or felt obliged to avail themselves on these occasions of the special aid and protection of the civil authorities to defend themselves against disturbances from evil disposed persons and wicked combinations. How far this necessity is owing to the allowance of an unrestrained expression of feeling, and a consequent intro-duction of some amount of disorder and confusion, of which the wicked avail themselves to work mischief—is worthy of grave consideration by that denomination.

Source: "Camp Meetings," *Christian Advocate*, July 18, 1831, 177.

The following, from the *Baltimore American* of Tuesday last, tells its own sad story. From other sources we learn that the mob was composed of about three hundred, mainly rebel soldrs, and that the whole movement was pre-concerted, the purpose being to murder several of the prominent whites connected with the meeting. . . .

During Thursday afternoon certain men were observed on the ground armed with revolvers, which they wore in belts around their waists; but no danger was apprehended until nearly midnight, when a party went into the colored people's meeting and knocked down a woman. The colored peo-ple soon rallied, however, and drove the rioters from the immediate vicin-ity, and the meeting again progressed; but while these in attendance were engaged in prayer, a man praying was knocked down, and as the colored people rose from their knees they were fired upon by these desperadoes, who attacked in front and on either flank, almost surrounding them. The attacked party again rallied, returned the fire, and charged upon their cow-ardly assailants, driving them within the circle formed by the colored peo-ple's tents, immediately in the rear of the preacher's stand at the principal camp. In a few minutes the roadies renewed their onslaught, but were again repulsed, firearms being freely used. At this time a young man named Milton Benson, a resident of the vicinity, while in front of the preacher's stand, upon his knees as a penitent, was mortally wounded by a pistol ball which struck him in the back of neck and passed out at his mouth. Surgical aid was immediately procured for him, but although he was still alive this morning, no hope of his recovery is indulged. The supposition is that this shot was intended for a certain preacher, as it was currently reported afterward that he had been fired at although he was not in the altar when the shot was fired.

Source: "Massacre at a Camp-Meeting," *Christian Advocate,* September 6, 1866, 245.

South Abington, [Mass.,] Jan. 30, 1847.

On Friday evening, Jan. 22, Mr. and Mrs. Foster commenced a course of anti-slavery lectures. They were invited here by special request of the old organized abolitionists of the town, and we have quite a goodly number of them here. Notice of the meeting having been circulated through the town, all manner of abuse and calumny were immediately in circulation by the pro-slavery portion of the town, in regard to Mr. and Mrs. Foster, the object of the meetings, &c. &c.

We have here four Orthodox churches, two Methodist, one Baptist, one Universalist, and one Swedenborgian. From there four Orthodox churches and the Baptist, came forth gross misrepresentations of us, and our movement. . . .

One Tuesday evening, the mob collected in large numbers, and a serious outbreak was expected. The police were present, but could not preserve order. The rioters commenced by clapping, stamping, coughing, &c. &c. Several eggs were thrown by them at Mr. and Mrs. Foster, and struck with great violence very near them; fortunately, no injury was done them. They finally succeeded in breaking up the meeting by their outrageous proceedings. Thus was free-speech struck down, and mob law and violence made triumphant in the town of Abington—a town noted for its evangelical religion, its meeting-house, its prayer meetings, its sermonizing, &c. &c.

But on whom rests the responsibility of this disgraceful outbreak? I say, unhesitatingly, it was an evangelical mob! And now for the proof.

Ministers and church members of the evangelical faith, in the town, have for a long time heaped all manner of abuse and gross misrepresentation on you and your religious sentiments, Mr. and Mrs. Foster, the come-outers, &c. Indeed, sermons have been preached, in an indirect manner, and some of them in a direct manner, in malignant disparagement of "old organized" anti-slavery, non-resistance, come-outerism, &c. Consequently, as soon as it was known that those awfully wicked disturbers and infidels, S. S. and

A. K. Foster, were coming to town, the wrath and indignation of the town, especially the "evangelical" portion of it, were strongly aroused.

Source: H. H. Bringham, "Mobocracy Triumphant in Abington," *Liberator*, February 5, 1847, 23.

Non-Believers

A number of state constitutions (e.g., Arkansas, North Carolina, South Carolina, Texas, Tennessee) prohibit persons who do not believe in God from holding public offices and from participating in some other public activities. The Arkansas Constitution of 1874 is cited here (in its 2008 form).

§1. Atheists disqualified from holding office or testifying as witness.

No person who denies the being of a God shall hold any office in the civil departments of this State, nor be competent to testify as a witness in any Court.

Source: Arkansas Constitution, art. 19, §1 (2008).

CHAPTER FIVE

Intolerance toward Native American Religions

During the early modern Age of Discovery Europeans organized their think-ing about indigenous peoples whom they encountered in the Americas and on other continents according to themes and categories drawn from their religious ideologies. The European experience of the Americas was one of enchantment. The New World was a place of wonders. Europeans discovered sublime landscapes, amazing populations of game, extraordinary creatures and plants, mysterious people, and wilderness that was both inviting and ter-rifying. Explorers and their parties of soldiers, missionaries, and colonists oriented themselves to the Americas and their indigenous peoples by draw-ing upon biblical images and stories. Adventurers scoured the Americas for the Garden of Eden and expected to discover it, as they anticipated finding the Fountain of Youth, whose curative waters were presumed to flow in some secret place deep within the lush jungle. What Europeans heard in their con-versations with North American natives was that there were cities of gold in the continent's interior, and some set out to find them. Such treasures—gold, youth, innocence—nevertheless lay concealed somewhere in a seem-ingly endless wilderness that was as terrifying and deadly as it was beautiful. To make sense of the stories that they collected from Indians, and to make sense of their own response to those stories and their firsthand experiences of the New World, they turned to religion. Religion supplied myths to explain the history of the Americas and to imagine the region's glorious Christian future. Religion also furnished explorers and colonists with understandings of their suffering as they crossed swamps, contracted malaria, died of starva-tion, fought with Native Americans, or were eaten by alligators. The New World, then, for all of its beauties, was also an enchantment of horrors, of ter-ror and tragedy. It could appear, as New Englander William Bradford wrote, as a "dungheap," or worse: for the Spanish missionary Bartolomé de las Casas the European slaughter of Native Americans was an eyes-wide-open journey into hell. The mystery and magic of America was powerful. It undergirded a European imaginary of the New World as a place where anything was possible and everything was in danger. Native Americans, as part of that mystery, were both fascinating as exotics and feared as evil savages. Most important, the European view of the New World as an enchanted place, including biblically derived explanations for the things of that world, objectified Indians' lives in a way that allowed Europeans to fit them into religio-cultural schematizations of order and power, and to define them in ways consonant with the goals of colonial empire.

In trying to fit the people they met in the Americas into biblically grounded ways of thinking about the past, many colonists came to the conclusion that Native Americans were descendants of the ten lost tribes of Israel. In the Old Testament stories about the history of the Jews, no further mention of those tribes is made after the narration of the destruction of Israel by the ancient Assyrians. Many Europeans came to believe that Native Americans were the descendants of those tribes. That made them, like all Jews, of particular interest to Christian missionaries, who took the task of bringing Jews to Christianity to be of paramount importance. Some theories about the origins of Indians went further, explaining that in fact Jesus had preached to the inhabitants of the New World, making them Christians, but that Indians had over time forgotten all but a small residue of their Christianity. Accordingly, for missionaries Indians were especially "prepared to receive the gospel." They were, in the patchwork, imaginative, and emergent European history of the New World, religious kin to the Christian explorers and colonists. They were judged ripe for proselytization, poised on the edge of converting and just needing a nudge to gather them back into the Christian fold.

But of course Indians were not religious kin. They did not convert immediately, or easily, or even at all in many places. They often fought with Europeans, resisting proselytization. They killed missionaries and burned down the missions. In 1680, along the upper Rio Grande in what is now the state of New Mexico, the Pueblo people threw out the missionaries, civil overseers, and soldiers in a widespread revolt. Europeans interpreted such events with reference to the Bible, and in many places came to the conclusion that Indians were "Amalekites," a reference to ancient enemies of the Jews who, for their duplicity and merciless raiding on the weakest of the Jews, earned the wrath of God. In Old Testament stories, God eventually commanded the Jews to exterminate the Amalekites—man, woman, and child—and to kill all of their livestock and destroy their belongings, and in so doing to "blot out" the memory of them from the world. The biblical accounts note that the sentence of extermination was passed in view of the fact that the Amalekites were "kin" of the Jews, and that turning on one's own—in other words, the Amalekites' betrayal of the Jews—was an especially terrible offense. Europeans saw Indians simultaneously as distant religious kin and as archenemies. When relations between Indians and Europeans went bad, the latter, viewing events through a lens ground by devotion to biblical images, were inclined to take Indians as Amalekites and to campaign against them with an eye to exterminating them.

In trying to make sense of their encounters with Indians, Europeans above all defined themselves as "Christians" and Indians as non-Christians, as "heathens." Europeans believed that Indians were not civilized and that making them Christians would lead to their becoming civilized. Accordingly, being Christian and being civilized were inextricably intertwined for Europeans. The process of establishing a colonial expire was always one of exploiting indigenous peoples for labor—to dig in the mines; tend agricultural enterprises; construct buildings, roads, and bridges; drain swamps; and manufacture a wide range of items for export, including beautiful violins. For Indians to play a role in any of these enterprises was, for colonial overseers, a sign of their advance toward being civilized, as was their religious improvement as Christians. With few exceptions, Indians were not treated as legal agents, as fully human, until they had become Christian. Tribes that earned the designation "civilized" were tribes that had converted to Christianity and had remained more or less Christian through several generations. The so-called Five Civilized Tribes that American historians referenced in the nineteenth century—Cherokee, Chickasaw, Choctaw, Creek, and Seminole—adopted in some measure the notion of private property, built houses, and engaged in farming, but the crucial element of their "civility" was their Christian religion. Unless a tribe was Christian, it risked having no status in land disputes, treaty interpretation, negotiations of trading rights, or in many other areas of contact and contestation with Euro-Americans. The legal history of land ownership, as nineteenth-century court cases illustrate, wrote Indians into a distinctly second-class status and affirmed as preeminent the conveyance of land from one "Christian" entity to another. As we see below, "heathens," according to the Supreme Court, did not figure as legitimate claimants when Christian claims were at stake.

Missionaries came in large numbers to the New World and undertook their task of converting Native Americans with remarkable energy and bravery. In some instances, Indians resisted their message of the gospel and were subjected to genocidal violence. In other instances, Indians gradually adopted a Christian life and came to live alongside Europeans in tentative and fluid arrangements of shared culture. Sometimes Indians appeared to convert quickly and in large numbers to the Christian faith, even in places where communication between missionaries and Indians was imprecise because of language differences. It was also the case that conversions among Indians frequently did not stick. The accounts of Jesuit missionaries in the St. Lawrence and Great Lakes regions include many reports of missionaries visiting converted tribes after the passage of a year or so only to find that little remained of Christian ideas or ritual. The same was true in the established missions of the Southeast and Southwest, where, in spite of established centers of Christian sacramental devotionalism and "civilized" ways of life, Indians still drifted from the faith that missionaries believed they had instilled. Such failures of the mission enterprise led many to conclude that Indians simply were not good candidates for conversion to Christianity. They were sometimes judged to be too stupid to truly learn and embrace Christian truths. At other times, they were cast as simpleminded children who needed constant and intense supervision in order to remain pious. Some Europeans also concluded that Indians were fakers who pretended to convert simply to avoid punishment or to achieve some gain in negotiations or trade with whites. The theory that Indians were cunningly duplicitous correlated well with Old Testament characterizations of the Amalekites and accordingly could serve to amplify ill will toward and fear of Indians and from there lead to extremely violent confrontation. In the long run, the idea that Indians calculatedly sought to give the appearance of conversion while secretly maintaining a vibrant connection to indigenous traditions did indeed contribute to intolerance toward Indians. Government officials, concerned about a slippery slope to conflict with Indians, learned to condemn virtually all Native American traditions as signs of a secretly practiced Indian faith that undercut the "civilizing" process. Such was the case well in evidence in South Dakota, when the growing popularity of the Ghost Dance among the Lakota Sioux caused federal military and civilian leaders to react in most extreme fashion—as if they were facing Amalekites—and massacre hundreds of Indians at Wounded Knee just after Christmas in 1890.

Religious persecution in many instances emerged as a response to complex interrelations of political, social, and cultural frictions between Indians and whites. There were some cases in which—perhaps because of the complaints of a missionary here, or a government official there—a problem emerged clearly out of the background of other frictions and was addressed largely as a religious issue. But in the development of Euro-Americans' attitudes toward Native Americans, it was more often the case that religious issues were blended together with other kinds of issues, all under an umbrella of "morality" or "justice," or "right." Historians sometimes have tried to untangle the strands of encounter, identifying what they believe to be largely political concerns, or ones involving specific secular themes: trade, land, sexual relations, and so forth. Sometimes such analyses have proven illuminating: politics, religion, social issues, gender relations, and other discrete areas of human life are certainly visible as we study events and ideas, and there is much to gain by interpreting them within contexts that are precise and limited. In the case of European encounters with Native Americans, however, we must remember that virtually everything in Native American cultures has a religious component to it. Everything is tied to a larger vision of ultimacy, sacred power, good and evil, ritual observance, a holy calendar, and religious meanings of space and place. It is hard to sort Native American religion from politics or abstract it from backgrounds of trade, gender, or material culture. When we study the interaction of Europeans with Indians, then, we must remember that what sometimes appears as Indian politics or sociality is often profoundly religious. And so, it is both telling and ironic that Europeans chose to identify Indians first and foremost as "non-Christians." In a sense, they were right, in as much as that view connoted a life that was informed top to bottom by religion. Of course, the reality was that by constructing Indians as non-Christians, Europeans denied them humanity, or at least a humanity equal to that Europeans imagined for themselves. Non-Christians could not be civilized, smart, moral, or perhaps even redeemable. But it is an open question as to how much Europeans saw the whole fabric of Indian life as religion, and to what extent they stopped short of seeing anything about Indian life beyond the fact that Indians were not Christians.

Government policy toward Native Americans developed as an extension of what more-informal relations had been. Those relations were characterized by the expectation among whites that Indians would recognize the superiority of white religions and culture and embrace them. In some cases where that did not happen, Indians were massacred. In other cases, whites assumed that Native American cultures were so retarded as to make unlikely the prospect that Indians would be able to acculturate. But the general trend was toward forced acculturation. Indians were brought to the mission by the Spanish, or preached to by the French, or organized as "praying towns" in New England, through intimidation, martial or otherwise. Whites persuaded themselves that they were doing Indians a favor by Christianizing them and compelling them to adopt European moralities and ways of life. Whites condemned as immoral numerous aspects of Indian life, from patterns of sexual relations and marriage to ritual performance to military conduct. In the latter part of the nineteenth century, when most Indians had been forcibly relocated to reservations and close government supervision (in the form of the Board of Indian Commissioners or the Department of the Interior) made possible greater control of Indian life, prohibitions of religious rituals became more common. The Sun Dance among the Plains Indians was made an offense in the 1880s and 1890s, and although it nevertheless was covertly performed on occasion, it was not legal again until the 1930s. Other dances were banned as well. The activities of medicine men and women—and even the office of "medicine man" itself—were sharply curtailed. Some Indian children were separated from their parents and placed in Indian boarding schools run largely by Christian missionary societies, where the practice of Native American religions (and languages) were forbidden and where participation in Christian worship and catechesis was required. The goal of these institutions was, according to Henry Richard Pratt, a leading figure in Indian education, to "kill the Indian and save the man" (see below).

In the twentieth century, Native Americans continued to fight battles against religious intolerance. Some of these drew national attention, such as the legal dispute, ending in a Supreme Court case and federal legislation, over the use of peyote in religious rituals of the Native American Church. Peyote became more widespread and important to the religious life of some Indians through the influence of the Comanche chief Quanah Parker (who founded the Native American Church Movement) in the late nineteenth century. In the late twentieth century, the church ran afoul of the much-publicized "war on drugs" that had become required dogma for most American politicians seeking reelection. The case took several twists and turns before federal legislation brought some remedy to the problem. In the late twentieth century the federal government also became involved in disputes about the excavation of Native American skeletons from their gravesites. The Native American Graves Protection and Repatriation Act (1990) set terms for the protection of burial sites and set in motion a process requiring museums and other institutions to inventory their collections of Native American human remains and artifacts and to plan for the repatriation of those items to Native American groups.

The history of encounter between Indians and Euro-Americans is a history of cultural genocide. Whites condemned Indian religion as superstition or outright devilry and sought to destroy it. Trusting in the superiority of their Christianity to all other worldviews, white Christians launched a systematic, powerful, and wide-ranging effort to cause Indians to forget their religious myths, rituals, and material culture. They largely succeeded. While tribal initiatives in the twentieth century managed to slow the deterioration of Indian religious cultures, much already had been lost to Christian hubris and the forced acculturation that it demanded.

DOCUMENTS

Pope Alexander VI, *Inter Caetera,* May 4, 1493

Immediately on the heels of the discovery of America the papacy formally declared that encounters with persons in the New World were to be appreciated as opportunities to convert indigenous peoples to the Roman Catholic faith. In the papal bull *Inter Caetera* (1493), those peoples were cast as barbarians whose conversion was expected to go hand in hand with their subjugation. The bull urged the Catholic powers of Europe to overthrow the religious, political, and social orders of indigenes and to impose Christianity. This bull, among others, set the tone for taking the religious lives of Native Americans, and all of the intertwined strands of the cultural worlds that they had created, as a whole. That is, it pressed on explorers, missionaries, and colonists a view of religion as identical to culture—and all of it barbarous. Religion, then, which was not separate from social authority, art, hunting, sexual moralities, dancing, war making, or any other cultural performances, was a problem to be addressed through force. The religious conversion of indigenes was a Christian responsibility coequal with the overthrow of all other aspects of the corrupt, profane, and inferior ways of Indian life.

Alexander, bishop, servant of the servants of God, to the illustrious sovereigns, our very dear son in Christ, Ferdinand, king, and our very dear daughter in Christ, Isabella, queen of Castile, Leon, Aragon, Sicily, and Granada, health and apostolic benediction. Among other works well pleasing to the Divine Majesty and cherished of our heart, this assuredly ranks highest, that in our times especially the Catholic faith and the Christian religion be exalted and be everywhere increased and spread, that the health of souls be cared for and that barbarous nations be overthrown and brought to the faith itself. Wherefore inasmuch as by the favor of divine clemency, we, though of insufficient merits, have been called to this Holy See of Peter, recognizing that as true Catholic kings and princes, such as we have known you always to be, and as your illustrious deeds already known to almost the whole world declare, you not only eagerly desire but with every effort, zeal, and diligence, without regard to hardships, expenses, dangers, with the shedding even of your blood, are laboring to that end; recognizing also that you have long since dedicated to this purpose your whole soul and all your endeavors—as witnessed in these times with so much glory to the Divine Name in your recovery of the kingdom of Granada from the yoke of the Saracens—we therefore are rightly led, and hold it as our duty, to grant you even of our own accord and in your favor those things whereby with effort each day more hearty you may be enabled for the honor of God himself and the spread of the Christian rule to carry forward your holy and praiseworthy purpose so pleasing to immortal God.

Source: *Inter Caetera* (papal bull), in *European Treaties Bearing on the History of the United States and Its Dependencies to 1648*, edited by Frances Gardiner Davenport (Washington, D.C.: Carnegie Institution, 1917), 75.

Christian Discovery and Dominion

In *Johnson and Graham's Lessee v. William M'intosh*, a case that came before the United States Supreme Court in 1823, the residue of the earliest European pronouncements about Native American inferiority—such as *Inter Caetera*—proved to be still powerful in organizing American thinking about Indians. In this instance, the court upheld a lower court's ruling that contracts conveying land ownership from Indians to Euro-Americans were invalid, except as were brokered by the federal government through its fidelity to colonial transmissions of land rights from the sovereigns of those European nations whose explorers had claimed the land in their names. Chief Justice John Marshall, in writing the opinion, argued that Indians had some claim of ownership but that their claims did not have the authority of European ownership that came with European discovery. The rationale for this, stated repeatedly in the text of the opinion, was that Indians were not Christian. European monarchs' commissions and grants to various trading companies and other colonial ventures were the foundation of legal ownership of land in the United States. The claims of non-Christians—in this case the American indigenes—were not.

On the discovery of this immense continent, the great nations of Europe were eager to appropriate to themselves so much of it as they could respectively acquire. Its vast extent offered an ample field to the ambition and enterprise of all; and the character and religion of its inhabitants afforded an apology for considering them as a people over whom the superior genius of Europe might claim an ascendency. The potentates of the old world found no difficulty in convincing themselves that they made ample compensation to the inhabitants of the new, by bestowing on them civilization and Christianity, in exchange for unlimited independence. But, as they were all in pursuit of nearly the same object, it was necessary, in order to avoid conflicting settlements, and consequent war with each other, to establish a principle, which all should acknowledge as the law by which the right of acquisition, which they all asserted, should be regulated as between themselves. This principle was, that discovery gave title to the government by whose subjects, or by whose authority, it was made, against all other European governments, which title might be consummated by possession.

The exclusion of all other Europeans, necessarily gave to the nation making the discovery the sole right of acquiring the soil from the natives, and establishing settlements upon it. It was a right with which no Europeans could interfere. It was a right which all asserted for themselves, and to the assertion of which, by others, all assented.

Those relations which were to exist between the discoverer and the natives, were to be regulated by themselves. The rights thus acquired being exclusive, no other power could interpose between them.

In the establishment of these relations, the rights of the original inhabitants were, in no instance, entirely disregarded; but were necessarily, to a considerable extent, impaired. They were admitted to be the rightful occupants of the soil, with a legal as well as just claim to retain possession of it, and to use it according to their own discretion; but their rights to complete sovereignty, as independent nations, were necessarily diminished, and their power to dispose of the soil at their own will, to whomsoever they pleased, was denied by the original fundamental principle, that discovery gave exclusive title to those who made it.

While the different nations of Europe respected the right of the natives, as occupants, they asserted the ultimate dominion to be in themselves; and claimed and exercised, as a consequence of this ultimate dominion, a power to grant the soil, while yet in possession of the natives. These grants have been understood by all, to convey a title to the grantees, subject only to the Indian right of occupancy.

The history of America, from its discovery to the present day, proves, we think, the universal recognition of these principles. . . .

The documents upon this subject are ample and complete. So early as the year 1496, her monarch granted a commission to the Cabots, to discover countries then unknown to Christian people, and to take possession of them in the name of the king of England. Two years afterwards, Cabot proceeded on this voyage, and discovered the continent of North America, along which he sailed as far south as Virginia. To this discovery the English trace their title.

In this first effort made by the English government to acquire territory on this continent, we perceive a complete recognition of the principle which has been mentioned. The right of discovery given by this commission, is confined to countries "then unknown to all Christian people;" and of these countries Cabot was empowered to take possession in the name of the king of England. Thus asserting a right to take possession, notwithstanding the occupancy of the natives, who were heathens, and, at the same time, admitting the prior title of any Christian people who may have made a previous discovery.

The same principle continued to be recognised. The charter granted to Sir Humphrey Gilbert, in 1578, authorizes him to discover and take possession of such remote, heathen, and barbarous lands, as were not actually possessed by any Christian prince or people. This charter was afterwards renewed to Sir Walter Raleigh, in nearly the same terms.

By the charter of 1606, under which the first permanent English settlement on this continent was made, James I. granted to Sir Thomas Gates and others, those territories in America lying on the seacoast, between the 34th and 45th degrees of north latitude, and which either belonged to that monarch, or were not then possessed by any other Christian prince or people. The grantees were divided into two companies at their own request. The first, or southern colony, was directed to settle between the 34th and 41st degrees of north latitude; and the second, or northern colony, between the 38th and 45th degrees. . . .

Thus has our whole country been granted by the crown while in the occupation of the Indians. These grants purport to convey the soil as well as the right of dominion to the grantees. In those governments which were denominated royal, where the right to the soil was not vested in individuals, but remained in the crown, or was vested in the colonial government, the king claimed and exercised the right of granting lands, and of dismembering the government at his will. The grants made out of the two original colonies, after the resumption of their charters by the crown, are examples of this. The governments of New-England, New-York, New-Jersey, Pennsylvania, Maryland, and a part of Carolina, were thus created.

Source: Johnson and Graham's Lessee v. William M'intosh, 21 U.S. 543 (1823).

Religiously Driven Violence

Europeans justified acts of violence against Native Americans through references to religion. Europeans understood themselves as "Christians" and identified Indians as non-Christians, described as "heathen," "barbarians," or in other ways that signaled their otherness to the Christian Europeans. Campaigns against Indians, in New France, New Spain, and in the English-speaking colonies, typically drew upon religious imagery in their rhetorical buildup to military or mob action. Assaults on Indian villages, or on groups of Indians living among whites, were imagined as performances of near-cosmic dimensions in their pitting of good against evil. A biblically grounded logic of extermination—Indians were Amalekites, betrayers of the faith, and therefore worthy of being "blotted out"—drove crusades against Indian opponents. Typically, frictions over land ownership, hunting rights, exchange processes, natural resources, alliances with competing nations or powers, or other such issues underlay the march to armed encounter. But in preparing for battle or reflecting on the fight after the fact, leaders referenced the Bible to make sense of their operations as religiously valid, indeed, as a requirement of their religious faith. Christians also sometimes perversely imagined their killing of Indians as a kind of sacrifice to God, an offering meant to indicate their fidelity to the tenets of their Christian faith and an example of their willingness to act in extreme ways in imagined defense of their faith. In some cases, Indians became both enemies—Amalekites—*and* a sacrifice. The massacre of twenty Indians by a Christian mob in Lancaster County, Pennsylvania, in 1763 was, in the view of commentator Benjamin Franklin, undertaken by a mob who appealed both to the command of the Old Testament God to annihilate one's enemies and to the belief that the extermination of Indians was a sacrifice to God. Franklin's narrative, which informed an 1818 account of the massacre that identified the culprits as Presbyterians, stressed that those who carried out such atrocities "despised government." In the latter part of the nineteenth century, this thinking was still in effect, as observed by an editorial published in the *New York Post* (and republished in various magazines).

> But it seems these People think they have a better Justification; nothing less than the *Word of God*. With the Scriptures in their Hands and Mouths, they can set at nought that express Command, *Thou shalt do no Murder*; and justify their Wickedness, by the Command given *Joshua* to destroy the Hea-

then. Horrid Perversion of Scripture and of Religion! To father the worst of Crimes on the God of Peace and Love!—Even the *Jews*, to whom that particular Commission was directed, spared the *Gibeonites*, on Account of their Faith once given. The Faith of the Government has been frequently given to those *Indians*;—but that did not avail them with People who despise Government.

Source: Benjamin Franklin, *Narrative of the Late Massacres, in Lancaster County* (Philadelphia: Benjamin Franklin and David Hall, 1764), 13.

But these people, being chiefly Presbyterians, seem to think that they have a better justification—nothing less than the *word of God*. With the Scriptures in their hands and mouths, they can set at nought that express command—"*Thou shalt do no murder*," and justify their wickedness by the command given to Joshua to *destroy the heathen*! Horrid perversion of Scripture and religion! To father the worst of crimes on the God of love and peace!" . . .

As this horrid massacre took place in Pennsylvania, and as it is known that the religious principles and pacific policy of William Penn had occasioned peace for 70 years between the white people and the Indians; it will be natural for many to ask—How came this peace to be interrupted? . . .

The Presbyterians, who murdered the harmless tribe, are represented as deluded fanatics. Under the influence of a malignant enthusiasm they destroyed their poor Indian brethren as an acceptable sacrifice to the FATHER OF MERCIES. But how dreadful is that delusion which led professed Christians to believe that God could be pleased to see them engaged in murdering his *heathen children*! This delusion however was not confined to the 57 murderers of the Conestogoe tribe, it was spread in a greater or less degree over the other provinces. It became, also, a kind of hereditary disease, which perhaps has not been wholly exterminated to this day.

Source: "Review of a Massacre," *Christian Disciple*, August 6, 1818, 3. Note that the account here adds "Presbyterians" to Franklin's original narrative.

Others put the same thing in the form of an assumption that the Pilgrims were by their faith the children of Abraham the faithful, and the aborigines, being heathen, were probably the descendants, or at any rate the proper representatives, of the devoted Canaanites, and therefore condemned by heaven to utter extermination. Other classes of settlers have taken a shorter cut in their reasonings, while agreeing to the practical conclusion that the

Indians as Incapable of Conversion to Christianity

A recurring theme in much European thinking about Native Americans
was that they were incapable of conversion to Christianity and therefore incapable of being civilized. Just as Spanish Catholics, after the expulsion of
Muslims from Iberia in 1492, came to suspect both Jews and Muslim of fake
conversions to Christianity—and so organized the Inquisition to root them
out—so also did Euro-Americans evidence skepticism about the possibility
of Indians becoming Christians. Accordingly, Indian conversions were often
suspect, thought either to be incomplete in some way or outright phony.
Drawing on Old Testament texts, and informed by a historical memory of
Spain and elsewhere, Euro-Americans sometimes took Indian performances
of Christian ritual to be tainted by the inability of Indians, in their alleged
childlike ignorance and mental inferiority, to know or appreciate what they
were really doing. The Russian explorer Otto von Kotzebue's reflections on
his 1816 visit to Spanish California states the European prejudice plainly. The
view of H. C. Cushing, in 1880, reiterates that opinion. The account of the
slaughter of ninety Moravian Indian converts at Gnadenhutten, Pennsylvania, on March 8, 1782, represents the view of some white Christians that Indian conversions did not "stick," and that Indians pretended to be Christians
in order to pursue covertly a nefarious agenda of stealing and murder.

On the clock striking ten we entered the church, built of stone, and neatly
ornamented, where we already found some hundreds of half-naked Indians upon their knees, who, although they neither understand Spanish nor
Latin, are not allowed to miss one mass after their conversion. As the missionaries, on their side, do not endeavor to learn the language of the natives, I cannot conceive in what manner they have been taught the Christian
religion; and the confusion in the heads and hearts of these poor people,
who only know how to mimic some external ceremonies, must indeed be
very great. The rage of converting savage nations is now spreading over the
whole of the South Sea, and produces great mischief. They never think to
humanize them before they make them Christians, and thus that which was
to have been productive of happiness and peace, becomes the ground of

bloody warfare: for instance, on the Friendly Islands, where the Christians and heathens constantly strive to exterminate each other. It struck me that during the whole ceremony, the unbaptized were not allowed to rise from their knees; for this exertion, however, they were indemnitied by the church music, which seemed to give them much pleasure, and which undoubtedly was the only part of the ceremony in which they felt interested. . . .

The missionaries assured us that their stupidity made it a very difficult task to instruct them; but I rather think the gentlemen do not trouble themselves much about it; they all told us that the Indians came far from the interior, submitting to them of their own accord, (which we also doubted) the religious instruction, they said, was then immediately begun, and, according to their capacities, they were sooner or later baptized. California costs the Spanish Government a great sum, without any other advantage than the annual conversion of some hundreds of Indians, but who soon die in their new faith, as they cannot easily accustom themselves to a new mode of life.

Source: Otto von Kotzebue, "Spanish Missionaries in California," *New Harmony Gazette*, March 21, 1827, 194.

It is to be assumed that the object we have in view is to transform the present Indian country into an abode for civilized people. To do this requires that its present population must either change entirely their mode of life or be removed out of it. That means civilization or extermination.

The latter plan has been, as we have shown, the most in vogue heretofore. It has been, however, an expensive method, and its morality is one of grave doubt. The Indian naturally objects to it, and formulates his objection in wars which shock the sense of the world. However regrettable they may be, it is urged that they are inevitable; that it is useless to attempt to civilize the race, and that being then cumberers of the ground, intractable and irreconcilable, the only logical method to adopt is to exterminate them. "You cannot civilize them," is the word. Our reply is that the proper methods have never been taken. We have invariably attempted to appeal to a nature insensible to our mode of appeal; we have employed an argument beyond his comprehension; we have sought to work on a species of selfishness which does not exist. Let us look at this matter outside of sentiment and in the light of business. We have some scores of thousands of barbarians to civilize. Why not take them as barbarians, and found our civilization on the barbarian substratum? As the situation stands, we cannot expect to effect much by religious means,—you cannot work on sensations if they do not exist, nor address yourself to the cultivation of moral qualities the germs of which are buried in layers of ferocity and habit. Exceptional instances there may be of

Indians who are Christians, or susceptible to religious influences, but the normal Indian is a fighter, a warrior, and we must recollect that he lives for war; that his occupation and source of greatest happiness is conflict with man or beast; and that the cardinal truth of religion is an absurdity to him.

Source: H. C. Cushing, "Military Colonization of the Indians," *United Service*, September 1880, 370.

The language of those White People who for that purpose had come to Salem, being here the same as at the former place: the Brethren and Sisters were easily persuaded to go with them; and the more so, as many of them professed to be *very* religious, admiring here their fine and spacious place of Worship; and keeping up a constant discourse on religion, both here and on the way to Gnadenhutten: frequently saying to the Indians: "You are indeed good Christians!" and making use of the same language to one another in the hearing of these. That some of them, had on leaving Salem, set fire to the Houses and Church, was not approved of by our Indians; they however pretended, that they meant no harm in this, and had merely done it to deprive the Enemy of a harbouring place. . . .

Being taken over to the Town—O how their prospect was changed! The language now held forth to them, was the reverse of what it had been at Salem, and on the road hither—the Gnadenhutten Brethren, Sisters and Children, already confined for the purpose of being put to death; these now no more being called Christians as before, but Warriors! . . .

The Murderers, impatient to make a beginning, came again up to them, while they were singing; and enquiring, whether they were not ready for dying: they were answered in the affirmative; they adding: "that they had commended their immortal Souls to God, who had given them the assurance in their hearts, that they should come to him:"—One of the party, now taking up a Coopers Mallet, which lay at the house (the owner of this House being a Cooper) saying: "how exactly this will answer for the business", began with Abraham, and continued knocking down one after the other until he had counted fourteen, that he had killed with his own hand, now handed this instrument to one of his fellow Murderers, saying: "My Arm fails me! Go on in the same way! I think I have done pretty well!"

Source: John Heckewelder, *Narrative of the Mission of the United Brethren Among the Delaware and Mohegan Indians* (Philadelphia: McCarty & Davis, 1820), 421, 422, 425.

Forced Christianization

Europeans attempted from earliest contacts to compel Indians to believe in the white man's god. In New Spain, the use of military force was especially important to the process of Christianization, and it was devastating to Indian ways of life. In America in the nineteenth century, the forced relocation of Indians to reservations went hand in hand with the separation of Indian children from their families and their sequestration at "Indian Schools." Those schools were established through the Board of Indian Commissioners after 1869 to acculturate Indians to what had emerged as a national culture—Christian (and strongly Protestant), democratic, legal, market driven, literate, English speaking, and white. The federal government, besieged by appeals from religious groups to allow them access to Indians on the reservations, brokered property and the rights to establish schools and religious missions to a wide assortment of denominations. The government at the same time welcomed the missionary arms of Christian denominations as de facto governors of reservation communities. The principle guiding the allotment of claims was ostensibly one of evenness among the denominations: Baptists were awarded a presence at one reservation, Presbyterians another, Catholics another, Methodists, or Lutherans, or Congregationalists others, until the entire geography of Indian reservations was accounted for, and the various Christian confessions dispersed among them. Children who were boarded at Indian schools were not allowed to practice tribal religions. They were required to learn their catechisms and to participate in the religious exercises of the governing denomination. Deviation from the program could lead to harsh punishment. Indian children often fled the schools. Richard Henry Pratt, a military officer who led in articulating the position that the Indian must be made Christian in order to take up a place in American society, in 1882 addressed an audience in Carlisle, Pennsylvania, where he had founded a nonreservation Indian school in 1879. He stressed that only by fully alienating Indians from their tribal "superstitions" and immersing them in a Christian educational and social environment through "forced" acculturation could they be transformed from savage to civilized. His theory nevertheless marks a departure from earlier beliefs that Indians were too stupid and religiously retarded to become civilized Christians.

A great general has said that the only good Indian is a dead one, and that high sanction of his destruction has been an enormous factor in promoting Indian massacres. In a sense, I agree with the sentiment, but only in this: that all the Indian there is in the race should be dead. Kill the Indian in him, and save the man. . . .

Inscrutable are the ways of Providence. Horrible as were the experiences of its introduction, and of slavery itself, there was concealed in them the greatest blessing that ever came to the Negro race—seven millions of blacks from cannibalism in darkest Africa to citizenship in free and enlightened America; not full, not complete citizenship, but possible—probable—citizenship, and on the highway and near to it. . . .

Left in Africa, surrounded by their fellow-savages, our seven millions of industrious black fellow-citizens would still be savages. Transferred into these new surroundings and experiences, behold the result. They became English-speaking and civilized, because forced into association with English-speaking and civilized people; became healthy and multiplied, because they were property; and industrious, because industry, which brings contentment and health, was a necessary quality to increase their value.

The Indians under our care remained savage, because forced back upon themselves and away from association with English-speaking and civilized people, and because of our savage example and treatment of them. . . .

We make our greatest mistake in feeding our civilization to the Indians instead of feeding the Indians to our civilization. . . .

It is a great mistake to think that the Indian is born an inevitable savage. He is born a blank, like all the rest of us. Left in the surroundings of savagery, he grows to possess a savage language, superstition, and life. We, left in the surroundings of civilization, grow to possess a civilized language, life, and purpose. Transfer the white infant to the savage surroundings, he will grow to possess a savage language, superstition, and habit. Transfer the savage-born infant to the surroundings of civilization, and he will grow to possess a civilized language and habit.

Source: Richard H. Pratt, "The Advantages of Mingling Indians with Whites," from an extract of *Official Report of the Nineteenth Annual Conference of Charities and Correction* (1892), 46–59, in *Americanizing the American Indians: Writings by the "Friends of the Indian," 1880–1900*, compiled by Francis Paul Prucha (Cambridge: Harvard University Press, 1973), 260–71.

Ritual Criminalized and Ethics Condemned

As part of the federal experiment with segregating Indians through their forced relocation to reservations, government officials deemed illegal certain activities that they believed were incompatible with a Christian civilization. Among those rituals and moralities that Indian commissioners found most offensive were the Sun Dance, plural marriage, and the healing and conjuring activities of "medicine-men." Missionaries had complained about nonmonogamous partnerships among Native Americans from the beginnings of the Spanish presence in North America. Given the chance to legislate against Indian codes of morality in the reservation setting, the government did so in no uncertain terms, punishing plural marriage with fines, hard labor, and revocation of all food rations. Indian medicine men and women, who could wear a number of different hats within the community as wise elders, leaders, healers, conjurers, and seers, could be confined to prison until they gave up their roles and status. The Sun Dance, the central religious ritual for males among Plains Indians, was rich in religious symbolism, framed profound religious visions for the participants, and lasted for several days. Although details could vary, it involved the penetration of breast tissue by wooden shanks, and a liturgy that ended in the dancer tearing open his flesh as he moved away from a post to which the shanks were tied. White observers were offended by the spectacle of pain and blood. They also associated it, incorrectly, with war dances. The massacre of over 150 Indians at Wounded Knee, South Dakota, in 1890 was precipitated by white anxiety about Indians engaging in the Ghost Dance. These items, among others, are listed on the 1883 Department of the Interior statement of rules governing the purview and procedures of the "Courts of Indian Offenses." Prohibition of the Sun Dance, as well as some other practices, was formally overturned in the 1930s.

> 4th. The "sun-dance," the "scalp-dance," the "war-dance," and all other so-called feasts assimilating thereto, shall be considered "Indian offenses," and any Indian found guilty of being a participant in any one or more of these "offenses" shall, for the first offense committed, be punished by withholding from the person or persons so found guilty by the court his or their rations for a period not exceeding ten days; and if found guilty of any subsequent offense under this rule, shall by punished by withholding his or their rations for a period not less than fifteen days, nor more than thirty days, or by incarceration in the agency prison for a period not exceeding thirty days.

5th. Any plural marriage hereafter contracted or entered into by any member of an Indian tribe under the supervision of a United States Indian agent shall be considered an "Indian offense," cognizable by the Court of Indian Offenses; and upon trial and conviction thereof by said court the offender shall pay a fine of not less than twenty dollars, or work at hard labor for a period of twenty days, or both, at the discretion of the court, the proceeds thereof to be devoted to the benefit of the tribe to which the offender may at the time belong; and so long as the Indian shall continue in this unlawful relation he shall forfeit all right to receive rations from the Government. And whenever it shall be proven to the satisfaction of the court that any member of the tribe fails, without proper cause, to support his wife and children, no rations shall be issued to him until such time as satisfactory assurance is given to the court, approved by the agent, that the offender will provide for his family to the best of his ability.

6th. The usual practices of so-called "medicine-men" shall be considered "Indian offenses" cognizable by the Court of Indian Offenses, and whenever it shall be proven to the satisfaction of the court that the influence or practice of a so-called "medicine-man" operates as a hindrance to the civilization of a tribe, or that said "medicine-man" resorts to any artifice or device to keep the Indians under his influence, or shall adopt any means to prevent the attendance of children at the agency schools, or shall use any of the arts of a conjurer to prevent the Indians from abandoning their heathenish rites and customs, he shall be adjudged guilty of an Indian offense, and upon conviction of any one or more of these specified practices, or, any other, in the opinion of the court, of an equally anti-progressive nature, shall be confined in the agency prison for a term not less than ten days, or until such time as he shall produce evidence satisfactory to the court, and approved by the agent, that he will forever abandon all practices styled Indian offenses under this rule.

Source: Department of the Interior, Office of Indian Affairs, *Rules Governing the Court of Indian Offenses* (Washington, D.C.: Government Printing Office, 1883), 1–8.

The "Problem" of Peyote

Native Americans have used peyote for centuries as a medicine to heal bodily ailments as well as in connection with spiritual exploration. The ritual use of peyote has long been practiced in the Native American Church, which began in the late nineteenth century and was formally established in 1918. The federal government began a campaign against it in the nineteenth century (through the Courts of Indian Offenses) and continued its opposition through the twentieth century, culminating in the case of *Employment Division v. Smith* (1990). In that case, which took several turns in interpretation at various levels of the judicial system, the prohibition of peyote use by two members of the Native American Church in the state of Oregon was upheld by the United States Supreme Court. In the aftermath of the case Congress passed the Religious Freedom Restoration Act (1993), which was a first step toward clarifying Indian religious freedom. It was amended in 1994 specifically for the purpose of addressing the sacramental use of peyote by Indians. Although part of the 1993 act later was overturned, the principle of free use of a regulated substance in religious ritual was upheld by the Supreme Court in *Gonzales v. O Centro Espírita Beneficente Uniao do Vegetal* (2006).

I am not informed as to whether this habit has taken any hold among the Indians of your agency. If it has, the following instructions issued to the Kiowa and Comanche Agency you will enforce among the Indians under your charge.

"It is the duty of the government peremptorily to stop the use of this bean by Indians. You will direct the police of your agency to seize and destroy the mescal bean, or any preparation or decoction thereof, wherever found on the reservation. The article itself, and those who use it are to be treated exactly as if it were alcohol or whiskey, or a compound thereof; in fact it may be classified for all practical purposes as an 'intoxicating liquor.'" ...

"The Court of Indian Offenses at your agency shall consider the use, sale, exchange, gift, or introduction of the mescal bean as a misdemeanor punishable under Section 9 [re intoxicants] of the Rules governing the Court of Indian Offenses."

You will please take some pains to inform yourself whether the Indians of your agency are using mescal or "woqui" in any of its forms, and if so, I hope you will be prompt, energetic, and persistent in your efforts to stamp out among them this evil practice.

Source: Letter from T. J. Morgan, Indian Commissioner, Bureau of Indian Affairs, to S. L. Patrick, U.S. Indian agent, Sac and Fox Agency, July 31, 1890, letter book, National Archives, cited in Omer Stewart, *Peyote Religion: A History* (Norman: University of Oklahoma Press, 1993).

American Indian Religious Freedom Act Amendments of 1994
§1996a. Traditional Indian religious use of the peyote sacrament

(a) Congressional findings and declarations. The Congress finds and declares that—

(1) for many Indian people, the traditional ceremonial use of the peyote cactus as a religious sacrament has for centuries been integral to a way of life, and significant in perpetuating Indian tribes and cultures;

(2) since 1965, this ceremonial use of peyote by Indians has been protected by Federal regulation;

(3) while at least 28 States have enacted laws which are similar to, or are in conformance with, the Federal regulation which protects the ceremonial use of peyote by Indian religious practitioners, 22 States have not done so, and this lack of uniformity has created hardship for Indian people who participate in such religious ceremonies;

(4) the Supreme Court of the United States, in the case of *Employment Division v. Smith, 494 U.S. 872 (1990)*, held that the First Amendment does not protect Indian practitioners who use peyote in Indian religious ceremonies, and also raised uncertainty whether this religious practice would be protected under the compelling State interest standard; and

(5) the lack of adequate and clear legal protection for the religious use of peyote by Indians may serve to stigmatize and marginalize Indian tribes and cultures, and increase the risk that they will be exposed to discriminatory treatment.

(b) Use, possession, or transportation of peyote.

(1) Notwithstanding any other provision of law, the use, possession, or transportation of peyote by an Indian for bona fide traditional ceremonial purposes in connection with the practice of a traditional Indian religion is lawful, and shall not be prohibited by the United States or any State.

Source: American Indian Religious Freedom Act Amendments of 1994, H.R. 4230, 42 USCS §1996a.

CHAPTER SIX

Anti-Semitism

While New England and Pilgrims often dominate our vision of America's settlement, if we shift our attention to the south and focus on New Amsterdam
instead of Plymouth Rock, on Jewish refugees rather than Puritan settlers,
different images of freedom and America emerge. Like the Puritans, the Jews
of Europe fled persecution. They, too, came to America in search of religious
freedom and civil liberty. Most historians agree that, in comparison with the
virulent anti-Semitism of Western Europe, the United States provided unparalleled possibilities for Jewish freedom; and the United States has indeed
been a more hospitable setting for Jews. But before we paint an even grander
portrait of American religious liberty, one in which the immigrant Jew stands
side by side with the iconic Pilgrim, we must investigate further, for in many
ways, the glorious vision of America as a "promised land" free of the prejudices that marked Jewish life in Europe proved to be an illusion. Unlike their
Protestant counterparts who achieved religious and political dominance
and secured their safety, Jewish immigrants to the United States have always
faced peril as a minority religio-ethnic group. In contrast to the image of the
Pilgrim that evokes visions of flight and freedom, the picture of the Jew in
the United States foregrounds different dimensions of American religious
history—social discrimination, religious persecution, theological invective,
and physical violence.

From the beginning, discrimination characterized the relationship between Jews and the land of liberty. For example, in 1654, the governor of
New Amsterdam, Peter Stuyvesant, fearing the negative effects of religious
diversity, wrote the West India Company requesting permission to deny
Jews entry into his colony. Given the company's desire for commercial success through settlement by various groups, it denied Stuyvesant's request.

In response, he let Jewish refugees from Brazil enter New Amsterdam but promptly curtailed their legal rights. In the eighteenth century, other colonies also used legal means to similar effect. They sought to minimize the threat of perceived religious outsiders through laws that consolidated power in the hands of the Protestant majority. In 1632, Virginia made church attendance compulsory and subjected violators to fines, imprisonment, or assault. While only enforced selectively, church attendance laws reveal the primacy of Christianity in America and the possible costs associated with challenging that dominant position. Similarly, later in the seventeenth century, the Massachusetts Bay Colony established the Congregationalist Church (granting it a privileged position it occupied until 1833); and in 1776, the North Carolina Constitution, like that of South Carolina and New Jersey, made Protestantism a requirement for holding public office. Despite the claims of the federal Constitution, these early laws proclaimed the Christian (if not the Protestant) character of America. However, the small number of Jews, fewer than 2,000, in eighteenth-century America protected them from widespread social discrimination and overt acts of violence. In many ways, the Jewish population appeared too small to be a significant social threat; nevertheless, in the eighteenth century religious difference did not go unchecked. Jews became a legal casualty of Protestant efforts to ensure and expand their dominance.[1]

The following century saw an increase in Jewish immigration accompanied by a decline in overt legal discrimination. States began to disestablish churches; test oaths faded from constitutions; and church attendance laws disappeared. As Jews in America experienced increasing civil liberties, those in Europe faced heightened persecution. In response, Jews fled Germany, then later Italy, Poland, and Russia. In ever larger numbers, they came to America seeking freedom. Between 1830 and 1860, the number of Jews in the United States increased over 3,000 percent, from 4,500 to 150,000. With the decline of legal discrimination, Jews gained unparalleled civil freedoms; however, social forms of anti-Jewish prejudice began to rise. Hotels barred Jewish occupancy; colleges established Jewish quotas; and neighborhoods prevented Jewish settlement. In response to the increasing presence of this religious and ethnic Other, some Christians sought to defend the religious and racial purity of America.

In the nineteenth-century United States, we see the rise of racial-ethnic prejudice against Jews and the emergence of what we now label anti-Semitism. Prior to 1873, the term anti-Semitism did not exist. Instead, intolerance of and hatred toward Jews came under the rubric of anti-Judaism, which denoted the ill will many American Christians held toward Judaism as a religion. In their eyes, the freedom, novelty, and faith of Christianity existed in sharp contrast with the legalistic, dated, and ritualistic nature of Judaism. Even more problematic for American Christians was the relationship between Judaism and Jesus. Jewish rejection of Jesus as messiah led to multiple charges by Christians, ranging from Jewish stubbornness, to Jewish clannishness, to the most damning accusation of all—deicide. In the nineteenth century, Protestant and Catholic alike compared Jews with their New Testament counterparts and remarked on the ill-favored resemblance between present-day Jews and their biblical predecessors. Sermons and textbooks upheld the guilt of the Jews for the death of Jesus, viewed the persecution of Jews as divine retribution for this act, and urged Christians to convert Jews and ultimately usher in the Kingdom of God.

For some observers, racial indictments of Jews appeared to supplant these religious charges. As the nineteenth century progressed, many grounded their attacks on Jews in ideas of racial-ethnic difference. They claimed that Jews were inherently different in myriad ways. In these polemical works, Jews were set apart by their greedy practices, their filthy bodies, their licentious behavior, and their isolationist tendencies. They were a race of people set apart. The virulence of this invective (then and now) has led some scholars to view anti-Semitism in the United States primarily in terms of racial prejudice. For example, Ernest Volkman makes no mention of religion as he defines anti-Semitism as the "hatred of the Jews as a people."[2] However, defining anti-Semitism solely in terms of perceived racial difference belies the complex nature of intolerance. Scholar Leonard Dinnerstein reminds us that when dealing with intolerance toward Jews, particularly in the United States, the category of religion matters. He writes, "It cannot be emphasized too strongly that all aspects of American anti-Semitism are built on this foundation of Christian hostility toward Jews."[3] While racial ideology plays a central part in modern and contemporary anti-Semitism, religion also continues to occupy a leading role. You need only to look at the heated debates over Mel Gibson's *The Passion of the Christ* for evidence of this phenomenon.

These various scholarly views of anti-Semitism illustrate how intolerance, like a veritable chameleon, disguises itself and blends in with its environment. As those who practice intolerance confront cultural shifts, they use new technologies, concepts, and vehicles to adapt and spread their hatred. The anti-Semitic treatise of the nineteenth century gives way to the white power website of the twentieth. Our task, then, is to recognize anti-Semitism in its various forms. This remains a challenge as opponents of "outsider" religious groups commonly translate religious problems and intolerance into a series of secular issues. By doing so, their attack appeals to a broader audience, and the attacker appears to uphold the virtues of the First Amendment and religious pluralism.[4] We must also keep in mind, as gender studies has taught us, that oppressions based on race, class, and gender, as well as sexual orientation and religion, are interlocking—they rely on and reinforce each other. Given the overlapping and cumulative effect of these oppressions, extracting one strand from the others is difficult and perhaps inadvisable. Rather than ranking these oppressions, we need to recognize and investigate how these strands work together to foster intolerance and hatred. Anti-Judaism does not simply disappear with the advent of racialist theories of difference. Rather, in anti-Semitism they combine in complicated ways to form a seemingly more formidable brand of intolerance, one that has only grown more pervasive in the twentieth century.

It is, perhaps, one of the great ironies of American religious history that the twentieth century, one associated with "progress," proved to be the most anti-Semitic in U.S. history. The twentieth century witnessed the rise of anti-Semitic religions, the bombing of Jewish synagogues, and the persistence of negative Jewish stereotypes. This increase in anti-Semitism demands our attention—it forces us to ask why. Scholars have attempted to answer this question; however, they have reached little consensus and continue to dispute the sources of anti-Semitism. Some name historical context the key to unlocking anti-Semitism's roots. They argue that anti-Semitism emerges from competition between socioeconomic and religious groups for rare commodities, including status, wealth, and prestige. In these scholars' view, such competition fuels the creation of stereotypes and sparks occasions of conflict. They add that societal crises—whether international war or domestic immigration, industrialization or urbanization—intensify hostility toward and intolerance of perceived outsiders such as the Jews.[5] Other scholars, however, remain unsatisfied with the seeming simplicity of this model and its failure to account for the pervasive nature of anti-Semitism. Frederic Cople Jahrer writes, "The persistence of anti-Semitism across time and around the globe raises doubts that its fundamental causes lie in specific historical forces or events." Similarly, Ernest Volkman states that anti-Semitism "will erupt in good times and bad, in times of great prosperity and times of tranquility, in times of quiet peace and times of great turmoil." He concludes, "anti-Semitism in all its guises is fundamentally irrational."[6] For him, there is no rational cause for intolerance and hatred.

Given the complexity of anti-Semitism in the United States, how then do we proceed? First, we must recognize that religious intolerance combines with other types of oppression and consequently takes many forms. As you read the following documents, consider how anti-Semitism changes over time, as well as attending to the ways it remains the same. Throughout the chapter, interrogate the definition of anti-Semitism as you examine the portrayal of Judaism as a religion and Jewishness as a racial-ethnic category. Second, rather than choosing one anti-Semitic cause—historical context or irrational hatred—combine these concepts and look for others as you investigate these manifestations of anti-Semitism in the United States. Ask, who are Jews being compared to, and what does this tell us about the perpetrators of religious intolerance and about the nature of religious intolerance itself? Third, reflect on how the documents define and use the concept of religious intolerance. Examine the consistent reversal of religious intolerance. Why does the perpetrator of religious intolerance see him- or herself not as a villain, but as a victim at the mercy of dangerous religious and political foes? Fourth, look for the ways anti-Semitism exists at multiple levels—individual, institutional, and national, as well as theological, cultural, and political. As Franklin Littell writes, "Unless political anti-Semites come to power, the main problem is the 'good people'—the theological and cultural anti-Semites who keep the fire smoldering under the surface."[7] In this chapter, analyze how our culture creates theological and cultural anti-Semites. Attend to the complex and varied role of the media in this process. What ideas about religion and about the United States go into the making of theological, cultural, and political anti-Semites? This leads to our fifth task. Interrogate the relationship between anti-Semitic beliefs and anti-Semitic actions. Scholar Michael Selzer writes, "Does anti-Semitism that fails to manifest itself in anti-Semitic behavior matter?"[8] This question necessitates interrogating the relationship between belief and action. It also challenges us to consider the possibility that the widespread nature of anti-Semitic belief in American culture, embodied most powerfully in enduring stereotypes of Jews and held by many ordinary citizens, fosters an atmosphere in which anti-Semitism, rather than religious liberty, flourishes.

DOCUMENTS

Nineteenth-Century Anti-Semitism

In the mid- to late nineteenth century, the Protestant-dominated religious landscape faced numerous challenges to its power, including the growth of Catholicism, the emergence of evolutionary theory, the rise of "higher" biblical criticism, the end of slavery, and an increase in Jewish immigrants. Nations, groups, and individuals respond to threats, whether perceived or real, in various ways. In the nineteenth century, one response was to combine racialist theories of difference with earlier theological views to create forms of anti-Semitism that continue today. Charges of deicide and rumors of blood libel (the belief that Jews sacrificed Christian children as part of their rituals) mixed with claims that Jews as a "race" were inherently stubborn and deluded or alternately lecherous and licentious. As you read these early documents, reflect on their understandings of religion and race. How do these people— whether Protestant or Catholic, native born or immigrant—use the biblical text and envision the relationship between Judaism and Christianity? Consider the implications of their positions and how they set the stage for future performances of religious intolerance.

Yom Kippur or "False Peace Leads to False Holiness"

Established in 1824, the American Sunday School Union (ASSU) sought to support Protestant Sunday schools through publishing curricular materials. While largely known for its periodical and children's literature, the ASSU also printed biographical and historical books, such as *The Jew, at Home and Abroad* (1845), to provide young adults with information about, in this case, an unfamiliar faith. In the following excerpts, the author describes the Jewish High Holy Day of Yom Kippur and then goes on to compare Judaism with Catholicism. As you read, ask yourself how the author portrays Judaism and why. What contrasts does he employ? And consider the influence this text might have on its nineteenth-century readers.

> Some held up their hands, others roared aloud, and all showed by their gestures the intense feeling of their heart. It was a grotesque scene, as well as peculiarly novel, to stand amid such a company each in his high fur cap, the tallith round his shoulders, and generally his beard flowing wide over the book he was reading. As we looked upon the crowds of worshippers that filled the spacious court of the synagogue, and saw their white eyes ever and anon turned up toward the bright moon, we were irresistibly reminded of the days when the fathers of that singular people forsook the worship of Jehovah, and "served Baal and Ashtaroth," and "made cakes to the queen of heaven." This service being done, they appeared as if relieved from the pressure of an overwhelming load, for they had fasted and prayed for twenty-four hours, and now they dispersed in all directions. Many went homewards

singing with great glee in the open streets, and shouting aloud to each other, "Peace to thee, and peace to thee!" This is said to be done because their sins are now forgiven. How little they know of pardon! Pardon obtained by God's method of justification, sanctifies and draws the sinner's heart to Him, instead of making the soul return again to folly. . . .

The resemblance between Judaism and Popery is clear and remarkable. They agree in principle in receiving tradition: in setting aside the right of private judgment for the interpretations of commentators; in maintaining that merit is stored up by prayers, pilgrimages, fasts and feasts; in the doctrine of a future "trial by fire;" in asserting that it is right to persecute, even to the death, any Jew who becomes a Christian, and in consigning all heretics to everlasting perdition. In practice, also, there is an accordance between Jews and Papists; in the constant offering of Hebrew prayers, however few may understand them; in supplications for the dead; in making the Sabbath when they are not engaged in the synagogue, a day of feasting and recreation; in the invocation of saints, and in pilgrimages to the tombs of rabbis, and to the Holy Land. The course of the modern Jew and that of the Papists, are therefore strikingly accordant. They alike displace the word of God by human inventions, and thus stand on the brink of a precipice, from which multitudes fall into the grossest superstition, or the most abject infidelity.

Source: *The Jew, at Home and Abroad* (Philadelphia: American Sunday-School Union, 1845), 85–87, 120–21.

Not So "Glad Tidings"

Shortly after the Great Chicago Fire of 1871, Protestant Dwight L. Moody (1837–1899) dedicated his life to evangelism. Moody's preaching, combined with Ira Sankey's musical stylings, touched a chord with the audience. After a successful series of revivals in England, the famous duo returned to the States much in demand. In 1876, New York City beckoned and Moody answered. Over the course of three months Moody gave a series of sermons, later published as *Glad Tidings*, to a daily average of 12,000 people. The following excerpt recounts the trial of Jesus. As you read, keep in mind that this excerpt follows Moody's claim that "Peter's heart was full, and he had the anointing of the Holy Spirit when he accused the Jews of having crucified the Lord." What implications might this sermon have for nineteenth-century Protestants and Jews?

They lead Him before the Sanhedrin, and Annas is sent for. He is taken before Annas and Caiphas; Christ is taken before the rulers of the Jews. There were seventy that belonged to that Sanhedrin. The law required that two witnesses must appear against a person on trial before he could be convicted. They secure false witnesses, who come in and swear falsely. Then the high priest asked Jesus what it was that those men witnessed against Him, but He said nothing. Then the high priest asked Him a second time and said, "Art Though the Christ, the Son of the Blessed?" Jesus answered, "I am, and ye shall see the Son of Man sitting on the right hand of power, and coming in the clouds of heaven." Then the high priest said, "What need we any further witnesses? Ye have heard the blasphemy from His own lips." And the verdict came forth, "He is guilty of death!" What a sentence! After a moment He was pronounced guilty of death. . . . About daylight they take Christ before Pilate. They are so eager for his blood they cannot wait. By this time the city is filled with strangers from all parts of the country. They had heard that the Galilean prophet had been brought before the Sanhedrin, that they had condemned Him, and that He was to die the cruel death of the Cross, and all they had to do was to get Pilate's consent and they would then put Him out of the way.

Source: Dwight L. Moody, *Glad Tidings* (New York: E. B. Treat, 1876), 296–97.

"Pilate Was a Weak Man"

Written by Catholic Bishop Richard Gilmour in 1881, *Bible History* was published as an instructional text on both the Old and New Testaments. In his account of Israel in the Old Testament, Gilmour described the "chosen people" as "perverse and stiff-necked." This theme seems to carry throughout the text as he describes their relationship to God in the New Testament. Like Moody's Protestant sermon, this Catholic text addresses Jews in relation to Jesus' trial and crucifixion. As Gilmour recounts the scene, he first states that "Pilate was a weak man." His portrayal of the Jews is not so favorable.

Pilate, seeing the pitiable condition to which Jesus was reduced, thought the sight of Him would appease the malice of the Jews. For this reason, he led the Son of God out on a high balcony, and, presenting Him in all His misery, said: "Behold the Man." But the barbarous, bloodthirsty, people only cried out the more: "Crucify Him, crucify Him." Pilate still continued irresolute, and hesitated what to do. But when the leaders of the people came and said to him, if he released Jesus, he was no friend of Caesar's he seems to have made up his mind. Hoping to quiet the stings of his conscience, he took a basin of water, and going before the multitude, washed his hands, saying: "I am innocent of the blood of this just Man." But the people cried out: "His blood be upon us, and upon our children."

For eighteen hundred years has the blood of Christ been upon the Jews. Driven from Judea, without country, without home, strangers amongst strangers, hated yet feared, have they wandered from nation to nation, bearing with them the visible signs of God's curse. Like Cain, marked with a mysterious sign, they shall continue to wander till the end of the world.

Source: Richard Gilmour, *Bible History: Part II* (London: Thomas Richardson and Son, 1881), 71–73.

"What Is Worshipped in the Ghetto Is Not the God of Moses"

A Greek immigrant to the United States, Telemachus Thomas Timayenis pursued a variety of careers in his new country, most notably teacher and author. Relying on the work of Frenchman Édouard Drumont, Timayenis's 1888 works, *The Original Mr. Jacobs* and *The American Jew*, introduced Americans to, as scholar John Higham writes, "race-thinking anti-Semitism." For example, throughout Timayenis's works, the Jew is a "born liar" and "malefactor," while the "Aryan" is the "child of Heaven." However, religion continued to play a vital role in his invective, as seen in the title to this excerpt from *The Original Mr. Jacobs*. As you read, consider how Timayenis combines the concepts of race and religion to indict the Jews. How does he portray Judaism and its relationship to Christianity? How are Timayenis's writings similar to or different from the explicitly religious texts of the American Sunday School Union, Moody, and Gilmour?

The sentiment that dominates the corrupt and passionate soul of the Jew is his hatred for the Church and its ministers. This hatred is, after all, natural. The vow of the missionary is a permanent mockery at the wealth of the Jew, who is incapable of buying with all his gold what the poorest Christian possesses—faith and hope, sentiments absolutely unknown among the Jews. Religion among the Jews is fidelity to tradition, an attachment to the race to which they belong. But there is not a word in the Hebrew language to express faith. . . .

Nothing has undergone change among the Jews. They hate Christ in 1887 precisely as they hated him in the time of Augustus. To lash the crucifix on Good Friday, to profane the consecrated wafers, to contaminate the holy images, was the great joy of the Jews during the middle ages, and the same is their joy to-day. Formerly they satisfied their venom by killing Christian children; to-day they assail them with their atheistic teachings. Formerly they bled them; to-day they poison them. Which of the two is the more criminal?

While affirming the persistency of hatred among the Jews, it may not be amiss to speak somewhat fully of their bloody sacrifices, accusations a thousand times proven, and against which the Jews always defend themselves with the impudence that characterizes them.

Source: Telemachus Thomas Timayenis, *The Original Mr. Jacobs* (New York: Minerva Publishing Company, 1888), 63–64, 241–42.

The Leo Frank Case

From April 27, 1913, until June 22, 1915, the city of Atlanta and much of America watched the Leo Frank case unfold. When fourteen-year-old factory worker Mary Phagan was murdered, suspicion soon fell on Leo Frank, the Jewish man who superintended the factory and the last known person to see her alive. Despite Judaism's deep roots in the South, Frank's "Jewishness" became a liability as the trial ensued. While Frank maintained his innocence and many irregularities marred the police investigation, a jury convicted Leo Frank, and he was sentenced to hang. However, on June 20, 1915, Governor John Slaton, troubled by the case's inconsistencies, commuted Frank's sentence from death to life in prison. Two days later, a group calling themselves the Knights of Mary Phagan lynched Leo Frank outside Marietta, Georgia (Phagan's hometown). While many denied that Leo Frank's religion played a role in the trial and its outcome, the following documents reveal its power in the minds of the public, if not the courtroom. This case highlights not only the growing influence of the media, but also the inextricable connections between racial and religious intolerance.

Leo Frank: Above the Law?
Georgian Thomas Edward Watson (1856–1922) was elected to the House of Representatives, as well as the Senate, but he is perhaps best known for his leadership of the Populist Party. While Watson defended the rights of the "common man," he increasingly criticized the common man's enemies; and in his eyes, these enemies—Yankees, Industrialists, blacks, and Catholics— were everywhere. In 1914, almost a year after Frank's initial trial, Watson added Jews to his list of foes and emerged as one of the most vocal opponents

of Leo Frank. Watson used his periodical, *Watson's Magazine*, to launch his attack. In the excerpt below, attend to his use of religion and characterization of the Jews. Also, recall that Leo Frank was lynched in June 1915, and Watson published this article in September 1915. Why would Watson continue his attack after Leo Frank's death?

Have the children of Moses the right to break the Sinai tables?

Do they deserve death when they slay Hebrews, only?

Is there some unwritten law, which absolves them, when their victim is a Gentile? They are taught in their Talmud that, "As man is superior to other animals, so are the Jews superior to all other men."

Do the Hebrews of today hold that, in their heart of hearts?

They are taught by their great teacher, Rabbana Ashi, that "Those who are not Jews, are dogs and asses."

Are the Hebrews true to Talmud, and to their learned Rabbana?

Was Mary Phagan—the Irish girl—legitimate spoil for the descendant of those who divided among themselves the daughters of the Midianites?

Is there a secret tenet of their religion, which compels the entire race to combine to save the neck of such a loathsome degenerate as Leo Frank?

They did not waste a dollar, nor a day, on the Jews who were electrocuted for shooting Rosenthal: was it because Rosenthal was a Jew?

If the victim in that case had been an Irishman, would there have been a Haas Finance Committee? a nationwide distribution of lying circulars? a flying column of mendacious detectives? a constantly increasing supply of political lawyers? the muzzling of daily papers? an attempt to enlist the Northern school-children, Peace Societies, and Anti-Capitial-Punishment leagues?

Money talks; and in this Frank case, money talked as loudly, and as resourcefully, as though Baron Hirsch's $45,000,000 Hebrew Fund had been copiously poured into the campaign.

Source: "The Official Record in the Case of Leo Frank, a Jew Pervert," *Watson's Magazine* 21 (September 1915): 292–93.

The Physiognomy of Abnormal Sexuality in Leo Frank or "The Jew Pervert"

Another Watson periodical, *The Jeffersonian*, questions the abilities of the country's most famous detective, William J. Burns, who was brought in by the Atlanta newspapers to solve Phagan's murder. Watson and the police took offense at the implied slight to local Atlanta law enforcement. Citing *Psycho-*

pathia Sexualis (1894), one of the foremost studies of sexual pathology at the time, the article attacks Burns's lack of knowledge about sexual depravity and at the same time introduces readers to the salacious topic. The article offers a sexualized interpretation of Leo Frank's Jewishness and echoes Timayenis's earlier claim from *The American Jew* (1888): "In many of the factories operated by the Jews throughout the country, the life of an honest girl therein employed is made simply a hell, by reason of the Jews' predominant lechery." This theme continued throughout Watson's various periodicals and can be seen in the second document, an image of Leo Frank, where the caption boldly proclaims Leo Frank's supposed sexual strangeness.

Thus the artless Burns drew public attention to Frank's horrible face, and provoked comment upon his abnormal features. No real detective would have stumbled like that. It was just such an asinine mistake as would come natural to a brassy pretender. I wonder if Burns ever studied any scientific work on morbid, diseased sexuality. Even he might learn something from standard books of that kind. He might begin with the monumental volume of Dr. R. v. Krafft-Ebing, German specialist, called "PSYCHOPATHIA SEXU-ALIS, a Medico-Forensic Study."

The physiognomy of Frank is altogether unusual. Burns himself confessed as much when he fished up the boy pictures of his client, showing his face prior to the age of puberty. Burns confesses this, also, by having recent pictures taken in such a way as to disguise the profile. In the recent pictures of Frank, those bulging, satyr eyes are covered by the lids, as Frank bends his head to read. In that pose, you miss the protruding fearfully sensual lips; and also the animal jaw.

Source: "The Leo Frank Case: Does the State of Georgia Deserve This Nation-Wide Abuse?" *The Jeffersonian* 11 (April 9, 1914): 7.

Source: Image of Leo Frank, *Watson's Magazine* 20 (March 1915): 257. Caption: "Note the horrible lips, the nose and the averted eyes of Leo Frank—A Typical Pervert."

Louis Marshall's Letter on the Leo Frank Case

As a lawyer and president of the American Jewish Committee, Louis Marshall (1856–1929) tirelessly fought for Jewish rights and equality. He worked to ensure the rights of Jewish Americans as well as other minority groups, including Catholics, African Americans, and naturalized citizens. He also opposed Henry Ford's anti-Semitic periodical the *Dearborn Independent* and worked to defend Leo Frank. In this letter to Simon Wolf (1836–1923), an equally prominent Jewish leader and fellow lawyer, Marshall shows an acute awareness of the perils facing Leo Frank and the larger Jewish community. What stereotypes or prejudices does Marshall cite in this letter? What is the role of the media in this controversy? What course does Marshall recommend?

September 27, 1913
To Simon Wolf

I consider this a very delicate matter. It is one which involves the good name of Georgia. Prejudices have been created which it is important to destroy. It is equally important that other prejudices should not be enlisted. Nobody knows better than you how sensitive the South is to criticism from other portions of the country, especially the North. If, therefore, through indiscretions, there should be published throughout the North and the West articles which would impliedly criticize the courts of Georgia and the fairness of the people of Georgia, it would inevitably injure the cause of Frank, it would be said that Jewish money and Jewish clannishness were engaged in creative sentiment and hostility to a sovereign state, and Frank would become the victim of the indignation which such a situation would promote.

Source: Louis Marshall, "Letter to Simon Wolf," in *Louis Marshall: Champion of Liberty*, 2 vols., edited by Charles Reznikoff, introduction by Oscar Handlin (Philadelphia: Jewish Publication Society of America, 1957), 1:295–96. © 1957 Jewish Publication Society. Reprinted with permission.

Media Depictions

In these 1915 images, *Watson's Magazine* takes on Strauss's *Puck*. Established by Joseph Keppler Sr. in 1877, *Puck*, an extremely popular periodical, was known for its colorful graphics, notably its political cartoons. At the forefront of political satire, *Puck* used artwork and editorials to condemn corruption at various levels—including the religious. While *Puck* and Watson both condemned Catholicism as a religion loyal to a foreign power, they ended up on opposite sides in the Leo Frank case. *Puck* graphically depicted its support of Leo Frank and its negative view of Georgia, including the example below. Watson, of course, felt compelled to defend his state and responded in kind. As you examine the images, analyze what "virtues" they invoke to indict their opposition and how they use dehumanization.

Source: "Almost Time for a Hog-Killing," *Puck* 77 (July 17, 1915): 4.

ALMOST TIME FOR A HOG-KILLING

Source: "Jewish Attack Upon a State Where No Jew Was Ever Mistreated," *Watson's Magazine* 21 (October 1915): 307.

The Legacy Left by the "Learned Elders"

Arguably the most powerful and persistent anti-Semitic document, *Protocols of the Learned Elders of Zion*, appeared in book form in Russia in 1905. Soon translated, it found its way across Europe, was popularized in the United States by Henry Ford, and continues to be a prominent component of anti-Semitic ideology. The documents in this section trace the legacy of intolerance left by this text. The *Protocols* claims to be an "accurate" record of a Jewish conspiracy that occurred at the first Zionist Congress, held in Basel, Switzerland, in 1897. However, the text is a hoax based on two earlier literary works, and was revealed as such by the *Times* of London as early as 1921. Framed as a series of Jewish "protocols" or plans for Jewish world domination, the text emphasizes the dangerous "otherness" of Jews. Framing the Jews as perpetrators of religious and cultural intolerance, the author of the *Protocols* casts himself (and Christian civilization) as the victim. This work then serves as a rallying cry for Christians to unite and protect themselves. The power of this rallying cry echoes throughout these documents.

Excerpts from Protocols of the Learned Elders of Zion

The *Protocols* is written as if it were an actual transcription of a supposed Jewish conspiracy to gain untold power. It recounts how the Jewish "race" will achieve its alleged goal through economic machinations, media manipulation, and religious chicanery. The text's introduction further emphasizes the religious component of the "conspiracy." The author writes, "There seethes between the lines [of the text] that arrogant and deep-rooted racial and religious hatred, which has been so long successfully concealed, and it bubbles over and flows, as it were, from an overfilled vessel of rage and revenge, fully conscious that its triumphant end is near." The excerpts below recount in more detail how the Jews are purportedly using religion, as well as other weapons, in their efforts to gain world domination. What is the role of religion in this alleged conspiracy? How does the text combine ideas of race and religion? And, lastly, the author puts the words of his text literally in the mouths of the Jews—why would the author make this choice and how does it affect the reader?

> In the days when the people looked on their sovereigns as on the will of God, they quietly submitted to the despotism of their monarchs. But from the day that we inspired the populace with the idea of its own rights, they

began to regard kings as ordinary mortals. In the eye of the mob the holy anointment fell from the head of monarchs, and, when we took away their religion, the power was thrown into the streets like public property, and was snatched up by us.

Moreover, among our administrative gifts, we count also that of ruling the masses and individuals by means of cunningly constructed theories and phraseology, by rules of life and every other kind of device. All these theories, which the Gentiles do not at all understand, are based on analysis and observation, combined with so skilful a reasoning as cannot be equaled by our rivals, any more than these can compete with us in the construction of plans for political actions and solidarity. The only society known to us which would be capable of competing with us in these arts, might be that of the Jesuits. But we have managed to discredit these in the eyes of the stupid mob as being a palpable organisation, whereas we ourselves have kept in the background, reserving our organisation as a secret.

Moreover, what difference will it make to the world who is to become its master, whether the head of the Catholic Church, or a despot of the blood of Zion?

But to us, "the Chosen People," the matter cannot be indifferent. For a time the Gentiles might perhaps be able to deal with us. But on this account we need fear no danger, as we are safeguarded by the deep roots of their hatred for one another, which cannot be extracted.

We set at variance with one another all personal and national interests of the Gentiles, by promulgating religious and tribal prejudices among them, for nearly twenty centuries. . . .

But until we have accomplished the re-education of youth by means of new temporary religions, and subsequently by means of our own, we will not openly attack the existing Churches, but will fight them by means of criticism, which already has and will continue to spread dissensions among them.

Generally speaking, our press will denounce governments, religious and other Gentile institutions by means of all kinds of unscrupulous articles, in order to discredit them to such an extent as our wise nation only is capable of doing.

Our government will resemble the Hindu god Vishnu. Each of our hundred hands will hold one spring of the social machinery of State.

Source: *The Jewish Peril: Protocols of the Learned Elders of Zion* (London: Eyre and Spottiswoode, 1920), 18–19, 64–65. The *Protocols* was published in numerous countries with many title variations. *The Jewish Peril* was used in the first British edition.

Henry Ford's Dearborn Independent

Best known for his enduring contribution to the automobile industry, Henry Ford (1863–1947) gave America its first mass-produced car—the Model T—and implemented the five-dollar, eight-hour workday (at the time, five dollars was the going rate for a ten-hour workday). He built a state-of-the-art manufacturing plant, funded the Henry Ford Hospital in Detroit, and left a powerful anti-Semitic legacy. Like Tom Watson, Ford began his own publishing venture, the *Dearborn Independent,* in 1919. A year later, in a desire "to awake the Gentile world," he began to use the *Independent* to popularize the *Protocols.* Later published by Ford as a four-volume set entitled *The International Jew: The World's Foremost Problem,* the work was translated into several languages and sold over ten million copies in the United States alone. While Ford apologized to the Jewish community in 1927, he was awarded the Grand Service Cross of the Supreme Order of the German Eagle by the German Reich in 1938, and the power of his publication endures. In the excerpts below, analyze the use of religious intolerance, the idea of "rights," the definition of patriotism, and the power of labels.

Here, however, is something for Jewish religious leaders to consider: there is more downright bitterness of religious prejudice on the part of the Jews against Christianity than could ever be possible in the Christian churches of America. Simply take the church press of America and compare it with the Jewish press in this regard, and there is no answer. No Christian editor would think it either Christian or intelligent to attack the Jewish religion, yet any six months' survey of the Jewish press would yield a mass of attack and prejudice on the other side. Moreover, no religious bitterness in America attains within infinite distances to that bitterness visited upon the Jew who becomes a Christian in his faith. It amounts almost to a holy vendetta. A Christian may become a Jewish proselyte and his motives be respected; it is never so when a Jew becomes a Christian. These statements are true of both the orthodox and liberal wings of Judaism. It is not his religion that gives prominence to the Jew today; it is something else. And yet, with undeviating monotony, it is repeated wherever the Jew takes cognizance of the feeling toward him that is on account of three things, first and most prominent of which is his religion. It may be comforting to think that he is suffering for his faith, but it is not true. Every intelligent Jew must know it.

Source: *The International Jew: The World's Foremost Problem,* 4 vols. (Dearborn, Mich.: Dearborn Publishing Company, 1920), 1:62–63.

Demands of NY Jewry. . . .

3. The suppression of all references to Christ by City, State and Federal authorities, in public documents or at public gatherings.

4. Official recognition of the Jewish Sabbath.

5. The right of the Jews in this country to keep open their stores, factories and theatres, and to trade and work on the Christian Sunday.

6. Elimination of Christmas celebrations in public schools and public places, police stations, and so on, public displays of Christmas trees, singing of Christmas carols and Christian hymns.

Source: *The International Jew*, 2:156–57.

Americans are very sensitive about infringing on other people's rights. The Jews might have gone on for a long time had they not overplayed their hand. What the people are now coming to see is that it is American rights that have been interfered with, and their own broad-mindedness. The Jews' interference with the religion of the others, and the Jews' determination to wipe out of public life every sign of the predominant Christian character of the United States is the only active form of religious intolerance in the country today.

Source: *The International Jew*, 2:168–69.

The Jew glories in religious prejudice, as the American glories in patriotism. Religious prejudice *is* the Jews' chief expression of their own true patriotism. It is the only well-organized, active and successful form of religious prejudice in the country because they have succeeded in pulling off the gigantic trick of making not their own attitude, but any opposition to it, bear the stigma of "prejudice" and "persecution." That is why the Jew uses these terms so frequently. He wants to label the other fellow first. That is why any investigation of the Jewish Question is so quickly advertised as anti-Semitism—the Jew knows the advantage of labeling the other man; wrong labels are most useful.

Source: *The International Jew*, 3:19.

Alma White: Pillar of Fire Preacher, Ku Klux Klan Promoter

Reared Methodist and influenced by the Holiness Movement, Alma Bridwell White (1862–1946) felt called to Christian ministry and claimed that the Holy Spirit commanded that she preach (despite Methodist opposition to female preachers). In 1901, she founded what became known as the Pillar of Fire Church and stands out as one of the first female bishops of an American denomination. However, at the same time, her Pillar of Fire denomination also bears the distinction of being the only one to officially and vocally endorse the Ku Klux Klan. Having reorganized in the 1910s and 1920s in Georgia, the Klan not only espoused racism, but also a virulent anti-Catholicism and anti-Semitism in its defense of Protestantism. Alma White allied herself with the Klan to promote this vision of a more Protestant America. In this excerpt from her book, *The Ku Klux Klan in Prophecy* (1925), White invokes familiar religious charges against the Jews, but also, as in the *Protocols* and the *Dearborn Independent*, frames Jewish action in terms of a larger racial and global conspiracy—one that, in her eyes, can only be combated by the Christianity of the Klan.

> The money-grasping Jew, who has no use for the Christ of Calvary, is doing all in his power to bring discredit on Christianity, and would be pleased to see the civil structure broken down, and in this way get rid of his responsibility for crucifying his Messiah and bringing the curse upon his race, which they have had to suffer since the beginning of the Christian era. The sons of Abraham have therefore become a strong ally to the papacy; they have nothing in common in religion, but they are one in their political propaganda against American institutions and principles.
>
> While no true Christian has anything against the Jew, it must be admitted that this alliance with the papacy is a dangerous menace to our flag and country. The Jew is insoluble and indigestible; and when he grows in numbers and power till he becomes a menace to Christianity and the whole moral fabric, drastic measures will have to be taken to counteract his destructive work, and more especially when he is in alliance with the old papal machine.
>
> The Knights of the Ku Klux Klan, who have sensed the danger, have been raised up by the Almighty at this critical time.
>
> Source: Alma White, *The Ku Klux Klan in Prophecy* (Zarephath, N.J.: The Good Citizen, 1925), 26–27.

Why Would You Believe the Protocols?

Journalist Burton Jesse Hendrick (1870–1949) wrote for the *New York Evening Post*, as well as the *New York Sun* and other area papers. While an associate editor at the *World's Work*, Hendrick wrote a series of articles on the rise of anti-Semitism and the power of the *Protocols* that was later published as *The Jews in America*. The book explores, as Hendrick writes on page two, "the increasing unfriendliness in the great liberty-loving Anglo-Saxon democracies." In the excerpt below, Hendrick attacks the *Protocols* and seems on course to defend Jewry; however, his "defense" soon falls far short of that ideal. In the end, to prevent the growth of anti-Semitism in the United States, Hendrick urges strict laws to block Jewish immigration.

Certainly this [the *Protocols*] is a scheme so magnificent in its iniquity that it is in itself almost a compliment to any racial group to which it is attributed, especially one so numerically inferior and so generally ostracized as the Jews. . . . [However] if there is one thing that the Jews have proved in their age-long wandering over the face of the earth, it is that they lack the power of cooperation. They occupy their present isolated position, not because they have been persecuted by Christians, but because they lack that aptitude for coherence and organization whose ultimate expression is nationality. The nomadic tendency of Israel is nothing new. It is not even modern. . . . The synagogue itself is perhaps the most outstanding illustration of Jewish individualism. There are 700 or 800 synagogues in Greater New York, but each one is a separate group, having absolutely no relation with the others. The Jewish religion is the only one in the United States which exists without an organization; there are no Jewish bishops, or presbyters, or conferences, or convocations; all attempts to create a Grand Rabbi, a functionary who would have a kind of pope-like supervision over all the Jewish congregations, have failed. In politics the same condition prevails.

Source: Burton Jesse Hendrick, *The Jews in America* (Garden City, N.Y.: Doubleday, Page, 1923), 46–47, 51–52.

"One Persecution Begets Another"

In the 1920s, Catholic priest Charles Coughlin (1891–1979) became a parish priest in Royal Oak, Michigan, a suburb of Detroit. To gain local acceptance and support in the predominantly Protestant landscape, Coughlin began broadcasting Sunday sermons on a local radio station in 1926. Eventually his sermons were broadcast to a national audience and heard by an estimated 40 million people per week. Like Tom Watson and Henry Ford, Coughlin used media effectively and promoted a message that appealed to the "common man." In the 1930s, as Coughlin grew disillusioned with Roosevelt's New Deal, his messages took an increasingly anti-Semitic turn and culminated in a radio address, "Persecution—Jewish and Christian," delivered on November 20, 1938, less than two weeks after *Kristallnacht*. Despite the undeniable knowledge that Jews were being persecuted and killed in Germany, Coughlin's address emphasizes the supposed Jewish roots of Communism and its subsequent persecution of Christians—"facts" that he insists gave rise to Nazi socialism and the current actions against Jews. He laments, "Thus, one persecution begets another as one injustice evolves into another."

Portugal and Spain, France and Germany, England and the northern countries, Italy and Russia—all, in turn, have taken their stand at the pillar of persecution to wield the leaden lash about the shoulders of Jews—for what reason I need not detail at the moment. I will satisfy myself simply by drawing to your attention that, since the time of Christ, Jewish persecution only followed after Christians first were persecuted—persecuted either by exploiters within their own ranks, as in the Middle Ages, or by enemies from without, as in our own days—the days of Communism. . . .

Why, then, was there this silence on the radio and in the press? Ask the gentlemen who control the three national radio chains; ask those who dominate the destinies of the financially inspired press—surely these Jewish gentlemen and others must have been ignorant of the facts or they would have had a symposium in those dark days—especially when students of history recognized that Naziism is only a defense mechanism against Communism and that persecution of the Christians always begets persecution of the Jews.

P.S.: I know that this address is particularly displeasing to those of communistic mind. I have it on definite information that these persons have organized to complain to the radio stations to stop my future broadcasts. Need I say more?

Source: Chas. E. Coughlin, "Am I an Anti-Semite?: 9 Addresses on Various 'ISMS' Answering the Question," in *Anti-Semitism in America, 1878–1939* (1939; reprint, New York: Arno Press, 1977), 43, 45.

1999: The Summer of Hate

Given our increasingly diverse society, along with our heightened sense of the world as a global village, we might imagine, or at least hope, that religiously motivated hate crimes ceased to exist on the eve of the twenty-first century. However, according to the FBI's Uniform Crime Reporting Program, religion continues to play a central role in hate crimes. In 1999, 18 percent of the 7,876 recorded hate crimes were motivated by religious bias (making it second only to racial bias). Of the 1,532 religiously motivated offenses reported in 1999, 1,198 of these acts were committed against Jews. In 1999, the number of anti-Semitic incidents increased, as did their virulence and violence in June and July, leading the Anti-Defamation League (ADL) to label it the "Summer of Hate." These facts and the documents below leave us asking why. Why has anti-Semitism in America increased over time? Why, in 1999, did more people act upon their anti-Semitic beliefs with violent intent? And, finally, what does the future hold: Will we see more summers of hate, or less? Why?

World Church of the Creator's Declaration of Independence

In 1973, Ben Klassen (1918–1993) established the Church of the Creator, later called the World Church of the Creator (WCOTC) and now known as the Creativity Movement (CM), a religion based on race—the white race. Unlike the Christian Identity movement, which "purifies" Christianity from its Semitic genealogy, Creativity rejects Christianity and other established religions and seeks to create a "religion where Race is the foundation, a religion that is rooted in Nature, and a religion that celebrates our past and secures our future."[9] For members of the CM and other white supremacist groups, rahowa—racial holy war—is inevitable. In this excerpt from Klassen's *The White Man's Bible* (1981), consider how he combines race, religion, and nation. Then examine how these views are enacted in 1999 during the Summer of Hate.

In the Name of the White Race a Declaration of Independence from Jewish Tyranny. Since a penetrating of both contemporary and ancient history has conclusively revealed the following situation:

1. The Jewish race by choice has waged deadly, unrelenting warfare against us, the White Race, in order to destroy us.

2. The Jewish people are banded together in a vicious racial, religious and political conspiracy to gain control of all the money, all the economic and financial resources, all the land and territory and real estate of the world, in short, its total wealth.

3. The Jews have made it their primary goal to mongrelize, kill, decimate and otherwise destroy the White Race.

4. The Jews are determined to enslave all the races of the world, including the final mongrelized product of the White Race that they intend bringing about.

5. The Jews have in the past successfully and successively destroyed our White Racial ancestors, to name a few: The White Egyptians; the highly creative and gifted Greeks of classical history; the great and noble Romans of ancient times.

6. The Jewish conspiracy now owns, and/or monopolizes, controls the majority of the White Man's industry, finances, educational facilities, news media, television networks, government, religion, and monopolizes all or nearly all instruments of thought control.

7. The White Race is now an occupied and enslaved people under the cruel heel of Jewish tyranny.

Now, therefore, we of the Church of Creativity, in the name of our White Racial Comrades throughout the world, proclaim this, our own Declaration of Independence.

We hereby resolve that it is our sacred duty and holy obligation, not only to ourselves, but also to our noble ancestors that produced us, and our precious progeny who will follow us, to bring about a world situation in which we are determined:

1. To throw off the yoke of Jewish tyranny and control.

2. To wrest control of the White Man's destiny into the loyal and capable hands of our own people.

3. To eternally fight for the survival, expansion and advancement of the White Race.

4. To shrink our enemies, namely the Jews and other mud races, and expand the territory, the power and the number of our own White Racial Comrades.

5. To make it impossible for the Jews and other mud races to ever again threaten the existence and well-being of the White Race.

To this, our Declaration of Independence, we forever pledge our Lives, our Sacred Honor and our Religious Zeal.

Source: Ben Klassen, *The White Man's Bible* (Lighthouse Point, Fla.: Church of the Creator, 1981), 410–11.

Benjamin "August" Smith

Brothers Benjamin Matthew Williams and James Tyler Williams inaugurated the Summer of Hate in June 1999, when they torched three Sacramento synagogues. Anti-Semitic literature published by the WCOTC was found at two of the three arson sites. Hoping to "cleans[e] a sick society" and initiate a revolutionary racial-religious war, the brothers, then ages thirty-one and twenty-nine, stated that they did not fear the death penalty, as they aspired to be "martyrs" to their cause. Over the Fourth of July weekend, less than three weeks after the Sacramento arsons, Benjamin "August" Smith (1978–1999) began a three-day shooting spree, crisscrossing the states of Illinois and Indiana while targeting Jews and other minorities. Smith killed two people, wounded nine others, and then took his own life. A criminal justice major at Indiana University, Smith belonged to the wcotc and distributed its literature on campus, as well as in the local Bloomington area. On July 2, 1999, hours before Smith began his violent assault, Illinois denied wcotc leader Matthew Hale's appeal to practice law within the state. Whether inspired by the Williams brothers, incited by Illinois's denial of his leader, inflamed by his wcotc ideology, or some combination thereof, Smith enacted his beliefs in a most violent manner. The first line of his journal, recovered by police, states, "anyone who knows the history of this plague upon humanity who calls themselves Jews will know why I have acted." The two excerpts below provide insight into the why and the how. Why would young, white men like Benjamin Smith and the Williams brothers be attracted to wcotc teachings? How does one become "young, white and racist"?

Indiana University sophomore August Smith doesn't look like he's brewing with malice but his hate list is lengthy: African-Americans, Hispanics, Christians, Jewish people, gays and lesbians.

As a member of the World Church of the Creator, a self-described "race religion" that espouses racism and totalitarianism, Smith is on a mission to whiten America. . . .

Creativity's creed is simple, Smith says. "White people are best and they deserve the best. We don't believe all races are equal. We see all inferior races breeding and the number of whites is shrinking. The mud people will turn this world into a cesspool."

When Smith speaks about his "faith", he speaks articulately, calmly, yet with a guarded flatness in his voice. A criminal justice major, he transferred from the University of Illinois to iu in June and immediately fired up his propaganda and membership campaign.

About three or four times a week—until iu officials clamped down— he walked around campus and Bloomington and tucked leaflets under car windshield wipers, earning him the moniker "the flier guy." "If we do nothing, we will condemn our children to live in an Alien Nation where there is no place to escape these non-White intruders," the fliers stated. "There is nothing wrong with wanting America to remain a racially and culturally European nation." . . .

Originally from Wilmette, Ill., a northern Chicago suburb, Smith began his personal journey to white supremacism when he entered college. "I looked through Aryan stuff and realized historically nations function best when there's one race. Otherwise it's a power struggle," he recalls. "This country was founded for and by whites and that's when I decided I had to become an activist." . . .

Although the church's webpage states that it will accomplish its goals without violence, Smith says there could be circumstances where it could be called for. "We believe we can legally come to power through non-violence. But Hale says if they try to restrict our legal means then we have no recourse but to resort to terrorism and violence."

Source: Lisa Sorg, "To Be Young, White and Racist," Bloomington Independent, July 8, 1999, 5–6.

"To want to live in a world where blacks have power over whites, where Jews are in control, I think that's a sickness and I'd like to eradicate that sickness. In some ways it's inevitable—racial holy war." . . .

In the inaugural "Creator Profile" section of the WCOTC newsletter, The Struggle (March 1999), Smith described his "Racial Awakening": "My genesis of racial awakening began in eighth grade. By law, all Illinois students in the eighth grade are forced to learn about the Jewish 'Holocaust' in National Socialist Germany. The best way to describe my eighth grade teacher is 'dirty Jew.' . . . The Jew teacher began with the 'slaughtering' of Indians by white pioneers and settlers. He then moved to the 'evils' of Black slavery and ended with the 'murder of six million Jews.' . . . The entire class was mind manipulation, pure and simple, but then it happened. . . . The LA Race riots broke out overnight. I saw scenes of niggers burning down the City of Angels and dragging whites from their cars for no reason other than the color of their skin. The experience was brutal and frightening. What if this happened in Chicago? What would Whites do if a full-scale Race War broke out?"

He told The Struggle, "I had read The Turner Diaries and Mein Kampf and still I did not feel satisfied, but after reading Nature's Eternal Religion, I knew at long last I had found what I was looking for."

Source: Devin Burghard, "'Creating' a Killer: A Background Report on Benjamin 'August' Smith and the World Church of the Creator," Special Report for the American Jewish Committee, July 1999, ⟨http://www.buildingdemocracy.org/reports/smith.pdf⟩ (accessed June 17, 2005).

Buford Furrow's Attack and a Mother's Response

On Tuesday, August 10, 1999, the Summer of Hate claimed yet more victims. Thirty-seven-year-old Buford Furrow Jr. opened fire on the men, women, and children attending the day camp sponsored by the North Valley Jewish Community Center in California. Targeting the center because of his anti-Semitic and white supremacist beliefs, Furrow, like the Williams brothers and Benjamin Smith, saw himself engaged in a "racial holy war." He called his actions a "wake-up call to America to kill Jews." After wounding five people at the center, Furrow then murdered Filipino American mail carrier Joseph Ileto. Furrow was a known member of the Aryan Nations, a subgroup of the Christian Identity movement, which preaches a version of Christianity devoid of its Jewish heritage. They believe the white Aryan race, not the Jews, represent God's chosen people and root this belief in the Bible. In their interpretation, Eve's sexual alliance with Satan produced Cain, the forefather of the Jews, while Adam fathered the white race through his son Abel. According to Identity adherents, the "satanic" Jewish seed line conspires against the "Adamic" seed line as it seeks to control the world. As a result, a battle between "good" and "evil" is inevitable. As you read the newspaper account below, reflect on the causes of Furrow's actions and the varied nature of white supremacy. How do we as citizens respond to this type of hatred? In "Mommy's Going to Take that Gun to School," Sarah Thompson, a Jewish psychiatrist, provides one type of response as she writes to reassure her daughter and rally American Jews in the wake of Furrow's actions.

In the world of white supremacy, Buford O. Furrow may represent the wave of the future: a new generation of racial warriors who believe in acting alone.

It is still unclear what combination of factors drove Furrow to open fire on a Jewish community center in Los Angeles Tuesday, and what precise mix of ideology contributed to that act. But judging from the trail of his associations in the white supremacy movement, the people who remember him and the books he read, Furrow was a "lone wolf" who distanced himself from the larger, organized elements of the movement. He may have considered himself one of the Phineas Priesthood, who initiate themselves individually, with a lone act of terrorism.

There are no membership cards for the Priesthood, no meetings, no central address, no organizational structure for the FBI and police to infiltrate. Instead, in this latest trend of Aryan resistance, "you anoint yourself," said

---

Brian Levin, an expert on hate groups, "by committing a violent act against a minority member."

The group's bible is the 1990 book *Vigilantes of Christendom* by Richard Kelly Hoskins. (Another of Hoskins's books was found in the van that Furrow drove to the community center.) The Lynchburg, Va., author urges his followers to follow the example of the biblical Phineas, grandson of the priest Aaron in the Book of Numbers, who kills a prince of Israel for marrying a woman from another tribe. In return for this deed, Phineas receives the "covenant of an everlasting priesthood; because he was zealous for his God."

The mission of the Priesthood, as Hoskins outlines it in his dozen or so books and newsletters, is to outlaw racial "inbreeding" and "root sodomites from the land." . . .

Furrow showed up on the neo-Nazi scene in the early 1990s, when he lived in the small foothill town of Metaline Falls, Wash., near the Aryan Nations headquarters in Hayden Lake, Idaho. . . . Floyd Cochran, a former spokesman for the Aryan Nations, recalled seeing Furrow at a Hitler youth festival in 1991. Furrow was at that time a member of the security team responsible for guarding Aryan Nations leader Richard Butler. Historically, the security guards are "the ones who have gone on to commit acts of violence," according to Eric Ward of the Northwest Coalition Against Malicious Harassment. . . . Cochran remembered Furrow was "anti-semitic, like everyone else," he said. "He was concerned that Jewish people were running the world and the media, and why don't people do something about it. He left it at that—do something about it."

Source: Hanna Rosin, "Suspect in Community Center Shooting Surrenders, Admits Hatred," *Washington Post*, August 12, 1999. © August 12, 1999 The Washington Post.

"We love you, and we're not ever going to let anyone hurt you. So to make sure you're safe, Mommy's going to stay at school with you today. So is Lisa's mommy. You know that we keep guns at home so no bad guys can come in the house and hurt us. Well, Mommy's going to take that gun to school, and Lisa's mommy will take her gun to school. In fact, there will be mommies and daddies with guns at the school every day. And we're going to teach the teachers about guns too, so they can protect you against bad guys. And when the bad guys find out, they'll be too scared to come to your school." . . .

People have hated Jews and sought to kill us throughout Jewish history—nearly 6000 years. It's not a new phenomenon. Yet is seems we are unable to learn from our experience.

Jews have never been "safe" for very long anywhere. Every so-called "safe haven" eventually turned on us and persecuted us: Egypt, Spain, Greece and Germany come to mind. Why do you believe you'll always be safe here? No government including that of the United States, has ever been willing to protect or defend us. Why are you so eager to surrender all means of self-defense? The police have absolutely no obligation to protect you or your children, and in case you forgot, they stood outside while children in Colorado were murdered. No one cares about Jewish children more than their parents. But if we're not willing to defend ourselves, no one will do it for us.

Source: Sarah Thompson, M.D., "An Open Letter to American Jews," Gun Owners of America, September 1999, ⟨http://www.gunowners.org/wv09.htm⟩ (accessed August 11, 2007).

On *The Passion of the Christ*

In 2004, controversy erupted over Mel Gibson's yet-to-be released film *The Passion of the Christ*. Gibson's film focuses on the last twelve hours of Jesus' life—his trial and crucifixion—and claims faithfulness to the biblical text. When these claims of authenticity combined with a leaked version of an early script, the American Jewish community voiced their concerns. Leaders of various Jewish defense organizations indicted the negative and stereotypical portrayal of Jews in the film. Concerned about the film's power to reinforce anti-Semitic beliefs and thereby fuel anti-Semitic actions, these Jewish leaders asked Gibson to amend the film. He did not respond. People of different faiths from all over the country weighed in on the controversy. Some defended Gibson's artistic and spiritual freedom, others decried the dangers of his depictions, while still others looked for answers in the biblical text. As you read these documents, consider how this twenty-first-century controversy again foregrounds the religious dimension of anti-Semitism and forces us to face tough questions about interpretations of the Bible, the power of the media, and the enduring nature of anti-Semitism.

ADL *Statement*
The Anti-Defamation League (ADL), established in 1913, is the leading Jewish defense organization in the United States. Its mission, as stated on the ADL website (⟨http://www.adl.org⟩), "is to expose and combat the purveyors of

hatred in our midst, responding to whatever new challenge may arise." Upon hearing of *The Passion* and its possible negative portrayal of the Jews, the ADL sought to meet privately with Gibson to discuss its implications. When these overtures failed, the ADL went public with their concerns. In an interview about the controversy, ADL Director Abraham H. Foxman stated that "after the Shoah (Holocaust), Jews no longer have the luxury to remain silent in the face of anti-Semitism." As a result, the ADL issued a press release, which is excerpted below. Consider how the ADL frames its concerns. What specific concerns does the ADL raise? How does the ADL view the relationship between the film's portrayal and the viewers' actions?

Throughout history Christian dramatizations of the passion, i.e. the crucifixion and resurrection of Jesus, have fomented anti-Semitic attitudes and violence against the Jewish people. During the past forty years the Roman Catholic and most Protestant churches have issued pastoral and scholarly documents that interpret the death and resurrection of Jesus in their historical and theological contexts. These churches repudiate the teachings that gave rise to Christian accusations that Jews were "Christ killers." They make clear that correct Christian readings and applications of the New Testament must avoid provoking or reinforcing anti-Semitic attitudes and behavior.

Based upon the scholars' analysis of the screenplay, ADL has serious concerns regarding Mr. Gibson's *The Passion* and asks:

Will the final version of *The Passion* continue to portray Jews as bloodthirsty, sadistic and money-hungry enemies of Jesus?

Will it correct the unambiguous depiction of Jews as the ones responsible for the suffering and crucifixion of Jesus? Will it show the power of the rule of imperial Rome — including its frequent use of crucifixion in first century Palestine?

Will the film reject exploiting New Testament passages selectively to weave a narrative that does injustice to the gospels, that oversimplifies history, and that is hostile to Jews and Judaism?

Will it live up to its promise "to tell the truth?"

Will it portray Jews and the Temple as the locus of evil?

Source: Anti-Defamation League, "ADL Statement on Mel Gibson's 'The Passion,'" June 24, 2003, ⟨http://www.adl.org/presrele/mise_00/4275_00.asp⟩ (accessed February 12, 2007).

"Passion *Elicits Unfair Conflict*" by Medved

Michael Medved, Orthodox Jew, film critic, and author of *Hollywood vs. America* (1992) does not shy away from controversy and has often chastised Hollywood for its overemphasis on violence and sexuality. Seeking a film industry more faithful and attuned to viewers' supposed values, Medved quickly entered the debate surrounding *The Passion*, and his article is a response to the ADL press release. Throughout, he questions their approach to the controversy, their interpretation of the film, and their definition of anti-Semitism. What is anti-Semitism according to Medved? How does Medved view the film? Whose interpretation—the ADL's or Michael Medved's—are you more inclined to agree with and why?

Any piece of pop culture that touches on serious religious themes inspires its share of controversy, but the noisy assaults on Mel Gibson's unfinished film *The Passion*, which describes the final 12 hours in the life of Jesus Christ, seem unfair and painfully premature. Indignant denunciations of a movie that its critics haven't even seen, coming nearly a year before that picture's scheduled release, suggest an agenda beyond honest evaluation of the film's aesthetic or theological substance. The explosive charges of anti-Semitism being directed at this project may even threaten the emerging alliance between devout Christians and committed Jews. . . . The Anti-Defamation League (ADL) and other groups devoted to combating anti-Semitism issued critical statements about *The Passion* based on an early draft of the screen play that the Gibson camp called a "stolen" script. Gibson insists that he has altered the screenplay substantially since that early draft, but this didn't stop the ADL from issuing an angry statement on June 24, asking: "Will the final version of *The Passion* continue to portray Jews as blood-thirsty, sadistic and money-hungry enemies of Jesus?" . . . In fact, the worries about anti-Semitic messages in the upcoming epic seem overblown based on known facts about the project. Of course, members of the religious establishment in ancient Judea come across badly in New Testament accounts, but beyond these villains, the new movie boasts a Jewish hero (or Hero)—not to mention many other sympathetic Judeans, including Christ's disciples and mother. Moreover, Gibson emphasizes the Hebraic identity of the Man from Nazareth. Production stills show actor Jim Caviezel as perhaps the most Semitic Jesus in cinema history—a welcome change from the Nordic Messiahs in many previous films.

Source: Michael Medved, "*Passion* Elicits Unfair Conflict," *USA Today*, July 22, 2003, A13. Reprinted with the permission of USA Today, a division of Gannet and Co., Inc.

Anti-Semitic Responses

While Jewish defense organizations, including the Simon Wiesenthal Center (SWC) and the ADL, feared that Gibson's film would lead to an outbreak of anti-Semitic violence, this outcome did not occur. However, that does not mean religious tolerance and freedom triumphed. Criticisms of the film by the SWC and ADL elicited a variety of negative responses. In the examples below, a church sign and a series of e-mails, consider the familiar accusations launched and stereotypes employed against Jews. How are religion, media, and intolerance intertwined in these vehement responses? Why would SWC and ADL criticisms of the film elicit these intolerant responses? What impact do "theological and cultural anti-Semites" have on the religious and political landscape of the United States?

> The Simon Wiesenthal Center urged Christian community leaders to rebuke the Denver Colorado, Lovingway United Pentecostal Church for posting a sign outside its church which reads: "Jews Killed The Lord Jesus . . . Settled!"
>
> Source: Simon Wiesenthal Center, "Wiesenthal Center Urges Denver Christian Community to Rebuke Pentecostal Church's Sign that Charges Jews with Deicide," February 23, 2004, ⟨http://www.wiesenthal.com/site/apps/s/content.asp?c=fwLYKnN8LzH&b=253162&ct=285881⟩ (accessed February 12, 2007).

> 1. You should be more concerned about the conduct of Jews in our government and financial markets . . . and stock scams promoted by Jews. The hypocrisy going on by Jews in this nation such as your radical Marxist liberal people in government . . . and the entire diatribe that opposes our Christian faith and daily tries to undermine our Constitution. . . . If a backlash comes it will be a result of that kind of conduct we see out of Jews . . . not a result of some historically based film. . . . Many people are just not going to be pushed around much longer.
>
> 2. I find it sad that you would attempt to censor Gibson. Whether you like it or not, the Jews of the time were instrumental in Jesus' death. We don't need anymore revisionist history. Didn't the Holocaust teach you anything?
>
> 3. Talk about the boy who cried wolf! Jews are among the most successful and disproportionately influential members of American society. . . . I accuse the liberal ADL of anti-Christian bias. . . . It's [expletive] like this that makes people anti-Semitic.

4. All anti-Semitism is the fault of Jews. If you would direct your people to quit being so dishonest, immoral, atheistic, and Marxist, this stigma would go away.... If you want people to quit their prejudice, then quit giving them reasons to be prejudiced. As long as you act like immoral heathens people will treat you the same way.

Source: Anti-Defamation League, "ADL Criticism of Mel Gibson's 'The Passion' Elicits Anti-Semitic Responses," August 13, 2003, ⟨http://www.adl.org/anti_semitism/anti-semitic-responses.asp⟩ (accessed February 12, 2007).

A Scholar Weighs In

Amid the controversy over *The Passion*, the public sought answers about the film's biblical interpretation from scholars. In response, Paula Frederickson, Aurelio Professor of Scripture at Boston University, joined the fray. In her article entitled, "Mad Mel" (a play on Gibson's starring role in the *Mad Max* movies), Frederickson tackles questions of truth and text. She explains her involvement in the controversy and her concerns about the film, and then addresses the biblical text. After addressing how each gospel portrays Jesus' trial and crucifixion differently, Frederickson offers historical-cultural insight into the practice of crucifixion and the motivations of the gospel writers. What does her perspective add to this controversy? How might the ADL or the vehement e-mailers respond to her interpretation?

The evangelists wrote some forty to seventy years after Jesus's execution. Their literary problems are compounded by historical ones: it is difficult to reconstruct, from their stories, why Jesus was crucified at all. If the priests in Jerusalem had wanted him dead, Jesus could have been privately murdered or killed offstage. If the priests had wanted him killed but were constrained from arranging this themselves, they could have asked Pilate to do the job. If the Roman prefect had simply been doing a favor for the priests, he could easily have arranged Jesus's death by any of the considerable means at his disposal (assassination, murder in prison, and so on).

The fact that Jesus was publicly executed by the method of crucifixion can only mean that Rome wanted him dead: Rome alone had the sovereign authority to crucify. Moreover, the point of a public execution, as opposed to a private murder, was to communicate a message. Crucifixion itself implies that Pilate was concerned about sedition. Jesus's death on the cross was Pilate's way of telling Jerusalem's Jews, who had gathered in the holy city for the paschal holiday, to desist from any thought of rebellion. The Gospel writers, each in his own way, introduce priestly initiative to apologize for Roman fiat, and the evidence suggests that the priests must have been somehow involved. But the historical fact behind the Passion narratives—Jesus's death on a cross—points to a primarily Roman agenda.

Source: Paula Frederickson, "Mad Mel: The Gospel according to Gibson," *New Republic* 229 (July 28 and August 4, 2003): 26.

CHAPTER SEVEN

Intolerance toward "New" Religions in the Twentieth Century

After encountering the Movementarians at the local airport, Homer Simpson and several other residents of Springfield want to learn more about this intriguing new religion. They file into the information session and sit down to watch an introductory film. Soon, a few audience members decide to leave, but the penetrating glare of the Movementarians' spotlight quickly makes them return to their seats. As the film ends six hours later, the audience, now captivated by the power and promises of the Leader, eagerly seeks to join the group. Unlike the other "brainwashed" residents of Springfield, Homer seems impervious to the film's message, as well as other Movementarian recruitment tactics—the insults of the circle of judgment, the daily diet of low protein gruel, and the power of the group's repetitive chant: "The Leader is good, the Leader is great, we surrender our will as of this date." However, their methods eventually succeed and Homer decides to join the group and signs up his wife Marge, as well as children Bart, Lisa, and Maggie. Upon paying the price of joining—their house, their life savings, and a contract for 10 trillion years of labor—Homer and the family move to the group's "agricultural compound." As Homer sees the face of the Leader in almost every lima bean he harvests, Bart, Lisa, and Maggie, at first reluctant, quickly convert. Bart's "Li'l Bastard General Mischief Kit" proves no match for the Movementarians' "Li'l Bastard Brainwashing Kit"; while the promise of good grades gains Lisa's support, and a Barney-like dinosaur lures little Maggie's love. Only Marge remains unhappy working in the fields as the Leader rides around in a Rolls Royce and promises that a spaceship will soon take them to the planet Blisstonia. Eventually Marge escapes the heavily guarded compound and seeks help from Reverend Lovejoy, neighbor Ned Flanders, and Groundskeeper Willie. The four agree that the Simpson family must be kidnapped from the compound and "deprogrammed" from the group's mind control. Once the quartet of rescuers impersonates the Rolls Royce–riding Leader and kidnaps the family, the process of deprogramming begins. Quickly the promise of "hover bikes" regains the children's allegiance, while beer proves to be Homer's salvation. In a final confrontation at the compound, Homer seeks to unmask the Leader's greed and trickery by opening the door to the "forbidden barn," whereupon a genuine-looking spaceship flies out. All too soon, however, the surface of the ship falls away to reveal the not-so-glorious leader riding away with his hoard of cash. In the end, the Simpson family returns to the "mindless happiness" offered by suburban life and FOX television.[1]

The Simpsons first aired in series format in 1989 and swiftly became a hit for FOX and a must-see for many Americans. In its long broadcast history, this Sunday night television staple has tackled a variety of religious and social issues as seen in the episode described above, entitled "The Joy of Sect." The episode embodies many of our culture's stereotypical views of "cults" and provides a starting point for our examination of the religious intolerance these groups have faced. The similarities between the fictional and the real begin with language. Language is a powerful weapon in the war waged against minority religious groups. Just as the Springfield residents consistently refer to the Movementarians as a "cult," many in our culture employ the same vocabulary in equally negative ways. These "deviant" groups are never recognized as legitimate religions. Denying these groups the status of religion means, in the eyes of their foes, that "cults" seek not spiritual power, but rather some type of material advantage, be it economic gain, political clout, or mind control. The "cult" label enables television viewers and cultural observers to "know" from the start that these groups, whether the fictional Movementarians or the actual Moonies, are "frauds." It causes people to rely on simplistic stereotypes rather than actively seeking the truth. While, as we will see, some members of the counter-cult movement (individuals who oppose "cults" on theological grounds) launch religiously based attacks, often the documents in this chapter demonstrate how "cult" opponents translate religious differences into a series of "secular" crimes—brainwashing individuals, defrauding followers, endangering cities, and harming America. To highlight and challenge these tendencies, this chapter places the word "cult" in quotes or refers to these groups as new religious movements (NRMs).[2]

The "Joy of Sect" episode vividly and accurately illustrates the enduring features of the "cult" stereotype, a stereotype that feeds religious intolerance. As Richard Dyer writes, "stereotyping—complex and contradictory though it is—does characterize the representation of subordinated social groups and is one of the means by which they are categorized and kept in their place."[3] For cultural opponents, the "cult" stereotype signals that these groups are not real religions. It denotes that they must be nefarious organizations led by up-to-no-good deviants, as seen in "The Joy of Sect." For example, characterizations of the Movementarian Leader as greedy and manipulative resonate with popular perceptions of "cult" leaders in the media. In fact, the episode does not fully exploit other common traits attributed to "cult" leaders, namely craziness and perversion. The title of the episode, "The Joy of Sect," plays on the word sex and the popular book *The Joy of Sex* and thereby subtly implies the sexual deviancy often associated with "cult" leaders; however, in this case, the Leader appears more criminal than crazy or perverted. Throughout this chapter, attend to the ways cultural opponents consistently attack NRM leaders to unmask their supposedly evil intent and thereby discredit their groups.

However, intolerance toward NRMs does not stop with their leaders. The fictional Movementarian members, like their real counterparts, are portrayed by the media and viewed in our culture as mindless sheep unable to resist a charlatan shepherd. This stereotype fuels intolerant views about "cult" members. It unfolds as follows: Given that the leader has no qualms about using nefarious methods, and as no sane, educated person could possibly believe a "cult" leader's "theology," "cults" must therefore prey on young, innocent people who do not know their own minds. The "cults" lure these "innocents" in and then, as the stereotype goes, "brainwash" them. Despite the lack of scholarly evidence for brainwashing, it remains a pervasive cultural and stereotypical explanation for conversion to "cults." As an explanatory device, brainwashing blames the "manipulative" leader even as it exonerates the "hapless" joiner. As you read the primary documents, consider how intolerance toward NRMs rests not only on exposing the "corruption" of a "cult" leader and the "true" aims of the group, but also on the construction of an "innocent" child or youth and a seemingly unshakable belief in brainwashing.

In addition, by including the deprogramming tactics of Groundskeeper Willie, the "Joy of Sect" episode highlights a central perpetrator of religious intolerance toward NRMs—the anticult movement (ACM). The twentieth century saw the rise of the ACM, whose organized efforts and rhetorical tactics set it apart from its counter-cult colleagues. While the ACM certainly disdains the beliefs of "cults," in keeping with its denial that "cults" are legitimate religions, the ACM does not launch theological attacks or hold heresy trials. Rather, the ACM frames itself as a pseudo-scientific business offering "psychological" resources and "rescue" services to its clients, typically concerned family members. Firmly convinced that brainwashing provides the only explanation for "cult" membership, anticultists believe that kidnapping and deprogramming, which they prefer to call "exit counseling," are the tools with which to save "cult victims." Like Groundskeeper Willie, for a fee, these anticultists offer to physically and mentally "liberate" the "brainwashed" from the clutches of "cults." As you read this chapter, reflect on how the ACM, as well as other opponents, attack "cults," construct "victims," and defend deprogramming.

Further, the "cult" stereotype propounded by the ACM and then fueled by the media results in another type of intolerance not explored in "The Joy of Sect." The Simpson family returns to their Springfield home without the aid of government authorities or litigious activity. However, the ACM frequently uses the legal system to discredit NRMs, and, in response, NRMs have gone to court to protect their rights. In the twentieth century, the rise in NRM litigation points to the increased role of the government in defining religion and religious rights. As scholar Phillip Hammond explains, "on issues not only of evangelizing but also of soliciting funds, tax exemption, and political involvement by religious groups, NRMs have stretched existing boundaries, with the consequence that government feels the need (or is asked) to intervene in matters that once were entirely internal to churches." For example, in *Cantwell v. Connecticut* (1940), the government adjudicated whether Jehovah's Witnesses had the right to distribute religious literature in a predominantly Catholic community. Hammond writes that "in upholding the right to proselytize in hostile neighborhoods, the court made explicit the right of the government to control proselytizing." Thus, even as individuals have gained religious rights, religion as an institution has become more and more entangled with and under the jurisdiction of the federal government.[4] As you read the documents in this chapter, consider the consequences of the American government's increasing power over religion and religious activity. How does the government wield this power? What constitutes a "legitimate" religion or an issue of the "public good?" In this chapter, and the next, examine how governmental power leads to implicit and explicit intolerance, and even violence, toward NRMs.

Given the power of the "cult" stereotype, government agents and agencies often align themselves with anticultists against NRMs. This occurs in two main ways, namely, the "use of the law as a weapon of harassment" and "the abuse of power by government agents."[5] Examples include "cult" opponents using zoning laws, criminal trials, city ordinances, and protest rights to hinder and interfere with NRMs. In addition, often police officers, influenced by the "cult" stereotype and the ACM, fail to catch the perpetrators of religious intolerance. In your reading of the documents, interrogate how legal codes become weapons and law enforcement officers become participants in this battle against new religions. Are laws biased against NRMs? How can the legal system be manipulated to discriminate against minority religions? Also, reflect on the role of law enforcement officers. How do they respond to religious differences, and what are the consequences? Throughout this chapter, analyze the constant negotiations between majority rules and minority rights, the tensions between mainstream religion and marginal "cult."

In conclusion, the intolerance experienced by twentieth-century NRMs reflects a more basic battle over the cultural ability to define religion in the United States, as well as the power to define the United States itself. Historically, minority religions often emerge as the casualties of this conflict as the majority seeks to preserve its image of America. As we examine this battle in, by, and for America, analyze at least two additional dimensions of this conflict. First, attend to the ways that intolerance toward NRMs serves and preserves the idea of a Christian America. Ostensibly a wall of separation divides church and state, but what is the reality? Is the United States a Christian nation? Consider how these documents assume (or not) the Christian character of America, as well as how they define what it means to be an American. Second, investigate how intolerance toward NRMs reveals societal tensions over "appropriate" levels of religious devotion. To return to *The Simpsons*, is it possible for us to see Homer's sacrifice of his independence and livelihood to join the Movementarians as a devout and legitimate act? Put another way, are we able or willing to recognize the validity of religious commitments marked by a level of devotion we deem as "abnormal" or "extreme"? As you analyze the documents included and issues raised in this chapter, consider how the dominant culture defines religious commitment and its consequences. Scholar James Beckford writes, "it is precisely the fact that large numbers of people are ignorant or apathetic about religion most of the time that makes the activities of those who are enthusiastic about their religion potentially more controversial." He continues, "I am arguing that a process of *polarization* is taking place between religiously energetic minorities and religiously apathetic majorities."[6] Or, as Larry D. Shinn writes, "Yes, America is still one of the most heavily church-going nations on the globe. Yes, our presidents still refer to our Judeo-Christian heritage in major speeches. But do we really understand or appreciate the kind of deep religiosity that produces a Mother Teresa—or a David Koresh?[7] To answer this question and to address the other issues raised, this chapter offers an in-depth examination of five NRMS in the United States—Unificationism, Wicca, Heaven's Gate, the Nation of Islam, and Santería. While we could have examined religious intolerance toward any number of "new" religions in the twentieth century, whether Jehovah's Witnesses, Buddhists, Hare Krishnas, Pentecostals, or even nontheists, these five groups provide a starting point for understanding and responding to this persistent brand of religious intolerance.

DOCUMENTS

Intolerance toward the "Moonies"

Unificationism, officially known as the Holy Spirit Association for the Unification of World Christianity or derogatorily referred to as the Moonies, preaches a "new" brand of Christianity built on the teachings of Korean minister Reverend Sun Myung Moon (b. 1920). At the age of fifteen, Moon received his first divine revelation, which informed him of his central importance in Christian history. As his visions continued, Moon refined his teachings and established Unificationism in Seoul, Korea, in 1954. Unificationism teaches that Reverend Moon and his wife are the "True Parents" of humanity inaugurating a new Eden, the kingdom of God on earth. In 1992, Moon confirmed that he is the messiah, or second coming of Jesus. In the 1960s, Unification missionaries started coming to the United States, but the movement began to attract greater numbers in the 1970s, when Moon himself moved to the States. However, with numerical growth came intense opposition. Anticultists repeatedly argued that Moon's "religious" teachings masked his "true" intent—political and economic power. These suspicions ultimately culminated in a federal investigation of Moon's financial dealings, and, in 1982, he was convicted of tax evasion and sent to prison for thirteen months. For Unification members, this conviction represented the culmination of a long history of religious persecution. Unificationism had, in fact, endured repeated attacks—literary and legal, spiritual and physical—in the 1970s. The documents below highlight these early struggles.

Youthnappers!

Intolerance toward Unificationism rose in the 1970s as the group attracted members from the "mainstream"—young adults from white, middle class, Christian families. In his 1977 book, *Youthnappers*, Christian writer James Hefley issues a wake-up call to America's parents. After detailing the beliefs and blasphemies of various "cults"—Moonies, Hare Krishnas, the Children of God, and more—Hefley urges churches and parents to recognize the cause of the problem. What, according to Hefley, is this cause? How does he portray America's youth? How will America win this fight for its children?

If the Eastern swamis and gurus should all pack their bags and return to India; if Sun Myung Moon should go into permanent eclipse; if "Moses" Berg should drown in the Red Sea; if all the cults that plague Western society should suddenly fizzle—what then?

New groups would surely arise to fill the void and we would simply see a rerun of the same chaotic religious show. It is not enough to expose the methods and doctrines of the cults, nor to prosecute those cult leaders who violate the law under the cloak of freedom of religion, nor to win present cult members back to ways more acceptable to their parents and society.

For the sake of future generations we must discover what makes our youth and others so vulnerable to the strange sirens of cultism. . . . Too many other congregations either neglect or underestimate the potential of their young people.

Adults tend to forget that Alexander the Great was only 21 when he conquered the Balkans, 22 when he crossed the Hellespont, and 24 when he built the city of Alexandria; that Ivan the Terrible was 17 when he won the Czar's crown; that Joan of Arc was 17 when her army captured Orleans; that Jesus' Twelve Apostles probably ranged in age from the late teens to early 20s.

Cultists such as Moon and Moses Berg have not forgotten. Nor have the Eastern teachers who are sweeping up drifting, emotionally insecure youths by the thousands.

Despite these tragedies, the cults which are causing so much commotion may in the long run serve to the advantage of our families and institutions. They will, if they mobilize us to mend the widening moral and spiritual holes in our national fabric.

Source: James C. Hefley, *The Youthnappers* (Wheaton, Ill.: Victor Books, 1977), 197, 204–5.

You Worship This Son of a Bitch!?

As parents feared for their "Moonie" children, many did more than write books and issue warnings; they assumed their children were brainwashed and sought the help of deprogrammers. The excerpt below, from *Let Our Children Go!* (1976), details the on-the-job exploits of one the best-known deprogrammers in the United States, Ted Patrick. First, Patrick discusses his view of "cults" and then shares his method of "liberation." How would you describe Patrick's tactics? Do his techniques resemble those he ascribes to "cults"? What are the implications of deprogramming for individual and religious rights? In the end, Patrick successfully "deprograms" Bernie, who eventually goes on to help Patrick deprogram others.

"The way they get them is by on-the-spot hypnosis. Once they get them, they brainwash them. The technique is the same as the North Koreans used on our prisoners of war," says Ted Patrick.... "They don't let a kid sleep, they don't let him eat. They hit him with tape recordings of Scripture, lectures, discussions, workshops—night and day. They wear him down, wear him out. Pretty soon he believes anything. Some kids go out fund-raising three days after they join."

"What about freedom of religion?" the reporter asks. "Moon's got nothing to do with religion!" he replies emphatically. "Moon's a crook, plain and simple. They're all crooks. You name 'em. Hare Krishna. The Divine Light Mission. Guru Maharaj Ji. The New Testament Missionary Fellowship. Brother Julius. Love Israel. The Children of God. Not a brown penny's worth of difference between any of 'em. I've taken 'em all on. Deprogrammed hundreds of kids from all those cults." ...

Moments later, sipping coffee, he remarks to the reporter, "See, he's [referring to Bernie] a robot right now." She does not take this down; she merely looks at him, quizzically, skeptically. "I tell the parents, 'You're not dealing with your son at this point. You're dealing with a zombie. You have to do whatever's necessary to get him back.'" ...

Seated in front of the boy [Bernie], so close that their knees almost touch, their eyes locked, Patrick gets right into it, disdaining preliminaries.

"You think you are a Christian. You think you are doing the Lord's work. You think you worship the Lord. But you don't worship the Lord. You worship Moon. Did the Lord ever tell you to hate your father and mother? Joe Franklin told me that when he asked you, 'Do you love Moon more than your own father,' you said, 'Yes.' You love Moon more than your own father and mother who birthed you into this world and gave you everything.

Where does it say in the Bible that you should hate your father and mother? Where does it say that? And where does it say in the Bible that you should spend all your life, twenty hours a day, out on the streets cheating little old ladies, lying to them, robbing them of their money? Where does it say that? Christ told the rich man to give away everything he owned. But he didn't say, 'Give it to Me.' And he certainly didn't say, 'Give it to Moon.'"

He talks quietly, slowly, almost inaudibly. As he talks, he works with a felt-tip pen on a photograph of Sun Myung Moon that he has taken from his briefcase. He draws a pair of horns on Moon's head, then a moustache, pointed ears, making a caricature of the Devil out of the image the boy has been conditioned to love and revere.

"Why would you give up your God-given mind, Bernie? God gave you that mind, a good mind, a brilliant mind. You are a brilliant boy, and you have everything going for you. Why would you give up that God-given mind to worship Moon? You're not doing the Lord's work. You worship this son of a bitch. See him?" He holds up the vandalized picture. The boy refuses to look—the rigor mortis smile is on his face again. "There's your god. There's the son of a bitch. Recognize him? That's who you worship. Satan the snake."

Source: Ted Patrick with Tom Dulack, *Let Our Children Go!* (New York: E. P. Dutton, 1976), 20–24.

Freedom or Abduction?

In response to the deprogramming endeavors of the ACM, members of Unificationism, as well as other victims of the practice, attempted to fight back through the legal system. Despite evidence that deprogramming amounted to kidnapping and violated individual rights, the courts rejected "cult" members' version of events and sided with parents and men such as Ted Patrick. Until the late 1980s, the courts aligned themselves with anticultists. Believing in the "brainwashing" theory, they placed "incompetent cult members" under the control of their parents. The court case described below, one of many, represents another example of how anticultists influenced the legal system to enact religious intolerance. The other document, from 1980, illustrates further legal attempts to deny individual religious rights (the bill was not approved by New York Governor Hugh L. Carey).

The U.S. Circuit Court of Appeals in Boston has upheld a lower court ruling favoring deprogrammer Ted Patrick in a suit brought by a Unification Church member involved in an unsuccessful deprogramming attempt.

The appeals court affirmed the rejection by District Judge Francis J. Boyle here last June of a charge by Leslie Weiss, 25, that she had been denied her constitutional rights in an unsuccessful deprogramming attempt on Thanksgiving Day 1974. In his June ruling, Boyle had said that Weiss had failed to prove her charge that she had been held captive by Patrick and Albert Turner of Warwick, R.I., in whose home the deprogramming attempt took place. He noted that she had testified that she was allowed to roam about the Turner home and that she had decided to pretend she was being deprogrammed to create the impression she was a willing listener.

Weiss had charged that she had been tricked into going to the Turner home by her mother and that she was forced to listen to denunciation of the Rev. Sun Myung Moon's Unification Church for nearly four hours in the Turner basement in an unsuccessful attempt to have her renounce her religious beliefs. She said she finally escaped by jumping from a window the next morning.

Judge Boyle also ruled that Turner and Patrick were motivated "primarily, if not entirely," by "the maternal concerns" of Weiss's mother, who hired Patrick because she feared her daughter's health and well-being were endangered by membership in the Unification Church.

The appeals court said it found no need to go into the constitutional questions raised by Weiss because she "was free to leave."

Source: Religious News Service, "Deprogrammer Upheld in Appeal by Moon Convert," *Washington Post*, December 29, 1978, D7.

The supreme court and the county courts outside the city of New York, shall have the power to appoint one or more temporary conservators of the person and property of any person over fifteen years of age, upon showing that such person for whom the temporary conservator is to be appointed has become closely and regularly associated with a group which practices the use of deception in the recruitment of members and which engages in systematic food or sleep deprivation or isolation from family or unusually long work schedules; and that such person for whom the temporary conservator is to be appointed has undergone a sudden and radical change in behavior, lifestyle, habits and attitudes; and has become unable to care for his welfare and that his judgment has become impaired to the extent that he is unable to understand the need for such care.

Source: State of New York Assembly Bill 11122-A, An Act to Amend the Mental Hygiene
Law, In Relation to Temporary Conservator, Introduced by Howard L. Lasher, et al.
(March 25, 1980). See Anson D. Shupe and David G. Bromley, *A Documentary History
of the Anti-Cult Movement* (Arlington, Tex.: Center for Social Research, 1985).

Intolerance toward Wicca

Scholars generally credit Englishman Gerald Gardner (1884–1964) with re-
viving the contemporary practice of witchcraft in the 1950s. Some Wiccans,
however, claim the antiquity of their religion and view themselves as inheri-
tors of the ancient healing traditions of Western Europe, traditions that survived the "Burning Times" (Christian persecution). Whatever its historic
origins, Wicca as a religion in the United States did not gain "official" recognition until a 1985 court ruling. In *Dettmer v. Landon*, the judge ruled that
Wicca was in fact a religion with doctrines and rituals like other recognized
religions. However, despite this ruling, many remain skeptical, critical, or
afraid. They see Wicca's use of magic and criticisms of Christianity as evidence of an alliance with Satan. In addition, the group's lack of a definitive
sacred text and any centralized authority has only fueled these accusations.
Despite Wicca's twofold moral code—the Rede, which states, "And it harm
none, do what you will," and the Law of Three, which states that all one's actions (for good or ill) return to him or her threefold—many continue to cast
Wiccans as enemies in league with the ultimate enemy, the devil. The documents below illustrate the pervasiveness of this misunderstanding of Wicca
and the actions taken to defeat this perceived ally of Satan.

"The Protocols" of Wicca

While the *Protocols of the Learned Elders of Zion* was written in the early 1900s,
the more recent "Seven W.I.C.C.A. Letters" bears an eerie resemblance. Like
the *Protocols*, the "Seven Letters" purports to be an accurate transcription of
a "nefarious" set of goals, these allegedly established at a Wiccan Convention
in 1981 and, it would seem, alarmingly close to being achieved. It also places
the conspiracy in the mouths of Wiccans, as the *Protocols* did with Jews.
However, like the *Protocols*, the "Seven Letters" is a hoax, one perpetrated,
according to a Wiccan site, by a San Diego policeman. As you read, analyze
how the text creates the alleged conspiracy and compare this text with its
predecessor. Attend to what ideas, institutions, and groups become weapons
in this war against Wicca.

1. To bring about the covens, both black and white magic, into one and have the arctress to govern all—ACCOMPLISHED;

2. To bring about personal debts causing discord and disharmony within families—ACCOMPLISHED;

3. To remove or educate "new age youth" by:
 —Infiltrating boys'/girls' clubs and big sister/brother programs
 —Infiltrating schools, having prayers removed, having teachers teach about drugs, sex, freedoms
  —Instigating and promoting rebellion against parents and all authority
  —Promoting equal rights for youth—ACCOMPLISHED;

4. To gain access to all people's backgrounds and vital information by:
 —Use of computers
 —Convenience
 —Infiltration—ACCOMPLISHED;

5. To have laws changed to benefit our ways, such as:
 —Removing children from home environment and placing them in our foster homes
  —Mandatory placement of children in our daycare centers
  —Increased taxes
  —Open drug and pornography market to everyone—NOT YET ACCOMPLISHED;

6. To destroy government agencies by:
 —Overspending
 —Public Opinion
 —Being on the offensive always, opposing, demonstrating, demoralizing—NOT YET ACCOMPLISHED;

7. (The seventh letter was not revealed until the Summer Solstice, June 21, 1986. Dep. Gaerin has been able to determine part of this letter, namely, that covens are sanctioned to abduct and sacrifice human adults or children on the 24th of each month for the next eleven years, at which time they expect to be in complete control. This amounts to new and unifying emphasis on blood-letting rituals.)

Peter Michas, a Christian pastor and expert in the area of Satanism and heavy metal music, says that goals five and six have since been accomplished, at least to a satisfactory degree, and that goal seven has been "announced" to the public on the album covers of popular Satanic heavy metal bands such as Ozzy Osbourne. By placing together bits of information from different album covers, Michas says that the seventh goal is to be a tremendous increase of blatant Satanic activity over the next thirteen years, culminating in the physical reign of Satan on earth on June 21, 1999.

Source: "The Seven W.I.C.C.A. Letters," ⟨http://www.holysmoke.org/wicca/wicca-letters-hoax.htm⟩ (accessed May 11, 2005).

Halloween: Holy Day or Hell's Day?

The Constitution guarantees the right to peacefully assemble, but does that right sometimes impinge upon the liberty of others? Many NRMs would answer emphatically, "yes." For example, in 1987, the Ku Klux Klan joined other residents of Jim Thorpe, Pennsylvania, to protest the proposed building of a "walled city" by the Hare Krishnas. Some protestors wore "Swami Buster" t-shirts and one Klansmen said, "If the cow worshipers get that mountain, all hell could break loose." The city was not built. In October 1990, Wiccans faced similar hostilities as they prepared to observe one of their sabbaths—Samhain or Halloween. The newspaper account below highlights this dilemma. As you read, consider the persistent misunderstandings of the Wiccan tradition and the invective employed against it. Why is Wicca so misunderstood? How do you balance Christians' rights to disapprove of Wicca with the rights of Wiccans to celebrate their sabbaths in peace?

As Halloween approaches, fundamentalists march to the Bay Area to begin a crusade against the devil and thousands of pagans and goddess worshippers prepare for the onslaught.

A peaceful prayer crusade? Or just another witch hunt?

The term "holy war" will take on a whole new meaning in San Francisco on Halloween, as Pentecostal Christians and goddess-worshipping pagans square off to prove who's holier than thou.

Texas televangelist Larry Lea is mustering 10,000 Christian soldiers in San Francisco's Civil Auditorium Halloween night, to do battle with the forces of Satan. And members of the normally low-key pagan community in the Bay Area—practitioners of Wicca, nature religions and New Age spiritualism—have launched a counter offensive, claiming Lea's spiritual warfare interferes with their constitutional right to practice their religion. . . .

Last month with the backing of 500 pastors of Bay Area churches, Lea announced a three-day San Francisco crusade to "reverse the curse" of Halloween and march through the city to convert those they consider possessed by Satan: drug addicts, gay people, the sexually promiscuous, believers in New Age "religions," and Wiccans: those spell-casting, Goddess-worshipping folks commonly called Witches.

"These are not just kids having fun," Lea said at the time. "There is actual worship of the devil."

Janet Christian, spokeswoman for the Bay Area Pagan Assemblies, an organization of Wiccans and nature-worshippers in the South Bay, is outraged. "We're Goddess worshippers: Witches don't have anything to do with

'Satan.' Who do these people think they are?" asks Christian. . . . "What if we brought some big-name Witch to town on Christmas day to do a ritual outside their churches? We'd never do that to them," Christian says. "Why are they doing this to us?" . . .

"I love people. I love all people. I think we have been misinterpreted; we don't want to be seen as confrontational," Lea says. "Every person has the right to believe what they want to believe. But I have the freedom to stand up and say they're wrong. To me, there are only two kinds of people in the world: Those who have found Christ and those who haven't found him yet."

The Rev. Dick Bernall, pastor of Jubilee Christian Center in San Jose is disappointed that the prayer warriors will not be a visible presence on the streets of San Francisco. Many of Jubilee's 5,000 congregants are expected to take part in the Lea crusade. . . . "Larry and I are beginning to look like a couple of wackos," says Bernal. "The misconception is that we're a bunch of narrow-minded goody-two-shoes. San Francisco's a city where everybody has parades; I wanted our people to be a presence, too. We weren't going to call down fire on anybody; it was not going to be a confrontation, just a little show of force."

"But the war on Satan will go on—inside the auditorium. There won't be any pussy-footing around," Bernal promises. "There'll be singing, preaching and speaking in tongues. It'll be wall-to-wall spiritual warfare."

Source: Joan Connell, "The Witching Hour," San Jose Mercury News, October 20, 1990, 1E.

"We Are Out to Kill!"

While many stay within the law when they enact religious intolerance, others disregard it and commit violent acts against NRMs. Unfortunately, as with anti-Semitism, arsons, bombings, and shootings targeting NRM members do occur. For example, in 1985, a Laotian Buddhist Temple in Rockford, Illinois, was pipe bombed and/or shot at on three separate occasions. As shown in the documentary, Blue Collar and Buddha, the culprits were never found. Similarly, in 1984, outside of Philadelphia, a Hare Krishna temple was bombed. Too often intolerant theological and cultural beliefs result in violent actions. The newspaper account below chronicles the violence undertaken against a Wiccan coven in Florida. Consider, again, what moves an individual from anticult belief to anticult action? What factors in American culture foster this progression? Encountering only the odd newspaper account of an act of violence against an NRM, people tend to explain such actions as aberrations. But when we place this violence alongside all the other examples of intolerance toward these groups, can we really be satisfied with that explanation?

New Port Richey, Fla.—A witches' ceremony came to an abrupt halt over the weekend when angry neighbors and members of the nature worshiping coven exchanged gunshots, authorities said. The witches said the attack Sunday was just the latest in a series of violent acts against their group and its island shrine near Moon Lake, just northeast of New Port Richey. Five witches from the coven Lothlorien told Pasco County deputies they had just finished a ritual seeking protection from threats when gunfire ripped through the trees surrounding their ceremonial grounds at about 11 p.m. No one was wounded and no arrests were made, the Pasco Sheriff's Office said. . . .

"We heard the bullets ripping past and we all crouched down on the ground and started crawling back to my house on our hands on knees," said Kassie Cornwell, a witch and a registered nurse. . . .

Members said Sunday's ritual was in response to threats they received the day before. Cornwell's house had been pelted with eggs, she said, and a note was left in her front yard Saturday. The note warned the group to stop their "Satan worshiping or be prepared for worse. Next time we won't stop at eggs." Another note said, "We are the ultimate enemy. We are out to kill!" Cornwell, 43, said she heard people cursing, calling them Satanists and other names during Sunday's attack. When the gunfire started, coven member Curtis Niles of Spring Hill grabbed a shotgun and fired several rounds in the air, Cornwell said.

Neighbor Art Gray, 39, told a sheriff's deputy he heard shots coming from Cornwell's property and he fired back, also in the air, to warn the people away from his house. Several of Cornwell's neighbors said they believed the group practices Satanism and sacrifices animals. But Cornwell said the group doesn't allow animals near their worshiping area.

She said the group's credo is to "do what you will, but harm none." Parshley said the group has "nothing to do with Satanism." The coven has worshiped at Cornwell's property since she bought her home a year ago. She said the worship area has been desecrated six or seven times.

Source: UPI, "Gunshots Exchanged" (1990), ⟨http://www.holysmoke.org/wicca/lothlor.htm⟩ (accessed May 11, 2005).

"Curse God and Die!"

Many Wiccans worship the duality of the divine—the Goddess and the God, her Consort. The Consort is often referred to and depicted as the Horned God. For those unfamiliar with this ancient deity and Wiccans' claiming of him, the Horned God resembles artistic renderings of the devil and thereby feeds the misconception that Wiccans worship Satan. In addition, some interpretations of the Bible provide fodder for this claim. For example, in 1992, the Bible verses below circulated on the Internet in an anti-Wiccan letter. How would you interpret these verses? How might the letter's author view the Bible? What are the implications of using the biblical text in this manner?

Leviticus 19:31 Regard not them that have familiar spirits, neither seek after wizards, to be defiled by them: I am the Lord your God.

Deuteronomy 18:10–12 There shall not be found among you any one that maketh his son or his daughter to pass through the fire, or that useth divination, or an observer of times, or an enchanter, or a witch, or a charmer, or a consulter with familiar spirits, or a wizard, or a necromancer. For all that do these things are an abomination unto the Lord: and because of these abominations the Lord thy God doth drive them out from before thee.

Isaiah 8:19–22 And when they shall say unto you, Seek unto them that have familiar spirits, and unto wizards that peep, and that mutter: Should not a people seek unto their God? For the living to the dead? To the law and to the testimony: If they speak not according to this word, it is because there is no light in them. And they shall pass through it, hardly bestead and hungry: And it shall come to pass that when they shall be hungry, they shall fret themselves, and curse their king and their God, and look upward. And they shall look unto the earth; and behold trouble and darkness, dimness of anguish; and they shall be driven to darkness.

Isaiah 44:24, 25 Thus saith the Lord, thy redeemer, and he that formed thee from the womb, I am the Lord that maketh all things; that stretcheth forth the heavens alone; that spreadeth abroad the earth by myself; that frustrateth the tokens of the liars, and maketh diviners mad; that turneth wise men backward, and maketh their knowledge foolish;

Isaiah 47:13, 14 Thou art wearied in the multitude of thy counsels. Let now the astrologers, the stargazers, the monthly prognosticators, stand up, and save thee from these things that shall come upon thee. Behold, they shall be as stubble; the fire shall burn them; they shall not deliver themselves from the power of the flame: There shall not be a coal to warm at, nor fire to sit before it.

Jeremiah 27:9, 10 Therefore hearken not ye to your prophets, nor to your diviners, nor to your dreamers, nor to your enchanters, nor to your sorcerers, which speak unto you, saying, Ye shall not serve the king of Babylon: For they prophesy a lie unto you, to remove you far from your land; and that I should drive you out, and ye should perish.

1 Corinthians 10:20, 21 But I say, that the things which the Gentiles sacrifice, they sacrifice to devils, and not to God: and I would not that ye should have fellowship with devils. Ye cannot drink the cup of the Lord, and the cup of devils: Ye cannot be partakers of the Lord's table, and of the table of devils.

Galatians 5:20, 21 Idolatry, witchcraft, hatred, variance, emulations, wrath, strife, seditions, heresies, envyings, murders, drunkenness, revellings, and such like: Of the which I tell you before, as I have also told you in time past, that they which do such things shall not inherit the kingdom of God.

1 Timothy 4:1,2 Now the Spirit speaketh expressly, that in the latter times some shall depart from the faith, giving heed to seducing spirits, and doctrines of devils; speaking lies in hypocrisy; having their conscience seared with a hot iron.

Job 2:9 . . . Curse God, and die.

Sources: Bible (King James Version); see also "A Fundamentalist Christian Speaks against Wiccans," ⟨http://www.holysmoke.org/wicca/anti-wic.htm⟩ (accessed May 11, 2005).

Intolerance toward Heaven's Gate

While many remained unaware of the existence of Heaven's Gate until their "suicide" in 1997, the group had existed since the early 1970s. Heaven's Gate falls under the broader umbrella of "UFO cults," a category of new religions that emerged after a reported UFO sighting in the 1940s. These groups tend to view life in terms of evolutionary growth and share a belief in communication with extraterrestrials. Heaven's Gate, founded by Marshall Herff Applewhite (1931–1997) and Bonnie Lu Nettles (1927–1985) (known in 1997 as Do and Ti, respectively), also held to these beliefs and blended them with elements of Christianity, as well as other religions. The duo preached that an ascetic life would lead to "Human Individual Metamorphosis"—transformation into a wholly spiritual being—and subsequent transportation aboard a spacecraft to the heavenly kingdom. Despite living in a gated community in Rancho Santa Fe, California, and having cordial relations with law enforcement, the group feared religious intolerance. They had faced negative media attention in the 1970s, and a later statement entitled "Our Position Against Suicide" revealed the fear that, like other NRMs, they would be persecuted for their faith. They wrote, "We could find so much disfavor with the powers that control this world that there could be attempts to incarcerate us or to subject us to some sort of psychological or physical torture (such as occurred at both Ruby Ridge and Waco)."[8]

It's Not Religion, It's Junk

Having prepared themselves for this eventuality, on March 27, 1997, thirty-nine members of Heaven's Gate committed suicide in the eyes of the world, an act that according to their beliefs would allow them to attain the Next Level of spiritual life and board the spacecraft they thought trailed the Hale-Bopp Comet. Baffled by such belief and commitment, many people responded with ridicule and derision. In the excerpts below, we once again see journalistic depictions and descriptions reduce a minority religion to a "crazy cult." Sociologist Anson Shupe argues that the news media depicts new religions in five progressive phases: Preconstruction (little or no coverage of the NRM), Benign (positive coverage of the NRM), Skeptical (suspicious coverage of the NRM), Malicious (negative coverage of the NRM), and Postmalicious (NRM becomes the butt of humor).[9] Test Shupe's theory as you examine these news magazine excerpts and the other documents on Heaven's Gate. If not faced with blatant discrimination during their lives, intolerance, it seems, characterized the treatment of this group upon their death.

So the worst legacy of Heaven's Gate may yet be this: That 39 people sacrificed themselves to the new millennial kitsch. That's the cultural by-product in which spiritual yearnings are captured in New Age gibberish, then edged with the glamour of sci-fi and the consolations of a toddler's bedtime. In the Heaven's Gate cosmology, where talk about the end of the world alternates with tips for shrugging off your fleshly container, the cosmic and the lethal, the enraptured and the childish come together. Is it any surprise then that it led to an infantile apocalypse, one part applesauce, one part Phenobarbital? Look at the Heaven's Gate Website. Even as it warns about the end of the world, you find a drawing of a space creature imagined through insipid pop dust-jacket conventions: aerodynamic cranium, big doe eyes, beatific smile. We have seen the Beast of the Apocalypse. It's Bambi in a tunic.

Source: Richard Lacayo, "The Lure of the Cult: Out Where Religion and Junk Culture Meet, Some Weird New Offspring are Rising," Time, April 7, 1997, 45.

What possessed this self-described "Next Level Crew" of 21 women and 18 men, ranging in age from 26 to 72, to go not only willingly, but apparently cheerfully? Judging from the abundant evidence—videotapes left behind, numerous written tracts and postings on the Internet—the followers of Heaven's Gate seem to have drunk from a delusional cocktail of just about every religious tradition and New Age escapist fantasy. They avidly watched old "Star Trek" episodes and "The X-Files" while cruising cyberspace looking for UFO sightings.

Source: Evan Thomas and Andrew Murr, "The Next Level," *Newsweek* (April 7, 1997), 30.

The Butt of the Joke

While Richard Lacayo of *Time* magazine referred to Heaven's Gate as an example of "junk culture," others responded to this little-known religious group's use of popular culture resources, including *Star Trek* and *The X-Files*, with humor. For Heaven's Gate members these television shows provided a literal and visual vocabulary. It helped them articulate their theological views to those unfamiliar with their complex cosmology. For cultural observers and critics, the group's use of television and belief in UFOs made them the butt of the joke. What does it mean to make fun of a religious group? Why is alright to make fun of some groups and not others? What is the effect of this humor? Are these documents—a cartoon, a "Top Ten" list, a fake Nike ad, and a "paper doll kit"—evidence of Shupe's argument about a postmalicious construction? What does this tell us about American culture and NRMs?

Source: Chris Sturhann, "Heaven's Gate Mass Suicide Cartoon" (1997), ⟨http://www.chrissturhann.com/nonsense/heaven.html⟩ (accessed April 20, 2005).

Top 10 Warning Signs Before Renting in Rancho Santa Fe, California
- 10. Ad in paper says "Sleeps 39."
- 9. No mention of return of security deposit.
- 8. Stereo plays only music by rock group "The Cult."
- 7. Amenities include gas oven.
- 6. References of main lessee include Dr. Jack Kervorkian.
- 5. Rental agreement asks for next of kin.
- 4. House vacant due to extended vacation in Guyana.
- 3. Four words: Matching pants and shoes.
- 2. Mailbox filled with forwarded mail from Waco, Texas.
- 1. Piped in music? Theme from "M*A*S*H."

Source: "Top 10 Warning Signs Before Renting in Rancho Santa Fe, California," ⟨http://www.planetproctor.com/index2.html⟩ (accessed February 21, 2006).

Source: "Fake Nike Advertisement," ⟨http://www.notbored.org/nike.gif⟩ (accessed February 21, 2006).

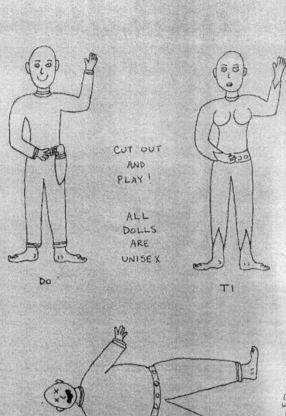

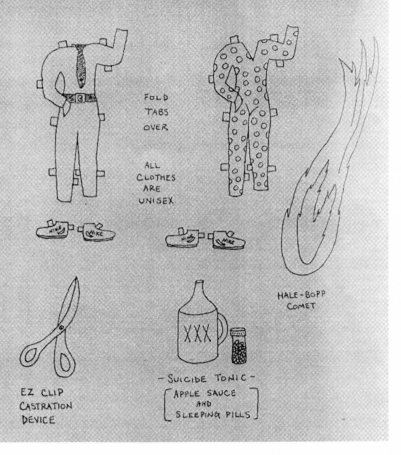

The Official
Heaven's Gate
Paper Doll Kit

Use the purple tissue paper to create death shrouds after mass suicide by cutting the tissue paper into equal pieces. Lay each piece over a cult member's paper doll and enjoy!

FOLD
TABS
OVER

ALL
CLOTHES
ARE
UNISEX

HALE-BOPP
COMET

EZ CLIP
CASTRATION
DEVICE

— SUICIDE TONIC —
APPLE SAUCE
AND
SLEEPING PILLS

Source: Artist unknown, "The Official Heaven's Gate Paper Doll Kit," ⟨http://spaceport666 .tripod.com/heavensgatePD.JPG⟩, ⟨http://spaceport666.tripod.com/heavensgatePD2.JPG⟩ (accessed February 21, 2006).

Heaven's Gate or Hell's?

Religious groups responded to the Heaven's Gate "suicide" in a variety of ways. For example, the Church of Euthanasia, which describes itself as "a non-profit educational foundation devoted to restoring balance between Humans and the remaining species on Earth," applauded the actions of Heaven's Gate members. ("Thou shalt not procreate" represents the group's one commandment, while abortion, suicide, cannibalism, and sodomy are listed as its four pillars of faith.).[10] Others, however, found nothing to applaud. In fact, in a sermon to his Baptist church, Pastor Marvin McKenzie issued a two-fold warning to his congregation—one about cults and the other about the media.

> There has been much interest lately about cults and the like. I preached a message this last Sunday night that I thought might be of interest to some of you. The Scriptures tell us that in the last days there will be many false Christs, many that try to turn people from the truth to follow "cunningly devised fables."
>
> The Christian should not be surprised nor alarmed at the rise of cultist type religious groups. Nor should we feel as if we must shrink from God given, Bible truth because of these cultist activities. We need to make a distinction at this point, from non Christian religions and Christian type or Bible-based cults. While many of the same things are true of each, our main difficulty is with those that use the same Bible we use, or at least a version of it.
>
> With the mass suicides of 39 people involved in the Heaven's Gate cult, there has risen a new thrust of conversation in journalism concerning the seriousness of cults and what they do to its people. I am as opposed to the cults as just about anybody I know. I believe they are devilish, destructive and disobedient to God. But, at the same time, I am concerned that the media is training the masses to believe that almost ANY church organization is cultish and dangerous.
>
> ***We have seen, in the last few days, video clips of cult leader David Koresh, teaching the Bible in much the same fashion (even if he was teaching a false doctrine) as we would in a Baptist church.
>
> ***We have heard them decry as a cultist mark, the idea of living for the "faith" seven days a week.
>
> ***We have heard them speak of the doctrine of "millennialism" or the coming of God to end this world as we know it and establish a new world as a cultist doctrine.

***Some of the clips of the cult leader, "Doe," aired in the news had him describing preparing to soon leave this world to go to the Kingdom of Heaven.

***Our church has been labeled a cult on at least two occasions I can think of.

Not by the media, but by people who disagree with our doctrines. That is not too much of a worry to me, because Baptists were branded a cult by the Catholics hundreds of years ago! YOU HAVE TO CONSIDER THE SOURCE!

With those things in mind, it would be wise of us to search the Scriptures and see what it would consider a true cult, or false faith.

Source: Pastor Marvin McKenzie, Bayview Baptist Church, Astoria, Oregon, "Heaven's Gate or Hell's?," Sermons.org, ⟨http://www.sermons.org/sermons/sermons57.html⟩ (accessed April 29, 2004).

Intolerance toward the Nation of Islam

In 1930 in Detroit, amid the struggles of the Great Depression and the persistent racism of the United States, Wallace Fard (1891–?) began a ministry to bring African Americans back to their "true" faith — Islam. Like Moorish Science Temple founder Timothy Drew, Fard taught that Christianity was the "white devil's" religion, designed to oppress the black community. Preaching his version of Islam, as well as black superiority and separatism, Fard began to attract followers, notably Elijah Poole, later known as Elijah Muhammad (1897–1975). Elijah Muhammad declared that Fard was Allah and quickly became his most prominent disciple. Upon Fard's mysterious disappearance in 1934, Elijah Muhammad, as the messenger of Allah, took over leadership of the Nation of Islam until his death. Opponents of the Nation, including the federal government, feared its demands for justice and its insistence on black superiority. The documents below illustrate the range of weapons its opponents used to fight what the FBI files initially called "The Muslim *Cult* of Islam."

"America Is a White Christian Nation"

Reborn in 1945, at Stone Mountain, Georgia, the Ku Klux Klan, like its previous incarnations, promoted racism, practiced anti-Semitism, committed violence, and instilled fear. As the civil rights movement gained ground in the 1950s, the Klan attracted ever greater numbers. For example, the success of the Montgomery Bus Boycott in 1956 was matched by the Klan's numerical zenith in 1958. The letter below, dated February 1957, reflects this racial-religious battle. Written by Jesse B. Stoner, a Klansman from Tennessee, the letter begins by citing two biblical passages—1 Thessalonias 2:14–16 provides fodder for his anti-Semitic beliefs, while John 8:44–48 reveals his vision of the Nation of Islam as it begins, "you are from your father the devil." Throughout, Stoner preaches Christianity even as he curses the rise of the Nation of Islam in the African American community. As you read, attend to Stoner's view of the relationship between race and religion, as well as his vision of America. In 1977, Stoner was indicted and later convicted for the 1957 bombing of Bethel Baptist Church in Alabama.

Infidels:

Repent of Mohammedanism or burn in hell forever, throughout eternity.

The Lord Jesus Christ is the only begotten Son of God and He is the only One Who can save your infidelic souls and lead you into Heaven. Read the Holy Bible. St. John 6:35—"And Jesus said unto them, I am the bread of life. He that cometh to me shall never hunger; and he that believeth on me shall never thirst." . . . Therefore, Muhammad can do you no good.

It does not surprise me to hear that Islam is growing among the Africans of America. It is easy to understand because Islam is a nigger religion. It has only been successful among Africans and mix-breeds and never among the white people never. As you probably know, Christianity was well established throughout North Africa by white people before Mohammad was born. As time went on more and more people in North Africa became mongrelized with African blood. Therefore, they were no longer able or willing to stand up and fight for Christianity when persecution came upon them from Arabia. Their faith in Christ was shallow and weak. Then came the bloody Islamic conquerors from Arabia who slaughtered the white Christian leaders but spared the black people and mix-breeds. The Africans quickly forgot Christ, the true religion, and became Mohammedans. Some scholars have wondered why, but not me. I know why. Islam is a product of the colored race. Islam is a dark religion for dark people. I don't know why Africans would support Islam for any other reason except race. . . .

America is a white Christian nation and no infidelic religion such as Islam, has a right to exist under the American sun. Your Islam, your Mohammedanism is not a white religion. Mohammedanism is a nigger religion. The white race will never accept it, so take it back to Africa with you. It is like the Holy Bible says about GOD's plan for the nations of men in Acts 16:31—"And hath determined the times before appointed, and the bounds of their habitation." Therefore you have no place in America with your African race or your Islamic African religion.

The Christian Party becomes stronger every day. When we are elected to power we will legally drive you out. Remember 1492 A.D. when those two great white Christian monarchs, King Ferdinand and Queen Isabella, expelled the Muslims from Spain. The Christian Party will be even more ruthless. We will not tolerate your infidelic Christ-hating religion on American soil. We will drive Islam into the ocean. America isn't big enough for the Christian Party and Black Islam, so Islam must go.

You Muslims should be ashamed of yourselves for trying to lead the poor darkies of America into your Mohammedan hell. If they are smart, they will shun Mohammed and follow the Lord Jesus Christ, the Son of God, into Heaven and a happy and everlasting life.

Repent and confess the Lord Jesus Christ or you will burn in hell forever, you infidels. Your false religion is an insult to the true living GOD.

May God have mercy upon your heathen souls.

With many wishes for the failure of Islam in America, I am, Yours for Christ, Country and Race, J. B. Stoner

Source: J. B. Stoner, "Letter," in *Message to the Blackman in America* (Chicago: Muhammad Mosque of Islam No. 2, 1965), 330–35.

Fard Is a Fake!

While the Klan threatened hellfire and hoped to instill fear through its letter, others tried to do damage in a more public and powerful way—by using the media. Media exposés often target the "notorious" activities of "cult" leaders. Accusations of financial misdeeds, sexual perversions, and deluded ramblings commonly characterize media coverage of NRM leaders, past and present. Implicitly or explicitly, these articles urge the government to respond in some way to the alleged crimes, thereby fueling further intolerance—state and federal governments' harassment of NRMs. Excerpted below is Ed Montgomery's exposé on Fard in the *Los Angeles Herald Examiner*, which appeared in 1963. As you read, consider how Montgomery attempts to discredit Fard. What areas does he attack and why? Shortly after this article appeared, Elijah Muhammad issued a scathing reply and offered to pay $100,000 to the newspaper if it could actually prove its inflammatory headline.

BLACK MUSLIM FOUNDER EXPOSED AS A WHITE

A Dope Peddler, Dodd Served Time in Quentin

Black Muslims by the thousands pay homage to Wallace Farad, their "Prophet from Mecca," in the mistaken belief that as founder of the black supremacy cult he is one of their own. It was Farad who composed the tenets of the Black Muslim faith. He is the "holy man and divine person" who must be remembered in one or more of the Black Muslim's seven daily prayers.

Yet Wallace Farad is, admittedly, an enterprising, racketeering fake. He is not a Negro. He is a white man masquerading as a Negro. His true name is Wallace Dodd. He was born in New Zealand on February 26, 1891. His father was British—arriving in New Zealand via Australia on a sailing schooner. His mother was a Polynesian native.

Dodd's police "rap sheet" includes a conviction for bootlegging and a San Quentin Prison term for the sale of narcotics. To the FBI he is No. 56062— and a man of many aliases. The California Bureau of Identification and Investigation lists him as Wallace Ford, No. 1797924. At San Quentin, as Ford, he was No. 42314. With the Michigan State Police his is Wallace Farad, No. 93076. Although the names and numbers vary, the fingerprints are always the same, be it Los Angeles, San Quentin or Detroit, birthplace of the Black Muslim movement. . . .

Released from San Quentin on May 27, 1929, he paused briefly in Los Angeles before walking out on his common-law wife and son. Dodd made his way to Detroit to become a Bible-toting itinerant peddler of silks. Dodd posed as a Negro and prided himself as something of a Biblical authority and mathematician. He had a tremendous gift for gab and soon attracted a depression-following of Negroes.

Dodd had no difficulty in convincing his followers they were descendents of the original man, that their forebears were of Islam and that they were Allah's chosen people. Realizing that he had a good thing going, Dodd began emphasizing Islam and black supremacy. Gradually he turned away from the Bible, eventually denouncing it outright through interpretations twisted to suit his purpose. He adopted the Koran as his cult's official religious text. He established a temple and conducted classes. During this period he met Elijah Poole, who he eventually ordained as minister of the Black Muslim faith under the name Elijah Muhammad, "Apostle of Allah."

By now Dodd was passing himself off as The Savior, born in the Holy City of Mecca. He claimed to have arrived in America on July 4, 1930. To excite interest among his followers and gain new adherents, Dodd published a crudely printed tract, the preface of which reads:

"This book teaches the Lost Found Nation of Islam. A thorough knowledge of our miserable state of condition in a mathematical way, when we were found by our Savior, W. D. Fard." . . .

Through contributions and expanding commercial endeavors, including the sale of "official" note paper, Dodd had what constituted a tidy financial racket.

Source: Ed Montgomery, "Black Muslim Founder Exposed as a White," *Los Angeles Herald Examiner*, July 28, 1963, Evening and Sunday Edition, A1–A2.

No Black Messiahs

In addition to garnering negative media coverage, the Nation of Islam's combination of religious fervor and racial solidarity quickly put it on the police and FBI radar. Fearing "black power," the FBI kept files on the "nefarious" activities of leaders such as Wallace Fard and Elijah Muhammad, as well as Malcolm X and Martin Luther King Jr. The document below reveals that the FBI did more than collect information on these men. They also used their power, as a government agency, to disrupt and harm groups such as the Nation of Islam. The excerpt below is an FBI memo addressed to the special agent in charge in Albany, New York, dated March 4, 1968 (three years after the assassination of Malcolm X and one month prior to the assassination of Martin Luther King Jr.). Why is the government (rather than the anticult movement) responding to the Nation of Islam? What about the Nation makes it such a threat in the eyes of police and the FBI?

The Counterintelligence Program is now being expanded to include 41 offices. Each of the offices added to this program should designate an agent familiar with black nationalist activity, and interested in counterintelligence, to coordinate this program. . . .

GOALS

For maximum effectiveness of the Counterintelligence Program, and to prevent wasted effort, long-range goals are being set:

1. Prevent the coalition of militant black nationalist groups. In unity there is strength; a truism that is no less valid for all its triteness. An effective coalition of black nationalist groups might be the first step toward a real "Mau Mau" in America, the beginning of a true black revolution.

2. Prevent the rise of a "messiah" who could unify, and electrify, the militant black nationalist movement. XXXX [blacked out] might have been such a "messiah;" he is the martyr of the movement today. XXXX all aspire to this

position. XXXX is less of a threat because of his age. XXXX [could] be a very real contender for this position should he abandon his supposed "obedience" to "white, liberal doctrines" (nonviolence) and embrace black nationalism. XXXX has the necessary charisma to be a real threat in this way.

3. Prevent violence on the part of black nationalist groups. This is of primary importance, and is, of course, a goal of our investigative activity; it should also be a goal of the Counterintelligence Program. Through counterintelligence it should be possible to pinpoint potential troublemakers and neutralize them before they exercise their potential for violence.

4. Prevent militant black nationalist groups and leaders from gaining respectability, by discrediting them to three separate segments of the community. The goal of discrediting black nationalists must be handled tactically in three ways. You must discredit these groups and individuals to, first, the responsible Negro community. Second, they must be discredited to the white community, both the responsible community and to "liberals" who have vestiges of sympathy for militant black nationalists simply because they are Negroes. Third, these groups must be discredited in the eyes of Negro radicals, the followers of the movement. This last area requires entirely different tactics than the first two. Publicity about violent tendencies and radical statements merely enhances black nationalists to the last group; it adds "respectability" in a different way.

5. A final goal should be to prevent the long-range growth of militant black nationalist organizations, especially among youth. Specific tactics to prevent these groups from converting young people must be developed.

Source: "FBI Memo," in *The Assassination of Malcolm X*, edited by Malik Miah (New York: Pathfinder Press, 1976), 182–85.

Intolerance toward Santería

Santería emerged as a new religion during the time of slavery in the Caribbean. Forced to convert to Christianity, slaves preserved elements of their traditional Yoruba beliefs by combining them with components of Catholicism. Practitioners believed in a high God, as well as number of intermediary deities or spirits called orishas. To maintain their bonds with these traditional Yoruba spirits, slaves associated them with Catholic Saints. For example, they equated the orisha Shango, linked to the natural powers of thunder and lightning, to Saint Barbara, while they likened Oggun, a spirit of war, to Saint Peter. Maintaining good relations with the orishas, through animal sacrifice and spirit possession, constitutes a vital part of Santería worship. Since Fidel Castro gained control of Cuba in 1959, the increasing Cuban refugee population has introduced Santería into the American religious landscape. As with other NRMs, Santería's reception has been less than hospitable. The documents below chronicle the persistent legal battles that have ensued over animal sacrifice, a practice essential to the Santería faith.

City Ordinances

In the late 1980s, the city of Hialeah, Florida, passed a series of ordinances to prohibit animal sacrifice. Though ostensibly meant only to address concerns that the practice endangered the public safety, exhibited animal cruelty, and potentially traumatized children who might witness the event or its aftermath, these ordinances were undoubtedly written with certain religious repercussions in mind. Local Santería practitioners were understandably upset and pursued legal action on the grounds that the Hialeah ordinances violated the free exercise clause of the Constitution. In 1992, *Church of Lukumi Babalu Aye v. Hialeah* was argued before the Supreme Court, and in 1993, the Supreme Court ruled in favor of the church. The court deemed the ordinances unconstitutional, stating that they specifically targeted a religious practice and thereby violated the precedent of "general applicability" (at this time, as long as a law applies generally to the entire population and does not target one specific religion it is deemed constitutional). As you read the ordinance below, which was the fourth in a series of six passed in 1987, analyze how it defines and restricts animal sacrifice. Also, consider how the ordinance attempts to circumvent the free exercise clause. Why would this religious practice be so feared?

City of Hialeah, Florida, Ordinance 87–52, adopted September 8, 1987, provides:

WHEREAS, the residents and citizens of the City of Hialeah, Florida, have expressed great concern regarding the possibility of public ritualistic animal sacrifices within the City of Hialeah, Florida; and

WHEREAS, the City of Hialeah, Florida, has received an opinion from the Attorney General of the State of Florida, concluding that public ritualistic animal sacrifice, other than for the primary purpose of food consumption, is a violation of state law; and

WHEREAS, the City of Hialeah, Florida, has enacted an ordinance (Ordinance No. 87–40), mirroring the state law prohibiting cruelty to animals.

WHEREAS, the City of Hialeah, Florida, now wishes to specifically prohibit the possession of animals for slaughter or sacrifice within the City of Hialeah, Florida.

NOW, THEREFORE, BE IT ORDAINED BY THE MAYOR AND CITY COUNCIL OF THE CITY OF HIALEAH, FLORIDA, that:

Section 1. Chapter 6 of the Code of Ordinances of the City of Hialeah, Florida, is hereby amended by adding thereto two (2) new Sections 6–8 'Definitions' and 6–9 'Prohibition Against Possession Of Animals For Slaughter Or Sacrifice,' which is to read as follows:

Section 6–8. Definitions

1. Animal—any living dumb creature.

2. Sacrifice—to unnecessarily kill, torment, torture, or mutilate an animal in a public or private ritual or ceremony not for the primary purpose of food consumption.

3. Slaughter—the killing of animals for food.

Section 6–9. Prohibition Against Possession of Animals for Slaughter Or Sacrifice.

1. No person shall own, keep or otherwise possess, sacrifice, or slaughter any sheep, goat, pig, cow or the young of such species, poultry, rabbit, dog, cat, or any other animal, intending to use such animal for food purposes.

2. This section is applicable to any group or individual that kills, slaughters or sacrifices animals for any type of ritual, regardless of whether or not the flesh or blood of the animal is to be consumed.

3. Nothing in this ordinance is to be interpreted as prohibiting any licensed establishment from slaughtering for food purposes any animals which are specifically raised for food purposes where such activity is properly zoned and/or permitted under state and local law and under rules promulgated by the Florida Department of Agriculture.

Source: "Hialeah Resolutions and Ordinances," Santería Web: The Supreme Court Ruling, ⟨http://userwww.sfsu.edu/~biella/santeria/doc1.html#87-40⟩ (accessed August 17, 2007).

The Barbarians Are Coming!

While the city of Hialeah at least attempted to disguise its bias against Santería, the following editorial makes no such effort. It reveals, albeit in an extreme way, how the concepts of "religion" and "America" played a central role in the controversy. In this text, Samuel Francis (1947–2005), an arch-conservative, nationally syndicated columnist, preaches a jeremiad, a lament for a lost America. In the document below, consider how Francis defines the Founding Fathers' intent regarding religious tolerance and the free exercise of religion. What, according to Francis, is the Hialeah case really about? What are the implications of his position?

The Church of Lukumi Babalu Aye is not your average pack of elderly Judaeo-Christian bingo-players. Based in Southern Florida, it's an organ of the Afro-Caribbean cult of Santeria, a polytheistic religion that propitiates its deities by the blood sacrifice of live animals. Santeria is one of the contributions to American culture made by recent immigrants from Cuba and points south, and when the good burghers of Hialeah got wind of it, they passed a law forbidding the killing of animals in religious rituals.

That was in 1987, and, since the adorants of Babalu assimilated to American customs quickly, they took the city to court. Indeed, after five years of court, they're still there. Federal judges have upheld the constitutionality of the Hialeah law repeatedly, and now the plaintiffs are going for the big one in front of the Nameless Nine who are as close to being gods as our political system allows.

The Babalu people claim that the law discriminates against their religion and violates the First Amendment, and some Christians agree. The latter argue that if the city can outlaw animal sacrifice, it and other cities can also forbid religious customs that are a bit more mainstream.

Lawyers for the Santeria cult say that "Hialeah has not interfered with the sale of lobsters to be boiled alive, and the record does not show that it has interfered with the practice of feeding live rats to pet snakes. . . . Religion is almost the only unacceptable reason for killing an animal in Florida." The city itself defends the law on the grounds that animal sacrifice might be unsanitary and cause health problems, that witnessing sacrifices could be disturbing to children and that the practice is cruel to animals. If those are the best reasons the city fathers can come up with, maybe they need the intercession of Babalu more than they think.

The real interest of the case has little to do with public health or disturbing kids, which are merely the excuses a decomposing culture finds convenient when it has forgotten how to defend itself. The case is important because it brings us at last to the very edge of constitutional government, suggesting that there may be some rough beasts lurking around in this country to which constitutional laws and procedures are not applicable.

If the rights and rules of the U.S. Constitution are anything, they are Western in their origin and meaning, and they presuppose a Western society reasonably unified in religious, moral, social and political norms. When the Framers drafted the language of the First Amendment and embraced the ideal of religious toleration, they were thinking mainly about Western religious conflicts that had all but burned themselves out.

They rightly saw no reason why various Protestant sects, Catholics and Jews couldn't practice their religions freely without having to kill each other or why the federal government had to endorse or ban one or the other. Whatever else the Framers believed about religion and the free exercise thereof, it is probably safe to say that they never had to think at all about Babalu or similar grim little gods who can be appeased only by spilling blood.

The citizens of Hialeah do have to think about it, and they decided that Babalu is a god up with which they will not put. In banning animal sacrifice, they publicly but tacitly affirmed their allegiance to Western norms, rejecting the ritual killing of animals as primitive, barbaric and cruel superstition. They rightly drew a distinction between, on the one hand, boiling a lobster or taking the Eucharist and, on the other, beheading a goat to ease your rheumatism.

The distinction, of course, escapes the lawyers for the cult, but then they're paid not to bring it up. What is more worrisome is that it also escapes the city of Hialeah itself and may not occur even to the Supreme Court. Hialeah still instinctively understands the distinction, but it or its own lawyers can't or won't articulate it.

When a culture and its leaders have forgotten how to distinguish between its own norms and those of barbarians and falls for the delusion that it can permit barbarians alien to its norms to enjoy the same protections the culture and its members respect, it has a problem. How the Supreme Court in its ineffable wisdom will resolve it only Babalu knows.

Source: Samuel Francis, "Blood Rites and Rights," *Washington Times*, March 31, 1992, F1.

From Florida to Texas: From Chickens to Goats

It would not be unreasonable to think that the 1992 Supreme Court ruling in favor of Santería practitioners' rights settled the animal sacrifice issue. However, such thoughts would be wrong. In 2007, the issue of Santería and animal sacrifice again came to the fore. In the newspaper account below, Michael Grabell chronicles the ongoing battle over this religious practice in Euless, Texas, a city located between Dallas and Fort Worth. As you read, consider how the city of Euless is attempting to use the legal precedent of "general applicability" to limit the rights of Santería members. How does the city define its "public interest"? And how would you interpret the city's "settlement offer"?

A Santería priest who is suing Euless over his religious practice of animal sacrifice would be allowed to kill chickens and hold small weekly gatherings at his home under a settlement offered by city attorneys. But the proposal would continue to prohibit the sacrifice of goats—a practice that Jose Merced says is as essential to Santería as communion is to Catholics. And it would limit the gatherings to 25 people. Mr. Merced said he will reject the city's offer as a restriction on his religious freedom. "You cannot do initiations without an animal with four legs. You cannot do it with just chickens," he said. "Without that, the religion ceases to exist." . . .

Mr. Merced filed a federal discrimination lawsuit against Euless in December after police and permit officials told him he couldn't kill goats for a ceremony initiating new members. Followers of the African-Caribbean religion believe that the energy contained in blood from animal sacrifice opens a channel of direct communication with the spirits, known as orishas.

In January, the city asked the judge to dismiss the lawsuit, saying that the city's slaughter ban applies to everybody and that making an exception for Mr. Merced would force the city to become entangled in religion. The case could call into question a federal land-use law that requires local governments to have a compelling public interest before enforcing an ordinance that could limit the practice of religion. Euless attorneys have argued that the land-use law is unconstitutional because it intrudes on a local government's right to regulate the health and welfare of its residents.

But Mr. Merced and his supporters say that the U.S. Supreme Court has already settled the issue of Santería animal sacrifice. In 1993, the court struck down an ordinance adopted by Hialeah, Florida, which prohibited animal sacrifice but made exceptions for hunting, fishing and the euthanasia of pets. Euless' ordinance, on the books since 1974, makes exceptions for the killing of chickens and turkeys for meals. The city also allows fishing and euthanasia of pets.

Euless' settlement offer would allow Mr. Merced to hold gatherings at his house. But they must not be visible to the general public, include more than 25 people or occur more than five times a month. The city said in a letter that the restrictions would comply with ordinances regulating assemblies in residential neighborhoods. Mr. Merced called the offer "ignorant" saying he doesn't hold regular gatherings. When he does have a gathering, he usually has about 15 people, he said, though once he hosted 200 people for a drum-playing ceremony for the orishas. "They probably think I'm holding Masses or church every Sunday," he said. "They just don't understand."

Source: Michael Grabell, "Euless Offers Settlement in Santeria Case," *Dallas Morning News*, March 21, 2007, B7.

CHAPTER EIGHT

The Branch Davidians and Waco

The Culmination of Religious Intolerance

April 19, 1993, Mount Carmel, Texas. By late afternoon on this day, ten miles outside Waco, Texas, the standoff between the Branch Davidians and the federal government was over. After fifty-one days, the FBI, convinced that negotiations had reached an impasse, ended the siege. In the aftermath, David Koresh and over seventy of his followers (men, women, and children) were dead from the fire that engulfed their home. Only nine Branch Davidians escaped. They later testified that the fires, which began in three separate locations and eventually overtook the entire structure, occurred when FBI tanks knocked over lanterns inside the building. In contrast, the FBI maintains that Koresh and his followers set the fires as part of their desire to commit mass suicide; while still others charge the government with murder (a charge that gained currency in 1999, when the FBI revealed that it had covered up its use of incendiary devices on April 19). These three versions of the final events—manslaughter, mass suicide, or murder—provide us with the dominant interpretive perspectives on Waco.[1]

Some view it as a government debacle, a poorly handled incident with disastrous results, but they find no evidence of government ill intent. Others see it as the typical outcome of a crazy "cult." They blame "unstable" and "criminal" "cult" leaders like Koresh, who take advantage of malleable adherents and lead them to their doom. While still others interpret events through the lens of conspiracy, claiming that Koresh and his followers became victims of the U.S. government's quest to curtail individual rights and consolidate its power. These perspectives reveal how, as scholar Catherine Wessinger writes, "every act of violence in the Branch Davidian case is disputed."[2]

Upon learning about these controversial events and divergent interpretations, one inevitably asks at least two questions. What really happened at Waco? And why? As it occurred less than twenty years ago—a relatively recent event in terms of American and world history—one would think that these questions would be easy to answer. Unlike research into the distant past, which is often plagued by a lack of sources and the challenge of entering a different historical-cultural world, the events at Waco occurred not so very long ago in a technological and cultural era aware of the importance of historical documents combined with the ability to preserve them. In 1993, we had computers, video cameras, twenty-four-hour news channels, a federal government sworn to uphold the First Amendment, and access to an ever-widening reservoir of knowledge. How is it, then, that the evidence from Waco continues to defy definitive interpretation? Why does this event continue to elude authoritative answers? How could events that occurred within our lifetime be shrouded in such mystery and steeped in such controversy?

This is the challenge of studying Waco. Despite its recent occurrence, evidence is missing, the interpretation of existing evidence is disputed, and people involved in the actual events tell vastly different tales. As a result, we as scholars are left adrift trying to navigate our way through the various droughts and floods of information, as well as the competing tides and currents of interpretation. Do a search about Waco on the Web and you will quickly be immersed in the flood—antigovernment conspiracy theories, Waco memorial sites, and anti–David Koresh propaganda. The sheer volume of information and competing perspectives can easily overwhelm, while the inability to determine whose information to trust frustrates. Studying Waco is not a task for the easily discouraged. Given these difficulties, this chapter provides you with insight into the turbulent waters that characterize these events. We may not be able to answer definitively the question of who shot first or who started the fires, but by placing Waco within the history of religious intolerance in the United States we can better understand why this deadly conflict occurred.

Where, then, do we begin? We could start our study at the end of the confrontation, as described in the first paragraph, but given the deadly results and conflicting interpretations, perhaps we need to begin by examining Branch Davidian history. Los Angeles, California, 1929. In this year, Victor T. Houteff, a devout Seventh-day Adventist, began a reform movement within his denomination. Calling for increased purity and morality, Houteff indicted his denomination's "worldliness" and called for a return to its roots. He saw himself as an Adventist prophet, like previous denominational leaders, to whom God had granted new insight into the Christian message. The Seventh-day Adventists rejected his teachings, which led Houteff to establish his own group, the Shepherd's Rod (incorporated as the Davidian Seventh-Day Adventists in 1942 and later, under the leadership of Ben Roden, known as the Branch Davidians). In the 1930s, Houteff began gathering his elect community of followers at Mount Carmel. Seeing himself as a "true" Adventist, Houteff adhered to basic tenets of the denomination (Saturday Sabbath, vegetarianism, a belief in Christ's imminent return, and pacifism); however, he also recovered elements from the denomination's earlier history. Notably, Houteff promoted belief in continuing revelation through a prophet (himself), and throughout his career he shared his prophetic messages. Houteff viewed his work as helping to usher in the Kingdom of God, and David Koresh came to see himself as the heir of this prophetic ministry and theological tradition. Like Houteff and the movement's subsequent leaders, Koresh viewed himself as a prophet, believed the second coming was imminent, and gained adherents through his ability to interpret scripture. Houteff and Koresh both believed the world stood on the edge of a cataclysmic event.

Perhaps, then, we need to begin our study with Vernon Howell. Mount Carmel, Texas, 1981. In this year, Vernon Howell, excommunicated from a local Seventh-day Adventist congregation for his disruptive teachings and seeking to grow in his faith, joined the community of Branch Davidians, then under the leadership of an aging Lois Roden. A handyman, musician, mechanic, and high school drop-out, Vernon Howell showed an aptitude for memorizing and interpreting scripture. In a short period of time, this gift helped him rise to prominence within the movement as he became a "consort" of Lois Roden and her eventual successor. Increasingly Howell was seen, by himself and others, as imbued with the prophetic gifts that historically characterized earlier Davidian and Adventist leadership. Howell's use of the "old" doctrine of continuing revelation allowed him, like his predecessors, to introduce "new light" into the community. Many of these new teachings were embodied in his legal name change to David Koresh in 1990. Claiming the names of God's favored King David, as well as that of King Cyrus (*Koresh* means *Cyrus* in Hebrew), David Koresh envisioned himself as a messianic figure, in the technical sense of one anointed by God to carry out a specific purpose. He would be a prophetic and messianic deliverer of the elect and help to usher in the Kingdom of God. Koresh believed that the righteous remnant at Mount Carmel would be vitally important in the upcoming final battle between good and evil and the subsequent establishment of the Kingdom. Koresh also believed that his biological children would rule God's coming Kingdom. Toward this end, he "married" several of the young women in the community (many under the legal age of consent), and, in 1989, began teaching that his male followers should espouse celibacy while he had sexual access to the community's married women. While many accepted Koresh's "new light," others left the group and voiced their disapproval through the anticult movement (ACM). Their claims of statutory rape, along with allegations of child abuse, mass suicide, and a large arsenal of weapons, put Koresh on a collision course with the United States government.

Perhaps, then, we should begin our study with the initial Bureau of Alcohol, Tobacco, and Firearms (BATF or ATF) raid. February 28, 1993, Mount Carmel, Texas. On this day, after months of investigating Koresh for weapons violations including converting semiautomatic weapons into automatic weapons without filing the proper paperwork, the ATF initiated operation "Showtime." Seventy-six ATF agents loaded in cattle cars approached Mount Carmel to arrest David Koresh and search the property. Having prepared for a dynamic entry raid, "despite the fact that the search warrant did not authorize a 'no-knock' surprise raid,"[3] the agents soon found themselves in a fire fight. Koresh and his followers, tipped off by the presence of the media, knew the ATF was on its way. Undercover ATF agent Robert Rodriguez testified that ATF commanders were aware that the element of surprise had been lost but persisted with the operation. In the aftermath of the battle, four ATF agents and five Branch Davidians were dead, while twenty ATF agents and four Branch Davidians, including Koresh, were wounded. In trying to ascertain who fired first, survivors from each group blame the other. Evidence is missing, and we are left with more questions than answers.

Perhaps, then, we should begin at an altogether different place—by revisiting the historical relationship between mainstream religions and new religious movements. Religions—"old" and "new," "familiar" and "strange," "normative" and "deviant"—have been at odds with each other throughout the history of the United States. As seen in previous chapters, religions that deviate from the perceived religious norm, whether Mormons or Catholics, Wiccans or Moonies, face myriad intolerant actions that range from seemingly innocuous stereotypes to deadly pipe bombs, from protracted zoning disputes to sensationalist media coverage. The "cult" stereotype, with all its negative components, produces real consequences in the world, and in the twentieth century those consequences increasingly involved state and federal governments. From court rooms to local laws to government agencies, the last century witnessed the increasing involvement of these forms of government in and over religious life. At times this has resulted in greater religious

Many of his followers are former Seventh-day Adventists. The Seventh-day Adventist Church strongly denies any connection with Howell's group. Howell's followers have come to 77 acres near the Elk community from Australia, New Zealand, Canada, England, Hawaii and throughout the continental United States. The end of the world is near, they believe. Howell, 33, is their salvation.

They pay dearly for those beliefs, say former Branch Davidians like Marc Breault, a one-time confidant of Howell's. An eight-month *Tribune-Herald* investigation that involved numerous interviews with Breault and more than 20 other former cult members and a review of court records and statements to law enforcement officials revealed complaints that Howell:

—abused children physically and psychologically.

—boasted of having sex with underage girls in the cult.

—claimed the divine right to take every man's wife.

—and has had at least 15 so-called "wives."

Authorities have not acted on the complaints. For various reasons. Some officials said former cult members making the allegations have not appeared in person to swear out a complaint against Howell, though they have mailed sworn statements to local, state, and federal authorities. Other officials said they needed evidence, not allegations.

Source: Mark England and Darlene McCormick, "The Sinful Messiah: Part One," *Waco Tribune-Herald*, February 27, 1993, 1A.

"Cult Experts"

Relying on the allegations and explanations of the ACM, the excerpt below from "The Sinful Messiah" series invokes the familiar charge of brainwashing. It discounts the validity of members' devotion and relegates it to delusion. In making this claim, the *Waco Tribune-Herald* not only considered ex-members to be reliable sources but also uncritically accepted the "expertise" of active deprogrammers and ACM organizations. Rick Ross, who has no educational training in psychology or religion, is a well-known deprogrammer. According to Ross's website, his "Institute" is "devoted to the study of destructive cults, controversial groups and movements."[6] In addition to Ross, from the 1970s until the mid-1990s, the Cult Awareness Network (CAN) stood at the forefront of the ACM. As you read the excerpt below, consider how the *Waco Tribune-Herald* relies on these "experts" and the "cult" stereotype to indict Koresh and his movement.

The Gospel According to Vernon Howell is a dangerous, volatile swerve out of the mainstream, say two cult experts who have talked to some of Howell's former followers. They say Howell's brand of religion constitutes a cult and that Howell controls the minds of his followers. "The group is without a doubt, without any doubt whatsoever, a highly destructive, manipulative cult," said Rick Ross, a cult deprogrammer who works in Phoenix, Ariz. "Vernon Howell is the absolute authoritarian leader of this cult. He controls everything and everyone in that compound, period."

Although he is not a mental health professional, Ross has developed an educational curriculum on the subject of cults and serves on a nationwide committee on cults and missionaries for the Union of American Hebrew Congregations in New York. He has been involved in more than 200 destructive cult cases, including the deprogramming of one of Howell's former followers, Ross said. Ross compares Mount Carmel, the Branch Davidians' base 10 miles east of Waco, to Jonestown, a settlement of American cultists in South America's Guyana led by the Rev. Jim Jones. On Nov. 18, 1978, more than 900 people there killed themselves by drinking cyanide or were murdered. Ross said, "I would liken the group to Jim Jones . . . from the standpoint that it's in a compound; it's isolated; it's extremely totalitarian. . . . "

Priscilla Coates, a 10-year Cult Awareness Network volunteer based at the organization's Glendale, Calif. Office also said Howell's group is "unsafe or destructive." The Cult Awareness Network is a non-profit group with chapters in 21 states that addresses the issue of cults. Coates was national director of the group when it was known as Citizens Freedom Foundation Cult Awareness Network.

Both Ross and Coates said they talked with two people who left the Branch Davidians. The two cult experts said they believe Howell practices mind control. Ross says Howell breaks down cult members to where they have little or no sense of self-worth or individuality. They are conditioned to be passive and obedient. Mind control comes from isolation, control of the environment and setting up doctrines that override an individual's needs, Ross said. He said Howell twists people's belief in God into a commitment to him. Ross said most people at Mount Carmel probably would not say they are committed to Howell as their absolute leader. They probably would say they are committed to God. Their commitment to Howell, in their minds, is synonymous to their commitment to God, he said.

Source: Darlene McCormick and Mark England, "Experts: Branch Davidians Dangerous, Destructive Cult," *Waco Tribune-Herald*, March 1, 1993, 7A.

"Charismatic Leader with a Pathological Edge"

Throughout the siege, the media, ACM, and government feared a repeat of what occurred on November 18, 1978, in Jonestown, Guyana. On this day, Jim Jones and his followers, a religious group known as the People's Temple, committed "revolutionary suicide." Nine hundred and eighteen men, women, and children died, many perhaps hoping in the process to define their lives and deaths on their own terms and to protest their continued harassment and persecution at the hands of the ACM and the United States government.[7] For the American public, media, and government, the Jonestown suicides epitomized the danger of "cults" and became the lens through which subsequent "cults" were interpreted. In fact, *Time*'s coverage of both Jonestown and Waco featured articles with the same exact title—"Cult of Death." Despite lack of evidence for the two group's similarities, the threat of mass suicide continued to influence the planning and interpretation of events at Waco. The articles excerpted below reveal the extent of this uncritical comparison and the continued construction of the Branch Davidians as a "dangerous cult."

> Equipped with both a creamy charm and a cold-blooded willingness to manipulate those drawn to him, Koresh was a type well known to students of cult practices: The charismatic leader with a pathological edge. He was the most spectacular example since Jim Jones, who committed suicide in 1978 with more than 900 of his followers at the People's Temple in Guyana. Like Jones, Koresh fashioned a tight-knit community that saw itself at desperate odds with the world outside. He plucked sexual partners as he pleased from among his followers and formed an elite guard of lieutenants to enforce his will. And like Jones, he led his followers to their doom.
>
> *Source:* Richard Lacayo, "In the Grip of a Psychopath," *Time*, May 3, 1993, 34.

> The cults to worry about, according to Rick Ross, an expert who advised the FBI during the confrontation in Waco, can be identified by the character of their leadership. The Branch Davidians, he says, were "totally dependent" on Koresh, who, like Jim Jones in Guyana, systematically brainwashed his followers and cut them off psychologically from the outside world.
>
> *Source:* Melinda Liu and Todd Barrett, "Hard Lessons in the Ashes," *Newsweek*, May 3, 1993, 31.

The ACM–U.S. Government Alliance

The depiction of the Branch Davidians as a dangerous "cult" continued throughout the fifty-one day siege. This repeated portrayal, led by the media and ACM, incited the public against the Branch Davidians. Numerous letters to the FBI called for action against the Branch Davidians and a restoration of government control. Scholar James Beckford writes, "If the mass media portrayals of NRMs, based mainly on the one-sided evidence supplied by activists in the ACM, are sufficiently numerous and disturbing, there is a strong probability that social control agents will have to be seen to respond."[8] Given the increasing involvement of the government in adjudicating religion and NRM cases throughout the twentieth century, its initial investigation of the Branch Davidians perhaps makes sense. However, the federal government's uncritical reliance on "cult experts" and anticultist propaganda remains disturbing. The documents below examine how the ATF and the FBI became allies of the ACM against David Koresh and the Branch Davidians—an alliance with deadly consequences.

"I'm Not Ready to Die"

In the years preceding the 1993 events at Waco, ex-member Marc Breault began his crusade against Koresh. Once a devoted Branch Davidian, Breault became an active anticultist and urged a government investigation of his former religious group. Despite having left the group in 1989, Breault claimed to have thorough knowledge of life at Mount Carmel and the plans of David Koresh. Interpreting the Branch Davidians through the lens of the People's Temple, Breault alleged that the group planned to commit mass suicide. To gain support for his cause and his claims, Breault took his story to the news media, as well as to the FBI. The excerpts below, from an April 1992 edition of the *Waco Tribune-Herald* and from 1992 FBI files, reveal how the ACM began its harassment of the Branch Davidians well before the eight-month ATF investigation and February 1993 raid.

> The leader of a religious group in Elk scoffed Friday at a rumor that he and his followers plan to commit suicide this weekend. David Koresh, who used to go by the name Vernon Wayne Howell, said the Branch Davidian Seventh-day Adventists have merely gathered at their 77 acre site 12 miles outside Waco to observe Passover, the Jewish holiday that commemorates the deliverance of the ancient Hebrews from slavery in Egypt.

He called the rumor "hogwash." "Hey, I'm not ready to die," Koresh said. " . . . It's all lies. Every year we've gathered here for Passover. Every year." "Look, the place is being built up. We're spending lots of money. A lot of people are putting time and effort in," he said. "When we got this place back from George (Roden) it was terrible. So we've been working three years out in California and other places to raise money to get this place back on its feet. "I've got the water well man coming in. I mean. . . . Two weeks in a row, we're supposed to be committing suicide. I wish they'd get their stories straight." . . .

Koresh said that's a rumor started by a former Australian member [Marc Breault] to smear the Branch Davidians. . . . Perry Jones, a long time Branch Davidian, said the rumor exasperated him. "It's not only insulting, but it's ludicrous," Jones said.

Source: Mark England, "Religious Group Denies Mass Suicide Rumor," Waco Tribune-Herald, April 18, 1992, 1C.

Date of Incident and Date of Complaint: 6/23/92

Synopsis of case: Vernon Howell, aka David Koresh, may have been planning a mass suicide for the members of his religious sect, "Branch Davidian Seventh Day Adventist." Allegations were also made against Howell of holding people against their will, which may constitute violations of the Federal laws pertaining to involuntary servitude and slavery.

Subsequent FBI Report 7/23/92

*** charge of the investigation conducted on a religious sect in Waco, Texas known as the "Branch Davidian, Seventh Day Adventist." An individual by the name of VERNON HOWELL, also known as DAVID KORESH, is the leader of the organization. Allegations had been made in the past by several ex-members that HOWELL was planning a mass murder/suicide event. Allegations were also made towards Howell that he was holding several members of the sect under conditions which may constitute violations of Federal law pertaining to involuntary servitude and slavery.

The CPS [Child Protective Services] was brought into the religious sect due to allegations from ex-members of child neglect and abuse. ***, as well as two other investigators, *** and ***, were involved in the investigation. Interviews were conducted with several members of the organization, children as well as adults, and also HOWELL himself. Those members interviewed indicated to the CPS that all individuals on the premises were staying with the religious sect on their own accord.

Through observation and interview on both announced and unannounced visits, the Department of Human Services (DHS), CPS had no indication that any children or adults were being held against their will by HOWELL. Investigation on 7/7/92 at Waco, Texas

Source: Federal Bureau of Investigation, "David Koresh: Part 1," ⟨http://foia.fbi.gov/foiaindex/davidkoresh.htm⟩ (accessed December 2, 2008).

"We Need More Information"

In 1992, much to the delight of anticultists, the ATF began to investigate David Koresh and his community for weapons violations, namely converting semiautomatic weapons into automatics without filing proper paperwork. The group bought and sold weapons to earn money, but they also increasingly saw themselves as playing a pivotal and perhaps active role in the coming final battle between good and evil. The group's gun inventory only increased anticultists' fears and fueled their actions. Below are two documents that demonstrate the ATF's reliance on anticultists as they investigated the Branch Davidians. The first is Marc Breault's description of a December 1992 conversation with the ATF, while the second indicts the ATF's dealings with "experts."

Special Agent Derek Anderson got straight to the point: "We need your help. I've read everything you've written. I've been working on this case for months and I've found all the stuff you've put together on David Koresh. We're impressed and we need more information." . . .

The ATF knew Koresh was dangerous. They knew he should have been behind bars. They were amazed that nothing had been done for years. But they needed to convince a federal judge that Koresh had illegal firearms. They needed a search warrant. . . .

One phone call to Koresh would blow the whole investigation. The last thing the ATF wanted was to alert Vernon. So they had to be extremely selective in whom they confided. They basically trusted David, Debbie and Robyn Bunds, along with Elizabeth and me. Later, the Jewells would be included. We were asked to tell no one of these proceedings. It was a request we honored. Lives were at stake.

So gathering evidence would be difficult. The ATF, however, had another problem. Once they obtained warrants to conduct raids, how were they to proceed? The Branch Davidians were not an ordinary group of criminals. They were religious zealots who would think nothing of dying for their leader. In many respects, they were like terrorists.

The ATF required psychological profiles on everyone. They needed to know who was with Koresh, who his most trusted people were, where they were, and how much military training they had. They needed to know everything about the man who called himself the Messiah. Using our computer, Elizabeth and I spent scores of hours compiling a comprehensive database on the cult. We had to glean information from people without letting them know we were working with the ATF. From Australia, we tapped into huge databases in America that contained property and phone numbers of every person listed in every phone book of the United States. We tapped into other resources as well to find information. We even had to spy on some of our best friends, and that was really painful. But it just had to be done.

Source: Marc Breault and Martin King, *Inside the Cult: A Member's Chilling, Exclusive Account of Madness and Depravity in David Koresh's Compound* (New York: Signet, 1993), 295–98. Reprinted with the permission of Penguin Group (Australia).

In the months that led up to the February 28 attempted "dynamic entry" at the Branch Davidian compound, the Bureau of Alcohol, Tobacco, and Firearms (BATF) apparently failed to solicit any social science background information about the nature of the group with which they were dealing. BATF has no internal behavioral science division and did not consult with any other behavioral science persons within the government. Nor did they consult with outside persons in religious studies, sociology of religion, or psychology of religion. There were, for instance, persons in the Baylor University Department of Religion who had studied this particular group for much of its history; they were not consulted. Investigators reviewing the Waco incident have repeatedly told us that BATF simply did not consult with anyone who might be considered an "expert" on this group or groups like it.

In their attempt to build a case against the Branch Davidians, BATF did interview persons who were former members of the group and at least one person who had "deprogrammed" a group member. Mr. Rick Ross, who often works in conjunction with the Cult Awareness Network (CAN), has been quoted as saying that he was "consulted" by the BATF. My suspicion is that he was merely one among many the BATF interviewed in its background checks on the group and on Koresh. However, it is unclear how information gained from him was evaluated. The Network and Mr. Ross have a direct ideological (and financial) interest in arousing suspicion and antagonism against what they call "cults." These same persons seem to have been major sources for the series of stories run by the Waco newspaper, beginning February 27. It seems clear that people within the "anti-cult" community had targeted the Branch Davidians for attention.

Although these people often call themselves "cult experts," they are certainly not recognized as such by the academic community. The activities of the CAN are seen by the National Council of Churches (among others) as a danger to religious liberty, and deprogramming tactics have been increasingly found to fall outside the law. At the very least, Mr. Ross and any ex-members he was associated with should have been seen as questionable sources of information. Having no access to information from the larger social science community, however, BATF had no way to put in perspective what they may have heard from angry ex-members and eager deprogrammers.

Source: Nancy T. Ammerman, "Report to the Justice and Treasury Departments," in *Recommendations of Experts for Improvements in Federal Law Enforcement after Waco* (Washington, D.C.: U.S. Department of Justice, 1993), 1.

The Ghost of Jonestown and the ATF

Unlike the People's Temple, which had developed a theological rationale and a ritual practice for "revolutionary suicide," the Branch Davidians had no such belief or practice. Nevertheless, the ATF relied on the "cult" stereotype and believed that the Branch Davidians, like the People's Temple, would commit mass suicide. Haunted by the events of Jonestown, the document below demonstrates how the ATF planned their raid with this anticult scenario in mind. As a result, they created the conditions for the very actions they hoped to prevent.

A high-level ATF source said law enforcement officials had ruled out ringing the compound from a distance in favor of the direct assault that resulted in the four deaths and many wounded. "The difficulty in this operation is that the group posed a threat not only to the community but also to themselves," the ATF official said, adding that if agents set up a good distance from the facility, Howell's followers might kill themselves, as happened in the 1978 Jonestown massacre in the tiny South American nation of Guyana. Nearly 1,000 followers of the Rev. Jim Jones died after drinking poison or were murdered by fellow adherents. The mass suicide occurred after a group investigating Jonestown led by Rep. Leo Ryan (D-Calif.) was attacked by some of Jones's lieutenants. Several, including Ryan, were killed.

About a half an hour into the morning firefight, agents were able to establish contact with the cult leaders and negotiated the cease-fire.

Source: Joan Biskupic and Pierre G. Thomas, "4 Agents Killed, 16 Hurt in Raid on Cult; Standoff Ensues at Texas Site," *Washington Post*, March 1, 1993, A01. © March 1, 1993 The

The ACM and the ATF

As we saw in the last chapter, government agents abusing their power represents one way intolerance toward NRMs is enacted. This abuse occurs at both the organizational and individual levels. For example, not only did the ATF as an organization choose to side with the cultural opponents of the Branch Davidians, ATF agents also believed anticult propaganda. These beliefs, in turn, informed both the agency's and agents' reactions to and interpretations of the Branch Davidians. As you read, consider the consequences of this ACM/ATF alliance.

Not religion but a con-man. Several agents expressed the view that David Koresh did not believe the religious ideas he preached to others. His followers, being psychologically vulnerable, were conned by his strong personality. In several briefings agents expressed the view that, in their line of work, "religion was often only a cover"—a dodge or smoke-screen for paranoid behavior, criminal pathology, derangement, or self-interested non-religious pre-existing motivations. It is possible that a view like this is widely shared in the federal enforcement agencies and perhaps even by the public at large. Whether that be true or not, it is not clear what process of evaluation, as a matter of standard operating procedure, leads to this conclusion. That there be such a process of reflection in cases like Waco seems crucial. Whatever the process has been, it has not seemed to take seriously the role of religion in the first place. If that is the case, the process in Waco arrived at predictable results overdetermined by blind spots in the process itself. This view of religion being used as a cover for a con runs the risk of dismissing religion as an issue. In the Waco case, the dismissal seems accompanied by underestimations of the deep-seated religious motives of the leader and the followers and by a resultant inability, on the part of federal law enforcement, to anticipate religiously-motivated responses to their own interventions.

Source: Lawrence E. Sullivan, "Recommendations Concerning Incidents Such as the Branch Davidian Standoff in Waco, Texas," in *Recommendations of Experts for Improvements in Federal Law Enforcement after Waco* (Washington, D.C.: U.S. Department of Justice, 1993), 12.

Tarnished ATF

In addition to anticultist influences, other factors played a pivotal role in the ATF's actions against the Branch Davidians. In the 1980s and early 1990s, the ATF faced threats to its very existence. Presidents and politicians pushed for the ATF to be merged into other government agencies. In addition, in 1992, the ATF faced numerous allegations, including charges of racism and sexism. Some also deemed the ATF a "lawless" and "rogue" agency after its botched investigation of Christian Identity adherent Randy Weaver, which left his wife and young son dead. Throughout the fifty-one day negotiations, the Branch Davidians questioned the ATF's reputation and tactics as they maintained that the ATF fired first. The document below, by scholar James R. Lewis, examines how the "ATF Cowboys" responded to these pressures and allegations by acting against the Branch Davidians at Mount Carmel.

As reported in *U.S. News and World Report*, the prospect of overcoming this tarnished image probably "influenced the decision to proceed with the high-profile raid" of the Branch Davidian community outside of Waco, Texas.

It has also been suggested that ATF began searching for such a high-profile operation soon after it became apparent that Bill Clinton would become the next president of the United States. Clinton had been broadcasting a strong anti-gun agenda. The Waco attack, if this suggestion is correct, was designed to attract positive attention to the ATF in a highly publicized raid. The raid was apparently planned with an eye to the Senate Appropriations Subcommittee on Treasury, Postal Service, and General Government that was slated to meet in early March.

Another factor playing into the Branch Davidian fiasco was the ATF's well-deserved reputation for initiating dramatic raids on the basis of ill-founded rumors.

Source: James R. Lewis, "Showdown at the Waco Corral: ATF Cowboys Shoot Themselves in the Foot," in *From the Ashes: Making Sense of Waco*, edited by James R. Lewis (Lanham, Md.: Rowman & Littlefield, 1994), 87–88.

"Conduct a Raid, Not Make an Arrest"

The ATF's commitment to conduct a high-profile raid, rather than an arrest of David Koresh, was further substantiated during the 1995 government hearings on Waco. Testimony revealed that in July 1992, David Koresh, through gun dealer Henry McMann, invited the ATF to come out and inspect his firearm inventory. The ATF declined. As news of this missed opportunity emerged, politicians and the public alike tried to fathom why this had occurred. The document below, a transcript from the hearings, examines this troubling occurrence and the ATF's rationale.

Mr. Shadegg: What disturbs me, and what I want to ask you about—and I want each of you to individually answer—is: In later testimony we establish that Agent Aguilera gave that information to his supervisor. He told his supervisor that, yes, in this conversation Mr. Koresh had offered to allow Mr. Aguilera and his companion who was there with him, an accompanying agent, to go to the compound and to look at all the weapons present in the compound and inspect them and make whatever ascertations they need to make with regard to firearms violations. Agent Aguilera had declined it at the time.

What troubles me is that at no time between when that conversation occurred did anyone in the ATF ever go back to Mr. McMann and say, gee, can you call David Koresh and ask him if we now can come in and look at the weapons. They did not call Mr. Koresh themselves and say you once made an offer saying we could come in and look at the operations. They did absolutely nothing ever, right up until the point where they walk up to the front door with their guns, and conduct and carry out the dynamic entry which results in the tragic death of several agents and the deaths of some people on the inside, and later ultimately, leads to the deaths of everybody involved. They never once followed up on that offer, never even tried to follow up on that offer.

Mr. Sanders, let me ask you, do you believe that was proper? Can you imagine a circumstance under which you would not even attempt to make such an offer?

Mr. Sanders: I cannot imagine any circumstances that I would not take up such an offer. It indicates to me not, you know, a willingness to accept the terms of Koresh's when to go out there, but it indicates a mindset that perhaps it was nonwillful. Perhaps what the ATF thought were violations of the law were really things that Mr. Koresh thought were legal.

Mr. Shadegg: It suggests perhaps that what they really wanted to do was to conduct a raid, not make an arrest or conduct a search.

Source: *Activities of Federal Law Enforcement Agencies Toward the Branch Davidians (Part 1)*, 104th Cong., 1st sess., July 19, 20, 21, and 24, 1995, Serial No. 72 (Washington, D.C.: Government Printing Office, 1996), 330–31.

The "Cult" Chasm: Misunderstandings and Failed Negotiations

Thus far, the documents have demonstrated that prior to the siege at Waco the ATF aligned themselves with anticultists. They believed in the validity of the "cult" stereotype promoted by anticultists, and it influenced their tactical operations. However, this stereotype also influenced the subsequent interpretations of the FBI, who took over negotiations after the raid. And David Koresh and his second-in-command, Steve Schneider, knew it. As Koresh told an agent early in the negotiations, "Jim, listen, listen, Jim, there's nothing that hurts me more than being called a cult leader, all right? I spoke the truth but you don't know that." In this section, we examine how the "cult" stereotype created a chasm between the negotiators and the Branch Davidians. James Tabor and Eugene Gallagher write, "From those first moments of the raid through the entire fifty-one-day siege, Koresh's adamant conviction that 'theology really is life and death' defined his approach to the government agents. What the FBI viewed as a complex Hostage/Barricade rescue situation drawn directly from their Crisis Management Program strategy manual, Koresh and the Branch Davidians saw as the beginning of the end of the world. Although there was conversation back and forth between Mount Carmel and the government agents during the prolonged standoff, neither side proved willing or even capable of bridging the great gulf between those two very different understandings of the situation."[9] This chasm led to frequent misunderstandings, failed negotiations, and ultimately, the deaths of the Branch Davidians.

Suicide Allegations, Again

Despite lack of evidence and repeated denials, negotiators continued to fear the possibility of mass suicide. The specter of Jonestown not only influenced the ATF's tactics, but also the FBI's strategies. In the excerpt below from March 1, 1993, negotiator Henry Garcia voices this concern explicitly. As you read, attend to David Koresh's denial of this claim, but also his knowledge of this accusation's source. The next day, Koresh continued to affirm this position as he told negotiators, "There's no reason to die. Because like I say, the truth is to give life. It's not to give death." However, the FBI did not believe Koresh and continued to consider suicide a likely possibility.

Henry: No. Our concern is that you're not going to come out and that you might commit suicide.

David Koresh: Oh, look, if I wanted to commit suicide, I would have done it already. Now let me explain something.

Henry: Well—

David Koresh: We were accused three times this last year of going to commit suicide. Three times. The authorities were roused up by letters from Marc Breault and all that. Here we, here we've been digging lakes in the front, fixing this place up from a rat hill, hoping that one day we might have this place finished, to be able to present it true to all those who want to come. But at the same time, knowing that as long as there were people who would not look at the truth, we could not sit with idle expectation and think that we're always going to be able to, to have this freedom that we've enjoyed.

We've never gone outside our boundaries. We've done things that are legal. You know, always suspicion on every hand, you know, but the thing of it is is that if there is anything in question, we need to take it to the Bible. Christians are supposed to take it to the law and the testimony of God's scripture. Now, otherwise, we are commanded by scripture to abide by the laws of the land in every degree, as long as those laws don't 100 percent conflict with the law of God.

Source: "Waco/Branch Davidian Compound: Negotiation Transcripts," March 1, 1993, Freedom of Information Act, Federal Bureau of Investigation.

I'm Listening??

During negotiations, the "cult" stereotype fueled numerous misunderstandings between the negotiators and the Branch Davidians. The FBI refused to see Koresh as a legitimate and sincere religious leader. As a result, they failed to understand his theological rationales and his decision-making processes. The excerpt below, from the negotiation transcripts, occurred after Koresh and his followers had agreed to come out but then failed to do so because Koresh claimed God told him to wait. This portion of the transcript reveals the FBI's inability to fathom Koresh and highlights the different religio-cultural worlds inhabited by the two sides. They clearly articulated different sources of authority and, as Koresh states at the end of this excerpt, the FBI failed to listen.

David Koresh: And I mean, you're, you're doing your talking and I'm, I'm doing my talking. I'm a mediator and you're a mediator.

John Cox: Yeah, but the bottom line is who is it up to? Who is going to have to make the decision?

David Koresh: Well, God is.

John Cox: You are.

David Koresh: God is—

John Cox: No, you are.

David Koresh: —and you are. No, God is.

John Cox: Is that so?

David Koresh: Remember, remember, I—

John Cox: The bottom line is you're the one that's going to hear God, right?

David Koresh: Yes, I'm the one listening to God and you're the one listening to the law, your system.

John Cox: And I'm listening to you.

David Koresh: That's not true.

Source: "Waco/Branch Davidian Compound: Negotiation Transcripts," March 5, 1993, Freedom of Information Act, Federal Bureau of Investigation.

"Not, Not Scripture . . . "

For the Branch Davidians, Koresh's ability to interpret the Bible, especially the book of Revelation and the seven seals, demonstrated his prophetic gifts and cemented his leadership role. Not surprisingly, Koresh's biblical interpretations permeated his discussions with negotiators. Throughout, he attempted to explain his complicated theology to alternately baffled and frustrated agents. For example, on March 2, 1993, FBI agent Henry Garcia told Koresh, "Don't talk to me about the scriptures. Not that I don't like to listen to you, I do. Honestly, I do. I like to listen to you, but I have to explain to my bosses here why you're not coming out." Garcia failed to understand the centrality of the Bible in Koresh's life. Similarly, the excerpt below shows the inability of the negotiators to deal with Koresh's unwavering commitment to his religion—and, as the selection reveals, it was an inability that Koresh recognized.

David Koresh: You got your Bible there?

Jim Cavanaugh: I'm sorry, no, I don't. I don't.

David Koresh: You didn't bring it today?

Jim Cavanaugh: No, I, there's, there was another guy here last night and I don't, don't see it here. But tell me, how can we—tell me about waiting. What's going to happen? Tell me. Just be straight with me.

David Koresh: Well, I'm, I'm trying to avoid [explain?] something here.

Jim Cavanaugh: Not, not scripture, David, I can't understand it.

David Koresh: Well, if you can't understand it there's no reason for me to talk to you anymore, Jim.

Source: "Waco/Branch Davidian Compound: Negotiation Transcripts," March 3, 1993, Freedom of Information Act, Federal Bureau of Investigation.

The Deadly Consequences of the "Cult" Chasm

David Koresh told a negotiator on March 1, 1993, "You know, I mean, this is a great nation, but, like I said, it's not bigger than my God." Similarly, Steve Schneider explained on March 3, 1993, "Safety is not the first thing in my mind. I mean, this world is not a safe place. You can do what you want to try to remain that, that way in some degree. No. My main goal is to make sure that I'm right with God if there is a God, that I may gain a better life that does not end." As we have seen, the FBI failed to take these claims and the religious world of the Branch Davidians seriously. They did not understand the priorities of David Koresh's life or the depths of the Branch Davidians' commitments. Throughout much of the siege, this "cult" chasm caused misunderstandings and frustration. Not surprisingly, then, in mid-April, the FBI failed to accord David Koresh's latest revelation any legitimacy. This failure resulted in the deaths of over seventy Branch Davidians. The documents below illustrate the deadly consequences of this decision.

Letter of April 14, 1993: Opening the Seven Seals

As the siege continued and frustration on both sides mounted, a seeming breakthrough occurred in mid-April. The letter below, from David Koresh to his lawyer Dick DeGuerin, documents a potential resolution to the stalemate. Koresh, who heretofore had only communicated his teaching orally, reveals that God has granted him permission to write down his interpretation of the seven seals. In many ways, for Koresh, this text symbolized his life's work. Through it, his message could reach the masses. Further, after finishing this text, Koresh promised to lead his followers out of their Mount Carmel home and face the consequences of his actions.

Hello Dick,

As far as progress is concerned, here is where we stand: I have received two messages, from God, to the FBI, one of which concerns present danger to people here in Waco.

I was shown a fault line running throughout the Lake Waco area. One angel is standing in charge of this event. Many people, here in Waco, know that we are a good people, and yet, they have shown the same resentful spirit of indifference to our "warnings of love."

I am presently being permitted to document in structured form, the decoded messages of the 7 *Seals*. Upon the completion of this task I will be freed of my "waiting period." I hope to finish this as soon as possible and to stand before man to answer any and all questions regarding my actions.

This written Revelation of the 7 Seals will not be sold, but is to be available to all who wish to know the Truth. The Four Angels of Revelation 7 are here, now ready to punish foolish mankind: but, the writing of these Seals will cause the winds of God's wrath to be held back a little longer.

I have been praying so long for this opportunity; to put the Seals in written form. Speaking the Truth seems to have very little effect on man.

I was shown that as soon as I am given over into the hands of man, I will be made a spectacle of, and people will not be concerned about the truth of God, but just the bizarrity of me—the flesh (person).

I want the people of this generation to be saved. I am working night and day to complete my final work of the writing out of "these Seals."

I thank my Father. He has finally granted me the chance to do this. It will bring New Light and hope for many and they will not have to deal with me the person.

The earthquake in Waco is something not to be taken lightly. It will probably be "the thing" needed to shake some sense into the people. Remember, Dick, the warning came first and I fear that the FBI is going to suppress this information. It may be left up to you.

I will demand the first manuscript of the Seals be given to you. Many scholars and religious leaders will wish to have copies for examination. I will keep a copy with me. As soon as I can see that people like Jim Tabor and Phil Arnold have a copy I will come out and then you can do your thing with this Beast.

I hope to keep in touch with you by letter, so please give your address.

We are standing on the threshold of Great events! The 7 Seals in written form are the most sacred information ever!

David Koresh.

Source: Report to the Deputy Attorney General on the Events at Waco, Texas: February 28 to April 19, 1993 (redacted version) (Washington, D.C.: Department of Justice, 1993), appendix E.

"Experts" Again

We have seen how the ATF relied on anticultists as they planned their February raid and how the "cult" stereotype exacerbated the FBI negotiation process. In addition, according to the document below, anticultists continued to act as "experts" to the FBI during the siege. Once again ex-member Marc Breault claimed a position of prominence and offered his "wisdom" to the FBI. The excerpt below delineates Breault's reaction to Koresh's letters and his insistence that the Branch Davidians would not come out peacefully. Given the FBI's "cult" bias and its alleged "experts," Koresh's claim that he would come out after writing down his interpretation of the seven seals had little chance of being believed.

> The FBI contacted us throughout the siege. They showed us Koresh's letters, which were nothing more than scriptural ramblings written down. After reading those we became more and more convinced that Koresh had no intentions of coming out. We told the FBI as much.
>
> Towards the end, Koresh's letters indicated to us he was getting desperate. The cult leader had been waiting for a sign from God for over forty days by then. Of course, nothing happened. By now Koresh had negotiated himself into a corner. He turned to his old theology, things he had abandoned years ago. He was grasping at straws. We told the FBI that Koresh was starting to lose his grip and that he would probably end the siege violently.
>
> Source: Marc Breault and Martin King, *Inside the Cult: A Member's Chilling, Exclusive Account of Madness and Depravity in David Koresh's Compound* (New York: Signet, 1993), 336–37. Reprinted with the permission of Penguin Group (Australia).

The Seven Seals: A Stalling Technique

While David Koresh worked on writing down his interpretation of the seven seals, Steve Schneider continued negotiations with the FBI. The excerpts below highlight the inability of the two sides to communicate effectively. In the first, the FBI agent doubts the Branch Davidians will ever come out and refers to Koresh's forthcoming text as a "stalling technique." To little avail, Schneider attempts to explain the importance of this text and the group's commitment to leaving once it is finished. In the second, we see how the FBI interpreted Koresh's actions as manipulation, and ultimately concluded that a successful negotiation process would not be possible. The FBI may not have believed that Koresh was writing, but on the final day of the siege, April 19, 1993, a Branch Davidian survivor brought out the beginnings of the text that

David Koresh was never allowed to finish. It is available on the Web at several different sites (see ⟨http://bdsda.com/koresh2.aspx⟩).

Dick: Well, I, I think one of the questions was asked, of course, is that, you know, the seven seals are not new to you folks out there, and all of a sudden he's waited till this point in time to go ahead and, and, you know, put some of his thoughts down on paper. You know, frankly, my, my belief is this is nothing more than a stalling technique. I mean— . . .

Steve: Dick, can I react to that?

Dick: Certainly. . . .

Steve: I, I'm, I'm telling you something. I'm, I'm going to say, about this whole stalling business. If, if you—if we did not believe in God and were waiting on him, I'd just come right out and— . . .

Dick: I don't doubt—

Steve: People—

Dick: —that you believe in God, that you have a great—

Steve: These people—

Dick: —belief in God.

Steve: No, no, but, Dick, these people do expect to come out. And if you think it's a stalling tactic, well, that—you know, think what you will. But I'm telling you that is not so.

Source: "Waco/Branch Davidian Compound: Negotiation Transcripts," April 15–April 16, 1993, Freedom of Information Act, Federal Bureau of Investigation.

Dick: David, let me tell you something. You know what? You missed your calling. You would have been one hell of a salesman, you know that? I mean you really would have been a great salesman. You—I know it's, it's a carnal interest. But you could have been a wealthy man, you know that? Because you have got a gift of what some people might call bullshit. But I'm not going to say that. I'm going to say you have a gift of gab that is probably as good as anybody I've ever heard. And that, you know, and I've been doing this job for a long time.

David: Um-hum.

Dick: You are very good at what you do. However, you know, my belief is that what you do is, is a very deliberate thing and is very manipulative. You know, it really is. I mean, let's face it. You're good at what you do, aren't you? I mean will you admit to that?

Source: "Waco/Branch Davidian Compound: Negotiation Transcripts," April 16, 1993, Freedom of Information Act, Federal Bureau of Investigation.

Ending the Siege

Despite David Koresh and Steve Schneider's assurances that the explication of the seven seals was not a stalling tactic, the FBI did not believe them. According to the *Report to the Deputy Attorney General on the Events at Waco*, the FBI even interpreted Koresh and Schneider's meetings with their lawyers as yet another stalling tactic. The report states that the lawyers "did not report anything of value to the FBI" after their visits, and Special Agent in Charge Jamar "revealed that Koresh had used the attorneys to buy time and make it appear that he was interested in resolving the standoff." The first excerpt below, from the same report, shows the FBI's deep suspicion and intense frustration. This brief chronology reveals how, in the end, Koresh's claims meant nothing to the decision makers. Even as Koresh tried to write his way out of Mount Carmel, the FBI undertook to end the siege with the approval of the U.S. attorney general. The second excerpt is part of the prepared script read over a loudspeaker on April 19th as the FBI inserted tear gas into the Branch Davidians' home.

> April 14
>
> From 10:21 a.m. to 11:32 a.m., DeGuerin and Zimmerman spoke over the telephone to Koresh and Schneider. The attorneys advised the FBI at the end of this conversation that Koresh had established a new precondition for his coming out. Koresh would only come out after he finished writing a manuscript which explained the Seven Seals.
>
> April 16
>
> There were eight conversations with four individuals for a total of 3.35 hours on April 16. The only conversation of relevance was Koresh's telling the negotiators that he had just completed the manuscript on the First Seal.
>
> April 17
>
> In the afternoon, the Attorney General approved the FBI's plan and directed that it be put into effect beginning Monday, April 19. The FBI commanders in Waco were notified of the Attorney General's decision at 7:00 p.m. The FBI began preparations for inserting the gas.
>
> Source: *Report to the Deputy Attorney General on the Events at Waco, Texas: February 28 to April 19, 1993* (redacted version) (Washington, D.C.: U.S. Department of Justice, October 8, 1993), 105–8.

We are in the process of placing tear gas into the building. This is not an assault. We are not entering the building. This is not an assault. Do not fire your weapons. If you fire, fire will be returned. Do not shoot. This is not an assault. The gas you smell is a non-lethal tear gas. This gas will temporarily render the building uninhabitable. Exit the compound now and follow instructions.

You are not to have anyone in the tower. The tower is off limits. No one is to be in the tower. Anyone observed to be in the tower will be considered to be an act of aggression and will be dealt with accordingly.

If you come out now, you will not be harmed. Follow all instructions. Come out with your hands up. Carry nothing. Come out of the building and walk up the driveway toward the Double-E Ranch Road. Walk toward the large Red Cross flag.

Follow all instructions of the FBI agents in the Bradleys. Follow all instructions.

You are under arrest. This standoff is over.

We do not want anyone hurt. Follow all instructions. This is not an assault. Do not fire any weapons. We do not want anyone hurt. . . .

We will continue to deliver gas until you leave that building. This has been done carefully so as not to injure anyone in the compound. We will continue to apply pressure. We will continue to put gas into that building. We are not going away. This is a non-stop effort until you leave the building. There is no longer a reason to remain in that building.

David, you and Steve lead those people from that building. You are the one that put those people in that position. It is time for you to bring those people out of there. Steven, you indicated to us over and over and over again that you're willing and able and ready to leave that building. Now is the time to do it. Do not depend on David Koresh's ability to make that decision. It's very clear, I think, that he is unable to make decisions. Vernon is finished. He's no longer the messiah. He is to leave the building now. Exit the building now.

Source: "Waco/Branch Davidian Compound: Negotiation Transcripts," April 19, 1993, Freedom of Information Act, Federal Bureau of Investigation.

In the Aftermath of Waco

It seems, despite examining all the reasons why Waco happened, we are unable to accept the answer. Even as this chapter has shown the power of the "cult" stereotype in American culture and its deadly consequences in the case of the Branch Davidians, the events at Waco remain difficult to fathom. To overcome this difficulty and enhance our understanding of these events, the documents in this final section offer additional reflections on the causes of Waco. All written or drawn in the aftermath of Waco, these sources—from government hearings to scholarly interpretations to political cartoons—provide additional insights into and commentary on this unfortunate event. In its own way, each source attempts to answer the "why" of Waco and challenges you to do the same. In the end, accepting the answer means acknowledging the deadly reality of religious intolerance in the United States.

[From testimony by Attorney General Janet Reno]

Mr. Schiff (Rep. N.M.): As you said a bit earlier, we are here to look to the future, to hope we don't have another situation, but to look at this one in terms of how things might be planned differently. And it is with that in mind that I have a couple of questions.

The first is with respect to your conclusion that Mr. Koresh did not intend to surrender. His attorneys, I believe, have been quoted as saying that he had inferred, at least that after he completed a biblical translation, that he did in fact intend to surrender. Are you familiar with that suggestion, and how did you decide that that was not going to happen?

Ms. Reno: That is a good question, Congressman, because I said, he is talking about when he finishes the Seven Seals he will come out. We went back over the lies that he had told the FBI up to that point, when their Passover was finished he would come out. The FBI felt that he had manipulated them and lied to them every step of the way. They can give you more of the details in terms of the notes and the information they had.

They also told me that based on their conversations and consultations with their behavioral scientists, that they concluded and the scientists concluded that he was a manipulator who would continue to manipulate.

Source: *Events Surrounding the Branch Davidian Cult Standoff in Waco Texas: Hearing Before the Committee on the Judiciary House of Representatives*, 103rd Cong., 1st sess., April 28, 1993, Serial No. 95 (Washington, D.C.: Government Printing Office, 1995), 48.

Source: © 1999 Monte Wolverton.
⟨http://www.wolvertoon.com/toons⟩.

The First Amendment to the U.S. Constitution legally proscribes the state from taking sides in matters of religion. Defenders of state action will no doubt emphasize the obligation of the state to enforce its laws. They already claim that this was the objective at Mount Carmel. But such a defense of state action is flawed. It would be one thing if cultural opponents and governmental authorities acted independently of one another, even if they shared an affinity of goals due to different interests. But the emergence of narratives about mass suicide shows something quite different. The degree to which certain governmental authorities consciously took up the cause of the cultural opponents remains an open question. Whatever the answer to that question, the connection of governmental action to cultural opposition runs much deeper. Mount Carmel does not just bear comparison to Jonestown as a similar but independent event. Instead, there was a *genetic* bridge between Jonestown and Mount Carmel. Specifically, the opponents of Koresh took tropes about mass suicide derived from the apocalypse at Jonestown, reworked them, and inserted them into accounts that they offered about the Branch Davidians. In turn, the opponents' reports about mass suicide directly structured the development of tactical scenarios for the BATF raid, and they may well have figured in the motive structures of BATF commanders on the day of the raid. In these direct yet presumably un-self-conscious ways, BATF operations became subordinated to the narratives of cultural opposition.

Meanings in the realm of public life are formed in part by the stories that people tell and the ways that other people hear these stories. On the basis of the stories they hear, along with their own personal and cultural structures of meaning, and in relation to their own reading of their resources and situation, people make new meanings in both their accounts of past events and their scenarios of projected actions. As is demonstrated by examining the conflict that developed between the Branch Davidians, their cultural opponents, and the state, personal narratives of salvation from the evil of a cult can shape cultural cries for help, and in turn become elements of official state discourse—with disastrous consequences.

Source: John Hall, "Mass Suicide and the Branch Davidians," in *Cults, Religion, and Violence*, edited by David G. Bromley and J. Gordon Melton (Cambridge: Cambridge University Press, 2002), 167–68. Reprinted with the permission of Cambridge University Press.

Few persons, however, have commented upon the twin factors of our culture that conspired to create the Waco tragedy: the increasing secularism and the increasing violence of American culture and institutions. These two factors had as much to do with the deaths at "Ranch Apocalypse" as did the seven seals of Revelation.

The first reason has to do with the fundamentally violent nature of our culture. It is not just that we lead the world in the rate of murder of our population; it is that violence, both overt and covert, lies at the basis of our very institutions. Whether in the home or in our legal and law enforcement practices, Americans often choose violence as a preferred means of self-expression. Gandhi led a movement for self-rule in India that took as its motto, "The means are the ends in the making." How else could the ATF "invaders" have expected an armed millennial religious movement to respond when they attacked with brute force? Violent means certainly lead to violent ends. Then, to compound an already botched initiative, the ATF and FBI proceeded to barrage the Koresh compound with light and sound and then expected those held captive inside to react "rationally." How could the highly informed Waco law officers neglect to consider the reciprocal response to the violent techniques *they* were using? Violence as a means of conflict resolution in America is seldom challenged and, in this case, led to predictable violent ends.

The second reason for the miscalculation by the ATF and FBI is the pervasive secularization of American culture. Yes, America is still one of the most heavily church-going nations on the globe. Yes, our presidents still refer to our Judeo-Christian heritage in major speeches. But do we really understand or appreciate the kind of deep religiosity that produces a Mother Teresa—or a David Koresh? Such deep devotion can be used for good and noble causes; it can also deteriorate into personal pathologies and evil outcomes, as history has taught us. Yet, do we understand in what ways troubled people in a culture that is secular and morally adrift seek simplistic answers and fundamentalistic retreats to an idealized past? Can we not see the substitutional values and images the ATF held when their fallen colleagues became the motivation to end the siege and bring to justice those who killed him? That the law enforcers were willing to sacrifice even the children for the righteousness of their cause when they decided to bring an end to the standoff reveals the same level of devotion to symbols and values that those inside the Koresh compound held. . . .

Could there have been another conclusion?

Source: Larry D. Shin, "Why *Did* Waco Happen?," in *From the Ashes: Making Sense of Waco*, edited by James R. Lewis (Lanham, Md.: Rowman & Littlefield, 1994), 185–88.

The single most damaging mistake on the part of federal officials was their failure to take the Branch Davidians' religious beliefs seriously. Instead, David Koresh and his followers were viewed as being in the grip of delusions that prevented them from grasping reality. As bizarre and misguided as their beliefs might have seemed, it was necessary to grasp the role these beliefs played in their lives; these beliefs were the basis of *their* reality. The Branch Davidians clearly possessed an encompassing worldview to which they attached ultimate significance. That they did so carried three implications. First, they could entertain no other set of beliefs. Indeed, all other views of the world, including those held by government negotiators, could only be regarded as erroneous. The lengthy and fruitless conversations between the two sides were, in effect, an interchange between different cultures—they talked past one another.

Second, since these beliefs were the basis of the Branch Davidians' sense of personal identity and meaning, they were nonnegotiable. The conventional conception of negotiation as agreement about some exchange or compromise between the parties was meaningless in this context. How could anything of ultimate significance be surrendered to an adversary steeped in evil and error? Finally, such a belief system implies a link between ideas and actions. It requires that we take seriously—as apparently the authorities did not—the fact that actions might be based on something other than obvious self-interest.

Source: Michael Barkun, "Reflections after Waco: Millennialists and the State," *Christian Century*, June 2–9, 1993, 596. © 1993 The Christian Century. Reprinted as an excerpted version with permission.

Final Thoughts, Prophetic Words?

This chapter ends with a March 1, 1993, exchange between negotiator Jim Cavanaugh and Branch Davidian leader David Koresh. The excerpt below seems fitting as it includes the "cult" theme of this chapter, as well as a disturbing foreshadowing of how it all would end. As you read, reflect on the label of "cult leader" and the charge of brainwashing. Formulate your own answer to the question of why Waco happened. Does this event signify the epitome of religious intolerance in American history? And, finally, reflect on how we can prevent another Waco.

Jim Cavanaugh: Well, what's going to happen to your people? Are they going to walk out?

David Koresh: We have to see, Jim. Like I said, I'm not a cult leader. I'm a Bible teacher, okay? Nobody ever is committed to do what I ask or do what I say, okay? People do what they want to do.

Jim Cavanaugh: Yeah.

David Koresh: Okay? Now, if you let the people think, you know, they're all scared around here now—

Jim Cavanaugh: Just—

David Koresh: You've shown them a big arm, you know.

Jim Cavanaugh: You know what I'm trying to do? I'm trying to let you— I'm asking you to let me look inside your people and you to see what's going to go on, because unless you do, then, you know, it's going to be hard to, to help.

David Koresh: Well, I'm telling you what you'll do. Just give us some time, give us time, you know. That's all I'm asking. Give us time. You know, you've all done—you've all been enraged a lot of times, you know. Don't burn our building down.

Jim Cavanaugh: No, we won't do that.

David Koresh: Don't, don't shoot us all up. Give these people a chance before God to weigh out whether what they've learned in the scripture is the truth or, you know, whether maybe they have second thoughts. But they've got to, they've got to have that time.

Jim Cavanaugh: David, if you die, you're leaving your people helpless.

David Koresh: Look, they're God's people.

Jim Cavanaugh: But if—

David Koresh: I'm just an instrument, okay?

Jim Cavanaugh: Yeah.

David Koresh: I'm just another human being, an instrument, okay? You don't understand. This is not no glory thing. This is life.

Source: "Waco/Branch Davidian Compound: Negotiation Transcripts," March 1, 1993, Freedom of Information Act, Federal Bureau of Investigation.

Changes and Challenges

In 2004, a group of German "patriots" initiated "Project Schoolyard," a program designed to distribute music CDs to school-age children. On the surface, the idea seems laudable—providing children with the gift of music. The problem, for the German government and others, rested in the lyrical content of the music, which promoted white power (an increasingly popular genre of music). This type of music advocates white supremacy and racial conflict, a common theme in groups such as Christian Identity and the Creativity Movement. For example, the song "Rahowa," meaning RAcial HOly WAr, by the band of the same name, provides a telling example.

> As I march into battle, my comrades I hail,
> Tonight the white race prevails —
> Death by our swords to the vile, alien hordes,
> Their every resistance shall fail.
> They see it, it's there in our eyes,
> We know it, it's time that we rise,
> Not one of their numbers shall be spared;
> The racial holy war has been declared.[1]

Emphasizing the purity of the white race and the necessity of violence toward others, this music frames the prophesied racial battle in religious terms. It is a "holy war." Built on similar ideas, the above initiative uses music as a weapon to transform the schoolyard into a battlefield. While initially shut down by the German government, Project Schoolyard backers soon found ways to distribute 25,000 copies of their musical message, and white supremacists in the United States followed suit. Panzerfaust Records created a Web site and produced 100,000 copies of the CD for distribution in the United States. According to a Project Schoolyard press release, "volunteers from every pro-White group and organization in the U.S. have signed up to assist us in this project, as well as numerous unaffiliated individuals, consisting mostly of our customers/supporters who are high school students themselves. These CDs will be handed out in middle schools, high schools, university campuses, shopping malls, sporting events, mainstream concerts, parties, etc." Not content to rely solely on music to spread their message, the site also features content areas entitled "The Truth Behind the Talmud," "Nigger's Owners Manual," and "Racist Jokes," as well as a message board. Notably, at the bottom of the Web site is the following message: "Panzerfaust: We don't just entertain racist kids . . . we create them."[2]

In 1994, Paul Hill (1954–2003) shot and killed physician John Britton and his security escort, James Barrett, while they were on their way into a Pensacola, Florida, abortion clinic. The shooting resulted from Hill's interpretation of the Bible and the Christian faith. In his article "Why Shoot an Abortionist?," Hill wrote, "I realized that using force to stop abortion is the same means that God has used to stop similar atrocities throughout history. In the book of Esther, for instance, Ahasuerus, King of Persia, passed a law in 473 B.C. allowing the Persians to kill their Jewish neighbors. But the Jews did not passively submit; their uses of defensive force prevented a calamity of immense proportions." Thus, Hill sanctioned violence through his appeal to biblical history, and he defined his shooting of Britton and Barrett as defensive and justifiable: The use of necessary force to defend unborn children. In addition, Hill later described the virtues of this violent act—it put his religious beliefs into practice, called attention to "the full humanity of the unborn," highlighted the "enormous consequences of abortion," and forced people to choose sides in the conflict.[3] He had no regrets. In 2003, Paul Hill was executed by the state of Florida for his crimes. His message and actions, however, live on. Michael Bray, leader of the anti-abortion group the Army of God, has memorialized Hill as a prophet on his Web site (www.armyofgod .com) and in his movement. Amid graphic images of torn fetuses, the site features Hill's writings as well as a "defensive action statement," which states, "we declare and affirm that if in fact Paul Hill did kill or wound abortionist John Britton, and accomplices James Barrett and Mrs. Barrett, his actions are morally justified if they were necessary for the purpose of defending innocent human life. Under these conditions, Paul Hill should be acquitted of all charges against him."[4] The site's valorization of Hill comes through clearly in Michael Bray's reflection, "The Murder of God's Prophet." Bray writes, "His [Hill's] was the message of a prophet to the civil authorities. This is the proper legal standard. This is justice. Murderers are to be executed. These children of the womb are true children. The aborting of them is the murdering of them. Those who abort them or assist in the aborting of them are murderers and accessories to murder. This ought to be the message of God's people to the government."[5] The site further reinforces this position by featuring Bray's writings, notably his book, *A Time to Kill: A Study Concerning the Use of Force and Abortion.* In this text, Michael Bray, like Paul Hill, spreads a militant interpretation of Christianity as he cites the Bible to legitimize the use of force against those supporting abortion.

The virulently antigay Reverend Fred Phelps (1929–) and his Westboro Baptist Church (wbc) launched an "attack" on West Virginia in 2006. A press release issued on their infamous Web site (www.godhatesfags.com) proudly proclaimed "Sodomite West Virginians, the Real Brokeback Mountaineers." The release compared West Virginia to the "Castro faggot district in San Francisco" and to "New York's sodomite Village" and concluded that West Virginia was "by far the worst," as apparently a number of West Virginians had threatened the Phelps organization. Phelps called for his supporters to picket the University of West Virginia during Gay Pride week and to protest at churches in the city of Morgantown. According to the release, these churches were really "sodomite whorehouses" that had "abandon[ed] God and the kjv Bible . . . thereby creating the hellish zeitgeist wherein fag activists and their enablers have seized control of America reducing the nation to a homo-fascist regime now irreversibly cursed of God."[6] Since 1991, Phelps and wbc have used picketing to draw attention to their message. Signs read, "God Hates Fags," "Aids Cures Fags," and "Fags burn in Hell." The wbc Web site explains, "Perceiving the modern militant homosexual movement to pose a clear and present danger to the survival of America, exposing our nation to the wrath of God as in 1898 B.C. at Sodom and Gomorrah, wbc has conducted some 20,000 such demonstrations during the last nine years."[7] They have picketed at the funerals of American soldiers and at services for the victims of the Virginia Tech shootings. When asked why he and his followers preach hate, Phelps replies, "because the Bible preaches hate."[8] For Phelps and his wbc, hatred constitutes part of the fabric of the Christian faith.

Browsing the Web site of a particular on-line retailer in 2008 reveals an apparel list like that of many a clothing store—belt buckles, shirts, jewelry, boots, as well as jackets and hats. However this Web site sells "Aryan Wear" (www.aryanwear.com), white supremacist clothing for children and adults in hate groups such as Christian Identity, the Klan, and the Creativity Movement. The site's homepage features a tank surrounded by a number of skulls in tones of black and gray. Below this artwork one encounters the following phrase—"Greetings Kamerad Welcome to Aryanwear.com"—and a number of different options, including t-shirts, hoodies, girls' gear, and boots. Youth may buy baseball-style shirts sporting the Aryan Wear Academy logo, while women may purchase tank tops featuring messages of "white pride" or "Nordic beauty." Male consumers can search through belt buckles in the shape of the iron cross or the rebel flag, while also looking at t-shirts with slogans such as "WWHD?" (What Would Hitler Do?) and "White Power: We Get the Scum Out!" In addition to clothing, the site also sells resources that support their white supremacist message—music, magazines, DVDs, as well as flags and stickers. If these objects do not suffice, one can also purchase items for the home. For example, in the "collectibles" section 1/20 scale figurines of Hitler, Mussolini, Patton, and Churchill, are available to consumers.[9] From t-shirts to CDs to figurines, this on-line store provides individuals with the material culture to create and support their religio-racist ideologies.

Similarly, if you start searching the web for religiously based antifeminism, chances are you will come across a recently released documentary film entitled "The Monstrous Regiment of Women" (www.monstrousregiment.com). Its attention-grabbing title features a quote from the sixteenth-century Protestant John Knox, who wrote a tract entitled, "The First Blast of the Trumpet against the Monstrous Regiment of Women." Knox, fearing that Mary the First's persecution of Protestants in England would spread to his native Scotland, used this tract (and the Bible) to rail against female rulers. The film's cowriter and narrator, Emily Gunn, states that she and her husband (cowriter and coproducer Colin Gunn) seek to "borrow his [Knox's] biblical perspective and apply his blast against those who rule in the wake of his monstrous regiment." Be warned, Gunn explains, the present monster [feminism] "far surpasses the queen's iniquities in both kind and degree." The various segments of the film claim to "document" how feminism stands in opposition to the Christian faith, and it uses interviews with a variety of antifeminist women to "prove" its allegations, including Phyllis Schlafly, who helped defeat the Equal Rights Amendment, as well as Stacey McDonald, author of *Raising Maidens of Virtue*, and Jennie Chancey, leader of Ladies Against Feminism (www.ladiesagainstfeminism.com). Using "egalitarianism applied to gender" as the definition of feminism, the film commences its attack. "The problem with egalitarianism," Gunn insists, "is that it extends equality beyond God's created order and forces equality in any and every circumstance no matter how unnatural, unrealistic or harmful the consequences may be." And, according to the film, the consequences are horrific: feminism, influenced by communism, is responsible for the victimization of women, the eradication of the family wage, the demoralization of the military, the "unparalleled holocaust" of abortion, and "the literal uncovering of American women." Splicing together biblical prooftexts and antifeminist interviews, the film insists on the virtues of "hierarchy." "The bottom line," according to Jennie Chancey, "is God created men for leadership." Female leadership in the home and in the public sphere, she insists, signals God's "curse on a nation." In fact, the film points to the Nineteenth Amendment, women's suffrage, as the harbinger of this curse. With its passage, "the father ceased to sit in the gates as a representative of his family's interests," which led to individualism, self-interest, and, ultimately, the rise of the "monstrous regiment." Unlike Project Schoolyard and Fred Phelps, the film does not employ the language of hatred, nor does it call for violence; but like its counterparts, it does use religion as a weapon. Further, its characterization of feminists as "monsters," its inflammatory accusations about the feminist movement causing "cultural suicide," and its claim that "it's time to do something about it" leave one wondering about the film's implications.[10]

The Web site entitled Teaching Tolerance: A Teacher's Guide to Understanding and Correcting Racial Hatred in the Classroom sounds like a wonderful resource for those navigating the waters of the multicultural classroom. The site asks, "Why do children hate?" and documents some of the conflicts besetting public schools. However, as one continues to read, the site takes a seemingly unexpected turn. It claims, "White students have become alienated as textbooks now promote minority pride, while texts focus on White guilt for slavery and past racial discrimination. Whites are collectively blamed for slavery even though only a very small percentage of Whites owned slaves. Blaming Blacks as a group for high levels of black crime would be considered hate speech. However, condemning the White race, as a group, for slavery is considered acceptable." The site urges schools to create policies "free of racial preferences" and recounts how "White students are just as likely to be victims of racial hatred." It then calls for "lesson plans that emphasize the positive European-American role in history," as well as segregated student associations and the elimination of apparent double standards—"if your school has a policy that prohibits students from displaying the Confederate flag on shirts or cars, a consistent policy must be in place to prohibit the display of shirts or symbols that offend White students such as Malcolm X, Martin Luther King, Jr., shirts which feature rap artists, or African flags."[11] Closer inspection of the site reveals that the Duke mentioned in the URL is not an educational institution, but rather David Duke (1950–), former Klansman, founder of the National Association for the Advancement of White People

(NAAWP), and current leader of the Euro-American Unity and Rights Organization (EURO). Like his Teaching Tolerance Web site, Duke's organization claims to disavow hate and casts its message in terms of advocating for white rights. The underlying racism in his message, however, is as apparent as the anti-Semitism on display in the title of his 2003 book, *Jewish Supremacism: My Awakening on the Jewish Question*, and that of a 2005 conference Duke participated in, "Zionism as the Biggest Threat to Modern Civilization." Duke's Teaching Tolerance site and his career provide an unsettling answer to the question he poses on the Web page: "Why do children hate?"

Throughout this book and in the examples above, you have seen the various ways religious intolerance adapts to the crises and fears of its social-cultural climate. Purveyors of hatred respond to perceived and real challenges to their religious, political, and social worlds with intolerance and violence.[12] As the issues that foster intolerance change depending on the specific group and the historical period under study, so too does the intolerance enacted against those labeled "dangerous." Even more unsettling, in the twenty-first century, religious intolerance remains a vital force in our world, and its tactics continue to evolve. The various examples described above reveal how religious intolerance in the United States is once again changing in at least five ways—in its method of transmission, its creation of community, the packaging of its message, the targets of its hate, and its use of religion.

First, all of these examples highlight the importance of technology, namely the prominent role of the Internet in disseminating religious intolerance. The Simon Wiesenthal Center calls the Internet "the new gatekeeper of information" and reports that it "provides re-tooled racists with an unprecedented marketing tool. They have populated the World Wide Web with hundreds of sites enabling them to promote their agenda in an attractive, yet unassailable way."[13] Similarly, Howard Berkowitz, chairman of the Anti-Defamation League, reports, "Hate groups and extremists have moved quickly to the Internet." He attributes the Internet's popularity among hate groups to four factors—cost, accessibility, efficiency, and anonymity. "As a vehicle for spreading hate, the Internet is more powerful than any extremist of the past decade could have imagined. Anti-Semites and racists use the Internet to recruit new members and threaten their enemies with violence. Online membership firms make it easy to join. Online, they become part of an electronic community of like-minded individuals which helps to reinforce their hateful convictions."[14] Throughout American history, we have seen how religious intolerance adapts to its environment—perpetrators align their cause with the crises of the time, and they use the technologies at their disposal. For example, the spurious and anti-Semitic *Protocols of the Learned Elders of Zion* was initially serialized, then published in book form, and now survives on white power Web sites. In each instance, the available technology afforded opportunities to disseminate the intolerant message.

Second, the Internet also provides contemporary hate groups with ways to create more-distinct yet dispersed subcultures—all the while shielded by the vastness and anonymity of the Web. The purveyors of religious intolerance can bridge geographic distances and create close-knit communities through Web sites that feature on-line forums, message boards, stores, literature, and blogs. In our current public discourse dominated ostensibly by political correctness and the disapproval of most types of bigotry, hate groups find little room for their voices or presence. However, on-line resources can provide communal ties that help foster a distinct group identity and a sense of belonging. "Collective identity," as one scholar writes, "is the shared definition of a group that derives from members' common interests, experiences, and solidarity."[15] Web sites can offer these resources, a feeling of affirmation and encouragement, the reality of community and solidarity. These sites provide validation. "The locus of collective identity is cultural; it is manifested through the language and symbols by which it is publicly expressed. We know a collective identity through the cultural icons and artifacts displayed by those who embrace it."[16] By creating their own Web sites, hate groups craft their theology, language, and symbols. Even more, they often provide the material culture to support it. For example, while you may find t-shirts or flags praising the Confederacy on the racks of local discount stores, you probably will not find more virulent messages of hate like the Aryan Wear WWHD? t-shirt. However, the Web provides these products and a way for hate group participants to purchase them—from books to t-shirts, from belt buckles to bumper stickers. Whether the products are for themselves, friends, or family, they reinforce a religiously intolerant ideology, equip members with the means to identify themselves with it, and provide a way to socialize their children into the faith. In addition, the commercial components of these sites afford hate group members the ability to participate in the culture of consumption so dominant in the United States, an act that in and of itself seems to bestow a sense of legitimacy on their cause. Media scholar Heather Hendershot writes that the ability to purchase products representative of one's own subculture is "to declare one's respectability in a country in which people are most often addressed by mass culture not as citizens but as consumers. In America, to buy is to be."[17] Further, all of this can be done behind the screen. The anonymity of the Web protects members or supporters of these groups from the censure of the wider public even as it creates a sense of solidarity with like-minded consumers. These products can be bought without fear of condemnation, and the purchaser can then use them where and when they desire. The Web's anonymity protects perpetrators of intolerance from unwanted detection; and when combined with its vastness, it allows those outside these groups to remain oblivious. Much of this intolerant activity remains unseen and unknown. If you do not intentionally look for hate sites, it is easy to remain ignorant of their existence and to deny the pervasiveness of religious intolerance on the Web and in our world.

Third, through their use of the Internet and the formation of dispersed-yet-unified communities, these hate groups are repackaging their messages in an attempt to reach the American mainstream. Carol Swain discusses this movement of hate from the periphery to the center: "Many former white supremacists such as Don Black and David Duke have changed with the times and reinvented themselves as white nationalists or white civil rights crusaders." She continues, "They are transforming themselves in order to widen their appeal."[18] The examples at the start of this chapter illustrate this transformation. For instance, while standing for similarly intolerant beliefs and practices, an Aryan Wear Academy t-shirt mutes the audibility of the message so loudly proclaimed by white Klan robes. Aryan Wear cloaks their racial and religious bigotry under the guise of normalcy and respectability—t-shirts and jeans. Similarly, sites such as Duke's Teaching Tolerance and Gunn's Monstrous Regiment do not employ the language of hate or advocate the burning of crosses or the torching of buildings (although those may be consequences). Rather, they frame their message in terms of celebrating one's heritage and protecting one's children. On the surface, these appear to be worthy goals; however, as we have seen, these groups' visions of celebration and protection rest on intolerance toward and persecution of others. Unfortunately, this more "mainstream" message seems to resonate with an increasing number of Americans. "What makes some of the newer organizations so dangerous," according to Carol Swain and Russ Nieli, "is that they address many important issues of race and nationality that are ignored in polite company, and they do so with a degree of candor and openness not found in more mainstream discourse."[19] By using new technologies, recasting their message, and addressing issues stifled in public discourse, contemporary hate groups have found a niche, a way for their message to reach the mainstream.

Fourth, people such as Fred Phelps, Michael Bray, Paul Hill, and Emily Gunn mainstream their message by expanding their targets. Perpetrators of religious intolerance often focus on particular religious or religio-racial groups—Catholics and Jews, African Americans and Asian Americans. Intolerance toward these groups combines religious prejudice with racial bigotry. Jews, for example, are not simply another religion, but in anti-Semitic rhetoric they also become a distinct and threatening race. While this pattern remains a prominent component of religious intolerance, contemporary hate groups have also added culturally charged "life-style choices" to the list of individuals and groups under attack. Some perpetrators now target those embracing feminism, homosexuality, and abortion—issues that have been and continue to divide Americans (politically and religiously). This focus provides contemporary hate groups with a way to broaden their appeal. If, as Swain and Nieli claim, a part of the American population feels that they cannot participate in public discourse on these issues or that their viewpoints will not be heard, then people like Phelps and Bray offer some segments of the population a listening ear, a validating voice, and a religious rationale. These hate groups use divisive cultural issues to unify people who feel alienated or marginalized, and they often do this through their appeals to the biblical text and American "ideals." For example, many contemporary hate groups have recast the American government's role in their ideologies to expand their attack. In the past, hate groups such as the Ku Klux Klan saw themselves as protecting and upholding the "ideals" of the American government. In these scenarios, the American government was besieged by various evils. However, current hate groups now connect their ideologies to visions of a corrupt American government. Christian Identity adherents view the government as an entity controlled by a Jewish conspiracy, while Bray and Gunn see it acting under the power of evil forces, namely the devil.[20] As a result, the government becomes an active villain that must be radically changed or destroyed. This logic then legitimates intolerance and violence. The result: Abortion doctors are shot, and military funerals are picketed.

Fifth, the opening examples reveal not only the proliferation of hate groups, but also a transformation in the relationship between religion and intolerance. Carolyn Petrosino describes it as "an increase in religious zealotry among hate crime perpetrators."[21] Many current hate groups, including the Army of God, WBC, Christian Identity, and the Creativity Movement, have explicitly included hatred, violence, and intolerance as the basis of or a prominent part of their religious visions. Take, for instance, Fred Phelps, who states, "What you need to hear is that God hates people, and that your chances of going to heaven are nonexistent, unless you repent. What you need to hear is a little fire and brimstone preaching, like Jesus preached. What you don't need to hear is that you're okay just the way you are, and God accepts every-one without exception."[22] For Phelps, hatred is a religious value. Similarly, Ben Klassen, founder of what is now known as the Creativity Movement, wrote in *The White Man's Bible*: "Let no man stand in our way in accomplish-ing our goal—the survival, expansion and advancement of the White Race. This is the ultimate, the highest, the loftiest, and to us the most sacred cause in the universe."[23] For Klassen and many white supremacist groups, race and racial conflict have become "sacred causes." While the Creativity Movement has divinized whiteness, anti-Semitism dominates the theology of Christian Identity. Scholar Michael Barkun writes, "So small a group would have little claim on our attention but for the fact that Christian Identity has created the most virulently anti-Semitic belief system ever to arise in the United States." Christian Identity defines Jews as "children of the devil."[24] These groups weave hatred and conflict into the fabric of their theology. Past perpetrators of religious intolerance certainly reconciled their religious beliefs with hatred and intolerance. For example, one cannot understand the Ku Klux Klan of the 1920s without recognizing its close ties to fundamentalist Protestantism. Similarly, in the nineteenth century, religious differences motivated main-stream Christian violence toward Mormons. The religious zealotry of these contemporary hate groups resembles the patterns of the past; at the same time, they are weaving religion and hatred together in ever more virulent and violent ways.

Continuations and Conclusions

Religious intolerance combines old accusations and new technologies even as it simultaneously grafts new charges onto old forms, patterns that dem-onstrate its ability to evolve and maintain its power. Thus, religious intol-erance changes; however, much of its staying power rests in its enduring forms.[25] Despite the passage of time or the differences between the groups being persecuted, religious intolerance often works in surprisingly similar ways. But perhaps this should not be surprising. As scholar Frederick Green-spahn writes, "All these diverse forms of religious hostility share certain characteristics. Although expressed in theological language, they reflect a sense of fear, fear that the other groups are not just wrong, but dangerous."[26] Religious intolerance works through the creation and promulgation of fear. According to the *Oxford English Dictionary*, fear means "the emotion of pain or uneasiness caused by the sense of impending danger, or by the prospect of some possible evil; an instance of the emotion, a particular apprehension of some future evil; a state of alarm or dread." Throughout this volume, we have seen the purveyors of religious intolerance respond out of fear and evoke fear to enact their agendas.

In large part, this fear emerges from the differences they perceive between themselves and others. Confronting difference constitutes a part of what it means to be human, and these confrontations inform how we construct our individual and cultural identities. Sociologist Robert Bellah describes this identity-formation process.

> It may seem obvious that in order for me to know who I am I need to know who I am not. I am not you; that is the beginning of the definition of me. It is the same with groups. In order to know what my group is, I need to know what it is not—I need to know its boundaries. Thus inclusion and exclusion are basic to the very idea of identity. Every society, every religious community and, indeed, every person is defined by a dialectic of inclusion and exclusion. Societies, religious communities, and persons, in order to have an identity, require an idea of boundary that defines them in relation to others.[27]

Identity formation necessitates the acknowledgement and articulation of difference. However, "we have all been programmed," Audre Lorde writes, "to respond to the human differences between us with fear and loathing and to handle that difference in one of three ways: ignore it, and if that is not possible, copy it if we think it is dominant, or destroy it if we think it is subordinate."[28] The religiously intolerant respond to difference, as Lorde describes, with fear and often destruction. Difference, to them, represents a threat to their safety, their security, their salvation, their power. They fear the loss of what they know, and to protect themselves, they define those who are different as "deviant" or "dangerous," as someone or something that threatens their existence and therefore must be controlled or destroyed.

To combat the threat of difference, perpetrators of intolerance seek to incite fear in others. By doing so, they hope to rally those like them and eliminate the perceived threat, that which is different. To provoke this fear they manipulate themes or issues that directly relate to who we are—to how people construct their identities—as human beings, as gendered individuals, as political bodies.[29] Throughout this book and its varied documents, we have seen how the religiously intolerant invoke central discourses of identity formation in American culture, namely the "proper" place of gender and sexuality, the relationship between power and victimization, the definition of Christianity, the idea of America, and the meaning of humanity.[30] They explore and exploit these categories—gender, victimization, religion, politics, and humanity—to incite fear and promulgate religious intolerance.

For example, throughout this volume, numerous documents reveal how perpetrators of religious intolerance raise fears about gender and sexuality to persecute other religions. These religions supposedly violate the mythical norms of the nuclear family—monogamy, heterosexuality, and patriarchy, all upheld through marriage. They call its status and form into question by problematizing constructions of masculinity and femininity, monogamy and heterosexuality. Catholic nuns reject "traditional" ideas of femininity—of cultivating beauty through dress and creating a family through marriage—and Wiccans reject patriarchal conceptions of God, promote feminist practice in daily life, and embrace diverse forms of sexual expression. Both, then, become the targets of religious intolerance as they question the centrality of men in our society and defy what women are "supposed" to be and do. Catholic priests also transgress this norm with their vow of celibacy, while fundamentalist Mormon men deviate with their practice of polygamy. The intolerant interpret the religious rationale for these choices as guises for sexual depravity, and the facts surrounding their sexual practices do not matter. Rather, what matters, in the eyes of the intolerant, are the ways Catholic and fundamentalist Mormon men are dangerously "deviant." They go against gender, sexual, and family norms, which represents a threat to both religious (Protestant) and American life. There can be no "real" religious reason for such threatening actions. Further, the supposed sexual deviance of these Others corrupts the "innocent," in most cases defined as white Protestant women. The purveyors of religious intolerance accuse Mormons, Catholics, and Jews alike of abusing and oppressing "pure" white women. They are the supposed victims, sexually, economically, and politically. The intolerant, then, define differences in gender and sexuality as an evil contagion that not only makes the minority group dangerous, but also threatens to infect and contaminate society. Something, the intolerant insist, must be done to stop this danger. These accusations work effectively because they play on existing cultural anxieties and fears. "Hostility," Frederick Greenspahn writes, "is a sign of underlying insecurity, a sense not only of personal danger, but religious uncertainty, with deep-seated social and psychological concerns masked by theological language."[31] These fears about gender and sexuality go to the heart of who we are and how we construct our identities—what does it mean to be a woman or a man? Are marriage and family the building block of American society? Perpetrators of religious intolerance foretell the supposed dire consequences that will come when we begin to ask these questions and expand their possible answers.

These accusations reveal another theme we have seen throughout this volume—the inversion of persecutor and persecuted or, put another way, the reenvisioned relationship between power and victimization. Historically, Protestantism has dominated the religious and political landscape of the United States. It has consistently held a position of social, cultural, and political privilege. However, the sources consistently show that this dominant religious group casts itself as the victim of religious intolerance, rather than as its most frequent perpetrator. For example, charges of sexual deviance function, in part, on the power of this supposed victimization. Other religions have used foul means to attain power and a place in American society. They then use this ill-gotten power to hurt "innocents"—again typically white Protestant women. "Over-sexed" black men allegedly lusted after and raped them; Catholic priests supposedly took advantage of and abused them; and Jews purportedly sexually harassed and exploited them. The religious groups vary, but the charge remains strikingly the same. Here we see how fears about sexual deviance gain meaning and power through the category of victimization. Despite the reality of Protestant dominance, Protestant perpetrators of religious intolerance insist that they are in fact its victims. They play on our fears about individual freedom and control, our notions about being in charge of our own destiny. Sociologists David Bromley and Anson Shupe came to similar conclusions in *Strange Gods*. They write:

> Did Catholic priests and Mormon leaders possess strange powers
> through which they were able to ensnare unwitting parishioners or
> enslave women or make them concubines? Was Quaker and Jehovah's
> Witness opposition to military service a treasonous act that would
> undermine America's capability to defend itself against foreign
> enemies? Were leaders of each of these new religions merely greedy,
> power-hungry despots who exploited their followers to further their
> own ends? From a modern vantage point, such past accusations range
> from exaggerated to ludicrous. However, the pattern of persecution
> ... indicates the very real fear and hatred felt by individuals who were
> caught up in those conflicts.[32]

As this quote and the sources in this volume illustrate, when confronting religions deemed Other, dominant individuals and groups fear the loss of their power and privilege. Their salacious accusations and intolerant acts, then, serve to create the boundaries of inclusion and exclusion of which Bellah writes. In this way, the rhetoric of victimization, with its inversion of reality, unifies the dominant group with its establishment of an "us-against-them" mentality. It feeds on the fear of possibility—of what could potentially happen if one loses power to supposed deviants. These accusations, then, become rallying cries. They are designed to move the dominant group from passivity to activity, from apathy to action. Acts of intolerance and violence are the result. Burning crosses and angry mobs, biased legislation and flawed court findings—intimidation, violence, prejudice, and fear—serve to keep Others in a position of peril. They are confined to positions of marginality and spaces of fear, while the dominant group maintains its place of power and privilege.

Throughout this text, we have also seen how gender and sexual deviance combined with the rhetoric of victimization result in another common pattern: The "deviant" practices and power of Other religions allegedly threaten the very foundations of American government and society. Put another way, these religions are decidedly un-American—they supposedly threaten everything for which America stands. They question the nation's gender norms, challenge its sexual practices, and consequently, undermine the very fabric of the country. One can see this connection between religious "deviance" and "American society" in *Reynolds v. the United States* (1879), a free-exercise case in which the Supreme Court upheld laws condemning the Mormon practice of polygamy. The court deemed polygamy "an offence against society" and stated that "marriage, while from its very nature a sacred obligation, is nevertheless, in most civilized nations, a civil contract, and usually regulated by law. Upon it society may be said to be built, and out of its fruits spring social relations and social obligations and duties, with which the government is necessarily required to deal."[33] In this view, to question the norm of monogamous heterosexual marriage is to oppress the majority and challenge the very structures of American society. Similarly, anti-Semitic ideology claims that Jewish economic success (allegedly gained through illegitimate means) represents only part of a larger conspiracy—that of American and world domination, while anti-Catholic propaganda often declares the un-American nature of that group. Accusations focus on the hierarchical nature of the Catholic Church and Catholics' supposed loyalty to the Pope over the American nation as evidence of their "undemocratic" agenda. The list of examples could go on. Here, we see that the perpetrators of religious intolerance use charges of sexual deviance and their own alleged victimization to invoke larger fears about the nation and democracy. This creates and sustains boundaries between the intolerant and the targeted and legitimates intolerance toward the latter. Similar to other charges, the accusation of being un-American unites the intolerant group and calls for them to "defend" their nation. The "American" group then defines their intolerant acts in terms of self- and national defense. In their minds, they have done nothing wrong.

This sense of being "right" illuminates yet another dimension of religious intolerance in the United States. The accusations against and fears of Others combined with a sense of moral "rightness" rest, in large part, on assumptions about what constitutes legitimate or real religion. The various sources in this volume reveal that historically those perpetuating religious intolerance in America define legitimate religion in very particular ways (often as an idealized Protestant Christianity). All of the patterns of accusation we have seen—gender/sexuality, victimization, and nationalism—gain additional currency in American culture by invoking religion and religious authority.[34] In this way, deviations from the heterosexual family norm, from the Protestant power structure, from so-called American ideals, are rooted in a more "sinister" cause—religious delusion or deviance, or quite simply, evil. These groups "pervert" or "reject" the truth of Christianity and embody all of the dangerous differences discussed thus far. They represent the ultimate threat, the divide between the "righteous" and the "damned." Further, these Other religions have led their followers astray; these gullible dupes then participate in the "deviant" actions that threaten American society and, equally horrifying, do so all in the name of their supposed religion. For the intolerant, such "evil" cannot be allowed to proceed unchecked or unchallenged. It must be stopped. The intolerant group, then, defines any action taken against these "deviant" religions as morally justified and divinely sanctioned. The intolerant claim to be acting in accordance with God's dictates; they are enacting God's will on earth.

This leads us to the last recurring pattern we have seen throughout these sources, namely dehumanization. If Other religions represent such dangerous deviance in all of these respects—gender, sexuality, victimization, nationalism, and orthodoxy—the perpetrators of religious intolerance ask: What kind of person could act this way? Their reply: None. "Real" religion does not act in such ways, and "real" people do not do such things. In *Authentic Fakes*, scholar David Chidester writes that religion "is engaged in negotiating what it is to be human," including "classifying persons into superhuman, human, and subhuman."[35] Those perpetrating religious intolerance negotiate definitions of religion and difference within a context of fear. The result is that the perpetrators of religious intolerance constitute what it means to be human, while their victims are defined as "monsters" or "demons," as sub-human or superhuman. Mormons are then depicted as cows, Catholics as crocodiles, and Jews as snakes or the "children of Satan."[36] They are wholly Other and must be destroyed. "It is this dehumanization," sociologist Mark Jurgensmeyer writes, "that allows a group to 'commit atrocities without a second thought.'"[37] Ultimately, the mutually reinforcing relationship that exists among these repeated charges of difference creates a culture of hate, a world in which intolerance becomes increasingly likely, if not normalized.[38]

Myths, Stories, and Narratives

Throughout this volume, we have seen how these recurring patterns of accusation rely on and reinforce one another. Allegations of Catholic sexual deviance rest on assertions of Protestant authority, which in turn invoke larger discourses about America and orthodoxy. Charges made against Mormons, Native Americans, NRMs and other groups work similarly. From these allegations, the religiously intolerant create a myth, an interpretive framework from which there seems to be little room or desire for escape. This is *not* to say that religious intolerance is a myth, but rather that religious intolerance functions and justifies itself like a myth or in mythic ways. The term myth generally denotes sacred stories of origin, which often include explanations for the state of the present world. Myths defy traditional categories of space and time, history and science. Originally from the Greek, "myth" literally means "word" or "speech," and we know from the documents in this volume that words are powerful. "In whatever cultural or religious tradition a creation myth is recited, it is paradigmatic in a special, one might even say pregnant manner, because of the many things to which its sheer force as a model is able to give birth."[39] Words, particularly those of myth, which claim divine or sacred authority, help us construct worlds; they provide us with motivations and prompt us to action, to good or evil.

The mythic framework or quality of religious intolerance seems to work similarly. For example, with its invocation of the divine, the rhetoric of religious intolerance "does not induce discussion; it does not argue, but presents."[40] It purports to be the "truth," so that "each individual story" or accusation "reinforces the overall stereotype of the enemy, and the overall stereotype in turn makes each story believable."[41] Myth presupposes one's belief, and in that way it is often circular. In religious intolerance, each accusation leads to another even as it leads back to itself, to its underlying fears and assumptions. Myths defy conventional notions of evidence. Religious intolerance works by citing vague generalities (sexual misconduct in convents), unlikely scenarios (the strangling of infants in convents), and little concrete evidence (the accounts of "ex-nuns" who were never really nuns). The perpetuators of religious intolerance claim this misinformation to be truth. They create a seemingly unassailable framework that functions through a "mythology of misinformation." However, even as we deem their information false, we must be aware that they believe in it (and convince others likewise).[42] As David Bromley and Anson Shupe write, "It is not a deliberate fraud, but it *is* a deliberate attempt to horrify and anger us. Stories are spread by a number of Americans who sincerely believe them and genuinely feel they have been victimized." They believe in their myth, and the fact remains that these Other religions do represent a challenge to the "values, lifestyles, and aspirations"—the power—of the intolerant.[43] As a result, this mythic framework, based on fear and false charges, wields power in our world. The contents of this book reveal the consequences of this "myth of misinformation." The mythology promulgated by the religiously intolerant gives birth to a "culture of hate," a society in which religious intolerance is a pervasive and constituent element.[44]

We started this book by examining the "founding myth" of the United States, with its persecuted Pilgrims and beleaguered colonists—all cast as the victims of tyranny in a grand drama of political freedom and religious liberty. This story extols the virtues of America, its exceptionalism in all areas, particularly religious freedom. These beliefs constitute a large part of American identity. They inform how we understand ourselves and our place in the world, as individuals and as a nation. However, this account also obscures the reality of religious intolerance in the United States, a reality that this volume documents. In fact, in some ways the rhetoric of American tolerance and liberty allows the mythic framework of the religiously intolerant to flourish. Those who unquestioningly believe in America's success in achieving tolerance have no explanatory mechanism with which to understand religious intolerance. "We will often see what our culture has trained us to see."[45] As a result, those blinded by the rhetoric of religious freedom do not "see" the reality of religious intolerance. Others may discern these events, but label them aberrant, as exceptions that prove the rule and one's own innocence. The rhetoric of tolerance allows us "to presume that hatred reflects a sick, pathological fringe," while "we see ourselves as innocent, blameless, and clean."[46] Believers in this American ideal have no other way to understand what has occurred. At the same time, people enacting religious intolerance, via their own mythology of misinformation, use the rhetoric of tolerance to bolster their claims. They appeal, as we have seen, to ideas of America, freedom, and agency. They invoke these ideals as they claim that their rights have been curtailed and that the nation sits on the brink of chaos or doom. These two frameworks, it seems, surreptitiously work together to protect the status quo.

To combat these myths and the culture of hate they produce, we need to remember our past in more accurate ways. We need to recognize the existence of tyranny and the reality of intolerance. With awareness comes the ability—the responsibility—to create new stories, myths, and narratives. Audre Lorde writes, "I have come to believe over and over again that what is most important to me must be spoken, made verbal and shared." She continues, "In the transformation of silence into language and action, it is vitally necessary for each one of us to establish or examine [his or] her function in that transformation and to recognize [his or] her own role as vital within that transformation."[47] So, as this book ends, the real work begins. We must acknowledge our past and the ways our stories, our myths, our histories matter. They negotiate power and construct identity.[48] We need new narratives, as they give birth to new possibilities. With these perhaps we will find, as Audre Lorde urges, "patterns for relating across our human difference as equals."[49] Maybe new and more accurate stories of the American past will help us respond to difference with interest or curiosity rather than fear. New narratives may help us understand ourselves and our nation in radically different ways. We must transform our silence into action to protect our freedoms, as "democracy is a continuing quest, not a stable condition or some finished end."[50] Right now, we have such an opportunity to tell new stories and to enact democracy. As the nation's religious landscape changes—76 percent of American adults identified as Christians in 2008, as opposed to 86 percent in 1990, and 15 percent of American adults now claim no religious ties, compared with 8.2 percent in 1990—the possibilities for both intolerance and tolerance remain.[51] At first glance, a decline in religious affiliation may seem like a harbinger of peace, as less-religious people could mean less religious intolerance. However, as we know from this volume, some could just as easily read these statistics with fear, finding in them a motivation to enact intolerance toward atheists, agnostics, and non-Christian religions. It is up to us to learn the lessons of this volume and lead the way. What will happen if we do not question and challenge the culture of hate that exists in the United States? A well-known saying by Reverend Martin Niemoller, a Lutheran pastor in Germany during World War II, evokes a necessary fear.

First they came for the communists, and I did not speak out—
because I was not a communist;
Then they came for the socialists, and I did not speak out—
because I was not a socialist;
Then they came for the trade unionists, and I did not speak out—
because I was not a trade unionist;
Then they came for the Jews, and I did not speak out—
because I was not a Jew;
Then they came for me—and there was no one left to speak out
for me.[52]

Ten Ways to Fight Hate

1 Act

Do something. In the face of hatred, apathy will be interpreted as acceptance—by the haters, the public and, worse, the victim. Decency must be
exercised, too. If it isn't, hate invariably persists.

2 Unite

Call a friend or co-worker. Organize a group of allies from churches,
schools, clubs and other civic sources. Create a diverse coalition. Include
children, police and the media. Gather ideas from everyone, and get everyone involved.

3 Support the Victims

Hate-crime victims are especially vulnerable, fearful and alone. Let them
know you care. Surround them with people they feel comfortable with. If
you're a victim, report every incident and ask for help.

4 Do your Homework

Determine if a hate group is involved, and research its symbols and agenda.
Seek advice from anti-hate organizations. Accurate information can then be
spread to the community.

5 Create an Alternative

Do NOT attend a hate rally. Find another outlet for anger and frustration
and people's desire to do something. Hold a unity rally or parade. Find a
news hook, like a "hate-free-zone."

6 Speak Up

You, too, have First Amendment rights. Hate must be exposed and de-
nounced. Buy an ad. Help news organizations achieve balance and depth.
Do not debate hate mongers in conflict-driven talk shows.

7 Lobby Leaders

Persuade politicians, business and community leaders to take a stand against hate. Early action creates a positive reputation for the community, while unanswered hate will eventually be bad for business.

8 Look Long Range

Create a "bias response" team. Hold annual events, such as a parade or culture fair, to celebrate your community's diversity and harmony. Build something the community needs. Create a web site.

9 Teach Tolerance

Bias is learned early, usually at home. But children from different cultures can be influenced by school programs and curricula. Sponsor an "I have a dream" contest. Target youths who may be tempted by skinheads or other hate groups.

10 Dig Deeper

Look into issues that divide us: economic inequality, immigration, homosexuality. Work against discrimination in housing, employment, education. Look inside yourself for prejudices and stereotypes.

Source: Southern Poverty Law Center, "Ten Ways to Fight Hate,"
⟨http://www.tolerance.org/pdf/ten_ways.pdf⟩ (accessed June 14, 2005).

APPENDIX   *Web Resources for Combating Religious Intolerance*

The Center for Religious Tolerance, http://centerforreligioustolerance.org/

Divining America, http://nationalhumanitiescenter.org/tserve/divam.htm

Lessons in Tolerance, http://www.ccsf.edu/Resources/Tolerance/index.html

Live Without Hate, www.cincinnati.com/nie/live_wo_hate/

Not in Our Town, http://www.pbs.org/niot/

The Pluralism Project, http://www.pluralism.org/

Portraits of Hate, Lessons of Hope, http://www.fightingreligiousintolerance.org/

Religious Tolerance, http://www.religioustolerance.org/

Southern Poverty Law Center, http://www.splcenter.org/

Teaching Tolerance, http://www.tolerance.org/

NOTES

INTRODUCTION

1 American Civil Liberties Union, *Jehovah's Witnesses and the War* (New York: American Civil Liberties Union, 1943), 15–17. For more on the persecution of Jehovah's Witnesses, see Shaun Francis Peters, *Judging Jehovah's Witnesses: Religious Persecution and the Dawn of the Rights Revolution* (Lawrence: University Press of Kansas, 2000).

2 S. T. Joshi, *Documents of American Prejudice: An Anthology of Writings on Race from Thomas Jefferson to David Duke* (New York: Basic Books, 1999), 423–24; and Thomas A. Tweed and Stephen Prothero, eds., *Asian Religions in America: A Documentary History* (New York: Oxford University Press, 1999), 159–62.

3 "President Franklin D. Roosevelt, "Executive Order 9066," in Tweed and Prothero, *Asian Religions in America,* 164–66.'

4 Tweed and Prothero, *Asian Religions in America,* 160.

5 "Testimony of the Honorable Earl Warren," in Joshi, *Documents of American Prejudice,* 449.

6 Daniel Dorchester, *Christianity in the United States* (New York: Phillips and Hunt, 1888), 121.

7 Albert Bushnell Hart, *National Ideals Historically Traced, 1607–1907,* vol. 26 of *The American Nation: A History* (Harper and Brothers: New York and London, 1907), 203.

8 Edward Eggleston, *The Household History of the United States and Its People for Young Americans* (New York: D. Appleton, 1890), 112–13, 199–200.

9 Oscar S. Straus, *Religious Liberty in the United States* (New York: Philip Cowen, 1896), 31.

10 Hart, *National Ideals Historically Traced,* 26: 199, 215.

11 Edward Channing, *The Period of Transition, 1815–1848,* vol. 5 of *A History of the United States* (Macmillan: New York, 1926), 287.

12 Joseph Henry Crocker, *Problems in American Society: Some Social Studies* (Boston: George H. Ellis, 1899), 206–7.

13 Ernest Hamlin Abbott, *Religious Life in America* (New York: Outlook, 1902), 264.

14 Leo Huberman, *We, the People* (New York: Harper and Brothers, 1932), 12–13.

15 Salma Hale, *History of the United States from their First Settlement as Colonies to the Close of the Administration of Mr. Madison, 1817,* vol. 2 (New York: Harper and Brothers, 1840), 262. The exceptions, of course, were any persons or groups judged by the majority faith to be ignorant, superstitious, erroneous, or fantastical.

16 John A. Nietz, *Old Textbooks: Spelling, Grammar, Reading, Arithmetic, Geography, American History, Civil Government, Physiology, Penmanship, Art, Music—as Taught in the Common Schools from Colonial Days to 1900* (Pittsburgh: University of Pittsburgh Press, 1961), 53–54; Ruth Miller Elson, *Guardians of Tradition: American Schoolbooks of the Nineteenth Century* (Lincoln: University of Nebraska, 1964), 54–61.

17 See Federal Bureau of Investigation, "Uniform Crime Reports," ⟨http://www.fbi .gov/ucr/ucr.htm⟩ (accessed December 1, 2008).

18 J. Hillis Miller, "Narrative," in *Critical Terms for Literary Study*, ed. Frank Lentricchia and Thomas McLaughlin (Chicago: University of Chicago Press, 1995), 69.

19 Paraphrased from Lynn S. Neal, "Hate and Hope," ⟨http://www.fightingreligious intolerance.org⟩ (accessed December 1, 2008).

20 For a list of anti-Arab and anti-Islamic attacks after September 11, 2001, see Hussein Ibish, ed., "Report on Hate Crimes and Discrimination against Arab Americans: The Post-September 11th Backlash," American-Arab Anti-Discrimination Committee, Washington, D.C., 2003. Available at ⟨http://www.adc.org/index.php?id=3302⟩ (accessed June 9, 2009).

21 Rev. A. W. Loomis, "Our Heathen Temples," *Overland Monthly*, November 1868, 461.

22 Tweed and Prothero, *Asian Religions in America*, 159.

23 "Letter to the Editor," *Cleveland Herald*, January 25, 1845, Column B.

24 Martha Nussbaum, "Religious Intolerance," *Foreign Policy* 144 (September–October 2004): 44–45; Susan Thistlethwaite, "Settled Issues and Neglected Questions: How is Religion to be Studied?" *Journal of the American Academy of Religion* 62, no. 4 (Winter 1994): 1037–45.

25 Barre Toelken, "Seeing with a Native Eye: How Many Sheep Will It Hold?" in *Seeing with a Native Eye: Essays on Native American Religion*, ed. Walter Holden Capps (New York: Harper & Row, 1976), 11, 23.

26 Ontario Consultants on Religious Tolerance, "Religious Intolerance: Introduction," ⟨http://www.religioustolerance.org/relintol1.htm⟩ (accessed December 1, 2008); Sexual Assault Centre of Brant, "Religious Oppression," ⟨http://www.sacbrant.ca/ religious_oppression.asp⟩ (accessed December 1, 2008). These definitions also explain that religious tolerance does not mean you must accept all religions as true or that you must agree with a religion's actions and claims.

27 Portraits of Hate, Lessons of Hope, "What is Intolerance?" ⟨http://fightingreligious-intolerance.org/user-guide/what-is-intolerance⟩ (accessed December 1, 2008).

28 Michael Cobb, *God Hates Fags: The Rhetorics of Religious Violence* (New York: New York University Press, 2006), 15; *Encyclopedia of Religion*, 2nd ed., vol. 14, ed. Lindsay Jones (Detroit: Macmillan Reference USA, 2005), s.v. "Violence" (emphasis added).

29 Simon Wiesenthal, quoted in James R. Lewis, *From the Ashes: Making Sense of Waco* (Lanham, Md.: Rowman and Littlefield, 1994), 213.

30 J. Gordon Melton and David G. Bromley, "Violence and Religion in Perspective" and "Challenging Misconceptions about the New Religions—Violence Connec-

tion," in *Cults, Religion, and Violence*, ed. J. Gordon Melton and David G. Bromley (Cambridge: Cambridge University Press, 2002), 1–2, 43, 54.

CHAPTER ONE

1 Perez Zagorin, *How the Idea of Religious Toleration Came to the West* (Princeton: Princeton University Press, 2003).

2 Sabine MacCormack, "Limits of Understanding: Perceptions of Greco-Roman and Amerindian Paganism in Early Modern Europe," in *America in European Consciousness, 1493–1750*, ed. Karen Ordahl Kupperman (Chapel Hill: University of North Carolina Press, 1995), 96, 98, 106, 80; Pacifique de Provins, quoted in Luca Condignola, "The Holy See and the Conversion of the Indians in French and British North America, 1486–1760," in Kupperman, *America in European Consciousness*, 196 (emphasis added); Abbé Bobé, *Mémoire sur la découverte de la Mer de l'Quest* (1718), 53, 72–75, quoted in Cornelius J. Jaenen, "'Les Sauvages Ameriquains': Persistence into the 18th Century of Traditional French Concepts and Constructs for Understanding Indians," *Ethnohistory* 29 (1982): 52. See Cotton Mather, *The Mystery of Israel's Salvation Opened* (London, 1669), 96. Mather seems to have had second thoughts about the theory at a later time (*Magnalia Christia Americana* [London, 1702], book 3, 192–93). For a discussion of Williams, Penn, and Samuel Sewall see Alden T. Vaughan, *Roots of American Racism: Essays on the Colonial Experience* (New York: Oxford University Press, 1995), 50-53 and 274n58, 63, 67. Jonathan Edwards, *A History of the Work of Redemption*, transcribed and edited by John F. Wilson (New Haven: Yale University Press, 1989), 155–56; Gerald R. McDermott, "Jonathan Edwards and the American Indians: The Devil Sucks Their Blood," *New England Quarterly* 72 (1999): 539–57.

CHAPTER TWO

1 Justin Nordstrom, *Danger on the Doorstep: Anti-Catholicism and American Print Culture in the Progressive Era* (Notre Dame: University of Notre Dame Press, 2006), 56; *The Menace*, quoted in Robert P. Lockwood, "The Evolution of Anti-Catholicism in the United States," in *Anti-Catholicism and American Culture*, ed. Robert P. Lockwood (Washington, D.C.: Center for Media and Public Affairs, 2000), 37.

CHAPTER THREE

1 Origen Bacheler, *Mormonism Exposed, Internally and Externally* (New York, 1838), 48, quoted in Spencer J. Fluhman, "Anti-Mormonism and the Question of Religious Authenticity in Antebellum America," *Journal of Religion and Society* 7 (2005), ⟨http:// moses.creighton.edu/jrs/2005/2005-9.html⟩ (accessed October 3, 2009).

2 Scott Keeter and Gregory Smith, "How the Public Perceives Romney, Mormons: Candidate Recently Discussed the Role of Religion in Public Life," Pew Forum on Religion & Public Life, December 4, 2007, ⟨http://pewforum.org/docs/?DocID=267⟩ (accessed October 3, 2009).

CHAPTER SIX

1 For overviews of anti-Semitism in the United States, see Leonard Dinnerstein, *Anti-Semitism in America* (New York: Oxford University Press, 1994); and Frederic Cople Jaher, *A Scapegoat in the New Wilderness: The Origins and Rise of Anti-Semitism in America* (Cambridge: Harvard University Press, 1994). See also Michael Selzer, ed., *"Kike!": A Documentary History of Anti-Semitism in America* (New York: World Publishing, 1972).

2 Ernest Volkman, *A Legacy of Hate* (New York: Franklin Watts, 1982), 10.

3 Dinnerstein, *Antisemitism in America*, xiii.

4 James T. Richardson, Joel Best, David G. Bromley, eds., *The Satanism Scare* (New York: Aldine de Gruyter, 1991), 104–5. Bill Ellis, *Raising the Devil: Satanism, New Religions, and the Media* (Lexington: University Press of Kentucky, 2000), 124. Massimo Introvigne, "Brainwashing: Career of a Myth in the U.S. and Europe," Center for Studies on New Religions, ⟨http://www.cesnur.org/conferences/BrainWash.htm⟩ (accessed October 21, 2003).

5 John Higham, "Social Discrimination Against Jews in America, 1830–1930," *Publication of the American Jewish Historical Society* 47, nos. 1–4 (September 1957 to June 1958): 1–33. Albert S. Lindemann, *The Jew Accused* (Cambridge: Cambridge University Press, 1991), 10–12.

6 Jaher, *Scapegoat in the New Wilderness*, 2. Volkman, *A Legacy of Hate*, 8, 300.

7 Franklin H. Littell, "American Protestantism and Anti-Semitism," in *Essential Papers on Jewish-Christian Relations in the United States*, ed. Naomi Coen (New York: New York University Press, 1990), 171, 175.

8 Selzer, *"Kike!"*, 5.

9 "Klassen's Teachings," ⟨http://www.rahowa.com/index.html⟩ (accessed May 7, 2007).

CHAPTER SEVEN

1 "The Joy of Sect," *The Simpsons* (Season 9, Episode 13), first broadcast February 8, 1998, by FOX. Written by Steve O'Donnell.

2 For more on the language of "cult," see Eugene V. Gallagher, *The New Religious Movements Experience in America* (Westport, Conn.: Greenwood Press, 2004), 3–15; Lawrence Foster, "Cults in Conflict: New Religious Movements and the Mainstream Religious Tradition in America," in *Uncivil Religion: Interreligious Hostility in America*, ed. Robert N. Bellah and Frederick E. Greenspahn (New York: Crossroad, 1987), 187–89.

3 Richard Dyer, *White* (New York: Routledge, 1997), 12.

4 Phillip E. Hammond, "Cultural Consequences of Cults," in *The Future of New Religious Movements*, ed. David G. Bromley and Phillip E. Hammond (Macon, Ga.: Mercer University Press, 1987), 268–69.

5 Catharine Cookson, "Fighting for Free Exercise from the Trenches: A Case Study of Religious Freedom Issues Faced by Wiccans Practicing in the United States," in *New Religious Movements and Religious Liberty in America* (2nd ed.), ed. Derek H. David and Barry Hankins (Waco, Tex.: Baylor University Press, 2003), 142–51.

6 James A. Beckford, "The Continuum Between 'Cults' and 'Normal' Religion," in *Cults and New Religious Movements: A Reader*, ed. Lorne L. Dawson (Malden, Mass.: Blackwell Publishing, 2003), 28–29.

7 Larry D. Shinn, "Why *Did* Waco Happen?" in *From the Ashes: Making Sense of Waco*, ed. James R. Lewis (Lanham, Md.: Rowman and Littlefield Publishers, 1994), 187.

8 "Our Position Against Suicide," ⟨http://religiousmovements.lib.virginia.edu/nrms/ heavensgate_mirror/let...⟩ (accessed April 29, 2004).

9 Anson Shupe, "Constructing Evil as a Social Process," in Bellah and Greenspahn, *Uncivil Religion*, 205–16.

10 Church of Euthanasia, ⟨http://www.churchofeuthanasia.org/coefaq.html⟩ (accessed September 16, 2009). Also see, "Heaven's Gate Sermon," ⟨http://www .churchofeuthanasia.org/e-sermons/heavensgate.html⟩ (accessed April 29, 2004).

CHAPTER EIGHT

1 Susan J. Palmer, "Excavating Waco," in *From The Ashes: Making Sense of Waco*, ed. by James R. Lewis (Lanham, Md.: Rowman and Littlefield Publishers, 1994), 104.

2 Catherine Wessinger, *How the Millennium Comes Violently: From Jonestown to Heaven's Gate* (New York: Seven Bridges Press, 2000), 57.

3 Ibid., 65.

4 Catharine Cookson, "Fighting for Free Exercise from the Trenches: A Case Study of Religious Freedom Issues Faced by Wiccans Practicing in the United States," in *New Religious Movements and Religious Liberty in America* (2nd ed.), ed. Derek H. David and Barry Hankins (Waco, Tex.: Baylor University Press, 2003), 142–51.

5 James A. Beckford, "The Mass Media and New Religious Movements," in *New Religious Movements: Challenge and Response*, ed. Bryan Wilson and Jamie Cresswell (New York: Routledge, 1999), 110.

6 The Ross Institute Archives for the Study of Destructive Cults, Controversial Groups and Movements ⟨http://rickross.com⟩ (accessed June 20, 2007).

7 David Chidester, *Salvation and Suicide: An Interpretation of Jim Jones, the Peoples Temple, and Jonestown* (Bloomington: Indiana University Press, 1988). See also, "Alternative Considerations of Jonestown and Peoples Temple," ⟨http://jonestown.sdsu .edu/⟩ (accessed December 2, 2008).

8 Beckford, "New Religious Movements," 111.

9 James D. Tabor and Eugene V. Gallagher, *Why Waco? Cults and the Battle for Religious Freedom in America* (Berkeley: University of California Press, 1995), 99–100.

CONCLUSION

1 Rahowa, "Rahowa," *Cult of the Holy War*, EMI Records, 1995.

2 "Project Schoolyard: About the Project," ⟨http://www.freeyourmindproductions .com/sampler/about.shtml⟩ (accessed March 13, 2006). This information can now be found at ⟨http://www.tightrope.cc/sampler/about.shtml⟩ (accessed September 17, 2009).

3 Paul Hill, "Why Shoot an Abortionist," ⟨http://www.armyofgod.com/PHillonepage .html⟩ (accessed March 11, 2008).

4 "The Second Defensive Action Statement," ⟨http://www.armyofgod.com/defense2
.html⟩ (accessed March 11, 2008). For more information on the Army of God, see
Mark Juergensmeyer, *Terror in the Mind of God: The Global Rise of Religious Violence*
(Berkeley: University of California Press, 2001), 19–43.

5 Michael Bray, "The Murder of God's Prophet," ⟨http://www.armyofgod.com/Mike
Bray.html⟩ (accessed March 11, 2008).

6 "Sodomite West Virginians, the real Brokeback Mountaineers" ⟨http://www.god
hatesfags.com/fliers/pickets.html⟩ (accessed March 13, 2006).

7 "Who are you, what do you do, and why do you do it?" from ⟨http://www.godhates
fags.com/faq.html#Who⟩ (accessed March 13, 2006).

8 "Frequently Asked Questions," ⟨http://www.godhatesfags.com/faq.html⟩ (accessed
March 13, 2006).

9 "Aryan Wear," ⟨http://aryanwear.com/⟩ (accessed March 12, 2008).

10 "The Monstrous Regiment of Women," Gunn Brothers, Gunn Productions, no date.
We first came across this documentary in 2008 suggesting a 2007 or 2008 release date.

11 "Teaching Tolerance: A Teacher's Guide to Understanding and Correcting Racial
Hatred in the Classroom," ⟨http://www2.davidduke.com/teaching_tolerance.html⟩
(accessed March 13, 2006).

12 Lawrence Foster, "Cults in Conflict," in *Uncivil Religion: Interreligious Hostility in
America*, ed. Robert N. Bellah and Frederick E. Greenspahn (New York: Crossroad,
1987), 189–90.

13 Rabbi Abraham Cooper, "Introduction," in *The New Lexicon of Hate: The Changing
Tactics, Language and Symbols of America's Extremists* (Los Angeles: Simon Wiesenthal Center, 1997).

14 U.S. Senate, "Hate Crime on the Internet," Hearing before the Committee on the
Judiciary on Ramifications of Internet Technology on Today's Children, Focusing on
the Prevalence of Internet Hate, and Recommendations on How to Shield Children
from the Negative Impact of Violent Media," 106th Cong., 1st sess., September 14,
1999 (Washington: U.S. Government Printing Office, 2001), 24–25.

15 Verta Taylor and Nancy E. Whittier, "Collective Identity in Social Movement Communities," in *Frontiers in Social Movement Theory*, ed. Aldon D. Morris and Carol Mc-
Clurg Mueller (New Haven: Yale University Press, 1992), 104–5.

16 William A. Gamson, "The Social Psychology of Collective Action," in Morris and
Mueller, *Frontiers in Social Movement Theory*, 60.

17 Heather Hendershot, *Shaking the World for Jesus* (Chicago: University of Chicago
Press, 2004), 30.

18 Carol M. Swain, *The New White Nationalism in America: Its Challenge to Integration*
(Cambridge: Cambridge University Press, 2002), 25, 27. See also Barbara Perry, *In the
Name of Hate: Understanding Hate Crimes* (New York: Routledge, 2001), 165.

19 Carol M. Swain and Russ Nieli, eds., *Contemporary Voices of White Nationalism in
America* (Cambridge: Cambridge University Press, 2003), 8.

20 Jurgensmeyer, *Terror in the Mind of God*, 178–82.

21 Carolyn Petrosino, "Connecting the Past to the Future: Hate Crime in America,"

in *Crimes of Hate: Selected Readings,* ed. Phyllis B. Gerstenfeld and Diana R. Grant (Thousand Oakes, Calif.: SAGE Publications, 2004), 12–13.

22   "Frequently Asked Questions: Why do you preach hate?," ⟨http://www.godhates fags.com//faq.html⟩ (accessed March 13, 2006).

23   Ben Klassen, *The White Man's Bible* (Lighthouse Point, Fla.: Church of the Creator, 1981), 7.

24   Michael Barkun, *Religion and the Racist Right* (Chapel Hill: University of North Carolina Press, 1997), x, 147.

25   Harvey Cox, "Myths Sanctioning Religious Persecution," in *A Time for Consideration,* ed. M. Darrol Bryant and Herbert W. Richardson (New York: Edwin Mellen, 1978), 3–19.

26   Robert N. Bellah and Frederick E. Greenspahn, eds., *Uncivil Religion: Interreligious Hostility in America* (New York: Crossroad, 1987), ix.

27   Robert N. Bellah, "Conclusion: Competing Visions of the Role of Religion in American Society," in Bellah and Greenspahn, *Uncivil Religion,* 219.

28   Audre Lorde, *Sister Outsider: Essays and Speeches* (Trumansburg, N.Y.: Crossing Press, 1984), 115.

29   Also see David Brion Davis, "Some Themes of Counter-Subversion: An Analysis of Anti-Masonic, Anti-Catholic, and Anti-Mormon Literature," *The Mississippi Valley Historical Review* 47 (Sept. 1960): 205–24.

30   See also David G. Bromley and Anson D. Shupe Jr., *Strange Gods: The Great American Cult Scare* (Boston: Beacon Press, 1981), 12.

31   Bellah and Greenspahn, *Uncivil Religion,* ix.

32   Bromley and Shupe, *Strange Gods,* 20. Also see Bellah and Greenspahn, *Uncivil Religion,* 183; and Perry, *In the Name of Hate,* 4, 39.

33   John F. Wilson and Donald Drakeman, eds., *Church and State in American History,* 3rd ed. (Boulder, Colo.: Westview Press, 2003), 159–60.

34   See also Jurgensmeyer, *Terror in the Mind of God,* 145–63.

35   David Chidester, *Authentic Fakes* (Berkeley: University of California Press, 2005), 18.

36   See "Portraits of Hate, Lessons of Hope," ⟨http://www.fightingreligiousintolerance. org⟩.

37   Jurgensmeyer, *Terror in the Mind of God,* 183.

38   The term "culture of hate" comes from Jack Levin and Jack McDevitt, *Hate Crimes: The Rising Tide of Bigotry and Bloodshed* (Boulder, Colo.: Westview Press, 1993), 34–44.

39   *Encyclopedia of Religion,* 2nd ed., vol. 9, ed. Lindsay Jones (Detroit: Macmillan Reference USA, 2005), s.v. "Myth: An Overview," 6363.

40   Ibid., 6359.

41   Bromley and Shupe, *Strange Gods,* 11, 19.

42   Ibid., 19.

43   Ibid., 4.

44   Perry, *In the Name of Hate,* 33; Petrosino, "Connecting the Past," 6.

45 Barre Toelken, "Seeing with a Native Eye," in *Seeing with a Native Eye,* ed. Walter Holden Capps (New York: Harper & Row, 1976), 17.

46 Levin and McDevitt, *Hate Crimes,* 42.

47 Lorde, *Sister Outsider,* 40, 43.

48 Thomas A. Tweed, ed., *Retelling U.S. Religious History* (Berkeley: University of California Press, 1997), 2.

49 Lorde, *Sister Outsider,* 115.

50 Bromley and Shupe, *Strange Gods,* 220.

51 Barry A. Kosmin and Ariela Keysar, "American Religious Identification Survey [ARIS 2008]: Summary Report," March 2009. Available at ⟨http://www.american-religionsurvey-aris.org/⟩ (accessed May 1, 2009).

52 See Franklin H. Littell, "First They Came for the Jews," *Christian Ethics Today,* February 1997, ⟨http://www.christianethicstoday.com/Issue/009/Issue_009_February _1997.htm⟩ (accessed May 6, 2008).

INDEX

Abbott, Ernest Hamline, 6–7

Abortion, 123, 248–49, 251, 255. *See also* Bray, Michael; Hill, Paul

"Absolute Proof That Romanism Desired the Death of Abraham Lincoln," 53

Abuse, 220; of children, 221, 225–26; of women, 258

Activities of Federal Law Enforcement Agencies Toward the Branch Davidians (1996), 230–31

"ADL Criticism of Mel Gibson's 'The Passion' Elicits Anti-Semitic Responses" (2003), 178. *See also* Anti-Defamation League

"ADL Statement on Mel Gibson's 'The Passion'" (2003), 175–76. *See also* Anti-Defamation League

"Advantages of Mingling Indians with Whites, The" (1892), 141

Adventists, 100; intolerance toward, 112–17. *See also* Branch Davidians; Seventh-Day Adventists

African Americans, 12, 52, 58, 69, 70, 107, 110, 111, 116, 117, 160, 171, 172, 204, 206, 208–14, 251, 254–55; intolerance toward, 12, 52, 70, 107, 110–12, 209–14; and Ku Klux Klan, 12, 52, 70; and race, 107, 116, 204, 206

African Methodist Episcopal Church, 107

African Methodist Episcopal Zion Church, 107

Agnosticism, 105, 264

Alexander VI, 131–32. *See also* Catholics; Native Americans; Pope

Allen, Richard, 110. *See also* African Americans

"Almost Time for a Hog-Killing" (1915), 161

Amalekites, 18–19, 21, 26–33, 127; and Bible, 18, 26–27; Catholics as, 19, 21, 28–29, 31, 32; Jews as, 18–19, 26; Mormons as, 21; Native Americans as, 19, 32, 126–27, 128, 135

America, 185, 211–13, 235, 257, 258; American destiny, 102–4; American identity, 204–6, 260, 263, 264; definition of, 185, 257; and exceptionalism, 5, 7; founding myth, 3; as Garden of Eden,

125; and Judeo-Christian heritage, 185–86; and religion, 211–13

American Catholic Quarterly Review, 55

American Civil Liberties Union, 116–17

American Ideals Historically Traced, 1607–1907, 6

American Indian Religious Freedom Act Amendment of 1994, 145. *See also* Government, U.S.; Native Americans

American Jew, The, 155, 158

American Jewish Committee, 160

American Nation: A History, The (1907), 5, 6

American Protective Association, 52, 67–68

American Protestant, The, 59–60

American Protestant Association, 59

American Republican Party, 51

American Revolution, 4, 6

American Sunday School Union, 152–53

"Am I an Anti-Semite?" (1939), 167–68

Ammerman, Nancy T., 227–28

Anglican Church (Church of England), 4, 18, 22, 40

Animal magnetism, 117

Animal sacrifice, 210–11, 213–14. *See also* Ritual; Santería

Anti-Catholicism, 49–72. *See also* Catholics

Anti-Christ, 22. *See also* Pope

Anticult movement, 183, 184–85, 221, 223, 224, 228, 229; and Branch Davidians, 218, 219, 224–31; and Unificationism, 186, 189–91

Anti-Defamation League, 169, 175–76, 177, 178–79. *See also* Gibson, Mel; Judaism

Antidote to Mormonism, 74

Antifeminism, 250–51

Anti-Judaism, 148–49, 150. *See also* Anti-Semitism; Judaism

Anti-Mormon Almanac, for 1842, The (1841), 75

Anti-Mormonism, 73–98. *See also* Mormons

Anti-Semitism, 147, 148, 149–51, 152–53, 155, 156, 162–68, 169, 173–80, 194, 204, 205, 252, 255, 256;

and hate, 149, 156; and Henry Ford, 164–65; and Ku Klux Klan, 204; and race, 149, 152, 155; and religion, 149, 256. *See also* Frank, Leo;; *Protocols of the Learned Elders of Zion*

Applewhite, Marshall Herff, 197. *See also* Heaven's Gate

Arena, 95–96, 115–16

Arkansas Constitution (1874), 124

Arminius, Jacob, 18

Army of God, 248, 255

Arson, 110, 111, 112, 113, 114, 170, 194–95, 205

"Article 2," in *New York Evangelist* (1879), 114

Aryan Nations, 173, 174

Aryan Wear, 249–50, 254

Ashby, Daniel, 84–85

Asian Americans, 8–9, 254–55

Asian Exclusion Act (1924), 9

Asian Exclusion League, 9

Assimilation, 6–7, 54; of Asian Americans, 9; of Jews, 54; of Native Americans, 24, 129–30, 140

Astoria, Oreg., 203–4

Atheism, 36, 105, 156, 179, 264; intolerance toward, 105, 124

Atkinson's Saturday Evening Post, 83

Atlanta, Ga., 53, 70, 156

Awful Disclosures of Maria Monk, 61

Bacheler, Origen, 74

Baptists, 4, 78, 203; and African Americans, 110, intolerance toward, 23; and Native Americans, 140

Barbarism, 29, 31, 33, 135, 138, 213. *See also* Native Americans

Barkun, Michael, 244–45

Barlow, Joel, 99

Barrett, James, 248

Barrett, Todd, 223

Battles, 63, 77, 84; Battle of Crooked Ridge, 82. *See also* Mormons

Bayle, Pierre, 18

Beaumont, Tex., 116–17. *See also* Jehovah's Witnesses

Beecher, Lyman, 66–67

Ben Israel, Rabbi Manasseh, 21

Benson, Milton, 122–23

Berg, Moses, 187

Bethel Baptist Church, 205. *See also* Arson

Bible, 18, 51, 102, 103, 105, 107, 126, 135, 136, 152, 175, 179–80, 196–97, 203, 205–6, 234–36, 237–38, 245, 248, 249, 250, 251, 255

Bible History (1881), 154–55

Bill of Rights, 4, 95, 193. *See also* Constitution, U.S.

Biskupic, Joan, 228–29

Black, Don, 254. *See also* White supremacy

"Black Muslim Founder Exposed as a White" (1963), 206–8

Black Power, 208–9. *See also* African Americans; Nation of Islam

Blasphemy, 36, 40, 74; Catholics as, 42; Jews as, 41, 42

"Blood Rites and Rights" (1992), 212–13

Bloomington, Ind., 171. *See also* Smith, Benjamin "August"; World Church of the Creator

Boarding schools, 130. *See also* Native Americans

Board of Indian Commissioners, 130, 140. *See also* Native Americans

Boggs, Lilburn W., 77, 82

Bombing, 194, 205. *See also* Arson

Book of Mormon, 73, 74, 92. *See also* Mormons; Smith, Joseph

Boston, 51, 55, 114

Boston Evening Telegraph, 61–62

Boundaries, 35, 257, 260–61

Bowers, Henry F., 67

Bradford, William, 125–26

Brainwashing, 97, 181, 182, 183, 184, 188–89. *See also* Anticult movement

Branch Davidians, 215–46; and Bureau of Alcohol, Tobacco, and Firearms, 218, 224, 226, 227, 228–29, 230–32, 237, 243; as cult, 215, 219–23, 224, 228, 233–34, 241, 243; and David Koresh, 215, 217–18, 220, 223–26, 230–31, 232–35, 237–38, 243, 244; and FBI, 215, 224, 225–26, 232–33, 237; and Jonestown, 222–23, 228–29, 232, 242–43

Bray, Michael, 248–49, 254, 255. *See also* Abortion

Breault, Marc, 221, 224, 226–27, 237. *See also* Branch Davidians

Brown, Lucretia, 117–18

Brownson, O. A., 87

Buchanan, James, 79, 86, 90–91; Buchanan's Blunder, 86. *See also* Utah Mormon War

Buddhism, 2, 9, 104, 186, 194

Bureau of Alcohol, Tobacco, and Firearms, 226–32, 237, 243–44. *See also* Branch Davidians; Government, U.S.

Burghard, Devin, 172

"Burning of Charlestown Convent" (1834), 61–62. *See also* Arson

Burning Times, 191

Burnt-over district, 73, 80

Butler, Richard, 174

Camp meeting, 105, 119, 120, 121, 122; intolerance toward, 119–24

"Camp Meetings" (1831), 122

Canaanites, 92, 136. *See also* Mormons; Native Americans

Cantwell v. Connecticut, 1, 184

Carey, Hugh L., 189

Carleton, James Henry, 88–89

Cartoons, 199–200

Castellio, Sebastian, 17–18

Castro, Fidel, 209–10

Catholics, 4, 50–51, 72, 80, 254–55; and African Americans, 209; as Amalekites, 19, 21, 27, 28–29, 31, 32; intolerance toward, 12, 18, 21–22, 23, 25, 27–29, 31, 32, 34, 49–72, 102, 218, 258, 259, 260; and Native Americans, 24, 32, 33, 44, 45, 58, 140; and Pope, 22, 29, 33, 38, 42, 70, 131–32, 260; and sexuality, 69, 70, 258, 259. *See also* Anti-Catholicism; Dominicans; Jesuits

Cavanaugh, Jim, 234–35, 245–46. *See also* Branch Davidians

"Chapter in the History of the Colored School, A" (1865), 112

Charlestown, Mass., 34, 51, 61–62. *See also* "Burning of Charlestown Convent"; Jones, Margaret

Chicago, Ill., 104, 153. *See also* Moody, Dwight L.

Child, Lydia Maria, 114

Children, 55, 97, 108, 110, 152, 182, 183, 187, 188–89, 192, 247; abuse of, 97, 217–18, 221, 223, 225–26; and Branch Davidians, 217–18, 221, 223, 225–26; Child Protection Services, 225–26; child sacrifice, 113, 114, 152; deprogramming of, 182, 183, 188–91; and Fundamentalist Church of Jesus Christ of Latter-Day Saints, 81, 97

Children of God, 187

Christian Advocate, 122–23

Christian Century, 244–45

Christian Disciple, 136

Christian Identity movement, 169, 173, 230, 247, 249, 255, 256. *See also* Race; White Supremacy

Christianity, 78, 92, 99, 106, 110, 137–39, 140–41, 142, 148, 162, 164–65, 168, 173, 176, 178, 193–94, 196–97, 204–6, 248, 249, 250, 256, 257, 261, 264; Christians as victim, 99, 162, 164–65, 168, 250; corruption of, 78, 110, 261; and Native Americans, 126–29, 132–34

"Christianity and the Church Identical" (1844), 87

Christianity in the United States (1888), 5

Christian Party, 206

Christian Science (Church of Christ, Scientist), 4, 100, 104, 106, 117–18; as demonic, 106, 117–18. *See also* Eddy, Mary Baker

Christian Secretary, 121–22

Christian Watchman, 121

Church of Christ, Scientist. *See* Christian Science

Church of England. *See* Anglican Church

Church of Euthanasia, 203

Church of Jesus Christ of Latter-day Saints. *See* Mormons

Church of Lukumi Babalu Aye v. Hialeah (1992), 210

Cieza de Leon, Pedro, 20

Civil authority, 43, 45, 54–55, 81, 86, 91; and Catholics, 54–55; and Mormons, 86, 91; and Native Americans, 43, 45, 54

Civilization, 77; and African Americans, 141; and Native Americans, 127, 137, 138, 142, 260

Civil liberties, 148. *See also* American Civil Liberties Union

Civil rights, 110–11, 254

Civil rights movement, 204

Civil War, 101

Clinton, Bill, 230

Clinton, Iowa, 67. *See also* American Protective Association

Cochran, Floyd, 174. *See also* Aryan Nations; Summer of Hate

Code Noir (1685), 46–47. *See also* African Americans

Columbus, Christopher, 23

Commerce, Ill. *See* Nauvoo, Ill.

Common Sense, 59

Communism, 168, 250, 265

Community, 31, 35, 73–74, 77, 78, 101, 103, 107, 217, 252, 253–54

Complaint against Daniel H. Spofford (1878), 118

Concerning Heretics, 17. *See also* Castellio, Sebastian; Heresy

Congregationalists, 4, 104, 140, 148

Congress, 3, 67, 75, 94–95, 156; and Native Americans, 144–45; and polygamy, 80

Connecticut. *See* Jones, Margaret

Connell, Joan, 193–94. *See also* Wicca

Constantine, 49

Constitution, U.S., 1, 3, 6, 63, 79, 80, 91, 95, 96, 115, 148, 161, 193, 210, 212–13, 242, 251

Constitution of New York (1777), 38

Conversion, 99–100; of African Americans, 209; of Jews, 137, 149; of Muslims, 137; of Native Americans, 43–45, 126–28, 137–39, 140–41; and revivals, 99–100

Coornher, Dirck, 18. *See also* Religious toler-
ance
Corruption, 49, 51, 77, 78, 110, 160, 183, 186, 220,
255, 258, 261
Coughlin, Charles, 167–68
Court of Indian Offenses, 142–44. *See also* Native
Americans
"Creating a Killer" (1999), 172
Creativity Movement, 169, 247, 249, 255, 256.
See also World Church of the Creator
Crime, 113, 116, 182, 260; and Branch Davidians,
215, 226; and Leo Frank, 156; and Native
Americans, 142–43
Crocker, Joseph Henry, 6
Cult Awareness Network, 221–22, 227, 228
Cult chasm, 232–40
Cults, 97, 182–83, 184, 187, 206, 232. *See also* Media;
New religious movements; Stereotypes
Cumorah, 98. *See also* Book of Mormon;
Mormons; Smith, Joseph
Curse of Ham, 107. *See also* African Americans
Curtis, Theodore W., 95–96
Cushing, H. C., 137–39

Dale, Thomas, 22, 35–36
Darwin, Charles, 105
"David Koresh: Part 1" (1992), 225–26
De Acosta, José, 20
Dearborn, Mich., 164–65. *See also* Anti-Semitism;
Ford, Henry; *Protocols of the Learned Elders
of Zion*
Dearborn Independent, 160, 164–66. *See also* Anti-
Semitism; Ford, Henry; *Protocols of the Learned
Elders of Zion*
Decker, Ed, 98
Declaration of Independence, 3, 55, 169–70
DeGuerin, Dick, 235, 236, 238, 239. *See also* Branch
Davidians
Deists, 99, 119
De Las Casas, Bartolomé, 20, 24, 43, 45–46, 126
De la Vega, Garcilaso, 20
Department of the Interior, 130, 142–43
"Deprogrammer Upheld in Appeal by Moon
Convert" (1978), 190
Deprogramming, 182, 183, 188–89, 190, 221–22, 228.
See also Anticult movement; Ross, Rick
Devil. *See* Satan
Dissenters, 41
Dorchester, Daniel, 5
Drumont, Edouard, 155
Dudley, Paul, 55

Duke, David, 251–52, 254. *See also* White
supremacy
Dulack, Tom, 188–89. *See also* Anticult movement
Dwight, Timothy, 100
Dyer, Mary, 39, 108. *See also* Quakers

Eddy, Mary Baker, 118. *See also* Christian Science
Education, 3, 4, 101, 172, 192; of African Ameri-
cans, 110, 172; of Native Americans, 172. *See also*
American Sunday School Union
Edwards, Jonathan, 103
Eggleston, Edward, 6
Eldorado, Tex., 97
Eliot, John, 21
Elizabeth I, 29, 56
Emotion, 101, 106, 256–57
Employment Division v. Smith (1990), 144–45.
See also Native Americans; Peyote
Enfield, N.H., 108. *See also* Dyer, Mary
England, Mark, 221–22
English Reformation, 19
Enlightenment, 18, 99, 100, 103, 104–5, 119
Equal Rights Amendment, 250
Erasmus of Rotterdam, 17
*Essay on the merchandize of slaves & souls of men,
An,* (1731), 56
"Euless Offers Settlement in Santeria Case"
(2007), 214
Euro-American Unity and Rights Organization,
252. *See also* Duke, David
Evangelicals, 97, 105, 119–24
*Everlasting Record of the Utter Ruine of Romish
Amalek, An,* (1624), 27–29
Executive Order 9066, 2. *See also* Asian
Americans
"Experts: Branch Davidians Dangerous, Destruc-
tive Cult" (1993), 221–22
Exposure of Mormonism (1838), 75
Extermination, 77, 82, 87, 127, 135, 136–37. *See
also* Missouri Executive Order Number 44;
Mormons

"Fake Nike Advertisement," 200
Family, 81, 192, 251, 258, 260
Fard, Wallace, 207
"FBI Memo" (1963), 208–9
Federal Bureau of Investigation (FBI), 168–69,
215, 232, 235, 236, 237, 239, 244
Feminism, 250–51
Finney, Charles Grandison, 99–100. *See also*
Revivals

First Amendment, 3, 5, 216, 242. *See also* Bill of Rights

"First Blast of the Trumpet against the Monstrous Regiment of Women, The," 250

Ford, Henry, 160, 162; and German Reich, 164; and *International Jew*, 164–65. *See also* Anti-Semitism; *Protocols of the Learned Elders of Zion*

Forgetting, 4, 5, 7–8; and Amalekites, 27; and religious intolerance, 263–64

"4 Agents Killed, 16 Hurt in Raid on Cult" (1993), 228–29

Foxman, Abraham H., 176

FOX Television, 181–84. *See also* Media; *The Simpsons*

Francis, Samuel, 211–13

Franciscans, 50. *See also* Catholics

Frank, Leo, 156–61; image of, 159; and sexual perversion, 157–58. *See also* Anti-Semitism

Frank Leslie's Illustrated Newspaper, 64

Franklin, Benjamin, 135–36

Fraud, 59, 182; David Koresh as, 229; Joseph Smith as, 74; Native American conversions as, 137; Wallace Fard as, 208–9

Frederickson, Paula, 179–80

Free exercise, 38, 119, 213. *See also* Constitution, U.S.

French and Indian War (1754–63), 22, 25, 50

Friends' Intelligencer, 136–37

From the Annual Letter of the Jesuits of 1655 and 1656, 57

Fundamentalism, 256

"Fundamentalist Christian Speaks against Wiccans, A," 196–97

Fundamentalist Church of Jesus Christ of Latter-Day Saints, 97. *See also* Abuse; Children; Mormons

Furrow, Buford, Jr., 173–75. *See also* Anti-Semitism; Aryan Nation; White supremacy

Garcia, Henry, 232–33

Gates, Sir Thomas, 134

Gender, 80, 250–51, 258, 260; and religious intolerance, 255, 257

"General Methodist Items" (1877), 112

Genocide: definition of, 13; of Native Americans, 128, 130

Gentiles, 163, 164; non-Mormons as, 87, 92. *See also* Mormons

Georgia, 37–38, 69, 156, 160

Georgia Charter of 1732, 37–38

Germany, 105, 164, 247

Ghost Dance, 128, 142. *See also* Native Americans; Wounded Knee

Gibson, Mel, 149, 178–79. *See also* Anti-Semitism; *Passion of the Christ, The*

Gilbert, Sir Humphrey, 134

Gilmour, Bishop Richard, 154

Glad Tidings (1876), 153–54. *See also* Anti-Semitism; Jesus Christ; Moody, Dwight L.; Pontius Pilate

Glorious Revolution, 50, 57–58

Gnaddenhutten, Pa., 139. *See also* Moravians; Native Americans

Golden plates, 73. *See also* Book of Mormon; Mormons; Smith, Joseph

Gonzales v. O Centro Espírita Beneficente Uniao do Vegetal (2006), 144. *See also* Native Americans; Supreme Court, U.S.

Government, U.S., 22, 77, 78, 135, 184, 192, 224, 239, 241, 255; and African Americans, 208; and Native Americans, 45, 129, 130, 136

Grand Service Cross of the Supreme Order of the German Eagle, 164. *See also* Ford, Henry; Germany

Great Awakening, 103, 105. *See also* Revivals

Grotius, Hugo, 18

Guiding mentality, 6. *See also* Religious tolerance

Gunn, Emily, 250–51. *See also* Feminism

Gunpowder Plot, 27

"Gunshots Exchanged" (1990), 195

Hale, Matthew, 171. *See also* World Church of the Creator

Hale, Salma, 7

Halloween, 193–94. *See also* Wicca; Witchcraft

"Hard Lessons in the Ashes" (1993), 223

Hare Krishna: as cult, 187; intolerance toward, 186, 193, 194. *See also* Arson; Cults

Hart, Albert Bushnell, 6. *See also* Separation of church and state

Harvard, Mass., 108

Harvard College, 55

Hate, 29, 57, 64, 70, 79, 95, 101, 173, 255, 264, 265; and anti-Semitism, 148–49, 155, 156, 171; and Bible, 249; and Fred Phelps, 249, 255–56; hate crimes, 8, 168–69; hate groups, 255; and race, 70, 148–49, 171, 251, 252, 255; and religion, 162, 255–56; and religious intolerance, 95, 252, 256; and Benjamin "August" Smith, 171

Haun's Mill, 77, 82. *See also* Mormons; Vigilantism

Heathens, 4, 9, 127; Native Americans as, 127, 135, 136, 138

Heaven's Gate, 197–204; as cult, 197, 203; and
Hale-Bopp Comet, 198; and humor, 199–202;
intolerance toward, 186, 197–204; and media,
197, 198, 199–202; and suicide, 197, 198, 199,
203–4. *See also* Cults; Media; Suicide
"Heaven's Gate Mass Suicide Cartoon" (1997),
199
"Heaven's Gate or Hell's?," 203–4
Heckewelder, John, 139. *See also* Moravians;
Native Americans
Hefley, James, 187. *See also* Anticult movement;
Cults
Hendrick, Burton Jesse, 166–67. *See also* Anti-
Semitism; Race
Heresy, 18, 38–39; and Inquisition, 24–25, 49;
intolerance toward, 17, 22, 23, 35, 36, 39, 49, 101;
Quakers as heretics, 23, 39; and Satan, 49
Heretics, 242. *See also* Heresy
Hialeah, Fla., 210–13. *See also* Animal sacrifice;
Constitution, U.S.; Santería
"Hialeah Resolutions and Ordinances" (1987),
210–11
Higher criticism, 151–52
Hill, Paul, 248, 254. *See also* Abortion; Murder
Hindu, 104, 163
Hispanics, 171. *See also* Hate; Race
Historical Memoirs of the Fight at Piggwacket
(1725), 33
Hoax, 162, 191
Hollywood vs. America (1992), 177
Holocaust, 178; and Anti-Semitism, 176; and
education, 172
Holy Spirit, 119. *See also* Pentecostals
Holy Spirit Association, 186
Holy War, 247
Homosexuals, 171. *See also* Hate; Sex
Hope for Israel (1650), 21. *See also* Jews; Native
Americans
"Horrors of Memphis, The" (1866), 111
Hoskins, Richard, 174
*Household History of the United States and Its
People for Young Americans, The* (1890), 6
Houteff, Victor T., 216–17. *See also* Branch
Davidians
Howard, Addie, 112
Howe, E. D., 74
Howell, Vernon. *See* Koresh, David
Huberman, Leo, 7
Huguenots, 115
Human Individual Metamorphosis, 197. *See also*
Heaven's Gate

Humanity, 261–62; of Native Americans, 127, 129
Humor: as intolerance, 199–202. *See also* Heaven's
Gate
Huntsville, Tex., 112. *See also* Arson

Identity, 257, 258, 260; and religious intolerance,
259–60
Idolatry, 35, 36, 113; of Buddhists, 9; of Catholics,
42, 55
Iews in America (1650), 21
Ileto, Joseph, 173. *See also* Murder; Race
Illinois Mormon War (1844–46), 85–86
Immigrants, 54, 61, 66, 148, 150, 151, 152
Immortale Dei (1895), 54. *See also* Catholics; Civil
authority
Imperial Night-hawk, 53
Independence, Mo., 74. *See also* Vigilantism
"Indian, The" (1867), 136–37
Infidelity, 18, 99, 105
Ingle, Richard, 56. *See also* Violence
Inquisition, 18, 24–25, 49, 137; and religious
intolerance, 24
Insanity: and cults, 183; and David Koresh, 215,
223
Inside the Cult (1993), 226–27, 237. *See also* Branch
Davidians; Breault, Marc
Inter Caetera (1493), 131–32
*International Jew: The World's Foremost Problem,
The* (1920), 164–65
Internet: and community, 253–54; and hate,
252–56
Internment, 2
"In the Grip of a Psychopath" (1993), 223
Intolerance, 1, 34, 79, 97, 116, 128, 149, 150, 223, 255.
See also Religious intolerance
Islam, 4, 204; intolerance toward, 8–10, 11, 23, 43,
49, 204, 205, 206. *See also* Nation of Islam
Isolation, 149, 197

James I, 134
James II, 57
Jamestown, 22, 35
Japanese Americans, 2, 3, 8, 9, 11
Jefferson, Thomas, 3, 39, 40–41, 99; and religious
freedom, 22–23
Jeffersonian, 53, 157–58
Jehovah's Witnesses, 1, 3, 8, 100, 112, 116–17, 184,
186, 219, 259; intolerance toward, 1, 8, 113, 116–17,
186; and law, 184, 219; and patriotism, 113, 219
Jesuits, 24, 128. *See also* Catholics; Native
Americans

Jesus Christ, 106, 107, 175, 179–80; and deicide, 149, 153, 154–55, 166; and Second Coming, 103–4, 107, 112, 175, 186

Jew, at Home and Abroad, The (1845), 152–53

"Jewish Attack Upon a State Where No Jew Was Ever Mistreated" (1915), 161

Jewish Peril: Protocols of the Learned Elders of Zion, The (1920), 162–63

Jews, 4, 62–63, 212, 213; and blasphemy, 41, 42; as Christ-killers, 41, 42; and conspiracy, 170, 255, 260; and Inquisition, 18, 24, 49, 137; intolerance toward, 8, 12, 18, 23, 41–42, 52, 70, 147–80; and Ku Klux Klan, 12, 52, 70; and Native Americans, 18, 20, 21, 126; as race, 69, 148, 149, 171, 255; and Satan, 262; violence toward, 147, 148, 150. *See also* Anti-Semitism; Frank, Leo

Jews in America (1923), 166–67

John Paul II, 55

Johnson and Graham's Lessee v. William M'intosh (1823), 132–34

Jones, B. P., 116

Jones, Jim, 222, 223. *See also* Koresh, David; People's Temple

Jones, Margaret, 34, 35. *See also* Satan; Witchcraft

Jones, Perry, 220

Jonestown, 222, 228–29, 232, 242–43. *See also* Branch Davidians; People's Temple

"Joy of Sect, The," 181–84

Judaism, 152–53, 155, 156; as religion, 151. *See also* Anti-Semitism; Jews

Junk culture, 198; and Heaven's Gate, 199–202

Kennedy, John F., 53, 71, 72

Keppler, Joseph, Sr., 160. See also *Puck*

Kidnapping, 189. *See also* Anticult movement; Deprogramming

King, Martin, 226–27, 237

King, Martin Luther, Jr., 208, 251. *See also* African Americans; Civil rights

King William's War, 32

Kirtland, Ohio, 74, 75. *See also* Mormons

Kirtland Safety Society, 75. *See also* Kirtland, Ohio

Klassen, Ben, 169–70, 256. *See also* Race; White supremacy

Knights of Columbus, 70

Knights of Mary Phagan, 156. *See also* Frank, Leo; Lynching

Knights of the Klan versus Knights of Columbus, 70–71. *See also* Ku Klux Klan

Know-Nothings, 51–52. *See also* Anti-Catholicism

Knox, John, 250. *See also* Antifeminism

Koresh, David, 215, 230–31, 232–35; and Bible, 203, 235–36, 237–38, 239, 245; as criminal, 215; and cult, 221–22, 243, 245; as fraud, 223, 229; as insane, 215; intolerance toward, 215–46; and prophecy, 217–18; and sexuality, 223; as terrorist, 226. *See also* Branch Davidians; Cults; Seven seals

Kristallnacht, 168

Ku Klux Klan, 12, 52–53, 70–71, 165–66, 193, 204–5, 206, 249, 251, 254, 255, 256; and anti-Catholicism, 12, 52, 53, 70; and anti-Semitism, 204; and David Duke, 251; and racism, 12, 52, 70, 204; and violence, 70. *See also* Anti-Semitism; Race

Ku Klux Klan in Prophecy, The (1925), 165–66

Lacayo, Richard, 198, 199, 223. *See also* Cults; Media

Ladies Against Feminism, 250

Lancaster County, Pa.: massacre at, 135

Lane Theological Seminary, 66, 93

Law, 4, 22, 23, 40, 41, 42, 43, 46, 47, 50, 57–59, 77, 78, 82, 87, 91, 96, 105, 114, 115, 116, 119, 120, 132–34, 142, 143–45, 148, 156, 184, 185, 186, 189, 190–91, 192, 193–94, 210–11, 212, 213–14, 218–19, 228, 243, 260; and expulsion, 41, 58; and Jehovah's Witnesses, 184, 219; and Native Americans, 43, 132–34, 142, 143–45; and polygamy, 77, 87, 142, 143; and religious intolerance, 22, 23, 189; and religious rights, 189, 190–91; and Santería, 210–11, 212, 213–14, 219; and Wicca, 191, 193–94

Law, William, 77

Lee, Mother Ann, 107. *See also* Jesus Christ; Shakers

"Leo Frank Case: Does the State of Georgia Deserve This Nation-Wide Abuse?" (1914), 157–58

Let Our Children Go! (1976), 188–89. *See also* Anticult movement

"Letter," in *Message to the Blackman in America* (1965), 205–6

Letter from Daniel Ashby to General J. B. Clark (1838), 84–85. *See also* Missouri Mormon War

Letter from Rebecca Gratz to Benjamin Gratz (1844), 63

Letter from the Devil to the Venerable Sister Maria Crocefissa (1845), 59–60. *See also* Satan

Letter from T. J. Morgan (1890), 144

Letter to a minister in London (1611), 35–36. *See also* Dale, Thomas

Letter to Dick DeGuerin (1993), 236. *See also* Koresh, David

"Letter to Simon Wolf" (1957), 160
Lewis, James R., 230
Liberal, 100
Liberator, 6, 53, 114, 123–24
Liberty, 64, 94, 95, 105, 115, 116, 119, 147, 167; and
religion, 105; and religious intolerance, 115, 116
Lincoln, Abraham, 53
Liu, Melinda, 223
Livesay, Richard, 75
Locke, John, 18
Loomis, A. W., 9
Los Angeles, Calif., 173, 216
Los Angeles Herald Examiner, 206–8
"Lure of the Cult, The" (1997), 198
Lutherans, 140, 264–65
Lynching, 70, 116; of Leo Frank, 52, 156

Madison, James, 3
"Mad Mel: The Gospel according to Gibson"
(2003), 179–80
Malcolm X, 208, 251. *See also* African Americans;
Nation of Islam
Marshall, John, 132. *See also* Supreme Court,
U.S.
Marshall, Louis, 160
Marxism, 178–79. *See also* Communism
Mary I, 250
Maryland, 4, 6, 22, 56, 112, 134; religious intoler-
ance in, 22, 56–57
Masons, 71
Massachusetts, 39, 71, 103, 117
Massachusetts Bay Colony, 19, 23, 29, 148
Massacres, 111, 122–23, 135, 136; at Mountain
Meadow, 79, 86; of Native Americans, 128,
135–36; at Wounded Knee, 142
"Massacre at a Camp-Meeting" (1866), 122–23
"Mass Suicide and the Branch Davidians" (2002),
242–43
Mather, Cotton, 21, 32–33, 41, 42
Mayhew, Jonathan, 55
McCormick, Darlene, 220–22
McDonald, Stacey, 250
M'Chesney, James, 74
McKenzie, Marvin, 203–4
Media, 53, 55, 160–61; and anticult movement,
184, 206, 219–20, 221–22, 223, 224, 228–29; and
Branch Davidians, 219–14; and Catholics, 167;
and Heaven's Gate, 197–202; and Islam, 11; and
Jews, 175–80; and Mormons, 74–75, 79, 81, 85
Medicine men, 142, 143
Medved, Michael, 177

Mein Kampf, 172. *See also* Race; White supremacy
Memory, 4, 5, 25, 27, 95, 127, 135; and religious
intolerance, 264
Mental healing, 117. *See also* Christian Science;
Witchcraft
Mescal, 144. *See also* Law; Native Americans
Messiah: David Koresh as, 217; Wallace Fard as,
208–9
"Methodist Camp-Meetings" (1825), 120
Methodist Error; or Friendly Christian Advice
(1819), 120
Methodists, 23, 78, 93, 119, 140, 165; and African
Americans, 110; and camp meetings, 120, 122–23
Michas, Peter, 192
Military, 50, 70, 79, 86, 113, 128, 129, 135, 208, 249
"Military Colonization of the Indians" (1880),
138–39
Militia, 63, 75–77. *See also* Missouri Mormon War
Millennialism, 103–4, 112, 203. *See also* Adventists;
Jesus Christ
Miller, William, 112–13
Millerites, 73, 100; intolerance toward, 112–17
Milton, John, 18
"Miscellany," in *Liberator* (1844), 114
Missionaries, 78, 126, 127–28
Missouri, 75–77, 83, 120
Missouri Executive Order Number 44 (1838),
77, 82–83
Missouri Mormon War, 82–85
Missouri Statute against Disturbing a Camp
Meeting (1879), 120
Mob, 78, 85, 108, 109, 113, 119–20, 121–23, 135, 163,
193, 260; at camp meeting, 119–20, 121–23;
and Ku Klux Klan, 193; at Nauvoo, 78, 85; and
violence, 108, 113, 117, 122–23
"Mobocracy Triumphant in Abington" (147),
123–24
Modell of Christian Charity, A (1630), 19, 29–31
Mohammedanism, 9–10, 205. *See also* Islam; Na-
tion of Islam
Money: and Jews, 166, 169, 176, 178, 260
Monster, 39. *See also* Dyer, Mary
Monstrous Regiment of Women, The, 250–51
Montgomery, Ed, 206–8
Montgomery Bus Boycott, 204–5. *See also* Civil
rights; Ku Klux Klan
Moody, Dwight L., 153–54. *See also* Revivals
Moon, Sun Myung, 186, 187, 190. *See also*
Unificationism
Moonies, 182, 186, 188. *See also* Moon, Sun
Myung; Unificationism

Moorish Science Temple, 204. *See also* African Americans; Nation of Islam

Morality, 5, 78, 79, 94, 99, 102, 104–5, 106, 113, 119, 129, 191, 248, 251, 261; decline of, 94, 113, 119, 251; and religion, 129

Moravians, 137

Mormonism Exposed, 74–75

Mormonism Unvailed (1834), 74, 76

Mormons (Church of Jesus Christ of Latter-Day Saints), 73, 74, 75, 77, 78, 79, 80; as cult, 81, 97–98; as false religion, 74, 79; intolerance toward, 8, 12, 21, 73–98, 100, 102, 104, 218, 256, 258, 262; and plural marriage, 80, 81, 85, 95, 260; *See also* Book of Mormon; Smith, Joseph

"Mormon Theocracy, The" (1877), 92–93

"Mormon War, The" (1838), 83

Moroni, 98

Morris, Rev. Dr., 93

Morton, Nathaniel, 39–40

Mosques, 4, 9

Mountain Meadows, Utah, 79, 86. *See also* Massacre; Mormons

Mount Carmel, Tex., 215, 217, 224, 235, 239, 242. *See also* Branch Davidians; Koresh, David

Muhammad, Elijah, 204, 206, 207, 208. *See also* Nation of Islam

Murder, 2, 42, 52, 74, 75, 78, 85, 114, 122–23, 135, 136, 137, 139, 156, 171, 172, 173, 215, 248

Murr, Andrew, 198–99

Muslims, 137. *See also* Islam

My Kingdom Come (2007), 98

Mystery of Israel's Salvation, The (1669), 42

Myth, 130; and religious intolerance, 262–63

Narrative of Strange Principles, Conduct and Character of the People known by the Name of Shakers, A (1782), 108–9

Narrative of the Late Massacre in Lancaster County (1764), 135–36

Narrative of the Mission of the United Brethren Among the Delaware and Mohegan Indians (1820), 139

National Association for the Advancement of White People, 251–52. *See also* Duke, David; Race

National Association of Evangelicals, 71–72

National Conference of Churches: and religious liberty, 228

National Conference of Citizens for Religious Freedom, 71

Nationalism, 208

Nation of Islam, 186; intolerance toward, 204–9. *See also* African Americans; Muhammad, Elijah

Native American Church Movement, 130, 144; and peyote, 143–45, 219

Native American Graves Protection and Reparation Act (1990), 130

Native American Party, 51. *See also* Nativism

Native Americans, 4, 20, 21, 23–24, 31–33, 102, 126, 132, 262; and civilization and savagery, 21, 33, 127, 129–30, 137, 138, 141, 142; as demonic, 20, 33, 130; as lost Jewish tribes, 20; and peyote, 130, 143–45, 219; religion of, 4, 21, 73, 129, 130, 131, 145; religious intolerance toward, 12, 18, 23, 25, 32, 39, 42–43, 125–45; and ritual, 128, 130, 135, 142, 143–45. *See also* Amalekites; Civilization; Conversion

Nativism, 51–52

Nature's Eternal Religion, 172

Nauvoo, Ill., 77–78, 82, 85. *See also* Mormons; Smith, Joseph

Nauvoo Expositor, 77

Nazis, 168

Nettles, Bonnie Lu, 197

New Age, 198–99

New Amsterdam, 147–48

Newbury Herald (1878), 118

Newburyport, Mass., 118

New Deal, 167

New England, 21–22, 38–39, 41–42, 57, 104, 106, 125–26, 129, 134–35, 147

New England's Memorial (1721), 39–40

New France, 24–25, 46–47, 135

New Harmony Gazette, 137–38

New Netherlands, 41

New Port Richey, Fla., 195

New religious movements, 182–83, 185–86, 193–95, 199, 206, 210, 218–20, 224, 262; as cult, 183, 218, 219; intolerance toward, 183, 185, 218

New Republic, 179–80

"News of the Day" (1835), 121

New Spain, 24, 42–46, 135, 140

Newsweek, 198–99, 223

New Thought, 106

New York, 38, 51, 57–59, 63, 71, 110, 134, 189

New York Act against Jesuits and Popish Priests, 57–59

New York Evangelist, 94–95, 114

New York Evening Post, 166

New York Post, 135

New York Sun, 166

New York Times, 71, 93, 162

"Next Level, The" (1997), 198–99
Niemoller, Martin, 264–65
Nike, 200
North Valley Jewish Community Center, 173.
    See also Summer of Hate
Northwest Coalition Against Malicious Harass-
    ment, 174

Oath of allegiance, 67–68
Occult, 75, 97–98
Of Crimes, 36
Office of Indian Affairs, 142–43
"Official Heaven's Gate Paper Doll Kit, The," 201–2
Official intolerance, 37–38
Official religion, 40
Oneida, 73
Ontario Consultants on Religious Tolerance, 12
On the Origin of Species (1859), 105
"Open Letter to American Jews, An" (1999),
    174–75
Orange Day Riot, 51, 63–64
Original Mr. Jacobs, The (1888), 155–56
Orishas, 209. See also Santería
Orthodoxy, 34–36, 79, 103
Osbourne, Ozzy, 192
"Our Heathen Temples," 9
"Our Position Against Suicide," 197
Outsiders, 54, 149–50

Pagans, 193–94
Paine, Tom, 59
Papists, 33, 38, 42, 56, 64. See also Catholics; Pope
Parker, Quanah, 130
"Passion Elicits Unfair Conflict" (2003), 177
Passion of the Christ, The (2004), 149, 175–80
Patrick, Ted, 188–90
Patriotism, 90, 94–95, 104–5, 113, 115, 164, 219, 247
Paul VI, 55
"Paul Denton, the Texas Missionary" (1850),
    121–22
Peace, 74, 264
Peale, Norman Vincent, 71–72
Peale Group, 71
Pearl Harbor, 2
Penn, William, 21, 38, 136
Pennsylvania, 6, 38, 134, 136
Pensacola, Fla., 248
Pentecostals, 100, 119, 178, 186, 193
People's Temple, 223–24, 228. See also Jones, Jim;
    Jonestown
Persecution, 147–49, 168, 250

"Persecution — Jewish and Christian" (1938), 168
Persecution of Jehovah's Witnesses, The (1941),
    116–17
Perversion, 157–59, 183, 261
"Peter Stuyvesant to the Amsterdam Chamber of
    the Dutch West India Company," 41
Peyote, 130, 143–45, 219. See also Native Americans
Phagan, Mary, 156–57. See also Frank, Leo
Phelps, Fred, 249, 251, 254–56
Philadelphia, Pa., 51, 62–63, 110, 194
Phineas Priesthood, 173–74
Physical violence, 1–2, 50–51, 74
Pilgrims, 3, 4, 136, 147, 263; and American found-
    ing myth, 3, 263
Pillar of Fire Church, 166
Pius IX, 54
Plea for the West (1835), 66–67
Pledge of Allegiance, 219
Plundering Time, 56
Pluralism, 18
Plural marriage, 77, 142–43. See also Mormons;
    Polygamy
Plymouth Rock, 147
Pocasset, Mass., 114
Poland, 148
Political cartoons, 160–61
Political freedom, 263
Political liberty, 66
Political parties, 51–52
Political power, 63
Politics, 53, 67, 70, 78, 81, 129, 186
Pontius Pilate, 154–55, 179
Polygamy, 77–81, 85–87, 94–95, 260. See also Plural
    marriage
Poole, Elijah, 204. See also Mormons; Muham-
    mad, Elijah
Pope, 22, 43–44, 53, 56, 67, 70, 131–32, 260. See also
    Catholics
Popery, 29
Popish Idolatry (1765), 55
Postmillennialism, 112
Pratt, Henry Richard, 130, 140–41
Praying town, 129. See also Native Americans
Prejudice, 137, 160, 164–65
Premillennialism, 104, 112–13
Presbyterians, 23, 66, 78, 93–94, 136, 140
Prison, 142, 148
"Proclamation on the Rebellion in Utah" (1857),
    90–91
Prohibition, 53
Project Schoolyard, 247–48, 251

Promised Land, 102, 147

Prophecy, 216–18, 235–36

Protestants, 12, 47, 49–50, 53–54, 57, 62–64, 66, 67, 71–72, 78–79, 92, 95, 97, 99–100, 102–3, 106, 147–49, 151–53, 166, 212–13, 250, 259, 261

Protestant Reformation, 49–50

"Protestant Unit Wary on Kennedy" (1960), 71–72

Protocols of the Learned Elders of Zion, 162–68, 191, 253

Psychology, 157–58, 184

Psychopathia Sexualis (1894), 157–58

Puck, 160–61

Punishment, 49–50, 140, 156, 186

Puritan Revolution, 50

Puritans, 17–22, 29–32, 50, 95–96, 102, 147

Quakers (Society of Friends), 4, 6, 8, 21–23, 38–41, 259. *See also* Dyer, Mary

Race, 46–47, 52, 70, 102, 107, 116, 148–49, 151–52, 155, 162–63, 167, 169–71, 173, 204–6, 247–48, 251–52, 254–56; and African Americans, 107, 116, 204, 206; and Jews, 52, 148–49, 151–52, 162, 171, 255; and whites, 162–63, 169, 173, 204, 247–48. *See also* Anti-Semitism; Racism; White supremacy

Racism, 69, 171, 204–5

"Rahowa," 247

Raising Maidens of Virtue, 250

Raleigh, Sir Walter, 134

Rancho Santa Fe, Calif., 197

Rand, Eleazar, 109–10

Reason, 108, 150, 198; and Enlightenment, 99, 103–5, 119; and religion, 75

Rebellion, 79, 86

"Recommendations Concerning Incidents Such as the Branch Davidian Standoff in Waco, Texas" (1993), 229

Reconstruction, 110

Reed, Rebecca, 61

"Reflections after Waco: Millennialists and the State" (1993), 244–45

Reformation, 19, 102

Refugees, 148, 209–10

Religion, 17, 21–22, 25, 34, 41, 63, 70, 73, 78–79, 99, 102–5, 125, 129–31, 145, 147–49, 151–52, 155, 160, 162–63, 168–69, 171, 173, 178, 182–85, 191, 198, 204–5, 211–13, 219, 229, 247–48, 250–52, 255–56, 258, 261–62; and African Americans, 204; and cults, 182, 183, 219; and hate, 162, 168–69, 255;

256; and Jews, 41, 147, 149, 169, 171, 255; and Native Americans, 21, 73, 129–31, 145

Religion in America (1902), 6, 7

Religious authority, 43, 54–55, 57, 119

Religious difference, 25, 81, 87

Religious diversity, 3–4, 8, 80

Religious freedom, 4, 22–23, 25, 38, 50, 66, 71, 144, 178, 212–13

Religious Freedom Restoration Act (1993), 144

"Religious Group Denies Mass Suicide Rumor" (1992), 224–25

Religious intolerance, 4–5, 8, 11–14, 17–19, 21–25, 27–29, 32, 34–35, 38–47, 49–51, 53–55, 70, 73, 80–81, 86–87, 93, 95, 101–2, 108, 113, 115–16, 130, 150–52, 164, 181–246, 252, 254–64; and boundaries, 260–61; definition of, 12–14; and fear, 256–58, 261; and forgetting, 263–64; as rhetoric, 55, 135, 262

"Religious Intolerance in the Republic: Christians Persecuting Christians in Tennessee" (1892), 115–16

Religious liberty, 3, 25, 66, 72, 147, 151, 218–19, 228, 263

Religious News Service, 190

Religious rights, 184, 189–91

Religious sects, 74–75, 80, 95–96, 104, 181–84

Religious tolerance, 7, 17–18, 212, 263–64

Religious violence, 11, 13–14, 19, 25, 30, 34, 43, 50, 56–57, 63, 71, 75–77, 93, 135–37

Reno, Janet, 239–41

Report of the Deputy Attorney General on the Events at Waco, Texas, 236, 239–40

"Report to the Justice and Treasury Departments" (1993), 227–28

Republican values, 91–93

Requerimiento (1510), 24, 43–45. *See also* Native Americans

Reservations, 130, 140, 142

Resolution of the Citizens of Warsaw, Illinois (1844), 85–86

"Review of a Massacre" (1818), 136

Revivals, 73, 99–100, 102–3, 105, 153

Reynolds v. the United States (1879), 260

Rhode Island, 6

Rigdon, Sidney, 74, 82

Rights, 132–34, 160, 164

Ritual, 98–99, 102, 106–9, 113–14, 119, 128, 130, 135, 142–45, 149, 152, 156, 195, 209–11, 213–14, 219, 228

Roberts, B. H., 80, 94–95

Robertson, Pat, 97

Rockford, Ill., 194

Roman Catholic Hierarchy, The (1915), 69–70
Rome, 29, 54, 66
"Rome's Tatooed Man," 53
Romish, 58, 69
Romney, Mitt, 8, 81
Roosevelt, Franklin D., 2, 167
Roosevelt, Theodore, 67
Rosin, Hanna, 173–74
Ross, Rick, 221, 223, 227–28. See also Anticult movement
Royal Oak, Mich., 167
Rules Governing the Court of Indian Offenses (1883), 142–43
Russell, Charles Taze, 113

Sabbath, 113
Sacramento, Calif., 170
Salem, Mass., 34, 117
Salem witchcraft trials, 34
Salt Lake City, 80
Salt Lake Valley, 78, 86
San Francisco, Calif., 193, 249
San Jose Mercury News, 193–94
Sankey, Ira, 153
Santería, 186, 209–14, 219
Satan, 49, 59–60, 70, 74, 97, 161, 173, 189, 191–97, 204–6, 255–56, 262
Savages, 21, 137
Scapegoats, 25
"Scene of the Riot at Elm Park" (1870), 64
Schlafly, Phyllis, 250
Schneider, Steve, 232, 235, 238–40
Science, 102–5, 184
Scribner's Monthly, 91–93
Second Coming, 103–4, 107, 112, 186, 217. See also Jesus Christ
Secrecy, 49, 50–51, 69, 70, 77, 107, 128
Secret Oath of the American Protective Association, The (1893), 67–68
Secularization, 244
Sedition, 58, 94
Segregation, 107
Self-defense, 85, 261
Senate, 80, 94, 156, 230
Separation of church and state, 6, 38, 54, 71–72
Servetus, Michael, 17
Seven seals, 235–39. See also Koresh, David
Seventh-Day Adventists, 113, 115–16, 216, 221
"Seven W.I.C.C.A. Letters," 191–92
Sex, 81, 103, 107, 119, 131, 157–59, 183, 217–18, 223, 249, 255, 257–60, 262–63; sexual abuse, 97;

sexual discrimination, 80; sexual impropriety, 69–70
Shakers, 73, 107–10
Shepard, James, 109
Shin, Larry D., 243–44
Shinto, 2–3
Short Account of the Destruction of the Indies (1542), 43, 45–46
"Showdown at the Waco Corral" (1994), 230
Simon Wiesenthal Center, 178–79, 252
Simpsons, The, 181–85
"Sinful Messiah: Part One" (1993), 221
Six Months in a Convent, 61
Slander, 54, 161
Slaton, John, 156
Slavery, 5, 45–46, 47, 57, 79–80, 82, 107, 113, 141, 152, 169, 172, 251, 259
Slosson, Jonathan, 109
Smith, Al, 52–53
Smith, Benjamin "August," 170–72
Smith, Hyrum, 78
Smith, Joseph (1805–44), 73–74, 77–80, 82, 85–86, 92, 97–98
Smith, Lucy Mack, 98
Smoot, Reed, 80, 94
Social class, 119, 187
Socialists, 265
Society, 78, 258, 260
Society of Friends. See Quakers
Society of Jesus. See Jesuits
Sorg, Lisa, 171–72
Souldiers counseled and comforted (1689), 32–33
South Abington, Mass., 123–24
Southern Poverty Law Center, 265–66
Spain, 29, 129, 131, 137, 206
Spalding, Solomon, 74
Spanish empire, 23–24
"Spanish Missionaries in California" (1827), 137–38
Special Report on the Mountain Meadows Massacre (1902), 88–90
Spiritualism, 73, 100, 104, 106, 114
Spofford, Daniel, 106, 117–18
Springville, Tenn., 115–16
Star Trek, 198–99
State of New York Assembly Bill 11122-A, 190–91
"Steps to Blot Out Mormonism" (1892), 93
Stereotypes, 150–51, 175, 182–84, 218–19, 221–22, 228, 232–34, 241, 262. See also Cults
Stone Mountain, Ga., 204
Stoner, Jesse B., 205–6
Struggle, The, 172

288 INDEX

Sturhann, Chris, 199

Stuyvesant, Peter, 41, 147–48

Subversion, 51, 70

Suicide, 114, 197–98, 203–4, 215, 218, 222–25, 228, 232–33, 242–43. *See also* Branch Davidians; Heaven's Gate; People's Temple

Sullivan, Lawrence E., 229

Summerfield, Charles, 121–22

Summer of Hate, 168–75

Sun Dance, 130, 142

Sunderland, LaRoy, 74–75

Superstition, 130, 140, 213

Supreme Court, U.S., 1, 79, 130, 132–34, 144, 213

"Suspect in Community Center Shooting Surrenders, Admits Hatred" (1999), 173–74

Suspicion, 8, 74, 77, 226

Swedenborgian, 123

Swiggart, Judge W. H., 115

Syllabus of Errors (1864), 54

Symmes, Thomas, 32–33

Synagogue, 4, 150, 152, 170

Tammany Hall, 63

Tar and feather, 2, 74

Taylor, Amos, 108–9

Taylor, Thomas, 27–29

Teaching Tolerance: A Teacher's Guide to Understanding and Correcting Racial Hatred in the Classroom Web site, 251–52, 254

Tennessee, 205–6

"Ten Ways to Fight Hate," 265–66

Terrorism, 173, 226

Testimonies of Mother Ann Lee (1816), 109–10

Texas, 121–22

Texas Supreme Court, 97

Textbooks, 6–8

Theft, 137

Theocracy, 77, 91–95, 113

Theosophy, 106

Thirty Years' War (1618–48), 4, 50

Thomas, Evan, 198–99

Thomas, Pierre G., 228–29

Thompson, Ga., 53

Thompson, Sarah, 173–75

Thorowgood, Thomas, 21

Threat, 2, 11, 41, 52, 257–58, 261

Time, 198–99, 223

"To Be Young, White and Racist" (1999), 171–72

Tolerance, 252

Tongues, 119

"Top 10 Warning Signs Before Renting in Rancho Santa Fe, California," 200

Torture, 45

Treason, 19, 21, 24–25, 49, 75, 80, 87, 259

Treaty of Paris (1763), 50

True religion, 78–79, 120

Turner Diaries, The, 172

Tydings from Rome or, England's Alarm (1667), 27–29

Tyranny, 3, 169, 263

UFO cults, 197

Unificationism, 186–91, 218

Uniform Crime Reporting Program, 169

Union Church of Africa, 110

Unitarians, 106

United Order, 75

United Service, 138–39

Universalist, 123

Ury, John, 58

USA Today, 177

U.S. News and World Report, 230

Usury, 41

Utah, 78–79, 86, 93

Utah Mormon War (1857–58), 86–91

Utopia, 107

Veneration of relics, 55

Vermont, 112–13

Victims, 162, 164–65, 184, 220, 250–51, 258–60, 263

Vigilantes of Christendom (1990), 174

Vigilantism, 1–2, 74, 82, 108, 174

Violence, 9–11, 56, 62, 70, 79, 82, 86–87, 107–8, 113, 116–17, 119–20, 122–23, 126, 128, 135, 137, 147–48, 150, 171–75, 194–95, 204, 215, 218–19, 243–44, 247–49, 251–52, 255–56, 260

Virginia, 22–23, 35–36, 39–41, 57, 148

Virginia Company, 22

Virtue, 248

Vishnu, 163

Volkman, Ernest, 149–50

Von Kotzebue, Otto, 137–38

Von Schiller, Friedrich, 4

Voting, 68

Waco, Tex., 97, 215–46

"Waco/Branch Davidian Compound: Negotiation Transcripts" (1993), 232–35, 245–46

Waco Tribune-Herald, 220–22, 224–25

War, 44–45, 49–50, 63, 82, 85–86, 169–70

Warren, Earl, 3

Warsaw, Ill., 85–86

Washington, D.C., 78

Washington, George, 3, 64, 99

Washington Post, 173–74, 190, 228–29

Washington Times, 211–13

Watson, Thomas Edward, 69–70, 156–57, 161, 164, 167

Watson's Magazine, 53, 156–57, 159–61

Westboro Baptist Church, 249, 255. *See also* Hate; Phelps, Fred; Religion; Sex

West India Company, 147–48

West Jefferson, Ohio, 1

We, the People (1932), 7

Whites, 169–71, 204–6, 247, 249–51, 254, 258–59. *See also* Anti-Semitism; Duke, David; Ku Klux Klan; Race; White supremacy

White, Alma Bridwell, 165–66. *See also* Ku Klux Klan

White, Ellen Gould, 113. *See also* Adventists

White Man's Bible, The (1981), 169–70, 256

White nationalists, 254. *See also* Duke, David; White supremacy

White supremacy, 16, 172–73, 247–50, 254, 256. *See also* Christian Identity movement; Creativity Movement; Duke, David; Race; Smith, Benjamin "August"

Whitney, Isaiah, 109

"Why *Did* Waco Happen?" (1994), 243–44

Wicca, 186, 191–97, 218, 258. *See also* Satan; Witchcraft

Wiccan Convention, 191

"Wide Awake Yankee Doodle," 64–65

Wiesenthal, Simon, 13

"Wiesenthal Center Urges Denver Christian Community to Rebuke Pentecostal Church's Sign that Charges Jews with Deicide" (2004), 178

William of Orange, 63. *See also* New York

Williams, Benjamin Matthew, 170

Williams, James Tyler, 170

Williams, Roger, 6, 21, 39

Wilmington, Del., 110

Winthrop, John, 19, 29–31, 34–35

Witchcraft, 34–36, 106, 108, 117–18, 191–97

Witches, 21, 32, 34–35, 39. *See also* Satan; Witchcraft

"Witching Hour, The" (1990), 193–94

Wolf, Simon, 160

Wolf in sheep's clothing, 78, 106

Wolvertoon, Monte, 242

"Woman's Board of Home Missions" (1898), 94–95

Women, 34, 53, 55, 61, 77, 108, 250–51, 258–59. *See also* Victims

"Word for the Mormons, A" (1899), 95–96

World Church of the Creator, 169–72. *See also* Creativity Movement

World's Parliament of Religion, 104

World War II, 1, 11

Wounded Knee, 128, 142. *See also* Native Americans

X-Files, The, 198–99

Yale College, 100

Yom Kippur, 152–53

Yoruba, 209. *See also* Santería

Young, Brigham, 78–79, 85–86. *See also* Mormons; Utah Mormon War

Young, Eugene, 94. *See also* Polygamy

Youthnappers (1977), 187. *See also* Anticult movement

"Zionism as the Biggest Threat to Modern Civilization" (2005), 252

Zionist Congress, 162

Zion's Herald, 112